THE ANARCHIC SEA

The Anarchic Sea

Maritime Security in the Twenty-First Century

DAVID SLOGGETT

PENTAGON PRESS

The Anarchic Sea: Maritime Security in the Twenty-First Century

First Indian Edition 2014

ISBN 978-81-8274-755-5

First published by C. Hurst & Co. (Publishers) Ltd., 41 Great Russell Street, London, WC1B 3PL. This edition published in arrangement

Published in India by

PENTAGON PRESS
206, Peacock Lane, Shahpur Jat
New Delhi-110049
Phones: 011-64706243, 26491568
Telefax: 011-26490600
email: rajan@pentagonpress.in
website: www.pentagonpress.in

Printed at Aegean Offset Printers, Greater Noida, U.P.

CONTENTS

ACKNOWLEDGEMENTS

The writing of this book was inspired by a number of people with whom I have worked and collaborated over forty years in the field. Iain Ballantyne, the Editor of *Warships International Fleet Review*, has been a constant source of encouragement. Sir Jeremy Blackham, the Editor of the *Naval Review* magazine and one-time Deputy Chief of the Defence Staff [Equipment Capability], has always been supportive and ready to allow my thoughts to appear within the Journal he so ably edits.

I would also like to thank Superintendent Brian Muir of the Lothian & Borders Police in Scotland for our wide-ranging discussions on maritime security and his insights into the challenges being faced in Scotland. His personal encouragement to me about my writing and efforts in the field has been sincerely appreciated. Detective Superintendent Andrew Lyttle of Kent Police has also been an inspiration to me as a practitioner whose knowledge of maritime security arises from his day-to-day involvement in the challenges faced by the Police in helping to secure the United Kingdom's coastline from Suffolk into Sussex. His insights and reflections have been hugely valuable as I have tried to study the United Kingdom and compare and contrast approaches with other countries throughout the world and document those as the Case Studies within the book.

Commander Steve Tatham [RN] also deserves thanks for his introduction to Michael Dwyer at Hurst Publishers. Michael has been an important source of encouragement and focus. Martin Murphy, Dave Mugridge and Assistant Commissioner Clarke of the Turks and Caicos Islands Police Force, have also given of their time to encourage me by reading ideas and providing feedback. I am grateful to all of them for their time and particularly their patience. Sym Taylor is also a good friend and colleague who should be thanked for reading the draft of the book and providing me with such encouraging feedback.

My opportunities to write have also been supported by James Green of the publishers IHS Janes, and through my long-term contacts with Jonathan Green, also of IHS Janes. The recent work they asked me to do updating the database on African navies was a source of inspiration for a renewed interest in maritime security at what has been a time of tremendous change, politically, economically and technologically. I am indebted to both of them for their friendship and support and for the opportunity to follow a lifetime's interest in naval matters through to writing this book. I wish also to acknowledge the important commentaries provided in this field for Janes by Tim Fish, Richard Scott and Jon Rosenfeld. I have referenced several specific reports they have published in journals such as Janes Navy International.

My colleagues at Dryad Maritime Intelligence Service have also provided valuable guidance and daily insights into contemporary challenges in the maritime security sector as they provide up-to-date threat assessment information to their ever-widening customer base. My friend Graham Gibbon-Brooks is a man of outstanding enthusiasm and energy. John Fusco has also been a great help providing his weekly update from open sources on maritime security. The publication that he produces from the New York State Office of Homeland Security is a weekly source of insights and reporting that I know he works hard to collect together. For anyone working in this field it is an invaluable adjunct to other sources and well worth taking the time to read.

Commander Paddy Green [RN] is a friend and colleague who has guided and moulded an enthusiast into someone who hopes that the insights within this book have value to professionals working in the field. His comments, always direct and incisive, are delivered in ways that are easy to understand and always add value. I am also grateful to many unnamed people serving within the Royal Navy for their help, and in arranging visits to various places to gain practical insights into the situations on the ground, both overseas and in the United Kingdom.

I also am lucky to have three sons, Richard, Christopher and Anthony, who provide a constant source of encouragement concerning my interests. I am hugely lucky to be their dad. Recently, Anthony wrote his first pieces for *Warships* under the excellent guidance of its Editor. It was a very proud dad that saw his son in print for the first time writing so eruditely about the activities of the United States Marines in Afghanistan and an assessment of the Russian Navy. Since then, Anthony has written about a range of topics, including a headline piece on the Iranian Navy. He has also read and provided helpful feedback on early drafts of this text, playing an important role as a reader and drawing upon insights he has gained from his studies at the Department of War Studies at King's College in London. I am delighted to have been able to collaborate with him on this project.

Finally, and most importantly, I must acknowledge the support and love of my wife Jo, whose tolerance of absences upstairs in my study writing is amazing. Without her encouragement and interest this project would not have got past first base. She has read every word I write, and that is no mean feat. I am truly lucky and privileged to have met my true soul mate. This book is dedicated to her and all she means to me.

Dr Dave Sloggett

ABBREVIATIONS

AIS	Automatic Identification Systems
AOR	Areas of Responsibility
APS	Africa Partnership Station
ASEAN	Association of South East Asian Nations
ASW	Anti-Submarine Warfare
BLEVE	Boiling Liquid Expanding Vapour Explosion
BM	Ballistic Missile
BMD	Ballistic Missile Defence
CBP	Customs and Border Protection
CBRN	Chemical, Biological, Radiological, Nuclear
CENTRIXS	Combined Enterprise Regional Information Exchange System
CNI	Critical National Infrastructure
CNTT	Coalition Naval Training Teams
CSI	Container Security Initiative
COIN	Counterinsurgency
C-TPAT	Customs Trade Partnership Against Terrorism
EEZ	Exclusive Economic Zone
ESA	European Space Agency
EUNAVFOR	European Union Naval Force
FPB	Fast Patrol Boat
FLTCYBERCOM	Fleet Cyber Command
FPV	Fisheries Protection Vessel
GDP	Gross Domestic Product
HALE	High Altitude Long-Endurance
IED	Improvised Explosive Device
IISS	International Institute for Strategic Studies

IMB	International Maritime Bureau
IMF	International Monetary Fund
IMO	International Maritime Organisation
IMOS	Integrated Marine Observing System
IOR	Indian Ocean Region
IPV	Inshore Patrol Vessel
ISPS	International Ship and Port Facility Security
ISTAR	Intelligence, Surveillance, Target Acquisition and Recognition
IUU	Illegal, Unregulated and Unreported fishing
JMSU	Joint Marine Seismic Undertaking
MDA	Maritime Domain Awareness
MEND	Movement for the Emancipation of the Niger Delta
MODIS	Moderate Resolution Imaging Spectroradiometer
MOOTW	Military Operations Other Than War
MRBM	Medium Range Ballistic Missile
MSO	Maritime Security Operations
MSRT	Maritime Security Response Teams
MV	Motor Vessel
NATO	North Atlantic Treaty Organisation
NEC	Network Enabled Capability
NEO	Non-Combatant Evacuation Operation
NIE	National Intelligence Assessment
NOA	Notice of Arrival
NOAA	National Oceanic and Atmospheric Administration
OPV	Offshore Patrol Vessel
PLAN	People's Liberation Army Navy
PSI	Proliferation Security Initiative
RDD	Radiological Dispersal Device
ReCAAP	Regional Cooperation Agreement on Combating Piracy and Armed Robbery against Ships in Asia
RMOP	Recognised Maritime Operational Picture
RPG	Rocket Propelled Grenade
SAR	Search and Rescue
SLOC	Sea Lanes of Communication
SRBM	Short Range Ballistic Missile
SSM	Surface-to-Surface Missile

TBMD	Theatre Ballistic Missile Defence
TMD	Theatre Missile Defence
UAS	Unmanned Aerial System
UAV	Unmanned Aviation Vehicle
UNCLOS	United Nations Convention on the Law of the Sea
USCENTCOM	United States Central Command
USCGC	United States Coast Guard Cutter
USCGS	United States Coastguard Service
USGS	United States Geological Survey
USNI	United States Naval Institute
VBIED	Vessel Borne Improvised Explosive Devices
VBSS	Vessel Board, Search and Seizure
VMF	Versatile Maritime Force
VTMS	Vessel Traffic Monitoring System
WBIED	Water Borne Improvised Explosive Device
WMD	Weapons of Mass Destruction

LIST OF TABLES

PREFACE

I have always enjoyed a sense of union with the sea, having been brought up along the south coast of England. I am fortunate to live in Ryde, on the Isle of Wight, where my study, in which this book was compiled, overlooks the Solent. The comings and goings of the commercial ships, and the ever-reducing number of Royal Navy vessels in and out of Portsmouth Harbour, rarely fail to bring a pair of binoculars to my eyes. I am really looking forward to the day when the Royal Navy's new aircraft carriers become a routine distraction from my writing.

Ships of all shapes and sizes pass through the Solent serenely making passage on their way to destinations that range across the world. I am fortunate to say that I am one of the few people that can speak of commuting by the sea to work when I visit the mainland. There are days when the view from my study is truly majestic, with the sun shimmering from the sea and racing boats being carried along by a gentle force 4–5. It is a sight, however, whose beauty can wax and wane; sometimes adopting a menacing atmosphere as the sea mist descends blanketing the mainland. The sound of foghorns always brings with it a sense of foreboding.

With such a vision of comparative tranquillity it is difficult to imagine the many areas of the world's oceans where this picture is anything but the case. The combined effect of transnational criminals, those engaged in illegal fishing, terrorism, piracy and the ubiquitous threat from nature combine to make seafaring, both historically and today, a hazardous trade that has many uncertainties. It was this fascination that led me to write this book. When I started to research it the very first issue that became clear is that the mere term 'maritime security' is one that has many different interpretations. It is therefore, in my judgement, an area wide open to the kind of systematic analysis I have tried to supply in this book by using case studies to provide a test of the various challenges that exist.

For some people, the subject is very clearly about the defence of ports and the concerns about terrorism. This is understandable in the aftermath of 11 September. I believe the term, however, needs to be reflective of a wider set of concerns. Events in Mumbai in November 2008 certainly caused some people to pause and reflect upon the implications for their maritime security of such a threat. For many others maritime security is seen through a slightly more dispersive lens, where the subject covers a much wider range of topics, such as biosecurity, piracy, invasion by potential adversaries and a variety of criminal forms of behaviour. In writing this book I have tried to look through the wider lens, commenting upon contemporary developments whilst signposting those excellent pieces of work that provide specific pieces of in-depth coverage to particular subject areas and historical perspectives.

In researching this book I rapidly concluded that it was important for maritime security to be seen through an all-encompassing lens. Many factors interact with each other and it takes a holistic viewpoint to start to appreciate the nature of those interactions. Seeing the various areas in isolation is unhelpful and does not allow for the development of a comprehensive approach in an era where criminals and terrorists exploit gaps in areas of state control to carry out their activities.

To attach the term 'maritime security' to one specific facet of the broad range of topics is, to my thinking, to take a myopic view of interactions between other dimensions that can have an impact upon the approach that is taken to securing the maritime environment.

This holistic approach, however, is difficult at a time of fiscal stringency. Priorities always have to be selected. This book attempts to lay out a framework, the seven dimensions of maritime security, that at least allow decision makers to be aware of the second and third-order interactions that are associated with specific primary areas that might be chosen as priorities. Navies and Coastguard services all over the world have to do more with less and to expect reduced, not increased budgets. Finding and understanding a focus, therefore, is hugely important.

This is also challenging at a time when great uncertainty plagues the international landscape. The world is a far from secure place. From what appeared to be a singularly dominant threat axis in the Cold War with some semblance of order, the international landscape has descended into chaos, and in some places such as Somalia where the country is close to anarchy, the international community appear powerless to act and reluctant to place military forces on the ground. There are many other countries whose maritime environments are insecure. The case studies developed within this book try to highlight their challenges, and they have been selected to illustrate the wide range of variables that exist in developing a clear strategy to secure the marine environment.

In the immediate aftermath of what some commentators described as the end of the Cold War, expectations were raised of reduced military budgets and greater spending on social priorities and international aid programmes. Too many people hoped that the attractions of democracy would smooth the pathway for nation states that wanted to make the change from oppressive regimes. Initial signs were hopeful as many countries from the former Eastern Bloc applied for and gained membership of the European Union and NATO, extending their reach and security to a much wider European population. But as other groups decisively rejected the path to modernity as conceived in the West, difficulties started to occur and the conditions were created under which transnational terrorism could plan and execute the attacks of 11 September. That was a profound moment and a wake-up call to those who thought the world was on a pathway to a new and golden age. Whilst many found the vision attractive, others with powerful religious and ideological foundations rejected that vision, offering an alternative concept for governance.

In such a fractured environment, criminality and terrorism thrived in the shadows of the global landscape. New threats quickly emerged and the conditions emerged that created those who carried out the attacks in Mumbai. The global media fuelled grievances and the Internet provided the means by which people could take up the franchises of transnational groups and conduct their own localised form of terrorism. The multi-dimensional nature of criminality also responded quickly to the opportunities the new world order created, as states with repressive security apparatuses fell foul of the uncertain world in which many found themselves as state-run economies faced up to the forces that dominate the market. The scene was set at the start of the twenty-first century for some serious issues to emerge. The sea, with all of its enduring characteristics that helped maritime force to be applied in aid of the world's population, also offered criminality and terrorism the flexibility and manoeuvre-room they craved to conduct their operations.

The first decade of the twenty-first century will become known for many events that will, in the fullness of time, shape history. One of those was 11 September and the other was Mumbai. These were cataclysmic events that had profound implications for world order and security. Moving upstream, something hitherto[1] practised by some elements of the security apparatus, was now something that was going to move into the remit of military forces and partner agencies seeking to help stabilise countries that were in danger of becoming failed states. In the wake of 11 September, a range of security initiatives were rapidly introduced to protect cargoes and the ports though which they move. This was one dimension of a multi-dimensional response to the terrorist attacks on the United States.

Some military forces were going to be asked to shift their focus from state-on-state wars to a new global policing role, conducting operations where local nation states fail to provide a secure environment. This was never going to be an easy task. Transformation became a task that was done in Iraq in contact. United States Counterinsurgency doctrine was developed in rapid order and applied on the battlefield. Laboratory testing and simulations were bypassed as the national priority was to make progress on the ground in what seemed to be an increasingly difficult and challenging situation. However, the application of these upstream activities has its political limitations. Despite being perhaps the most famous of all failing states, there seems little appetite in the world's political arena for an intervention on land in Somalia. Attempts to curtail the activities of pirates operating from the lawless environment ashore are limited to the multinational naval forces seeking to protect the vital sea lanes of communication off the Horn of Africa, used for more than 30,000 transits of the area each year by vessels carrying a wide range of cargoes and also cruise liners.

Maritime transformation to the new world order, however, was perhaps not seen to be as challenging. After all, at the end of the Cold War the threat from the Russian Navy and their considerable submarine fleet had all but disappeared. It may have appeared to some commentators that navies were no longer required in the form developed in the Cold War. With their ability to project global maritime power on the world stage, a new form of navy was required, perhaps one that operated through collaboration across the world's navies to secure the marine environment. Surely as the maritime environment was the world's common highway for trade, its importance having increased after the Cold War, it at least could be secured with the participation of many nation states.

The concept of a 1,000-Ship Navy (a grand international coalition of naval forces) has been suggested, with many obvious and apparent attractions. Contemporary military operations off the coast of Somalia[2] bear testament to the enduring appeal of this idea, despite its obvious drawbacks in its application in a wider sense. The need to harness the naval and coastguard forces across the world to tackle the growing use of the maritime environment by criminals and terrorists is a vital element of a global approach to security in an age in which the ever-present threat of a terrorist group gaining access to weapons of mass destruction haunts the nightmares of many Western politicians.

Bizarrely, as this text was being finalised, the world witnessed the mysterious events that surrounded the reported disappearance of the Maltese registered wood carrier *Arctic Sea*, with rumours circulating that it was smuggling weapons to another country, such as Iran,[3] as well as carrying a cargo of wood; an allegation the Russian authorities involved in the investigation of the event clearly reject. The vessel had checked in with Dover Coastguard on 28 July 2009 in what appeared to be a routine call. Later that day the coastguard in Zeebrugge contacted Dover Coastguard to inform them that Interpol had apparently issued an alert to say the vessel had been hijacked. This report probably originated from an earlier report suggesting the vessel had been boarded in Swedish waters off the Island of Gotland on 24 July. The apparent delay in passing on this information was crucial in preventing an intervention whilst the vessel was in the English Channel.

The uncertainty prompted a multinational effort that included nuclear submarines from the Russian Navy that spanned the North Sea, Baltic Sea and Atlantic Ocean, to find the vessel that seemed to have disappeared. Portuguese coastguard authorities reported that the vessel had not passed through their waters and the Malta Maritime Authority commented that the *Arctic Sea* had not passed through the Straits of Gibraltar *en route* to what it had claimed was its destination in Bejaia in Algeria, suggesting that it had in fact headed out into the Atlantic Ocean. Its discovery off the coast of West Africa, near the Cape Verde Islands, whilst not difficult to predict, leaves many questions unanswered; after all, the sea is a big place and if the vessel had truly disappeared it would be remarkable for it to be found by a Russian naval task force. It is very tempting to think there is more to this story than meets the eye. Time, no doubt, will provide some of the answers.

With the reverberations from the commando-style assault on Mumbai still creating waves in the security apparatus of many countries, it is not difficult to see why some people's imaginations were being quickly put to the test in trying to explain what might have been behind such a hijacking. Could it have been carried out to provide a floating platform from which to launch a major attack on a Western country? Was Hollywood fiction about to become reality?

Many commentators have reasoned that a vessel—not necessarily the *Arctic Sea*—could be hijacked and used to mount an attack on a major seaport or to blockade a narrow waterway. Their arguments have often apparently fallen on deaf ears. The reported hijacking of the *Arctic Sea*, in what can be regarded as our own back yard, highlights the art of the possible for those who are sufficiently determined to cause harm. Whilst this episode is more than likely to have a far more mundane explanation, it does highlight the enduring need for those charged with maritime security to maintain their alert levels. If, as the United Kingdom seems to favour, we should depend upon an intelligence-led approach to maritime security, then the apparent lack of knowledge at the Dover Coastguard about the vessel's hijacking off the coast of Sweden provides some insights that should not be ignored.

A further testament to the dynamic nature of the maritime environment came in the form of reports of the deaths of nearly 100 people aboard the *Princess Ashika* inter-island ferry that sank on 5 August 2009 off the coast of Tonga. Its loss is one of many hundreds that could be catalogued throughout history—some more famous than others—that vividly illustrate the unforgiving nature of the maritime environment. A similar event occurred off the coast of the Philippines when the *Super Ferry 9* sank in September 2009. The loss of life on that occasion was minimised by the rapid reaction of the Philippines Navy and several commercial vessels that rescued 926 of the 928 passengers aboard the ferry; the remainder were reported as missing.

I have often sat and thought about the term maritime security in the context of a globalised twenty-first century world. What does it mean? What is the difference between maritime security and maritime strategy? To seafarers this might all seem quite academic. To them the answer may appear to be obvious. I am less sure. For me the issue of maritime security has often been overlooked, and seen as something that is not of immediate concern. Many commentators, in trying to capture this sense that the sea is taken for granted by many political leaders whose priorities often seem hampered by a myopic and land-centric view of the world, speak of a sea-blindness that has developed.

It is my viewpoint that the changes in the world's security landscape have been so dramatic since the end of the Cold War that it is necessary to fundamentally re-evaluate what the term maritime security means. Unsurprisingly, most of the recent books published in this field have originated from the United States, still understandably traumatised by the events of 11 September 2001. Their contributions, whilst important and insightful, are often quite parochial and viewed through quite narrow lenses, highlighting threats and potential solutions that reflect the immediacy of their concerns for the homeland of the United States.

It is my contention that the sea links nearly all of us in daily activities, be they social or for commercial purposes. It is not difficult to imagine the implications of an act of terrorism that was aimed at one of the megaports or one of the major nine choke points, such as the Bosphorus or the Strait of Hormuz. The apparent terrorist attack on the Japanese oil tanker the MV *M. Star* in August 2010 in this area provides further evidence, if any is needed, of the potential for terrorists to strike in the maritime domain. For groups intent on creating havoc, the sea provides a large area of room to manoeuvre. The fact that the attack took place where seventeen million barrels of oil a day transit a well-known maritime check point just adds to the need to develop a comprehensive approach to maritime security. Any major interruption of sea trade through the disablement of a major port facility, such as through an attack by a large-scale radiological device or biological weapon, would rapidly create a chaotic situation in the world's trade with dire economic consequences compounding an already weak global marketplace.

Transnational criminals and terrorist groups see the sea in a similar light, as a highway on which to ply their trade in misery, and to prepare and enact criminal behaviour and execute apocalyptic visions of jihad upon Western societies. This holistic viewpoint aims to see maritime security through a much wider lens. It tries to explore the relationships that exist between the sea and the land in ways that seek to inform those developing security policies of the enduring and ever-changing nature of the threat.

This is quite a difficult task. It requires a systematic approach that breaks the problem down into manageable tasks that can each be considered in detail. A range of questions can be asked. What can we learn from history that may help shape our response to the obvious threats to the maritime environment? What threatens the maritime environment and its users today? What should be the strategic approach to addressing these problems, and what are the solutions that could be developed?

There was a time when seafarers would derive security from the sheer scale of the oceans. It was unlikely that a merchant vessel would come into contact with a potential enemy. As more formal trade routes developed, based upon critical nodes, those seeking to disrupt those routes for commercial gain or as part of a national attempt to deny wealth to other potentially hostile nations honed into key areas of the oceans where their chances of locating vessels improved. The furthest end points of the trading routes became a magnet for pirates and buccaneers that targeted the weak points in the world's emergent trading networks. Theirs was a ruthless pursuit of financial gain using violence in its most extreme forms. Today's pirates and maritime terrorists, far from being the mischievous and yet likeable caricature played by the actor Johnny Depp in the series of films *Pirates of the Caribbean*, are more than content to resort to extreme forms of violence and intimidation if it suits their purpose.

Navies developed, in part, to try and address these problems and capture and bring these individuals and their crews to trial. Early forms of maritime security focussed upon the protection of the early forms of communication at these critical points from which trade originated. The wider benefits of naval power became recognised in the eighteenth and nineteenth centuries and navies took on a broader role, which led to the development of alternative theories concerning their application given the size of the maritime domain. Navies became an instrument capable of delivering maritime security in a number of different ways. Combat power was the *sine qua non* of creating a secure maritime environment. Today that is simply not the case. Securing the maritime environment requires more than simply kinetic approaches and also needs to recognise that there is a land-sea interface where many solutions to problems at sea lie on the land, such as in economic development and giving people some hope of a more sustainable future.

PREFACE

In April 2009 the USS *Theodore Roosevelt* visited the Solent. The amazing image of her appearing through a mist over the Solent will stay with me for a long time. Yet, despite all of the combat power and maritime capability, pirates using little more than an AK-47 and some Rocket Propelled Grenades (RPGs) are disrupting one of the world's major sea lanes of communications with wide-ranging ramifications for global trade and the international economy. This is an illustration of the nature of the globalised world in which we find ourselves today. The threats are dynamic, adaptable and determined, in many cases quite willing to die for their causes.

It is clear that there are many dimensions to maritime security and that some very specific challenges exist to the freedom of use of the oceans and the protection of coastal waters. Many of the challenges facing the maritime environment have been addressed in other publications. They each bring specific and often detailed understandings to particular areas of concern. However, the picture that emerges can be fragmented and can lack an over-arching framework. This text attempts to bring some coherence and clarity to the problems posed by the myriad threats to states with an interest in the sea. Its aim is to provide insights into the nature of the issues and ways of addressing the associated insecurities, thereby developing potential solutions that build frameworks for local, regional and international cooperation.

Drawing upon history and recent trends, this text tries to provide a holistic vision of how single and multi-state coalitions can work and cooperate to provide increased security to riverine, coastal and bluewater maritime operations. However, in this complicated world with its protean threats, it is difficult to argue that hard power alone will deliver solutions. A balance between the application of hard and soft power needs to be developed.

This text reflects both upon the application of hard and soft power in trying to secure the maritime domain, and in creating the conditions in which secure environments can be developed. Frameworks for multi-agency and multi-state cooperation can form the basis for the development of a modular approach to maritime security that can be a blueprint for nations to cooperate irrespective of their immediate local needs and focus.

Of course, a one-size-fits-all approach does not work and nation states with coastal waters will need to adapt the ideas to what they can afford and need. But my sincere hope is that within this book they can at least find a few ideas that might help them in their quest to develop secure maritime environments that reflect their national needs and priorities. It is a sad fact that many people across the world are stuck on the horns of a dilemma: live on the increasingly meagre harvest from the ocean or turn to terrorism or piracy. A comprehensive approach to maritime security needs to take, as an example, the mandate of the European Union Naval Force (EUNAVFOR) operating off the coast of Somalia. They not only provide security for ships bringing much needed humanitarian aid to Somalia, but also keep watch on fishing activity in the coastal region. This additional focus is important. Secure the present whilst helping the countries to conserve and manage their food supplies for the future. It is not only a worthy aim, but a vital part of a sensible and pragmatic approach to addressing the problems that beset many coastal states around the world.

INTRODUCTION

What we may be witnessing is not just the end of the Cold War, or the passing of a particular period of post-war history, but the end of history as such: that is, the end point of mankind's ideological evolution and the universalisation of Western liberal democracy as the final form of human government.

Professor Francis Fukuyama, 1992

The twenty-first century dawned with a terrorist outrage that would shape its first decades. When terrorists attacked the United States on 11 September the world changed. Those who argued that the world was a different place after the end of the Cold War were suddenly faced with a large dose of reality. The security landscape of the world morphed from a bilateral world dominated by two superpowers into a multilateral one, where the concept of the nation state began to diminish. Transnational actors and social movements aligned with developments on the Internet to create a world where events could be transmitted to target audiences all day, every day.

The dramatic images of that autumn day in New York and Washington so vividly depict a new world where terrorist groups with evil intent can reach out from their remote and isolated hillside sanctuaries in inaccessible parts of the world and inspire people to commit acts of mass murder. Whilst those attacks were hardly conventional in nature, using passenger aircraft as missiles, they did not employ nuclear weapons. Throughout the Cold War the image of a nuclear exchange haunted political leaders. The potential for the end of the world literally was never more than fifteen minutes and one mistake away. The end of the Cold War was supposed to bring that chapter of history to an end. Paradoxically, it did quite the reverse. The irony of this was captured by President Obama when he observed in Prague on 5 April 2009: 'In a strange turn of history, the threat of global nuclear war has gone down, but the risk of a nuclear attack has gone up'.

Despite the huge international effort to ensure no repeat of those harrowing scenes, Al-Qaeda and its affiliates remain a viable international terrorist group. They have shown agility in changing the nature of their organisation. It continues to evolve whilst still maintaining its core message that the West has embarked upon a war with Islam and seeks its destruction as a religion; a narrative that gains traction with many communities that feel disenfranchised and remote from the kind of world that is emerging in the twenty-first century.

With its leaders largely isolated from activists on the ground, resorting to systems of trusted couriers to convey messages and instructions, and increasingly infrequent media appearances, the ability for the Al-Qaeda to function as an organisation is being disrupted. For some this is a sign of progress. For others, it presages a new and more dangerous evolution of the threat from franchises of Al-Qaeda who support the central ideology of the organisation, but choose to implement their own localised interpretations of how that should be achieved. The ways in which terrorism may evolve are increasingly unpredictable. Strategic shocks may well still occur, and law enforcement and military leaders must not let down their guard.

While the attacks on the United States on 11 September arrived from the air, the great fear is that the next strategic shock will arrive from the sea. Al-Qaeda, and its affiliates, have shown themselves to be a manoeuverist organisations. They use the global media to send messages to vulnerable target audiences to incite violence; manoeuvring in the cognitive domain. In parallel they also make pacts with drugs smugglers in West Africa and leverage relationships across the Sahel, the Maghreb, the Caucasus, and in places like Iraq, Yemen, Afghanistan and other areas of Southeast Asia.

They balance the ability to manoeuvre at the strategic level with criminal activities at the regional and local level. When operating across such a large area, the maritime domain, and its essential freedom of manoeuvre, becomes increasingly important. For transnational terrorist groups like Al-Qaeda and Hezbollah, who use the sea to import weapons from countries such as Iran, these freedoms are a relatively new-found extra dimension to their activities. As they increase their use of the maritime environment there is a danger that it will become increasingly ungovernable and anarchic in character.

Whereas in the recent past, mariners could sail the world largely unchallenged by the threat of piracy, nowadays people and narcotics smugglers, and those moving weapons, make some areas of the sea increasingly dangerous. This situation is compounded by other factors such as climate change. Admiral Nelson's observation that 'I cannot command the winds and the weather' is an enduring reminder of the vagaries of the maritime environment and the threat it poses to shipping. Maritime security should not simply be viewed through the lens of the impact of criminals and terrorists. It is a multidimensional problem.

For transnational criminal groups, such as those involved in the illegal movement of narcotics and people, this is a tried-and-tested domain in which to operate and they enjoy the freedom of the seas. One potential danger for us all is that a nexus emerges between terrorist groups and those involved in crime that creates the circumstances that help deliver a new and more deadly form of terrorism to Western society. Disrupting their freedom of manoeuvre of the sea is crucial.

That is easy to say, but not so easy to achieve. The sheer scale of the problem of trying to secure the maritime environment from those engaged in criminal activities is difficult, as the international task force operating off the Horn of Africa will attest, especially at a time when the world's economies are in such a poor state of health. Cooperation by nation states with converging agendas, aimed at disrupting the activities of criminals and terrorists, is vital. Admiral Roughead, the United States Chief of Naval Operations, has offered many insights in his various speeches on the subject. The notion of the 1,000-Ship Navy, made up from component parts contributed by various nations, is a sensible vision of the future. As Darwin noted: 'in the long history of humankind (and animal kind, too) those who have learned to collaborate and improvise most effectively have prevailed'. His observation chimes with political and military leaders in the twenty-first century who are trying to tackle problems that are increasingly malign. Admiral Roughead rightly argued in an address to a regional symposium in Argentina in April 2006 that 'no nation can do everything, but all nations can do something', continuing 'Maritime security starts with every nation's capacity to contribute and expands from there'. In his testimony to the

Senate Subcommittee on Appropriations on Defence on 28 March 2010 Admiral Roughead opined 'I believe an international "1000-Ship Navy" offers a real opportunity to increase partner-nation capabilities while reducing transnational crime, Weapons of Mass Destruction (WMD) proliferation, terrorism and human trafficking'.

International collaboration amongst military and civilian organisations involved in securing the maritime environment, such as the United States Coastguard and its international partners, is part of the solution to these challenges, but it is not a silver bullet that magically solves the problem. The answer, if indeed one exists, has to be found from a number of sources. The French writer and historian Alexis de Tocqueville pithily noted that 'history is a gallery of pictures in which there are few originals and many copies'. If his perceptive comment is true, it is to history that we should look, in part, for insights and solutions.

Sir Walter Raleigh, writing in the *Discourse of the Invention of Ships* in the early part of the seventeenth century, summed up the importance of controlling the oceans when he observed: '[W]hosoever commands the sea, commands the trade, whosoever commands the trade of the world, commands the riches of the world, and consequently the world itself'. The passage of time has not diminished the power of his argument. Arguably it has increased it, with 90 per cent of the world's trade now being carried out by sea.

Julian Corbett is well known for being one of the great maritime strategists. His work, *Some Principles of Maritime Strategy*, remains a defining source of insight and wisdom on the nature of defining approaches to the control of the sea. Set against the backdrop of the nineteenth and early part of the twentieth century, when control of the sea had a much greater military focus, his work retains its relevance, even when the context has fundamentally shifted. Perhaps his unique contribution to the field was to add the important link that set maritime strategy within a wider framework of human conflict. The sea was not to be seen on its own. It was part of a greater system of links, all of which interacted, with the coupling between the land and sea environments being crucially important. Admiral Roughead acknowledged this point when he said 'Pirates don't live at sea. Pirates live ashore. What needs to happen is a broader interagency approach that goes beyond a maritime or naval approach'. Looking at the globalised nature of the twenty-first century, his analysis seems prescient. True scholarly insight transcends time and maintains its relevance.

The End of State-on-State Conflict?

Many people thought that the end of the Cold War presaged a new 'golden era' in human history in which large-scale state-on-state conflicts would be behind us. And yet there are many parts of the world where the ever-present threat of a local spark igniting a regional conflagration dogs progress towards a more liberally-minded and tolerant world. The sinking of the South Korean naval vessel, the *Cheonan*, on 26 March 2010, is an example of rhetoric expressing itself through specific physical actions. The loss of the *Cheonan* and the death of forty-six South Korean sailors was the latest in a number of clashes that had occurred at sea off the Korean Peninsula and in its immediate coastal waters. The maritime environment can, it appears, be used as a place where localised battles can be fought and people can die without immediately igniting a regional conflagration. That said, a tipping point may well be reached at which repeated confrontations turn into full-scale war. Managing that situation is far from straightforward, where regional political alliances lack transparency.

It was the eminent political economist Francis Fukuyama who coined the phrase 'the end of history' when in an article he declared, perhaps precipitously, that History (in the sense that the word is spelt with a capital letter) was over; liberalism had won and the markets ruled the way the world would operate in the future.[1] The backlash against his apparent assertions led to quite a heated debate.

It appeared to some commentators that he was declaring that the Western liberalism model had triumphed emphatically over the models of communism. Many people were unhappy with the inference, as it also reflected a viewpoint that if you propagated the democratic model globally, wars would come to an end. His argument followed a particular line of reasoning: liberal democracy replaces the irrational desire to be recognised as greater than others with a rational desire to be recognised as equal. A world made up of liberal democracies, then, should have much less incentive for war.

This seemed to some commentators a somewhat optimistic viewpoint. It is clear that several did not fully understand the point that Fukuyama was making; his was a view that is supported by some empirical evidence, that in time (irrespective of how long it takes and any short-term setbacks), democracy will be the favoured approach taken towards governance.

For some parts of the world this goal is a long way in the future, as their current societal structures, customs and creeds do not readily map onto those traditionally associated with a democracy. Political leaders in the West often place too high a reliance upon gaining an elected leader (such as in Afghanistan), and assume that the rest will follow. The swift imposition of Western political models can have immediate impacts upon societies, as insurgents use the adoption of such models as a means to create uncertainty in local populations unfamiliar with change. To fail to understand the underlying societal landscape and its associated customs, creeds and traditions, is to miss vital points in the ways in which future confrontations can be managed.

In many ways, the confrontations in the Balkans, Iraq and Afghanistan have been clashes of civilisations as very different societal landscapes confronted each other as a result of many underlying factors. Arguably a new genre of warfare has been created to deal with the results of these clashes, as Counterinsurgency (COIN) operations have had to be reshaped to cater for the ubiquitous presence of the media and its impact upon target audiences.

It is axiomatic that events shape mindsets. To be more nuanced, however, it is necessary to appreciate that events are often viewed through a magnifying lens whose focus is controlled by prior perceptions, attitudes and beliefs. People can see what they want to see and hear what they want to hear. Terrorists and insurgents understand this phenomenon and play on it in the way they direct messages to the wider world. When Israeli gunboats intercepted the convoy heading for Gaza with relief aid in June 2010, these problems of perception and reality were drawn into sharp relief as claim and counter-claim were played out to an international audience, some of whom would have been particularly receptive to one side's view of the events. It is easy to see how attitudes can be polarised in such situations. Developing political solutions when the airwaves of the world are full of such graphic imagery is difficult. The imagery has a direct effect upon public opinion and can galvanise support for both parties.

Top-down solutions often do not readily map onto the kind of complex societal structures that will inevitably form the backdrop to future confrontations and conflicts in many areas of the world. The United Nations recognises over thirty states that are either seen to be failing or are in danger of being unable to deliver the kinds of basic social services that characterise the form of state that is at the heart of the democratic model. Bottom-up approaches are as important as having leadership in place. Local people need to buy into a form of democracy if it is to gain traction throughout societies that are sometimes reflective of feudal approaches to governance, where patronage provides leverage and influence. President Obama recognised this when he said 'each country gives life to democracy in its own way' in his speech in Ghana.[2] Sloggett and Sloggett have also shown how this rhetoric is part of a new approach to international relationships that is based upon engagement in contrast to intervention.[3] President Obama recognises the potential for Fukuyama's message to become reality and for major conflicts to break out across the world as civilisations move from ideological confrontation to military conflict.

Fukuyama's arguments are complex, and a matter of philosophy and debate in other more suitable forums. However, they do reflect a viewpoint often associated with those of a neo-conservative persuasion; that one of the basic essences of the human character is a wish to be free and to enjoy the benefits of self-determination. For many, that vision is one with which they readily associate but cannot enjoy, as states deploy the full force of the security apparatus to suppress any ideas of changing local political landscapes. For them, life is a daily struggle to survive, which forces many to become engaged in criminal activities and even more extreme forms of violence. This battle to survive is at the heart of the forces that drive some into engaging in behaviour that threatens the maritime environment and its users, and creates the potential for areas of the maritime environment to take on an appearance of being unregulated, uncontrolled and even anarchic in character.

For some commentators and politicians this hope of no future warfare is one that is entirely politically motivated. Their distaste for war is well known and they recoil from becoming embroiled in its complexities. For them warfare and conflict is miasmic and something to avoid at all costs. Their solution is to resort to an ever-increasing level of threatening rhetoric, which is aimed at deterring specific behaviour. International efforts are made to develop a consensus to try and act in concert, with the United Nations in the lead. For the pragmatists, history does not provide many good examples of where such escalated levels of rhetoric have actually succeeded in changing the mindsets of often despotic leaders of states embarked upon a specific course of action, which first and foremost is designed to ensure their regime stays in power. Theirs is a hopeful vision of a world living in peace and harmony, punctuated by the occasional incident where terrorists (inconveniently for their vision) mount a major attack and temporarily grab a headline. They regard such events as unfortunate distractions from their greater liberal purpose and find it necessary to assuage public opinion by acting against the perpetrators of the attack. As events in Iraq and Afghanistan have shown, such responses can have significant long-term consequences for military engagements in far-off lands. While the argument that fighting 'terrorists' before they can attack the homeland resonates with the public at first, enthusiasm diminishes as the insurgents find ways to alter their tactics, fight asymmetrically and maintain their presence on the battlefield. One lesson from Iraq and Afghanistan is that there are no quick fixes to twenty-first century COIN operations.

Theirs is also a narrow, dogmatically formed vision that fails to grasp the realities of the twenty-first century and the rapid changes that have occurred after the end of the Cold War. It fails to acknowledge the importance of the maritime environment and the important links that exist between the land environment and the sea, the land-sea boundary.

There are few political leaders who understand the maritime environment. Politics tends to focus on the here and now and on the land. The sea is a distant sphere, an area over which political leaders have little jurisdiction. 'The great commons', as it is often called, is the place where organised crime, terrorist groups and others who would harm our societies manoeuvre. Disrupting their activities has become increasingly important in a world where the technologies of weapons of mass destruction can be smuggled by sea to a range of state and non-state actors whose desire to use the technologies knows no bounds. Countries across the world are grappling with these problems, and many are publishing revised strategies concerning their overall approachs to warfare and their specific ideas of maritime security. Australia is one example that, due to its role on the international stage, has been in the forefront of developing its ideas.[4]

With 70 per cent of the world's population living close to coastlines, failed states are going to be an enduring problem for the land-sea interface and for potential operations in the littoral. Stabilisation operations and conflict prevention activities will require naval forces to go into potentially difficult situations where one wrong step may aggravate tensions and rapidly move a confrontation into a conflict—helping to create anarchy rather than avoid it. Mapping the societal landscapes in areas of the world that have not been a traditional focus for naval operations will be problematic, although on occasion, historical connections, routed in empires (with all of that associated baggage), will provide some degree of understanding of an area. While insights derived from colonial experience can aid understanding of the characteristics of such societies, giving insights into local customs, creeds and traditions, they can also be problematic, as it is easy for former colonialists to be portrayed as having an alternative agenda. Mapping societal landscapes of such countries is complicated. The capability to integrate information derived from a range of open sources and intelligence material gathered from more sensitive sources, and developing local maritime and land-based domain awareness is going to be a crucial element of any coherent maritime response to emerging international points of tension and potential conflict.

The maritime domain starts and ends on the horizon and is often out-of-sight and out-of-mind;[5] a situation that can lead to political leaders and populations being unaware of the strategic priorities that need to be focused upon the maritime domain to create a secure maritime environment. Challenges such as those that arise from the unregulated nature of the oceans and the opaqueness and amorphous nature of the domain create opportunities that terrorists and criminals enjoy exploiting.

Drift and Uncertainty in the Wake of the Cold War

It can be argued that in the collective euphoria that followed the end of the Cold War, many holding these views started openly to challenge the so-called defence spending being allocated to navies. In the current economic climate these arguments are resurfacing[6] and questions are being asked as to where to place priorities in defence spending.[7] What purpose did navies perform when the Cold War had ended and the world was moving into a new era of peaceful co-existence? This period was one when, in the absence of a huge and globally visible Russian Navy, some naval leaders initially struggled to define a new role for maritime power.[8] Till argues[9] that in such situations navies become even more important, with their role in defending the Sea Lanes of Communication (SLOC) becoming vital, as it is the building block upon which the global economy depends.

Ironically, at the very same time, international trade and the developing global markets were becoming increasingly vulnerable to disruption, as events in the Gulf of Aden have highlighted. The threat does not start and stop in the SLOC; it also drives at the main ports and their nearby facilities. Mumbai was a harbinger of a much wider set of issues for maritime security, many of which had already been recognised after 11 September,[10] albeit from a quite narrow and parochial perspective. Countries with large coastlines will find it hard to erect barriers to protect their populations from acts of terrorism. Isolation is, in reality, not an option.

The political reaction to the 11 September attacks made intervention upstream in countries that harboured terrorist training camps a necessity. Intervention upstream, in places like Afghanistan became de rigueur. With the long term political and economic consequences of those interventions now becoming apparent, new ways of deploying military power are being sought that are based on reducing the footprint on the ground. There are simply too many places where terrorists can hide around the world for the current approach to intervention to continue.

Public opinion in many Western countries simply does not buy the message that you need to project force into a country and suffer the inevitable combat casualties over a long-term war. Investment in facilities that disrupt and interdict the operations of terrorists, insurgents and organised criminals at sea is less dramatic and less costly in terms of human lives. The problem with this is that agile terrorist groups know just how to manoeuvre, to use the sea as a means of smuggling people to places such as Mumbai, and across the Red Sea into the Yemen, and onwards into Saudi Arabia. The sea is a haven for terrorists who can blend into the often complex background of dhows and other activities to hide their own activities and manoeuvres.

Latterly, this argument about the role of navies has developed further, questioning the purpose of maritime power when the world seems to be faced by land-centric threats, such as those experienced in Iraq and Afghanistan. Moreover the issue of how to use navies to project both soft and hard power has also been the subject of much debate. Many navies around the world have become masters of using the manoeuvre room and agility afforded by the sea to influence people's behaviour. The deployment of a British nuclear submarine off the coast of the Falkland Islands in 1977, conducting Operation Journeyman, is one example of where the rumoured presence of a major naval asset was sufficient to avoid the escalation of a tricky situation. This tactic was reused in March 2010 when reports emerged of HMS *Sceptre*—a 5,000 tonne Swiftsure-class submarine—being dispatched to the same area, as tensions over oil exploration rights threatened to reignite the long-standing dispute. The decision by the Dutch Navy to deploy a submarine off the coast of Somalia in the autumn of 2010, as part of the international effort against piracy, shows the enduring flexibility afforded by submarines in the maritime environment as a potential intelligence-collection platform. Not knowing where the submarine might be operating at any instant in time may provide another factor for the pirates to consider as they launch their attacks against merchant shipping in the area. The deployment of the Royal Marine Commandos into Kuwait had a similar deterrent effect in 1961.

To become too land-centric in our analysis is to miss some important aspects of a wider role that navies will have to adopt in the future for conflict prevention. Equally, protecting SLOC will increasingly become more diverse, with the opening of new trading routes as a result of climate change, and also as new oil and gas fields come online. This will have implications for energy security, and will be important for preventing situations that have the potential to escalate.[11]

The established patterns of movement of energy supplies will change. New discoveries will open up new trading routes, and in a climate where economic development in countries such as China and India becomes increasingly important, the potential for confrontation over access to such resources becomes clear. International concerns over threats to important SLOC, where intervention in the land environment is politically constrained, has led an international task force of over thirty warships to be deployed off the Horn of Africa.

The decision taken by so many countries to contribute to this task force was not taken lightly. It is a harbinger of future maritime security operations. As global trading routes evolve it is difficult to predict where the next outbreak of this form of piracy or new threats from criminality may occur.

Navies in the future will not just protect SLOC. Their traditional roles will have to be maintained as they use the freedom of the sea to provide security in other forms. President Obama's decision to cancel the deployment of the Ballistic Missile Defence (BMD) system in Europe, announced in September 2009, relies on the forward deployment of the

Aegis-class warships that have a Theatre Missile Defence (TMD) capability into the Eastern Mediterranean Sea and, if required, the North Sea.[12] The deployment by the US of Aegis-equipped destroyers into the Gulf provides reassurance to countries such as Saudi Arabia that fear Iranian efforts to obtain nuclear weapons, and the ballistic missile capabilities that might deliver such weapons.[13] By deploying the Aegis-class platforms in the Persian Gulf and off the coast of North Korea, the United States is providing an additional layer of defence capability against actions by what it regards as rogue states. It is now a tool being used in a managed escalation of the diplomatic pressure being brought against Iran. The attraction of such platforms is clear, and South Korea has announced its intention to acquire six scaled-down Aegis destroyers in 2019.[14] The new ship design is designated KDX-3A. These will follow on from the three Aegis-equipped destroyers, one of which was commissioned in December 2008, that are already progressively being introduced with a total of six being on order eventually. This will provide South Korea with its own indigenous capability to deploy TMD and use it as part of its response to any confrontation with North Korea.

Navies also have an important role in projecting expeditionary operations across the oceans to distant locations and ensuring the safe delivery of the initial amphibious force into theatre to fight the entry battle. Countries such as France, with its thirteen geographically distributed colonies (including French Polynesia, New Caledonia, Wallis et Funtuna and Clipperton in the Pacific Ocean, several in the Caribbean and three in the Indian Ocean), require an expeditionary capability to ensure the protection of these colonies in times of crisis. France's decision to acquire four new re-supply ships for delivery in 2020 is easy to understand.[15]

China is a country that places huge importance on asymmetric approaches to warfare, especially in the maritime domain. It has also taken the first tentative steps towards the development of an anti-ballistic missile capability,[16] as it embarks upon a comprehensive programme to establish itself as a maritime power.[17] China depends upon its SLOC to obtain its energy supplies and the experience[18] it is gaining from participating in the operations off the coast of Somalia are important for its ability to develop a navy that has regional influence. India will not have ignored the significance of these developments and is being very clear in its own ambitions to be able to manage what goes on in the Indian Ocean.[19] The potential for the economic rivalry to turn into a confrontation in the Indian Ocean is very real.[20]

Given the strategic nature of some of the world's most important choke points, such as the Strait of Hormuz, projecting amphibious forces ashore to secure those routes in a time of tension or conflict cannot be ruled out. In the event of such an operation, naval forces would find it hard to resist the deployment of sea-based TMD to prevent attacks being mounted on the task force before sending the amphibious forces ashore.[21]

At a time when many defence politicians are heavily focused on the land-environment, they would be wise to remember the teachings of naval strategists such as Alfred Mahan and William Corbett, who showed how very different the land and maritime domains are when it comes to warfare.

Ironically, this has been an era in which the threat has become vastly more difficult. Instead of massive force-on-force engagements, (where revolution in military affairs was heralded by some to provide the battle-winning tempo and decision superiority required to defeat an adversary), the threat dispersed and became point-targets that were much more difficult to detect. Our adversaries have understood how to deceive us of their intentions and how to camouflage their assets. The Intelligence, Surveillance, Target Acquisition and Recognition (ISTAR) problem has just become a vastly different challenge in the maritime domain.

Instead of looking for large naval formations, the threat morphed into smaller boats, like the skiffs used by pirates, the boats and tactics employed by the Iranian Navy,[22] and similar vessels that move economic migrants across the world's oceans.[23] Their ability to paint their boat a specific colour, to blend into the background, and attack at dawn or dusk to reduce their ability to be detected, suddenly introduced a whole new challenge for those that push the case for investments in ISTAR and the concepts of developing situational awareness based upon the idea that an adversary could be detected. The issue of persistence, and the resolution of sensor systems to detect such small and immersive targets, is increasingly vital in developing any response.

Off the coast of Somalia, vessels under threat have to maintain a level of vigilance that may seem to the uneducated observer as quite extraordinary. In the end, the protection of a vessel threatened by pirates is often in the hands of the master and the ways in which he conducts manoeuvres[24] to counter any attempted boarding by pirates. The development of such tactics has seen the number of successful hijackings reduce towards the end of 2009; although the overall statistics for the year are appreciably worse than in previous years. Encouragingly, despite the development of new tactics by pirates, the trend in overall seizures of vessels did not escalate rapidly in the first six months of 2010. This is a testament to the increasing cooperation across the international naval forces deployed into the region.

The idea of Maritime Domain Awareness (MDA) is all well and good when one has cooperating targets that carry transponders that provide helpful information in an internationally recognised format, the Automatic Identification System (AIS), which is mandated for all vessels over 300 tonnes. But crucially, it is very different indeed when a naval unit is faced by an adversary that knows the environment, and employs camouflage, deception and swarming tactics to achieve its objectives. Systems that use the advantages of space-based observations are still in their early phases of development and deployment, and have yet to reach a level of maturity where real-time information on the location of all vessels on the ocean is available.[25]

The problems surrounding the hijacking of the *Arctic Sea* in the Gulf of Bothnia on 24 July 2009 highlight enduring communications difficulties and a lack of a comprehensively joined-up approach in the United Kingdom, which is indicative of a broader range of issues concerning developing integrated views of what is actually happening around coastlines. With the arrival of the Olympic Games in the United Kingdom in 2012, the lessons emerging from the *Arctic Sea* incident need to be understood.

As time has gone by, it has become clear that information was clearly available to some authorities, who felt it unnecessary to pass it onto others who had the responsibility to interdict such activity and may well have needed to know. As the *Arctic Sea* passed Dover, information percolated through various authorities that should have placed the vessel on a watch list or at some heightened state of alert. Reports indicate that Interpol was certainly aware that all was not well aboard the vessel after the agency had been contacted by its owners.

The *Arctic Sea*, after it had been hijacked by pirates, went past several major elements of the United Kingdom's Critical National Infrastructure (CNI), such as the Isle of Grain, two nuclear power stations and the oil refining facilities at Fawley on Southampton Water, over a period of three days. The fact that the ship was not under the control of its Captain throughout that journey is at best worrisome. What if the pirates had had a very different intent? What if they had been carrying some form of explosive device aboard?

The incident surrounding the *MV Nisha* on 21 December 2001, just months after 11 September, when it had to be assaulted in the English Channel by Special Forces, also seems to have been forgotten. Intelligence reports indicated that the *MV Nisha* was carrying some form of Chemical, Biological, Radiological, Nuclear (CBRN) device, which was loaded whilst it was in Djibouti. Whilst the intelligence as to the chances of a second attack was not clear in the heightened state of alert in the aftermath of 11 September, it was a very rash decision to ignore the specific warning that had been given.

The dividing line between terrorism and piracy is often a semantic one as some commentators argue that there are established links between various transnational groups and pirate activity. Whilst these links are often difficult to prove, the fact that the *Arctic Sea* made its passage past such a number of high profile assets unchallenged may have sent out signals to a range of terrorist groups as to the lack of a joined-up approach to maritime security in the United Kingdom.[26] This unfortunately is just one example of the many problems faced by countries around the world. Developing a comprehensive picture of activities around coastlines is not easy and takes a lot of resources.

Governments often argue that they base their deployment considerations upon intelligence. This is often referred to as an intelligence-led approach. In practice, this is often used as an argument to avoid difficult investment decisions that would otherwise be required. Intelligence failures do happen; but a failure to pass on information that is available to the authorities that can carry out an interdiction operation smacks of complacency and a failure to appreciate the current multidimensional nature of the threat.

Was the *Arctic Sea* incident an intelligence failure or an indication of far more systemic failings at the heart of the United Kingdom's approach to maritime security? One thing is clear: the incident was a wake-up call for those involved in the maritime security sector, where piracy may have been characterised as a problem that does not happen in the United Kingdom's coastal waters. The broader implications of the *Arctic Sea* incident are, however, more profound and highlight the highly fragmented nature of the databases and systems that might, if integrated, help form a comprehensive viewpoint of activities in and around the United Kingdom's coastline and also provide important pointers for other countries with similar concerns.

Those who pose threats to the maritime environment do not stop with simple measures such as using paint and local environmental factors that inevitably reduce visibility and warning times of a potential attack. Discerning pirates in a 2 metre skiff with insufficient warning time for a captain to commence evasive manoeuvres is already difficult enough. The new tactics simply make the task immeasurably more difficult and cry out for the installation of masthead optical systems that can zoom in on a number of skiffs that might be approaching a vessel.

Criminals have started to use midget submarines, and terrorists used rubber inflatable boats to attack Mumbai. Simple mines have also made a comeback and the deployment by organisations with close ties to Hamas of floating devices, found off Hofit beach in Ashkelon,[27] seemed to be of a similar design to land-based improvised explosive devices or IEDs that are used in Palestine against the Israeli Defence Forces.

Proliferation of weapon systems, such as the supply of missiles from recognised nation states to non-state actors has made the threat environment even more difficult. The detection problem has also become very difficult. The sea provides a large area to hide if you do not wish to be found. The International Monetary Fund (IMF) estimated in 2005 that transnational criminal organisations currently earn between $1–2 trillion a year from their activities; this is the size of a number of the world's leading economies.

Maritime Security and the World's Economy

At the start of the twenty-first century the world's economy depends upon the sea. The problem is that the world's oceans, which represent 70 per cent of the total surface area of the earth, are unregulated and vulnerable. The world's merchant fleet carries 90 per cent of global exports (estimated at $8.9 trillion in 2004). An additional $400 billion is generated in freight rates, and some 300 million containers move the goods across the seas on over 45,000 merchant vessels. This highway of the sea is guarded by just over 6,000 naval vessels of varying types and capabilities, operated by 160 nation states with some naval, coastguard and maritime constabulary function, with around forty nation states having a capability to project naval power over significant global distances. Most of these are the ones engaged off the coast of Somalia, trying to protect the 20,000 ships every year that use that maritime highway to move goods in and out from the Indian Ocean and beyond into the economically vital area of Southeast Asia.

The maritime environment is also a hugely important source of food, and with fish stocks dwindling across the world and demand outstripping supply, aquaculture industries that are increasingly important to local economies have sprung up in places such as Norway, Chile, Scotland and New Zealand.[28] This industry is hugely vulnerable to environment events, such as harmful algae blooms, which can have a devastating impact upon a wide area. Satellite-based observations, originally based upon the National Oceanic and Atmospheric Administration (NOAA) series of satellites, allowed blooms to be detected, as they discoloured the water. Newer sensor systems, such as Moderate Resolution Imaging Spectroradiometer (MODIS), provide greater spatial and spectral resolution of the features detected in the water, allowing the type of bloom to be discerned.

The world's economy is hugely dependent on oil and anything that threatens oil supplies can have a major impact on it. Operations, such as those successfully conducted by naval units in the Gulf during the Iran-Iraq War to escort tankers,[29] or the projection of air power over the conflicts in the Balkans from platforms based in the Adriatic Sea, somehow did not grab the attention in the same way as the ones carried out against the Russian Navy in fighting the Second Battle of the Atlantic.

Media focus, so often prominent at the outset of military campaigns, fades as the conflict draws out into a longer-running affair. The public loses connectivity with the aims and objectives of the military effort and can become critical of what appear to be protracted and unsophisticated approaches to warfare that involve too many civilian casualties. Impatience often characterises public perceptions of war. If war is to be conducted then it must be fast, effective and involve few casualties.

The First Gulf War (1990–1991) set expectations in this regard that are perhaps unrealistic in the medium term; they appeared to confirm the line of reasoning being developed at the time, that technology would provide a battle winning edge, and that the ubiquity of knowledge of the battlefield provided by ISTAR would ensure all future wars would be short duration affairs. The more recent experiences in Iraq and Afghanistan, and the complex nature of the maritime situation off the Horn of Africa, have tended to highlight just how unrealistic those views were at the time.

This attitude permeated the collective psyche of many in the West and defence spending per se became less of a focus for governments than during the Cold War. This was the start of the form of sea-blindness that now pervades the majority of Western political thinking, with the notable exception of Norway and Canada,[30] who are increasingly focusing their vision towards the north and the riches of the Lomonosov Ridge.[31] The issue of energy security is inexorably linked to maritime security, as so many potential areas of interest for the exploitation of assets on the continental shelf are linked to potential disputes and conflicts. Securing the national Exclusive Economic Zone (EEZ), when its definition allows areas to be defined over the proven extent of the continental shelf, is going to be a vital role for some national navies.[32]

Whenever operations to counter terrorism were mentioned, it appeared to some as grasping at straws, latching onto anything that justified maintaining naval forces at the levels enjoyed during the Cold War. Against this background and an emergent general economic malaise, what had been ambitious plans to sustain naval power, became victim to piecemeal cutbacks in forces, as a number of platforms were trimmed back and programmes cancelled and deferred. This narrow vision of the enduring utility of maritime power and the perception of a safe and stable maritime environment, however, is not one shared by those involved in criminality and terrorism. They understand the abiding characteristics and benefits enjoyed by those who seek to manoeuvre using the maritime environment to hide their nefarious activities.

Much of what we know about the activities of those who use the sea in this way is anecdotal. Hard evidence is often difficult to come by, as the maritime domain is so huge that it is simply difficult to create an accurate picture of the activities on the sea. This leads to many problems. Political leaders are known for their inability to understand and master a nascent threat, and Somalia is a case in point. It took the hijack of a vessel loaded with tanks bound for East Africa to galvanise the necessary political will to act. Fishermen complaining of their livelihoods being denuded by foreign fishing vessels were simply not enough to get political leaders in the West to sit up and pay attention.

Therein lies an important lesson. It is axiomatic that prevention is better than cure. In the twenty-first century, one of the major issues the world faces is an inability to master the rhetoric or dialogue of early intervention and apply soft power approaches to solve problems before they escalate to a level where military resources need to be deployed. These are often required in significant numbers, as by the time political leaders wake up to the issue, the level of chaos that has already gained a foothold in an area is very difficult to suppress. This applies to the land and sea environments. Early action is essential if situations are to be contained.

The problem is that such early action costs money and resources and appears to provide little in return. Classic risk-based modelling does not fit the bill. Traditional approaches to developing the political will to intervene suffer from inertia. New approaches to risk-based modelling that can provide for situations where a number of factors can suddenly align with catastrophic consequences need to be developed. Each element of the increasing anarchy on the seas can make its contribution to such an outcome. A person with specific materials is smuggled by sea, using one of the established routes for illegal immigrants, arrives at a destination and meets up with another person who has particular skills. They have had prior contact on the Internet. Two pieces of a jigsaw puzzle come together at a place and time below security agencies' radar horizons. The ingredients for a catastrophic outcome are being assembled and the basis for a large-scale terrorist attack is being created.

Is this fact or fiction? Unfortunately only history can tell what it is. But the chance of a major terrorist attack is what motivates many whose job it is to disrupt and interdict the channels by which such outcomes could occur. It is generally accepted that we only have to get it wrong once. In contrast, terrorists can try and fail many times. Professor Paul Wilkinson summed this up quite well when writing in the *Daily Telegraph* in 1992, 'Fighting terrorism is like being a goalkeeper. You can make a hundred brilliant saves but the only shot that people remember is the one that gets past you'.

Attack planning takes time, but time is what terrorists and their insurgent friends have in abundance. The Taliban in Afghanistan have a saying: 'you have the watches, we have the time'. Political leaders should reflect on the implications of such a statement, which would find traction with any insurgent or terrorist around the world. Criminals are often motivated by short-term gains, so their attitude may be quite different. Legal frameworks back up this myopic view of the maritime environment with statements that encourage the perspective that the freedom to navigate the seas is available as a right.

Transnational criminals use the sea to smuggle people,[33] weapons and drugs and to steal from seafarers and their vessels.[34] Pirates use the sea to bunker oil reserves and hijack vessels. Terrorists use the freedom of manoeuvre on the seas to maintain their presence on the international security landscape, as highlighted by the attacks on Mumbai. Given the impact each of these forms of criminality has had on the international landscape, there are genuine fears about the implications of a nexus being created where the two forms of criminality merge their efforts.

There are at least two schools of thought on this that prevail today. The first dismisses a nexus as unlikely, as the objectives of criminals and terrorists differ markedly. The second highlights the pragmatic nature of the way the insurgent environment in Iraq responded to being disrupted and destroyed, by forming temporary alliances that crossed what might have been regarded as ideological fault lines in order to maintain the fight against what rapidly became classed as the common enemy: the forces of the West who were trying to impose their ideas of democracy upon Iraq.

One facet from the maritime perspective is the apparent line that exists between piracy[35] and terrorism.[36] Semantic arguments do form a large part of the discussion that arises, with the inevitable ongoing debates about the definition of the term terrorism. The jury is out on this debate at the moment, but the consequences of alliances developing between terrorist groups and transnational criminals, who already use the maritime environment extensively, would be quite profound, further complicating what is already a complex multi-dimensional environment.

Enduring Characteristics of Maritime Power

Time alone will tell if those who have an insular view of the world in the twenty-first century are right or wrong. History, however, does not bode well for those who seek to dismiss the utility of maritime power. The speed, flexibility, agility and scalability of maritime forces offer political leaders an ability to gradually escalate a response to a crisis. These are the enduring characteristics of maritime power. They offer a dynamic and responsive approach, allowing a flexible means of intervention on a global basis by providing options and potential break-points to diffuse difficult situations and to support Maritime Security Operations (MSO).[37]

This operational agility of maritime power has been illustrated throughout history, no more so than in the multinational evacuation of Beirut in the summer of 2006 as the Israeli Defence Force and Hezbollah confronted each other in a conflict that lasted thirty-three days. The rapid ability to mount such an operation, massing naval units from a wide range of participating countries that had previously been widely dispersed, was a true indication of one of the applications of contemporary maritime power on an international basis.

When tensions flared off the coast of North Korea, after it conducted its second nuclear test, naval vessels quickly responded and provided a tactical shield,[38] should South Korea or Japan have been directly threatened if the rhetoric spilled over into direct confrontation, and some of North Korea's extensive arsenal of ballistic missiles launched as a precursor to a wider initiation of hostilities. The presence of the missile defence shield provided options to the politicians as they tried to manage a very unpredictable situation. The events surrounding the sinking of the South Korean naval vessel, the *Cheonan*, provided further evidence, if it were needed, of just how situations can unexpectedly arise out of left field. The deployment of South Korean naval forces and the immediate planning of naval exercises with the United States Navy provided a maritime-based response to the incident that could easily have got out of control if land-based military activity had escalated. The magnifying effect of the world's media watching large scale land-based military manoeuvres is far more dramatic than a number of ships sailing on the sea. Situations like this must be seen through the magnifying glass of perception where potential adversaries can rapidly conclude that the only course of action open to them is to strike first to gain an advantage.

Where Western liberal democracies are faced by threats from unpredictable and autocratic leaders for whom war might be a whim, the ability to scale a response and to act defensively in the first instance is really important. The TMD shield provided by the Aegis Class destroyers offers just the kind of flexible response often associated with the application of maritime power;[39] it helps defuse what might have been a difficult situation and provides options for political leaders, as it is purely a defensive deployment[40] having no aggressive capability. Security was delivered from the sea to protect domestic infrastructure and military facilities located on the land. The introduction of this capability is an example worthy of future detailed study.

The responses to other more desperate humanitarian operations highlight the enduring flexibility associated with maritime power. This was amply demonstrated in the immediate response to the terrible earthquake that took place in Haiti on 12 January 2010. The magnitude of the earthquake, at 7.0 on the Richter Scale, was sufficient to devastate most of the country's already crumbling infrastructure. Maritime-based assistance was able to provide swift and tailored help in areas in the initial search phase, and also when that moved into longer-term recovery and reconstruction activities. The efforts of the United States Navy and Coastguard, after Hurricane Katrina had so mercilessly battered the south coast of the United States, have left a profoundly different set of perceptions in the minds of those who reflect carefully upon maritime security. The potential for major battle groups, such as a Nimitz-class carrier formation to provide support in the aftermath of a major disaster, brings another perspective to the less kinetic applications of combat power. The signals of climate change are becoming clearer, even if controversy still surrounds the exact interpretations of the science. In the last decade the frequency of hurricanes has reached anomalous levels, according to an article published in *Nature* in August 2009.[41] Evidence, as reported in *Nature* in September 2008, suggests that the frequency of hurricanes is increasing, as is their ferocity.

If this is an indicator of climate change it may well presage more events such as Katrina, and a greater need to be able to deliver security from the sea to the land when communications, roads and infrastructure have been disrupted, and in some cases destroyed.

The Royal Navy has a similar recent history of providing much-needed and prompt assistance to Caribbean states when they have experienced real difficulties. During both Hurricane Gustav[42] and Hurricane Ike in September 2008,[43] the Royal Navy deployed surface and airborne units to bring relief to the local population. The Indian Navy provided similar assistance to the people of Sri Lanka after the Tsunami in December 2004.[44] The ability to quickly deliver assistance from the sea is a crucial demonstration of the enduring versatility of maritime power, and is causing some navies to review the utility of their current fleets and propose new concepts for vessels.[45]

In his address to the Seventeenth Seapower Symposium, then Rear Admiral (Select) Charles Martoglio remarked, in his comments on the *United States Navy's Strategic Plan*, remarked how in the wake of the devastation left by a natural disaster like Katrina in the maritime environment, relief workers can gain 'infrastructure access', bringing with them everything they need, even the Post Office. The maritime domain has played a similar role in the aftermath of the Haiti earthquake in January 2010. As local populations struggle to cope with the consequences of a major hurricane, maritime power can help deliver a sense of security from the sea to the land, bypassing many of the infrastructure failures that would inevitably delay purely land-based responses.

A key question is how that security should be developed. With over 6,000 naval vessels in operation around the world an idea was floated of creating a 1,000-Ship Navy as a global maritime partnership. This United States-led initiative gained a lot of supporters as it made a great deal of sense conceptually. Given the scale of the problem, and the protean nature of the threat, harnessing naval power from across the world's navies could well have a unifying effect upon the political landscape; integrating naval power for the common good against transnational criminals, terrorist groups and those who represented emergent threats. The concept was based upon some basic ideas:

- That coalitions of the willing would be formed to provide maritime security or a deterrent effect in areas of the world that were too unstable to prevent terrorist groups or criminals from exploiting that instability for their purposes.[46] The model for this form of naval cooperation was already available from existing operations within NATO, such as the various Standing Naval Forces that routinely operated in the Mediterranean Sea and their wider application in the Gulf of Aden.[47]
- That countries without specific deployable naval resources should provide funding and support for other countries in the forefront of such operations. The funds made available by the United Arab Emirates to support the doubling of the Seychelles Coastguard fleet to ten vessels in July 2010 is an excellent example of such cooperation. While Abu Dhabi is not directly threatened by the piracy, it has clearly recognised the possible impact this criminal behaviour may have upon its role as a major hub for commercial shipping.
- In such an uncertain world no single navy can protect the world's oceans from the range of potential targets, ranging from small boats that suddenly appear from a mother craft, to those that shuttle drugs using powerful outboard motors to move quickly across the ocean.
- Trying to counter the activities of transnational criminals and terrorist groups requires local knowledge of the coastline, where these peo-

ple may use the freedom of rivers and other natural features to hide and disperse—hence the need to coordinate with local coastguard, constabulary and naval units.

- Developing a mix of capabilities, where some naval units can bring specific skills and expertise to the coalition units operating under the umbrella of the 1,000-Ship Navy, allowing the full-spectrum of threats to be countered, including ballistic missiles where these may be deployed. Coalitions would be formed quickly to utilise maritime power to provide humanitarian relief in the wake of a natural disaster, as in the case of the huge international effort that went into the Indian Ocean after the December 2004 Tsunami.
- That a simple communications environment would be created based upon contemporary and readily available technologies based upon international communications standards and widely adopted by maritime nations A model for this already exists,[48] and is called the Combined Enterprise Regional Information Exchange System (CENTRIXS). This allows countries to plug-and-play naval units into information sharing environments that allow national commanders to share maritime domain awareness to assist them in making decisions.[49]
- Creating the frameworks whereby naval forces could congregate and remove any overlaps in their activities, thus making the best use of the coalition assets (including any organic air capabilities) that were deployed to protect specific areas of the world's oceans.

Constraints on Maritime Power

The international response to the activities of pirates off the coast of Somalia provides some insights into the problems of developing a secure maritime environment, and illustrates what arguably is a major challenge—that of persistence when trying to secure an area of the ocean. At the time of writing, thirty-five warships from sixteen countries are operating in a naval coalition in the Gulf of Aden and into the western end of the Indian Ocean, an area of over 2 million km.[50]

On 5 August 2009, a South Korean warship rescued a Bahamian-registered commercial ship from a pirate attack, highlighting the transnational nature of the response being mounted by the international community. The South Korean warships are present to help the estimated 500 vessel-journeys a year flagged to their own country to conduct a safe passage through the dangerous waters off the coast of Somalia; of these, 150 are thought to be particularly vulnerable to pirate attack.

The anti-piracy efforts involve the naval forces of Canada, India, South Korea, Japan, Russia,[51] the United States, Turkey, the United Kingdom and many others.[52] Securing this vitally important trading route has created an interesting, and somewhat eclectic, coalition of the willing that has seen Iranian warships[53] operating alongside those from the United States, with the latter notably saving one of Iran's major tankers, the MT *Hadi*, from being hijacked on 28 June 2009. Strategic diplomacy between the two countries might be emerging from a somewhat dormant state, but tactical cooperation on the high seas to secure sea lanes of communication is alive as warships from the Royal Saudi and United States navies quickly offered assistance to the Iranian vessel.

On 5 May 2009, a South Korean warship, *Munmu the Great*, provided assistance to a North Korean vessel that was being threatened by pirates. The efforts at sea have been complemented by the efforts of the Yemenis, for example, to increase maritime security along their coastline following the commissioning of new radar systems in June 2009 to monitor their coastal waters. This is truly an international cooperative effort to secure one of the world's most important sea lanes and possibly a role model for future wider-ranging MSO activities involving international cooperation.

A crucial question that has emerged from the international efforts to secure the SLOC through the Gulf of Aden has been the discussion of whether to arm vessels transiting the area. There are a wide range of views on this subject, with the French and Spanish governments' authorisation of the deployment of security forces on their fishing boats in the area. The Dutch government, in contrast, did not agree to proposals to place marines on slow moving and particularly vulnerable merchant vessels operating in the area. Events surrounding the release of Captain Richard Phillips of the *Maersk Alabama* acted as a catalyst for developments in this area for the United States.

The situation deteriorated when the Syrian Captain of a vessel bound for Mogadishu was shot by pirates on 25 September 2009, after he refused to turn the ship away from the port.[54] This event represented an escalation in the violence associated with piracy in the Horn of Africa; this and other developments suggest that some pirates, with specific links to the Al-Qaeda,[55] are planning to specifically target Indian vessels operating in the Gulf of Aden, presumably in an effort to increase tensions in the region.[56] The situation in the area is in a fluid state and has the potential to deteriorate further if pirates find they are unable to sustain the lifestyles to which they have become accustomed.

Paradoxically, at a time when the problems of maritime security are highlighted through the media nearly every day off the coast of East Africa, there seems to be a reluctance in some circles to address the implications of an absence of maritime security in the strategically important sea lanes of the Gulf of Aden and out into the Indian Ocean on the global economy. As a direct result of piracy in the Gulf of Aden, international insurance premiums increased to between 0.5 per cent and 0.175 per cent of the value of their cargos in July 2009. In May 2009 these levels varied by up to 0.05 per cent. The potential for such costs to rise still further is clear. If the level of insecurity prevails, shipping companies will move their goods over the longer route off the coast of South Africa. This will consequently impact international trade routes and ports that service those routes as part of the international hub-and-spoke architecture. Aden is one port that has suffered from these increases in insurance premiums, with important implications for its local economy and employment. Local people driven out of work can turn to criminal activities, mimicking the very actions of the pirates whose attacks have created the problem in the first place; this is a vicious circle that needs to be broken.

This is a prominent example of the way in which the land and sea environments interact in what is a tightly coupled interface whose linkages are often not fully appreciated. As maritime trading routes evolve in the future, the wider implications of the potential impact of criminality threatening other important SLOC should not be forgotten. The issue of persistence is one that criminals rely upon to manoeuvre at sea; developments in technologies that are able to provide increased levels of surveillance are likely to have an important impact upon the ways in which a secure maritime environment develops.[57]

Persistence is a crucial issue, but there is little point in being able to detect targets if units do not exist on the ground that are deployed to reduce response times and to disrupt the activities of those who enjoy the freedom of the seas for their own criminal activities. Sea power does have its constraints if navies have their platform and hull totals significantly reduced. There is clearly a need for the development of a class of vessels that can perform constabulary tasks in the EEZ. Their design and performance will have to reflect local issues on basing, response times and likely sea states in which they will have to operate. The rise of the Offshore Patrol Vessel (OPV), being procured by many countries around the world, is an indicator of the importance of this role to police the EEZ.[58] However, many of these vessels are only lightly armed and likely to be able to disrupt criminal activity and those planning terrorist attacks, where they can be impeded at sea. Variants will appear that will allow OPV to engage in protecting sovereign territory where confrontation turns to local conflicts. The potential for these to be a repeat of the Cod Wars conducted off the Icelandic coast in the 1950s and 1970s between the Royal Navy and the gunboats of the Icelandic authorities is clear. For those deploying this capability an understanding of the lessons to emerge from that crisis—where NATO nations were all but at war over a dispute over natural resources—may well provide some important insights to help shape their operational doctrine.

Whilst it is highly likely that the OPV will become an ubiquitous element of future naval planning for many countries seeking to create secure maritime environments, for those with interests in protecting SLOC beyond the EEZ, very different decisions about the nature of their navies will have to be made. Frigates and destroyers will still have a role for some blue-water navies that seek to protect their SLOC on the world stage. After 2020, as oil and gas supplies increasingly become a focus for countries trying to maintain their economies, the potential for blue-water navies to become involved in confrontation on the high seas should not be ignored. The Indian Ocean, the South Atlantic and the new sea routes that will open up as the Arctic ice caps continues to recede, will challenge the extent to which navies can deploy on a global basis to protect their SLOC.[59]

Coupling the Land and Sea Domains

The ignorance of this critical linkage between the land environment and the sea can be illustrated by a recent commentary provided by the International Institute for Strategic Studies (IISS), one of the foremost academic bodies addressing the issues of the post Cold War international security landscape. Adelphi Paper 400–401, which is entitled *Perspectives on International Security: Speeches and Papers from the 50th Anniversary*

Year of the International Institute for Strategic Studies, brings together a range of contemporary commentaries on the subject of international security to celebrate the fiftieth anniversary of the formation of the Institute, but barely finds any room for meaningful debate upon the issues associated with maritime security. It is apparent from the discourse presented that a form of malaise exists when it comes to discussing maritime security in an international context. Too many assumptions are made, whilst disturbing patterns and trends in the maritime environment that have links to the land domain are being ignored.[60]

The analysis presented by the IISS is very land-centric, and this is echoed throughout the text that purports to analyse and provide a critical commentary upon the emerging international security landscape. A passing reference is made to a speech concerning how Southeast Asia is a potential crucible for future state-on-state conflict and the development of Chinese strategic capabilities.

It may be that this land-centric approach reflects the strategic nature of political thought and its focus upon where populations live. It is unwise, and indeed short-sighted, to appear to ignore the significance of the maritime environment and the role it plays in helping to provide security for economic growth and development. In one relatively simple example, several major operators of cruise liners have decided that the waters of the Gulf of Aden are now simply too risky. By rescheduling their cruises they have had an impact upon the local economies of several countries that look to the tourist trade as an important source of foreign currency.[61] Ironically, this very act of withdrawing the cruise liners and their vital revenue from an area actually creates greater instability, as people who are no longer able to earn money from legitimate enterprises related to the tourist trade resort to criminal behaviour to ensure their families are supported.

At the heart of the problem is the need to have an accurate and current picture of the maritime domain. This requires persistence of observation and is difficult to achieve. Once a comprehensive picture of activities in the maritime environment has been formed, units can be deployed to areas seen to be at risk. Creating what is often referred to as 'MDA' requires, above all, continuity of observation, and cooperation between multi-agency partners in both the military and civilian sectors of a nation state, to analyse the results and develop the Recognised Maritime Operational Picture (RMOP). This represents maritime domain awareness and needs to be updated at intervals commensurate with the nature and characteristics of the threats, some of which can be fleeting targets.

These are crucial elements of any framework that might be created, either alone, or with regional or international partners. The sheer size of the maritime environment provides those with malevolent intent a great deal of room to manoeuvre. As the pirates operating off the coast of Somalia have shown, even people with limited resources can extend their reach over wide areas using mother ships to provide platforms from which smaller craft can be launched.[62] The formation of pirate action groups has been one development in tactics that has seen the pirate adapt to the measures being introduced by the international maritime task force. It is unlikely that these measures will be the last. Biology provides a good analogy for the ways in which the tactics between the naval task force and the pirates adapt to each other; it is called co-evolution, wherein each party evolves in ways that try to improve their survivability.

While the survivability of the international maritime force is not in doubt from a combat viewpoint, it might not survive political pressures to scale back the operations and commitments. For many of the pirates, however, in the absence of a lucrative fishing industry upon which to fall back, the confrontation with the international maritime task force is literally a question of survival. The risks and privations they endure to put meals on their family tables is understandable to many. Solving the problem, however, is not so straightforward in countries where governance structures have broken down. Somalia is a basket case, but unfortunately for the maritime environment, it may not be the last country whose chaotic political structures create lawlessness and disorder along its coastline. These circumstances produce exactly the kind of breeding ground for lawlessness and anarchy that spread from the land to the sea.

The Focus of this Book

This book takes a different viewpoint on maritime security and tries to look at the problem holistically.[63] Building upon the dimensions already discussed, from historical and contemporary perspectives since 11 September, the book looks out into a wider world and considers the impact of other aspects of security, such as food, economic and energy security. There are many challenges to establishing a secure maritime environment,[64] hence the title of the book, *The Anarchic Sea*.

Countries, such as Iran, are known to use the sea to supply weapons to various groups that act as their proxy-partners in promoting instability in various regions. The arrest by the Yemeni authorities of the *Mahan-1* on 26 October 2009, when it was found to be carrying a containment of anti-tank weaponry, illustrates the nature of such weapons smuggling. The Israeli Defence Force seized a similar vessel, the Antiguan-flagged *Francop*, on 4 November 2009 off the Israeli coast, carrying hundreds of tonnes of weapons for the Hezbollah.[65]

Many countries in Africa are having their fish stocks depleted by the activities of commercial trawlers. In Nigeria, pirates siphon off and bunker oil resources, denying important income to the central government. Australia is facing a new wave of economic migrants from Indonesia. Vietnam and China are involved in various disputes with countries such as Malaya and Taiwan concerning claims over the Paracel and Spratley Islands in the South China Sea.[66]

To build a picture of the contemporary situation concerning maritime security around the world, this text is based upon a series of detailed case studies that have both geographic and thematic focus. The thematic case studies provide specific insights into maritime security issues around the world, from the use of the tactics of asymmetric warfare, to the proliferation of WMD, to the need for TMD capabilities using the sea to protect the land.[67] The geographic case studies explore the challenges posed on particular countries, such as Chile, Canada, the United States, Australia, and the United Kingdom in protecting their coastal waters.[68]

One particular case study addresses the international footprint used by the French government to offer security to its protectorates in the Caribbean and the Pacific Oceans, as well as the close ties it has developed with a number of countries in the Middle East. The approach to maritime security being taken by France merits a detailed examination. Its basis is an appropriate and significant permanent presence in the various areas it believes are important to its national security. As part of its new approach, the French government commissioned a new military base in Abu Dhabi, which includes an important naval element that illustrates the French emphasis in maritime security on forward-basing and presence. This shows a clear recognition by the French government of the importance of the area, and the ability to be able to respond quickly, should the need arise. France also contributes to international coalition efforts to provide humanitarian assistance, and needs to be ready to evacuate its own and European Union citizens, should any crises arise.

The case studies highlight the polymorphous nature of the threat environment. Each case study provides specific insights, some of which are generic, and others that are quite specific to the local situation. The aim is to compare and contrast the case studies and draw from them ways of creating secure marine environments that can be developed both by individual nations and by those operating in coalitions. By adopting this comprehensive approach, the aim is to try and be sure that whilst the specific nature of the threats posed to a particular country's coastal waters is acknowledged, elements that are germane to the broader regional and international considerations are also appreciated. The analysis presented through these case studies, based as it is on a holistic approach, provides the basis of the 'seven dimensions of maritime security' that are the themes of this book.

This book also develops its perspectives on maritime security through a thorough analysis of what the term means and how that fits alongside a broader national security strategy, and any maritime security strategy that is a component of the overarching text. It is based on a holistic approach, but in adopting such an approach there is an inherent danger of repetition, of recycling old material through a slightly different lens. This book tries to avoid repeating previously published analysis, except where the analysis adds specific value to the discussion laid out herein, as this would be counterproductive. There have already been many texts that have brought important insights into the area of maritime terrorism; these are acknowledged and key points drawn from their analyses.

The aim is to build a substantive new work that provides contemporary perspectives on the issue of maritime security, looking at illegal fishing, the Mumbai attacks, TMD and humanitarian relief operations. These are all fertile areas and little existing material has been published concerning the ways in which these factors have an impact upon maritime security. Particular case studies, drawn from a wide range of international perspectives, have been drawn up to reflect upon the nature of these threats. A number of excellent reference works are also cited for further detailed examination in a chapter that reviews the contemporary perspectives that are available on maritime security. Having looked at the spectrum of threats, the book moves on to consider responses to those threats and, through the use of some specific case studies, illustrates how some countries are approaching the task and collaborating with other nation states on a regional or international basis to deliver maritime security, both for the sea and from the sea to the land. The text ends with a series of conclusions that have been developed from the analysis discussed within this book, drawing out a model of an architecture that would help create a secure maritime environment.

1

CONTEMPORARY PERSPECTIVES ON MARITIME SECURITY

Maritime security is the ongoing condition in the maritime environment where international laws are adhered to, the right of navigation is preserved, and citizens, vessels, infrastructure and resources are protected.[1]

Defining Maritime Security

Maritime security at the start of the twenty-first century is not an easy concept to define. It is a globalised era where so many things are becoming ever more tightly coupled, and differentiating maritime security from wider-ranging political, military and economic issues is difficult. So many things appear to be linked.[2] Maritime security covers a wealth of perspectives and agendas; a point illustrated by the United States Navy setting up Fleet Cyber Command (FLTCYBERCOM) at the end of 2009.[3]

The United States Navy's posture of being forward-based allows it to respond quickly to crisis, but also inevitably places a huge reliance on the operations of its networks, and their reach back into the United States to allow it to function effectively. It is therefore understandable that the initial focus of the new command will inevitably be on the security of its current massive investment in global communications networks. The potential for FLTCYBERCOM to move into other applications of cyber-based technologies, perhaps using the cyber domain as part of its toolkit to project power and influence ashore, may not be too long in being forthcoming. In an era that will be defined more by the ideas associated with conflict prevention, anything that allows power to be projected using soft means is going to have a rapidly increasing profile.

Maritime security also concerns seafarers and commercial organisations that move goods and people by sea, military commanders, national governments and their governance structures and agencies, their citizens and those who exploit the potential of the sea for their living, such as fishermen and those engaged in the offshore industry. Inevitably, given the diversity of such a community, priorities and agendas vary. This challenging array of viewpoints creates problems for developing a coherent legislative approach to the maritime environment at home and on the international stage. Core principles are required, such as the freedom of navigation and respect for human rights.

Yet those very freedoms that offer such flexibility to legitimate users of the sea are at the same time its major weakness, enabling criminals to exploit the environment to manoeuvre and avoid detection, and to operate in the shadows and margins. With many nation states unable or unwilling to prosecute pirates operating off the Horn of Africa, the lack of sanctions that can be brought to bear to deter or change behaviours of the people and groups involved, frustrates the efforts of those charged with bringing maritime security to the region. In this major area, the international community has thus far failed to produce a coherent and widespread response to the issues of prosecuting those involved in piracy. While legal loopholes are not closed, the problems will not abate. Putting sticking plaster over the problems by supplying Kenya, for example, with some additional resources to put more people accused of piracy through a due legal process is not a sustainable solution. International efforts to create a long-term solution to this problem are an essential development in addressing the current problems, and any spread of the activity that might arise in other geographic areas. Concerns are also growing about the threats from Al-Qaeda linked groups in Yemen and Somalia, creating a link-up across the Bab el-Mandeb Strait at the bottom of the Red Sea. Threats have been issued by groups in both the countries to attack merchant vessels in the area and for the vital sea lane to be closed. Whilst much of the rhetoric might be hyperbole, it is a worrying development.

The marine environment is a hugely important domain upon which the global economy depends for over 90 per cent of its trade; yet its sheer vastness makes it difficult to secure.[4] There are vast tracts of the marine environment about which we have little idea as to how it is being used. Admiral Mullen was right when he observed at the opening of the Seventeenth International Seapower Symposium[5] that one consequence of today's security challenge is the realisation that the ungoverned and under-governed parts of the maritime domain can no longer be ignored.

As a direct result of the lack of governance, a number of major vulnerabilities of the maritime domain are accentuated, gradually making it more anarchic in nature, such as:

- Illegal and unreported fishing and its impact upon local coastal communities.
- The aftermath of major natural events, such as tsunamis, typhoons and hurricanes.
- The potential for acts of terrorism against merchant vessels, offshore installations and major elements of maritime and civilian infrastructure, such as Mumbai in November 2008.
- The trade in drugs and psychotropic substances.
- Piracy and armed robbery conducted against ships under way or at anchor,[6] where the 2,500 attacks reported in the period from 2000 to 2007 contrast markedly with the 209 in the period from 1994 to 1999.
- Pollution incidents that degrade the natural environment, such as Red Tides and the discharge of oil.
- The movement of a variety of weapons, from ballistic missiles to weapons of mass destruction.
- Economic migration using the sea.
- The results of major shipping disasters and their associated loss of life.
- The ever-changing nature of bathymetry and the need to monitor the movement of the seabed.
- The issues of infestations arising from the transport of non-indigenous species into local aquatic environments.
- Differing claims over the ownership of the sea at the boundary areas of nation states' EEZ.
- The transport of a variety of hazardous waste materials.

Maritime security is all about trying to bring governance to these potentially anarchic situations, so that their impact can be controlled and managed for the benefit of local people and the wider international community. This is an important holistic viewpoint and the focus of this book—looking at maritime security from the widest possible perspective. Insecurity in the maritime environment is unhelpful to the global economy in many ways and the situation, if not tackled, is likely to get worse, as a developing nexus appears between transnational terrorists and criminals who learn to put aside their ideological differences to work more closely together. There are indications, in places like Guinea Bissau, of a greater pragmatism that is emerging in what was previously a formal adherence to Islamic teachings, allowing Islamic extremists to have some latitude in the ways in which they interpret the canon of Islam, to enable local people on the ground to work closely with criminals and overcome what might have been ideological barriers to their cooperation. Paradoxically, as the world's governments make efforts at improving maritime security, the potential for them to force these two apparently separately motivated and ideologically polarised groups into each other's arms increases, in a case of 'the enemy of my enemy is my friend'.[7] As improvements are made to the security of the maritime environment, governments and their various intelligence agencies need to be watchful as to where terrorists and criminals will try to manoeuvre next. Success in creating a stable maritime environment may well shift the focus of security operations into the cyber world.

The Seven Dimensions of Maritime Security

There are many aspects to maritime security. Table 1.1 provides an analysis of these into what are referred to as the *Seven Dimensions of Maritime Security*, which cover a spectrum of threats and situations from state-on-state confrontations over access to offshore resources, to the issues arising from natural disasters. In presenting these seven dimensions the aim is to provide a comprehensive framework in which all aspects and linkages in the maritime domain can be envisaged as policymakers try to develop priorities and understand the links that occur; for example, between the dimensions in the maritime security domain and those that exist across the land-sea boundary. The aim of this is to be more holistic and to avoid the obvious pitfalls of being focused into one or two rather narrow areas.

The seven dimensions comprise six that are specific (or vertical) and one that links with all of the other six, that of oceanography. This plays an important role in understanding the physical, chemical and biological

Table 1.1: The Seven Dimensions of Maritime Security.

Dimension	*Comments*	*Topics Covered*
State-on-State[8]	That any threats emerging to a country's sovereignty or vital interests that can be deterred or destroyed before they threaten the integrity of the country or its interests, including disputed areas of EEZ or traditional state-on-state confrontation over other economic or political issues and where a state's citizens are caught up in a combat zone.	Invasion of Territory, Theatre Missile Defence from the sea, mines, the employment of asymmetric tactics (swarming), traditional State-on-State Conflict (Maritime Dimension), confrontations over ownership of the EEZ.
Trade Protection	To ensure that vessels and their cargoes (including cruise liners) leaving a port of origin arrive at a destination port unhindered and that their vessels and seafarers are rescued if they get into difficulty. This is the protection of the Sea Lanes of Communication (SLOC) and requires a comprehensive and multi–national regional approach to cooperating against the threats that exist to shipping.	CSI, PSI, Piracy & Hijack, Robbery, the threat from mines and Vessel Borne Improvised Explosive Devices (VBIED), Search and Rescue (SAR), Coastguard, Navigation Aids and Pilot Services, Automatic Identification Systems (AIS), Vessel Board, Search and Seizure procedures (VBSS) and Vessel Traffic Management (VTS) and convoy routing schemes.
Resource Management	To ensure that resources within an EEZ of a country are managed in a sustainable way; covers renewable (fishing, wave and wind power) and non-renewable resources	Illegal Unreported and Unregulated Fishing, regulated exploitation of Oil, Gas and Mineral resources (countering oil bunkering), offshore power generation (wind and

	(oil, gas and minerals) and the potential for tourism. This also includes coastal defence from rising sea levels.	wave), opportunities for countries to earn foreign currency from tourism.
Smuggling	To counter any use by smugglers of a country's EEZ.	The smuggling of people, money/bonds, narcotic substances and weapons and the activities of Coastguard authorities to counter the threats.
Terrorism	Threats to specific near-shore & shore-based facilities, ports, bridges, ferry and cruise liner facilities, oil refineries, power stations, major cities from acts of terrorism launched from the maritime domain, such as Mumbai.	Terrorist attacks on ferries (such as the *SuperFast 14* Ferry), cargo vessels (such as the M.V. *Limberg*), oil and gas refineries, power stations, ports, anchorages, major cities and other important elements of critical national infrastructure and environmental terrorism.
Disasters	Natural and man-made and mitigating their impact upon the coastal zone.	Extreme weather events, Tsunami, flooding, chemical spills, illegal dumping of toxic waste.
Oceanography	This covers tidal, current, bathymetric aspects of the nature of the maritime environment, the issues of algae blooms, biosecurity and mapping the extent of the continental shelf and surveys to recover from disasters.	Bathymetry, tidal gauges, salinity measurements, thermal gradients, current streams, river discharges, algae blooms, charting the continental shelf and the issues of the introduction of non-native species into the aquatic environment and the potential impact of that upon the indigenous population.

effects that arise in the littoral and out into the deeper areas of the ocean, and the impact of climate change, such as rising sea levels. The nature of these dimensions is worth exploring through some specific examples.

Illegal fishing and discharges of pollutants harm the environment and test the vulnerability of marine wildlife; transnational criminals ply their trade, moving around economic migrants and narcotics, whilst terrorists use the shadows of the sea to hide and plot the fall of a globalised economy.

Robert Kaplan foresaw this development when he wrote about the idealism that followed the end of the Cold War.[9] The scale of displacement of the threat had not yet become clear and the horrors of 11 September were still in gestation in Afghanistan when he wrote that 'after the World War I and World War II, our victory has ushered in the next struggle for survival, in which evil wears new masks'.

Echoing that view, Admiral Mullen used similar language in stating 'the most serious threat all nations share is the threat of irregular and unrestricted warfare—warfare with no rules, nothing forbidden'. He went on to observe that the chief problem was that their goals were global, citing the increasing links between acts of piracy and other forms of criminality. Hill thought something similar when he explored how to deter people motivated by a fanatical desire to die, and the potential role that can be played by maritime forces using both hard and soft power to create a more secure international environment.[10] Hill's analysis is important, as it develops arguments about the role that can be played by maritime forces in helping create the conditions that ultimately undermine insurgencies and this form of criminal behaviour.

Whilst the interaction between the oceanographic dimension and the other six dimensions is apparent, other cross linkages occur between the six vertical dimensions. These occur to first, second and third orders, depending upon the nature of the coupling between the various elements. Table 1.2 provides an analysis of the coupling between the various dimensions as well. It is important to recognise that decisions taken about ways of improving maritime security in one area will inevitably have a knock-on effect in another; the degree of coupling at least provides a signpost as to factors that need to be considered. To illustrate this, any state-on-state conflict is bound to have an impact upon the ability to protect trade moved by sea; hence this linkage is seen to be a first order coupling between the dimensions.

It is understandable, given the events of 11 September, that in the United States a great deal of emphasis has been placed upon the ability of terrorists to mount an attack from the sea,[11] despite statistics which show that only 2 per cent of terrorist attacks since 1968 have involved a maritime target.[12]

Concerns were raised in the aftermath of 11 September as to the ability of the United States Coastguard Service (USCGS) to interdict potential terrorist attacks being mounted from the sea. Congressman Russ Carnahan captured the sense of things when he noted, '[f]rom protecting our natural resources to providing maritime security and national defence, the Coastguard's duties are broad in scope, and the performance of those duties has never been more important'. Port security operations became a new focal point for an organisation whose task load remained high, as other threats from criminality remained important. Priorities had to be established and resources tasked to those seen to have the greatest concerns.[13] Before 11 September, the USCGS had repeatedly raised concerns over its inability to raise funds to support its long-term cutter replacement programme, Deepwater.

Perhaps surprisingly, this situation hardly changed in the immediate period following 11 September, even when the wider range of missions conducted by the USCGS over and above countering narcotics smuggling, such as alien interception and fisheries enforcement, were highlighted. The United States is not alone in asking its coastguards to do a lot more with far less resources; it seems an endemic problem that limits the ability of nation states to create the kind of secure maritime environment that will constrain and restrict the operations of terrorists and criminals.

Despite the apparent lack of interest in terrorism in the maritime domain, there are signs that this area could receive more attention as pressure on the land environment restricts the freedom of movement of transnational terrorist groups,[14] the attack on Mumbai being a contemporary example. The Indian authorities were clearly unprepared for an attack of this magnitude, and have been trying to catch up quickly by making various new investments in maritime security. The Indian Coastguard is one agency that is receiving significant new investment, with the acquisition of twenty-one fast patrol vessels, forty-one interceptor boats, twelve Dornier coastal surveillance aircraft and seven offshore patrol vessels.[15]

Clearly the Indian authorities are reacting to the attack on Mumbai and building a layered approach to maritime security, with the deployment of offshore patrol vessels and the Dornier coastal surveillance aircraft at the outer reaches of an architecture that offers several different opportunities to intercept suspect vessels. A key element of any new approach by the Indian authorities is to establish as part of this architecture a number of data fusion centres where information from various agencies can be combined and analysed to determine patterns of behaviour of vessels operating in Indian waters. Just before the attack, even though the information was not directly linked to the events that unfolded, local Indian fishermen had reported what they perceived to be the presence of unusual vessels in the area to the authorities.

Local seafarers can play a significant role in getting an integrated approach to maritime security in place, as they can spot unusual behaviour that may be indicative of a forthcoming attack. Developing insights into what is known in intelligence circles as 'pattern of life indicators' is vital if the unusual has to stand out. Presence patrols by the elements of the Coastguard help, but information on specific sightings are very important.

With the attacks in November 2008, Mumbai became spoken of as India's 11 September moment by some commentators, and the enduring nature of this threat is not difficult to comprehend.[16] Citing major terrorism attacks in the maritime environment,[17] Parfomak and Frittelli explore the nature of the threat to the United States and where its focus may lie, documenting the 360 port facilities which may be vulnerable to attack.[18] They note the potential for attacks on ferries and cruise liners if the objective is to create mass casualties, despite the fact that this industry makes up only 4 per cent of the United States' commercial inventory.

In one part of the report they document the various means by which a port facility can be attacked, highlighting the range of options available to terrorist groups, such as the use of mines, taking hostages, the use of Improvised Explosive Devices (IED), the detonation of a Radiological Dispersal Device (RDD) and specific targeting of port storage facilities.[19] A nuclear explosion in a major port area would result in catastrophic economic consequences, massive casualties and a virtual shut-down of major ports facilities in the United States.[20] This would have a rapid and dramatic knock-on effect, as a backlog of trade and goods would rapidly develop throughout the supply chain and the 165 trading partners with whom the United States exchanges goods and materials.

Barnes and Oloruntoba explore this subject in greater detail, where they examine[21] the implications of the vulnerability of the entire maritime supply chain, underscoring the need to screen and identify high-risk containers before entry into United States ports, and addressing the economic consequences of having an insecure maritime environment. In their paper, they develop a model for crisis recognition highlighting the existence of both internal (Type 1) and external (Type 2) vulnerabilities within maritime trading systems, citing the need to maintain vigilance across a broad spectrum of areas to reduce the potential for incidents that may disrupt the economically important supply chains. They also address how the incidents may be anticipated and their consequences managed through the use of environmental scanning techniques, focusing on the development of a crisis management skill-set.

Viewing the problem from a slightly different perspective, Gooley and Cook reported on the two-week industrial strike in late 2002 on United States west coast ports, and the blowback that it had on trade routes, as 200 container ships (carrying 300,000 containers) remained unloaded. The effect upon the entire transport network resulted in a 0.4 per cent impact on the Asian economies' GDPs.[22] This was quite a significant impact for a two-week, highly localised strike and shows the consequences of any interruptions to the just-in-time system of delivery that now supports the global market place.

Environmental terrorism would also have a major effect on the state's ability to manage its resources. For instance, valuable reefs might be devastated by such an act, and create serious economic impact upon a country, hence the need for an integrated approach to biosecurity.[23] The term biosecurity is often used in a wider context to include threats from biological weapons, such as anthrax, being employed by terrorists. In this book our use of the term biosecurity is in a purely maritime context, and relates to events where species can be accidentally introduced into aquatic environments with devastating consequences for local indigenous populations and subsequent adverse economic side-effects.

The tsunami of December 2004 was a major shock to the local ecosystems around the Maldives, with a great deal of coral being lost in a single incident. The linkage between terrorism and smuggling (only one aspect of a broader set of criminal behaviour) is suggested as being of a

Table 1.2: Coupling Between the Dimensions of Maritime Security.

	State-on-State	*Trade Protection*	*Resource Management*	*Smuggling*	*Terrorism*	*Disasters*	*Oceanography*
State-on-State		1	1	2	1	2	2
Trade Protection	1			2	2	1	1
Resource Management	1	2		3	1[24]	1	1
Smuggling	2	2	3		2	3	3
Terrorism	1	1	1	2		2	3
Disasters	2	2	1	2	2[25]		1[26]
Oceanography	2	1	1	3	3	1	

second order, as often the ideology of terrorists and the aims of criminal groups are divergent. Several commentators have discussed the potential for a nexus to develop between these two entities that would provide some additional manoeuvre room for terrorists, who could use the contacts and connections available through transnational criminal groups to help move weapons and money in support of planned attacks.

The solution in Somalia lies in the hands of people, who wish to rejoin the international community and do not want their state to be seen as a pariah requiring the long-term presence of maritime forces. Their ability to deliver a secure maritime environment, in the presence of what is close to anarchy on the ground in many areas of Somalia, is constrained.[27] International support for the creation of an effective coastguard to restore governance to the waters in which pirates currently operate, may yet be undermined by a range of practical difficulties. The problems with insecurity in the increasingly important Gulf of Guinea are also unlikely to be solved simply by the application of a military solution.[28] Long-standing problems exist in the area and environmental degradation is a source of great resentment in the local population, causing them an estimated $2 billion annual loss of income.[29]

In developing any approach based upon the application of soft power, messages that resonate with core values and beliefs held within the target societies are an essential element of the tools that should be employed. Developing a nuanced understanding of the underlying anthropology, societal norms and behaviour can provide important insights that can then be used to develop narratives that have a greater chance of changing the behaviour of target groups within a society, setting the conditions for reconciliation and reintegration.

One of the major problems with maritime security is that the strength of the global economy, with its hub-and-spoke architecture based upon thirty mega-ports (which are the critical nodes) and 'just-in-time' philosophy, is also its key weakness and most vulnerable point. An openness and desire to reach out to enjoin the world in the benefits of globalisation is a great strength, but it also makes huge assumptions about global desires for freedom, democracy and the desire to live within a globalised world. The inter-connectivity that is globalisation, with all its inherent media overtones, is also its greatest weakness. The West celebrates efficiency and productivity and 'just-in-time' suits this model as its philosophy. For others, the weaknesses in being confronted with using methods that focus on 'aesthetics', and can potentially send global markets into meltdown, are all too evident.

Simple acts by criminals and terrorists groups can send shockwaves throughout an already weakened global economy. Acts of piracy and terrorism on the high seas, whilst themselves individual news items that in their own right have little detrimental impact given the scale of the problem, can generate perceptions created by the media that can carry and sway opinions in international markets with quite irrational consequences and commercial effects.[30] The acts are not discriminating, as vessels from all nations may be hijacked if they happen to be in the wrong place.[31]

The North Korean vessel *Ryu Gyong* was approached by pirates four times over the period 20–23 March 2009. The omens for the Captain and his crew were not good. Pirates, quite non-discriminating and opportunistic when it comes to seizing vessels, have suffered great setbacks on the few occasions they have made mistakes and attacked coalition warships. Some anecdotal evidence is emerging of pirates gaining access to increasingly sophisticated devices, such as portable AIS transponders, that might allow them to become more selective in targeting specific high-value vessels developing an ISTAR capability. The potential for the pirates to benefit from the availability of such technology should not be dismissed too easily. It is not too difficult to think of pirates being given advance warning of vessels that might command a high ransom passing through the Suez Canal *en route* to the Gulf of Aden. The tactical agility that pirates have shown to date in manoeuvring across the southern Red Sea to over 1300 nautical miles (nm) away, highlights the extent to which they will adapt to fund their new-found lifestyles.

Paradoxically, tackling this phenomenon can create politically unusual partnerships, such as between Iranian and South Korean warships operating alongside and cooperating with NATO warships.[32] At a time when tensions between North and South Korea have rarely been higher, in the wake of the sinking of the South Koran warship *Cheonan*, and Iranian nuclear ambitions are fuelling concerns across the Middle East, the defence of important sea lanes of communication can bring together coalitions that might otherwise not be possible.[33] The maritime world can certainly be a place where purely national, polarised viewpoints, can be put aside, if the circumstances and priorities demand an approach that involves unorthodox coalitions of the willing to protect the SLOC in key economic areas, such as in the Gulf of Aden. Securing the maritime environment from the common threat of piracy and criminality is something all states that might be fiscally affected can take on board as a priority.

The Vulnerability of the Marine Environment

There are many threats to the maritime environment and often they have complex linkages that need to be appreciated. It is a focal point for what can be regarded as the 'dichotomy of globalisation',[34] where the fault lines between globalised views of the world, with all their intended benefits, come into stark relief with issues of poverty, non-state terrorism and criminality.

In his famous and often quoted work, Samuel Huntington spoke of a 'clash of civilisations' to describe the apparent conflict that exists at the start of the twenty-first century, between major religious and political fault lines that exist in the globalised world.[35] This, he argued, is the nature of things when globalised Western liberal models of freedom, democracy and human rights come into direct confrontation with value and belief systems that are based upon deep religious convictions. Resolving those contradictory views is proving to be difficult and will remain a challenge for the foreseeable future.

The marine environment provides many illustrations of this stark contrast in world visions. For instance, the fishermen of Africa desperately seek to harness a living from small wooden boats in coastal waters,[36] where fish stocks have been ravaged by deep sea commercial trawlers who plunder the seas to fill burgeoning world populations on the other side of the planet. Their inability to follow in the footsteps of their predecessors creates the conditions in which they change their behaviour and become involved in criminality and piracy, with the potential to spread their activities along coastlines into adjoining regions, threatening important natural resources.[37] If globalisation does not provide for them and their families, the rewards from engaging in robbery and other forms of criminality just might. For some, it is not a difficult equation to resolve. The opportunity of moving out of poverty is simply hard to resist.

Paradoxically, given its crucial importance, the marine environment can often be forgotten and taken for granted by political leaders, who appear to be transfixed by the complex mosaic of the international security landscape that exists in the post Cold War world. This viewpoint is not just one shared by political leaders. In what was quite an extraordinary set of remarks on the subject of piracy, the Senior Vice President of the Maersk line argued[38] that piracy is not a threat to international shipping, stating that the definition of the term piracy is being too loosely applied in respect to activities off the coast of Nigeria and highlighting the differences between that and the piracy that has developed off the coast of Somalia. His points are reiterated in the results reported by McGinley and Berliner, which provide insights into the proximity of the piracy attacks that occur in the Straits of Malacca and in the Gulf of Guinea.[39]

Pirate attacks dropped by 61 per cent in the first half of 2010, with only thirty recorded in the first quarter of the year. The United Nations have taken this figure and linearly extrapolated it to an estimate of 120 for the full calendar year of 2010, in contrast to 217 recorded in 2009. This reduction can be attributed to a number of factors. The presence of warships from over thirty nation states is important, with plans to increase local patrolling and resources by the Seychelles Islands authorities and their neighbours from Madagascar, Reunion Island, Mauritius and Comoros. The operation of the transit corridor and the presence of naval patrols are equally important. However, the rate of successful hijackings has also been reduced as captains of vessels have learnt to increase speed and manoeuvre their vessels to hinder the pirates' attempts to board their vessels. The patterns of attacks of pirates reflect local conditions. The monsoon has a major impact upon the ability of pirate action groups to operate when wave heights at sea go above 2.5 metres. Attempting to board a target vessel in that kind of a sea state is dangerous. Evidence is also emerging of a switch in tactics, with pirates using swarms of between six and ten skiffs against single merchant vessels. Over the Christmas period in 2010, the pirates altered their tactics again. This time, merchant vessels such as the MV *York* had been hijacked into the Arabian Sea and the Indian Ocean to act as mother craft and also to provide an extended ISTAR capability for the pirates.

In June 2010 the pirates mounted a series of attacks to the north of the Bab el-Mandeb Strait, where weather conditions and sea states were more moderate. Even during the monsoons, there are days when the winds in some areas in the Gulf of Aden ease for periods of time, reducing the inclement sea state. Pirates have shown themselves to be adept at exploiting this local knowledge. Off the Gulf of Guinea the pattern of pirate attacks is quite different. Hostage-taking and hijacking are not nearly as common. Robbery appears to be the main way in which local people supplement their meagre incomes. In the Malacca Strait, another well known location for pirate attacks, concerted efforts by the Malay, Singapore and Indonesian authorities have seen dramatic falls in the levels of successful hijackings and robberies taking place at sea, although in the middle of 2010 a very large spike in robbery in three distinct areas, Pulau Subi Besar in Indonesia, the Anambas Islands near Malaysia and Horsburgh Light east Singapore Strait, was noted. The cause of this remains to be determined, but it appears that piracy is on the rise again in the South China Sea.

The global pattern of piracy is clearly modulated by local factors and generalisations about patterns of piracy and the scale of its problem should not be avoided. The International Maritime Bureau's report for 2009 shows that eight seamen were killed, sixty-eight injured and 1,052 taken hostage in 2009, and that attacks off the coast of Somalia increased from 111 in 2008 to 217 in 2009; of which forty-seven vessels were actually hijacked with 867 crewmen on board. The report notes a surge in activity from October 2009, with thirty-three incidents being recorded including thirteen hijackings, with some attacks taking place over 1,000 nm off the coast of Somalia.[40] In the early part of 2010 this was extended still further, with attacks out to 1,300 nm from the Somali coast. While pirates are showing an ability to manoeuvre, recognising the constraints this places on naval forces, the response of the coalition, with the use of marines on amphibious landing craft, the planned deployment of a Dutch submarine in September 2010 and the use of maritime patrol aircraft, are helping to move the operations of the coalition in-shore to the point where pirates launch their activities. This avoids placing boots on the ground but provides a very visible presence just off the coast in full view of the pirate training camps. These moves by the coalition in the early part of 2010 have had a clear impact on the rate of successful attacks that have been achieved in the first part of the year. In March alone, the European Union Naval Force (EUNAVFOR) disrupted eighteen pirate action groups. The pirates' response was to increase their efforts, attacking ten vessels in a week, with only the MV *Iceberg 1* being successfully hijacked 10 nm off the coast of Aden. The pirates also attacked and hijacked a number of Indian fishing vessels in the same period.

In a spate of incidents, five attacks were carried out in the week beginning 7 November over a large area of the Indian Ocean. A Hong Kong-flagged crude oil tanker, the *BW Lion*, was approached 400 nm to the north-east of the Seychelles Islands and 1000 nm to the east of the Somali capital Mogadishu. Given the range involved, it is clear that the attacks came from ships that had been transported to the area on mother vessels. These were often fishing trawlers that had also been hijacked. Hours later in the southern part of the Somali Basin, a container ship was attacked 530 nm to the east of the Tanzanian capital Dar es Salaam, and 420 miles to the west of the Seychelles Islands. The area over which pirates now operate has grown significantly as their tactics have changed in response to the deployment of the international task force.

Elsewhere, twenty-eight incidents were reported off the coast of Nigeria with twenty-one vessels being boarded, attacks in this area being far more violent in nature. Strategies to counter piracy clearly need to be developed against a local context that considers environmental, geographic, economic and political factors.

Carmel's arguments are obviously an attempt to add a viewpoint to the debate, which he feels is aggregating too many criminal acts under the banner of piracy. He wishes to see criminal acts that threaten maritime security broken down into better categories, in effect disaggregating the nature of the threat and breaking it up into smaller, more manageable pieces. Through this process, local security measures, tailored to the needs of specific geographic and demographic concerns, can be implemented and the hysteria associated with what is becoming an international problem can be avoided.

As a commercial operator of ships at sea, his need to talk down the threat to avoid irrational increases in insurance rates with its impact upon commercial rates, is even more pressing when the global economy is already severely weakened. A hike in insurance rates associated with an apparent break-out and spread of piracy on a wider scale would be a strategic shock that the world's economy can ill afford at this moment.

He argues that piracy off the coast of Somalia is not a systematic threat to global shipping, but in making these remarks he clearly fails to acknowledge the potential for piracy to spread and become a much wider geographically dispersed phenomenon. The agility of the pirates operating in the Indian Ocean has been a surprise to many involved in the international shipping industry. Attacks now reach out over an area estimated to be 2 million square miles as mother ships are used to project the pirates' own smaller skiff boats out over ranges of 1000 nm from the coast of

Somalia. The events surrounding the hijacking of the *Arctic Sea* might provide a cause for that position to be re-evaluated. Whilst the *Arctic Sea* incident has failed to produce a strategic shock to the global system in terms of it being used as a platform for a terrorist attack, the ease with which it was seized and moved through busy sea lanes without intervention provides, if nothing else, a strategic warning that piracy has the potential to spread a lot further than the coastlines of Nigeria,[41] Malaysia, Indonesia and Somalia.

Carmel rightly highlights the issue of linkage and collateral damage that can occur to economies that are apparently geographically disconnected from a trouble spot. His point on the impact of piracy in the Gulf of Aden on the Egyptian economy is well made. Some 11 per cent of Egyptian government revenues are raised from tolls on those using the Suez Canal.[42] Anything that has the potential to reduce that may have a detrimental effect on an already weak economy and have a knock-on effect on tourism, leading to a down-spiral into instability.

Transnational terrorist groups have long tried to ferment problems in countries like Egypt, which they regard as apostate regimes. Anything that might sow the seeds of discontent into the population is something that groups such as Al-Qaeda, with their strong Egyptian connections, would welcome. The balance between striking the so-called near enemy (the regimes in the Middle East that they feel are propped up by the West) and the far enemy, the West itself, has always been a key discussion within groups like Al-Qaeda.

The global nature of the world's economy in the twenty-first century is highlighted by this example, which shows the high degree of coupling that exists between what might appear, superficially, to be geographically disconnected areas. The sea and the land environments are indeed connected and this is something that continues to baffle many political leaders who fail to grasp the innate, and often highly complex, linkages that occur in our globalised economy.

The potential threat from transnational groups of criminals and terrorists seems to be viewed through a lens that is biased towards their work on the land. It appears that the superficial analysis developed at the strategic level suggests that terrorism and criminality only work on the land and that maritime incidents are rare. Ironically, this land-centric and short-sighted viewpoint fails to grasp a key essence of that landscape; the sea not only provides the highway for the world's nations to trade, it also provides transnational criminals with a space in which, in the absence of any coherent maritime security, they can operate. These groups are also able to exploit gaps that appear in the approach to maritime security, requiring a comprehensive response to be developed that involves the participation of the widest possible community of people using the maritime environment for recreational and business purposes.[43]

Such global security, however, comes at a price in terms of national effort and political will through local, regional and international cooperation.[44] Given its high profile today, it is easy to see piracy as the main issue for maritime security and thus ignore the potential for events such as Mumbai to occur at locations where the appropriate catalysts exist. Shashikumar has analysed the gaps in maritime security that existed in Mumbai prior to the attacks, highlighting the problems in inter-agency cooperation and describing the information that was apparently available before the attacks.[45]

Shashikumar claims that for a year before the Mumbai attacks, intelligence had been available about the activities of a group known as Lashkar-e-Tayebba (sometimes also referred to as Lashkar-e-Toiba or LeT), which intended to use sea routes from Pakistan to attack major oil facilities at Bombay High, located 160 km offshore from Mumbai, which produces a third of the national oil requirements. Other targets of interest include nuclear power stations and port facilities that are important to the Indian economy. His reporting claims that intelligence agencies warned the Indian government that up to 500 terrorists were being trained in the Azizabad coastal camps near Karachi to execute attacks against high-valued targets along the 7,000 kms of India's coastline. This training had started in October 2006.

His report is a damning indictment of the preparedness of Indian security authorities, concluding that the coastal police service was absolutely ineffective and that the coastguard was grossly under-equipped with only sixty vessels to patrol 7,000 km of coastline.[46] Despite the warnings ahead of the Mumbai attacks, the Indian authorities appeared to have been focused upon other threats from the maritime environment, such as gun-running, drug trafficking and piracy; they were not prepared for the possibility of terrorists crossing the sea and attacking a major city. In what are regarded as belated efforts to improve maritime security, the Indian authorities are making investments in coastal radar systems and new fast patrol craft.[47]

The attacks on Mumbai must therefore be classified as a strategic shock, as they originated from outside the threat assessments that had been carried out by the central authorities at that time; hence the lack of preparedness to confront a determined attack by a group of people intent on causing mass casualties.

The Aftermath of Mumbai

Mumbai was a watershed for maritime security[48] and has created an increasing awareness of the potential for terrorism to be launched from the sea.[49] Commentators such as Shashikumar have suggested that the attack requires the widening of the original definition of maritime terrorism to include attacks on port facilities mounted from the sea.

This is now considered by many authorities to be one of the major threats that exist to coastal states, allied perhaps with the potential for transnational terrorist groups to smuggle Weapons of Mass Destruction (WMD).[50] Whilst WMD may remain beyond the realm of some groups for the foreseeable future, there are ways in which similar visual effects can be achieved, such as through the use of Boiling Liquid Expanding Vapour Explosions (BLEVE), where the aftermath in terms of the cloud has all the hallmarks of a small nuclear device, with its potential for creating a serious reaction from the public. It highlights a key point: that to create the impact of a nuclear explosion it is not necessary to actually detonate one. Terrorists are innovative in their approaches to attacks and it is quite possible that they may wish to attack a major energy storage facility. After all, it would not be a new departure in terms of tactics; insurgents did try to disable the major oil terminals used to export Iraqi oil, and the MV *Limberg* attack was an act of maritime terrorism in its own right.

These weapons could be used to mount a major attack upon a coastal region or port facility using surface (fast boats or jet skis) or sub-surface platforms or swimmers whose task is to mine harbour entrances or major facilities, such as refineries. In an increasingly globalised world, where trade is so dependent upon free access to the seas, the threat of terrorism from the sea is one that is likely to endure and remain attractive.

There are many complex and interacting systems in play in the maritime environment. A traditional analysis of maritime security might tend to focus upon a military perspective. The end of the Cold War was heralded by many as being the start of a new era, in which military threats would be significantly reduced and the potential for large-scale naval combat would all but come to an end. Contemporary history, however, is rapidly providing us with a different viewpoint, wherein the protean nature and diverse complexity of threats paint a more chaotic and unpredictable picture. The potential for state-on-state conflict looms in a world faced with ever-increasing problems of energy security, climate change, and inevitable natural disasters.

At the start of the twenty-first century a wider definition of maritime security is appropriate in the light of the use of the maritime domain, both to launch terrorist attacks and also to move the weapons, materials and money needed to support the activities of those engaged in transnational crime and terrorism. Writing before the attacks on Mumbai, Sugandha provides an important insight into the issues of maritime security from an Indian perspective, setting her analysis against an historical backdrop.[51] The main thrust of her analysis focuses upon the potential sources of state-on-state threats and the geo-strategic perspective that existed in the Indian Ocean, with a detailed emphasis upon the economic importance of its sea lanes of communications.[52]

Her somewhat narrow interpretation of maritime security highlights an element of tactical blindness that existed in India prior to the Mumbai attacks, and is common to many commentators' analysis prior to November 2008, such as Roy-Chaudhury[53] and Singh and Singh.[54] Bhanu Krishna Kiran has also explored the Indian dimensions of maritime security, emphasising the need for constabulary forces to be developed within the immediate maritime environment of the coastline, whilst not neglecting the key role that needs to be played by the Indian navy in defending the SLOC.[55]

The parallels with a similar narrow viewpoint of the threat to the homeland of the United States before 11 September are easy to make, and this shows the nature of the strategic surprise that arose from the attacks mounted on Mumbai. While many other coastal states have a similar limited perspective, some such as Singapore, realising the major negative impact terrorism has upon eco-prosperity, have moved quickly to address any apparent weaknesses in their domestic maritime postures. The slow response of the Indian authorities to the nature of the threat highlighted their obvious lack of preparedness for this type of attack. The events in Mumbai set new parameters, requiring an out-of-the box approach, which security organisations of the world are only just beginning to come to terms with. Sugandha's analysis also looks at contemporary concerns that exist about maritime security, citing specific issues about the need to strengthen overall security frameworks that exist in India. This is a particular feature of the post-Mumbai analysis conducted by the Indian authorities, who rapidly recognised the gaps that appeared between the various elements of their security apparatus.

Sadly, it is all too apparent that analysts are well aware of these gaps.[56] The simple lack of political will to address them ultimately results in the events taking place,[57] and leads to the concerned government seeking to prevent any further occurrence.

Rear Admiral Tay of the Republic of Singapore Navy was right when he said that 'transnational terrorists and non-state actors not only disregard national boundaries, they often exploit the margins'.[58] His analysis brings attention to the ways in which terrorists and criminal gangs seek to operate on the fringes of our societies, and exploit vulnerabilities in the security frameworks provided by multi-agency and international cooperation to achieve their goals. They understand and try to operate in the grey areas that exist between intra-government and inter-government agencies and departments, exploiting their rivalries and innate inability to share intelligence material.

The problem is that our governance structures and approaches are often incapable of bringing the spotlight to bear upon these gaps, as rigid and inflexible approaches to managing budgets and resources inevitably create the margins which criminals and terrorists utilise to such profound effect. The appointment of national coordinators, whose task is to draw together the efforts of such agencies, can often be thwarted by petty internal politicking, as departments vie for position and resources. Bureaucracy can indeed help to create the very margins in which criminals can thrive.

This situation is compounded by what Nye refers to as the 'diffusion of governance in the twenty-first century', which exacerbates the lack of clarity that exists at the margins.[59] What used to be fairly clear dividing lines and hierarchical relationships of governance and legal frameworks, have been clouded and flattened out as information technology has changed the societal landscapes of many countries. Whilst these changes bring many benefits, many governmental organisations have yet to make the transition to being able to exploit the flexibility allowed for by such approaches. This creates a differential rate of take-up, that sees organisations fully enabled by technology operating alongside those who have yet to change their operating processes and procedures to fully derive the associated benefits.

Wider Perspectives

Securing the maritime environment is vital for any country that has direct access to the sea. Any eyewitness accounts of the events in Mumbai in 2008, the attack on the USS *Cole* and the MV *Limburg* in 2000 and 2002 respectively, and the sinking of the *SuperFerry 14* in the Philippine Islands in 2004, will attest to the catastrophic consequences of terrorism. The attacks were visually dramatic, and heralded a new and wider thinking on the nature of maritime security. After a comparatively short interlude, terrorists in the Philippines have returned to the maritime environment, by attempting to bomb the ticketing office of the busy port of Nasipit at Butuan on 25 May 2009. In a subsequent security operation on 26 July 2009, Philippines security officials found twelve bombs hidden inside a bathroom on the inter-island ferry, the *Blue Water Princess*. Vigilance is clearly an enduring issue, as the lack of actual attacks does not mean the potential for terrorism has suddenly declined.

Chen and Edwards provide a local perspective on the problems of maritime security in Taiwan.[60] Their analysis provides important generic insights as Taiwan is faced by a range of threats across the 200 km of the Taiwan Strait from mainland China, which has embarked upon an ambitious programme of naval development, including the deployment of ballistic missiles which can reach Taiwan in a few minutes. This kaleidoscope of threats to Taiwan mirrors the problems faced by South Korea and Japan, as they consider similar threats from North Korea. Nations that operate in the Persian Gulf may also come to rely upon the mobility and agility inherent in such platforms as they face an increasingly difficult situation with Iran. The utility of maritime forces in responding to such threats and quickly moving a shield into place from the sea, is one that political leaders are beginning to appreciate.

Piracy is another major concern for those vessels at sea; the seizure of vessels such as the *Sirius Star* on 15 November 2008,[61] when it was 830 km off the southeast coast of Kenya, for which it gained notoriety as the largest ship that had ever been seized by pirates, and the *Maersk*

Alabama on 8 April 2009 when it was 440 km off the coast of Somalia,[62] being two high profile incidents out of a catalogue of attempted and successful hijackings in the area around the Gulf of Aden. One of the root causes of piracy is that it is a reaction from the coastal people of Somalia trying to earn a living[63] after their fish stocks have been plundered by commercial trawlers. Bearing down on the problem of piracy is clearly something that maritime power alone cannot solve.

What started as a series of local hijacks and ransom demands against commercial fishing vessels has spiralled into an international threat to the basic freedom of the seas upon which the global economy depends. The maritime environment comprises of a linked series of interacting agents, some of which are related, and others, such as the reported links between terrorist groups and transnational criminals, perhaps have yet to be proven fully.

Transnational criminals enjoy the freedom of the seas to smuggle drugs and people. Local criminal elements, such as those operating off the coasts of many countries, often raid boats at anchor, robbing them of cash and other commodities. Criminality, pollution and terrorism deter tourists and economic development. This damage to economies lowers their potential to invest in their navies to maintain maritime security and deter illegal discharges of pollution. These processes are cyclical and self-sustaining in nature. The increasingly diverse nature of threats is amply illustrated by these examples.

Interrupting this behaviour is difficult and can require outside support and assistance to develop basic governance over local seas where indigenous infrastructure, such as the regional response to piracy developed in the Strait of Malacca, is not available. The Africa Partnership Station (APS) initiative by the United States and the European Union is one example of the way in which outside assistance is given to countries in Africa to help them develop indigenous capabilities to monitor and police their own coastlines.[64] This approach, which minimises the intervention levels and associated footprints on the land, is directly in keeping with the overall approach to international diplomacy being developed by the Obama administration. Obama's administration prefers to help countries establish such capabilities, breaking the downward spiral that means they have limited capacity to intervene in their own maritime domain, and by instead increasing this capability ensuring that their economic development enables them to sustain that effort in the medium to long term. This provides a model that has many attractions and may well form the basis for future interventions designed to prevent states from failing and creating havens for terrorists and those involved in organised crime.

Contemporary Viewpoints on Maritime Security

The wider context and definition of maritime security is one that has yet to receive the specific attention of many writers. Works such as the Oxford Encyclopaedia[65] provide a detailed chronicle of events that have shaped the history of the maritime environment and are an excellent source of reference material. Maritime security is not a recent topic that has emerged somewhat chaotically from the high profile terrorist attacks that have been witnessed in the media. Mumbai was an attack launched from the sea and provides a new dimension to an already complex picture that merges routine criminal activities, such as the boarding of vessels at anchor to steal goods and money, at one end of a spectrum of threats, with the potential for a terrorist event utilising WMD smuggled in through a maritime entry point at another, more extreme position.

In the wake of the terrorist attacks on the United States in September 2001, several authors have addressed the wider implications of securing the maritime environment, as concerns quickly spread about the potential for using the sea to deliver a more devastating attack involving the smuggling of nuclear weapons. Given the dramatic nature of the attacks of 11 September, it is understandable that the United States has become a source of many of the international initiatives that were introduced as the repercussions of the attack from a maritime viewpoint were considered.

The issues that arose concerning maritime security after 11 September can be broadly divided into three groups. The first of these addresses port security as a subject and provides descriptions of the measures that need to be taken to ensure the safe loading and unloading of cargos and their management into and out of the port facilities, including securing the port itself, to ensure cargos are not tampered with whilst they are in transit and prior to loading. This group also includes discussions on the threats to vessels whilst they are in port or at anchor, such as from swimmers and from small boats with the intent of mounting an assault upon a specific vessel.

The second of these groups involves looking at the procedures and processes that ensure the smooth arrival of cargos into ports, such as those in the United States. Vesky et al. also emphasise the concerns over port security from a United States viewpoint, drawing attention to the over 300 sea and river ports in America and the 3,700 cargo and passenger terminals for which maritime security is a priority.[66] Frittelli et al. provided earlier coverage of this subject, noting the six million container vessels that enter United States ports every year and the issues associated with only 2 per cent of the containers being physically inspected.[67] Their work specifically notes security legislation and the gaps that, at the time, could provide opportunities for terrorists to attack the United States, providing a commentary on the implications of changes for public safety, the United States' and the global economy, and federal, state and local homeland security initiatives. In the United Kingdom even lower rates of inspection have been achieved in the past, much less than 1 per cent of arriving containers, as rummage teams have tended to focus upon the smuggling of vehicles, drugs and other commodities.

Vesky et al. draw attention to the measures implemented by the Bureau of Customs and Border Protection to determine potential cargos that might be at risk and the increase of the Notice of Arrival (NOA) from 24 to 96 hours to provide time for security officials to screen vessels, their crews and cargo. They also describe the wider maritime security measures adopted within the Container Security Initiative (CSI) and also the Customs Trade Partnership Against Terrorism (C-TPAT), which offers importers faster processing of their cargo if they comply with Customs and Border Protection (CBP) measures.[68] Vesky and his colleagues provide a parochial, and yet detailed, perspective on maritime security addressing the threat of terrorist nuclear attacks on seaports and the response, some background and issues for the United States Congress from a legislative viewpoint. They also provide a wider overview of maritime security and the enhancements that have already been made to mitigate the perceived risks.

The third of the three groups focuses upon the passage of cargo ships through the highway of the sea to their destinations, and just prior to when they complete the formalities of entering territorial waters. Concerns regarding the activities of the A.Q. Khan network based out of Pakistan (see Corera),[69] and the ways in which they used the sea as a means of delivering component parts of a national nuclear weapon development programme to Libya, for example, underscored a wider concern about proliferation.[70] In 2009, concerns had been specifically raised about the activities of a number of vessels flagged by North Korea and their involvement in smuggling material to countries such as Myanmar, highlighting the enduring nature of this threat and the wider need to maintain a global viewpoint on the use of the sea by some maritime nations.[71] This is one of the driving forces behind the creation of the Proliferation Security Initiative (PSI),[72] and the deployment by NATO of its warships in the Mediterranean Sea to look at potential proliferation routes into and out of the Middle East and off the northern coast of Africa.

Jones[73] has provided a practical perspective on the issues of maritime security, offering in-depth analysis alongside that provided by McNicholas upon the maritime security issues from the viewpoint of the United States.[74] McNicholas chose to concentrate upon providing practical insights drawing on his own personal experiences in the field and providing pointers to the development of port security plans and assessments.

The term 'maritime security' is one that should be explored in further detail. It has several dimensions that need to be considered and has multi-disciplinary considerations. It is perhaps too easy to think about the term today through the lens of the acts of piracy being committed in the Gulf of Aden, its nearby waters and off the coast of Nigeria. That would be too narrow a lens. An excellent book by Martin Murphy provides a contemporary viewpoint of the situation, exploring the alleged emerging nexus between piracy and terrorism in the maritime domain.[75] In his work, Murphy explores, in detail, the nature of piracy and terrorism and then considers the circumstances that could bring them together, leading to alliances that might threaten weaker states and destabilise vulnerable regions, creating insecurity and instability and providing a platform for new terrorism attacks on countries in the West.

Adam Young has also explored the problems associated with piracy in Southeast Asia, providing a causal analysis that shows how policy formulation needs to draw on the lessons of history to ensure that initiatives are framed in ways that are likely to succeed.[76] Citing a mindset that 'piracy is a thinkable option', he goes on to suggest that through the development of appropriately shaped policies, the threat from piracy can be reduced. The joint efforts of local maritime security forces, both seaborne and air-based assets, has had a notable impact upon the level of piracy specifically in the Malacca Strait in the last few years.

One facet of maritime security concerns the ability of the nation state to rescue seafarers that have got into difficulty. Search and Rescue (SAR) capabilities are an important aspect of maritime security. Being able to mobilise quickly to reach the scene of a disaster and save lives is a critical capability for nation states to possess. Whilst it lacks the sense of drama associated with countering terrorism and related topics within the broader maritime security domain, it is nevertheless a vital aspect and topic to address. Countering pollution in the coastal waters is important, as, if it reaches the shore, it can have dire consequences for sensitive areas such as beaches and eco-systems, which are protected either internationally or through local laws.

This aspect of maritime security is the focus of works such as that edited by Rupert Herbert-Burns, Sam Bateman and Peter Lehr and published through the Lloyd's Maritime Intelligence Unit.[77] Their work, which harnesses contributions from authors working in the field of maritime security, provides a broader base of insights into the world of maritime security. It seeks to provide a reality check for the developments and new mechanisms, measures and procedures, that were introduced in the wake of the terrorism attacks on the United States. Given the plethora of initiatives that have been developed as the potential risks from the maritime environment emerged, this book provides a timely datum point from which to build. However, naturally enough for an organisation like Lloyd's, their analysis focuses upon the measures being taken to manage and reduce risks to the movement of goods on the high seas.

This book makes its first point with a series of reviews of the emerging maritime security environment in the aftermath of the terrorism attacks in the United States on 11 September 2001, chronicling key events that help to contextualise the spectrum of threats that now exist in the maritime domain, such as developing new forms of improvised explosive devices (IED), underwater swimmers and documenting responses to these threats such as the development of the AIS. Their work also explores the industry sectors and its responses to the changes in the maritime environment and the increasing diversity of threats that now exist to international shipping. Legal frameworks, which are constantly evolving, are also brought to the fore with detailed analysis of the regulatory framework, which provides the basis for law enforcement and military operations in the maritime domain.

In a slightly more focused analysis, Greenberg et al. of the RAND Corporation provide their own analysis of the specific implications and risks associated with maritime terrorism, tabulating the major events that have occurred in the period from 1961 to 2004. One particular aspect of the analysis presented is the vulnerabilities that arise at specific choke points, such as the Malacca Straits, the Straits of Gibraltar and the Straits of Hormuz.[78]

The Bab el-Mandeb is also one of the world's major choke points, and the impact that piracy has had on this region is an indicator of the types of threat that might arise in the maritime domain should terrorist groups choose to focus increasing resources in this area. At the start of 2010, Islamist extremists in Yemen and in Somalia threatened to work together to blockade the Strait. This would have been difficult for them to achieve in a permanent sense. Nevertheless, operations aimed at the 25,000 ships a year that pass through the Straits onto the Gulf of Aden could have considerable nuisance value and could impact the levels of maritime traffic in the area. The author's focus is upon the risks and liabilities associated with specific acts of terrorism in the maritime environment that are aimed at creating mass casualties. I highlight the consequences of maritime terrorist incidents citing human, economic and intangible effects upon nation states and the population at large. The intangible effects are those that are difficult to measure but nevertheless affect confidence and can change people's behaviour markedly with significant implications for the economies of countries.

My argument is based, in part, on the need for terrorist groups to use the maritime domain to manoeuvre, as they have come under pressure through military operations being undertaken in Iraq, Afghanistan and Pakistan.[79] This is a form of threat displacement that pushes terrorists to use the maritime environment as constraints apply on the land. Terrorist groups need publicity if they are not to become irrelevant and therefore need to continue to mount attacks.

In their analysis Greenberg et al. also see increasing access to maritime leisure activities and the development of offshore industries as being catalysts in the development of the skill-base from which terrorist groups can draw, to plan and execute viable maritime attacks. Maritime terrorism, however, does have its limitations. Its impact can be less than that of those attacks which occur on land, as the media is often not able to immediately mobilise to the scene. Camera shots of the *Limberg* took time to get to the screens and the initial impact of the attack began to wane. The USS *Cole* attack gained increased coverage as it was carried out in a way such that the full glare of the international media could be rapidly mobilised to cover the event. Brian Jenkins of the RAND Corporation has referred to terrorism as 'theatre', drawing out the obvious psychological impact it is supposed to have on the population. In part, this analysis may help explain why the maritime environment, in a blue-water sense, appears to have less attraction for terrorists, as it lacks immediacy in terms of potential media coverage.

Taking another perspective on the subject of maritime security, Michael Richardson looks specifically at the implications associated with smuggling weapons of mass destruction.[80] Tabulating a series of events, Richardson builds a picture of the potential use of the maritime environment by terrorist groups, citing the anecdotal evidence associated with the existence of an Al-Qaeda navy[81] that provides the ability for the organisation to exploit the maritime domain. Whilst reporting via open sources provides largely anecdotal information on the existence of such a capability, it would not be the first time that terrorist groups resorted to manoeuvring in the maritime domain; this practice was vital for the Tamil Tigers, whose resupply routes relied on the sea, and their basing of many weapons and other forms of supplies at sea on a number of small freighters, a novel form of 'sea basing'.[82]

The various publications cited provide some important and contemporary context to the world of maritime security. Other publications address specific topics in greater detail. Stopford provides a hugely important analysis of the economics that lie behind the exploitation of the maritime domain.[83] Highlighting the 5,000-year history of shipping, he provides an exhaustive analysis of the maritime trade sector and its operations, drawing out some specific analysis of shipping cycles that date back to 1741. Stopford provides detailed models, and charts the operations of the maritime sector.[84] He provides an analysis of the cost base of operating sea transportation systems from a market and company viewpoint, addressing bulk, specialised and general cargo. His analysis allows the implications of an insecure maritime environment to be observed and its impact assessed. It is this commercial environment, with all its importance from a global standpoint, which the various elements of maritime security must protect.

Providing Solutions

The agility, audaciousness and adaptability of the pirates operating off the coastline of Somalia highlight the durability of the threat. Financial rewards and an improved lifestyle await those who are successful in hijacking vessels. However, rich rewards are reserved for the few who direct and control the operations. Many of the people involved receive little in the way of benefits. They risk arrest and even death in some judicial systems. However, resorting to piracy in the face of a near famine, when the sanctions imposed by the international community are so unclear, appears to be worth the risk.

Couple this with the scale of the problems facing the international task force trying to secure an area of around 2 million square kilometres, and the difficulties in creating a stable and orderly maritime environment become clear. It is also worth considering that maritime combat power, per se, does not act as a guarantor of maritime security. Its ability, however, to deter other nation states from embarking upon a military adventure is well understood. An interesting issue then arises as to the degree to which maritime power can adapt and deter asymmetric forms of conflict and criminal behaviour. To what extent might soft power be applied by maritime forces?

Joseph Nye recognised the broader issues with the application of combat power in his book *Soft Power*, in which he analysed a nation state's ability to attract and persuade, contrasting that with the coercive nature of combat power.[85] Writing against the backdrop of the terrorist attacks in September 2001, Nye was in part trying to address the issue of why people appear to hate the United States. His analysis reflects what is often perceived to be a paradox. Ask many people in the Middle East where they would like to live and they answer the United States. Ask them who they dislike and distrust the most and the answer appears to be the same. How can people apparently love and hate a nation simultaneously?

The answer to this lies, in part, in the ways in which the world's only superpower is perceived, and the ways in which it appears to conduct itself on the world stage. In today's media dominated world, governments must exercise military power alongside the additional flexibility afforded by the application of economic and diplomatic power. The flexibility afforded by the maritime domain provides options for governments who may wish to intensify situations in a managed environment. Soft power has its advocates, even in a maritime environment. Operations, such as those offering humanitarian assistance, are a good example of the application of soft power.

The United States Navy created huge amounts of goodwill and positive public reaction through its efforts in Aceh in the aftermath of the tsunami in December 2004; arguably helping shape the environment for the subsequent reconciliation efforts that took place between the Indonesian government and the separatists that had previously been causing problems in the region. Other navies were also quick to respond to the tsunami, prompting reflections on the need for the development of rapid reaction forces by the Indian Navy, for example, to address further incidents or other unforeseen events in a regional context.[86] This one example deserves to be studied extensively by naval scholars in the coming years. President Kennedy's handling of the Cuban Missile Crisis is another obvious example of how the manoeuvre room afforded by the use of maritime power helped to create the conditions in which a diplomatic solution could be developed.

'Soft power', as envisaged by Nye, has its limitations and can result in an escalation of rhetoric and some undiplomatic remarks being made about people and their states.[87] Belligerent states run by autocratic rulers tend not to get too intimidated by the ideas and statements that apply soft power. 'Hard power' will continue to have a long-term role in helping deter and resolve international crises. Navies the world over and throughout history have epitomised the application of hard power, bringing enemies to battle and destroying their capabilities. In the twenty-first century, as the inexorable rise of transnational criminals and terrorists threaten the very foundations of international order, finding ways of persuading people to change their behaviour, in contrast to using coercion, is an important facet of a world order that is hesitantly emerging from the aftermath of the Cold War. The application of soft power is an avenue that needs to be explored off the coast of Somalia and in other areas, such as along the African coastline, where the risk of piracy spreading is high.

Given the polymorphous nature of the threat to maritime security and the need to balance local, regional and international dimensions from a national viewpoint, one overriding requirement for any solution is that it needs to be adaptable, agile and flexible. International cooperation is essential, and it has to come in forms that are compatible with regional cultural sensitivities.

In addressing the issues in the immediate aftermath of the attacks in America in September 2001, Nye highlights what he refers to as the paradox of American power.[88] His analysis shows that despite its position as the world's superpower and pseudo-guardian of democratic values, the

United States cannot go it alone in a globalised world. The United States needs to form and join international coalitions of the willing that will deploy the full panoply of instruments—economic, military and political—to developing frameworks and approaches that reduce the manoeuvre room of those that threaten the global economy, nation states and maritime order.

International cooperation is the *sine qua non* of any approach to creating a secure international landscape, as the authors that compiled the analysis of maritime security from the Lexington Institute point out in their analysis.[89] They highlight the application of CENTRIXS in providing an agile communications infrastructure that can readily be deployed to create a networked environment, based on enclaves, that allows information collected on maritime domain awareness to be shared amongst cooperating naval units. This inter-operability between maritime units underpins the political initiatives taken by countries to act jointly in response to what they see as a threat to their own national interests, and ensures that strategic decisions can be carried out at the operational and tactical levels of command.

Countries such as the United States, Japan, Russia and many European countries, such as Norway and Sweden, have shown their willingness to provide solutions to maritime security problems, by deploying forces into the Gulf of Aden and the nearby waters of the Indian Ocean. They have been joined, in what is truly an international effort, by warships from South Korea, India, Australia and China. This highlights versatility, or perhaps flexibility, in a political sense. Seeing Iranian and United States warships cooperating in the defence of a merchant vessel threatened by pirates is important. Maritime security can be a unifying force, bringing together nation states in support of common goals and good.

The vital nature of the SLOC off the coast of Somalia is clear from the international effort being put forward, sometimes with quite narrow national interests at heart. The projection of global sea-power is a capability that is the purview of a relatively small number of countries. China and India are working hard to further develop what is currently a nascent capability to project power as blue-water navies. In 2009, the Indian Navy deployed units to work alongside the Royal Navy, French Navy and German Navy in joint exercises in European maritime waters, in what clearly illustrates their desire to be seen to be a blue-water navy and to show the steady progress they are making in towards that objective aim.

Many countries, however, simply cannot afford to become involved in such ventures. The initial reticence of South Africa, with a highly capable navy with a distinct blue-water capability, is perhaps surprising. But countries such as many of those in Africa, like Kenya, have a quite limited capacity to work outside their own area, and provide what would be a regional contribution to the problem. Kenya has sought to mitigate this situation by offering to provide the legal framework through which pirates can be tried and brought to justice.

Maritime security can sometimes comprise a myriad interacting elements, to provide a comprehensive response to the ongoing nature of guaranteeing security. For many African countries, simply getting boats to sea is a major issue. Maintenance problems and maintaining the skills of their naval officers and crews poses real problems. APS offers part of the solution for providing investment in sea-based and land-based facilities, which can help develop the degree of MDA that is required to deter transnational criminals and terrorists from exploiting apparent gaps in the levels of security maintained in the maritime environment.

2

HISTORICAL PERSPECTIVES

Historical Context

The problems associated with maritime security are nearly as old as civilisation. The focus of this book precludes a detailed analysis of the history of maritime security; that would be a text in its own right. History however, provides important insights that contextualise contemporary situations. Today's world is a product of its past. Black, in what is an informed guide, has produced an excellent analysis of the application of naval power since the start of the sixteenth century to the present-day, that provides just the level of insight that is required to help set the following contemporary perspectives in context.[1]

However, it is important to chart some of the developments that have occurred to highlight the enduring nature of the maritime environment, such as the long-standing threat from piracy, criminality and those states seeking to conquer the territories of others for economic or political reasons, and to develop some insights from history that remain pertinent even today.[2] This analysis confirms that many facets of maritime security, such as the protection of SLOC and the importance of maritime choke-points, are as relevant today as they were in antiquity.

Evidence chronicling the migration patterns of early humans reaching Australia shows the first use of boats to cross from Java to Australia 60,000 years ago. The exploitation of the sea is well documented in history, with the practice of fishing thought to date back to the Palaeolithic period, 40,000 years ago. Archaeological finds of shell middens, discarded fish bones and cave paintings highlight the importance of fisheries at a time when settlements were just emerging as a means of mutual support. There is also early evidence of the importance of shellfish as part of the Japanese diet from 10,000 BCE. The earliest treatise on fishing, which has survived to the modern day, is perhaps a work compiled by Oppian of Corycus between 177 and 180 BCE. The coast had a particular attraction for people who had been hunter-gatherers and were constantly on the move. Developing settlements on the coast and along rivers would prove to have its benefits and vulnerabilities.

Invasion from the sea or the disruption of trading patterns has been a source of concern to cities and states since the Phoenicians first set out to colonise the Mediterranean Sea. Between the ninth and sixth centuries BCE, the Phoenicians established the first trading system to encompass the entire length of the Mediterranean Sea. Starting from their coastal bases in locations such as Tyre and Arvad, they spread their influence as far as southern Spain.

In her detailed review of this, drawing upon archaeological research, Maria Aubet provides some insights[3] into the geographic considerations that drove the creation of these settlements. The settlements were located on islands close to the coast, which transformed them into impregnable fortresses as long as they kept control of the sea. At the time, the main threat to the Phoenicians came from the Assyrians, and also from internal conflict within their own loose arrangements of city-states along the coastline of what is now Lebanon. In many ways, this idea of a loose arrangement of trading states was to last until the decline of famous mercantile states, such as Venice in the sixteenth century, as it was unable to guarantee the security of its SLOC. The key to maintaining trading routes was the ability to sustain and protect the fortresses that stood guard over the key parts of the supply chain. This approach somewhat mirrors the ideas of what are called ink spots today in Afghanistan, from which control over certain geographic areas is exerted as part of a clear, build-and-hold approach to creating security.

The ancient Greeks had similar problems infusing their city-states into a coherent entity that could project power in defence of what was to become Greece. Depending upon the viewpoint on the veracity of the sacking of Troy, which has been attributed by some authors, such as Herodotus, to a period circa 1200 BCE, it is possible to argue that concerns about maritime security date back yet further into history.[4] The whole legend of Troy depends upon the arrival of the Achaeans by sea, led by Agamemnon, the King of Mycenae, and Odysseus.

Whilst it is true that the Persian Empire was largely created through warfare between various states on the land, its leaders—such as Alexander the Great—understood the power of manoeuvring in the maritime domain and its implications on the overall campaign. The use of naval power to provide another domain in which to fight wars and win campaigns was about to show its hand decisively, with profound effects in history for maritime security.

In the fifth century BCE, the Persian Empire dominated the Greek world. The Ionian Revolts, in response to the taxes levied by the Persians, were triggered by Aristagoras, the leader of the city of Miletus at the end of the sixth century BCE. In a war that lasted from 499 BCE to 492 BCE, most Greek cities rebelled against their Persian rulers. But the Ionians were defeated at the Battle of Lade in 494 BCE. The cities were reconquered by the combined might of navies drawn from Egypt and Phoenicia. In 490 BCE the Athenians defeated a Persian naval invasion at Marathon on the north coast of Attica. In 481 BCE the Great King of Persia, Xerxes, attempted to mount an invasion by land and sea to conquer all of Greece. His aim was to finally open up the western Mediterranean Sea to Persian rule.

To the surprise of many, the Greeks managed to overcome the Persian naval forces at the Battle of Salamis, where over 200 Persian ships were captured or destroyed. By luring them into the cramped space of the Straits of Salamis, the Persian fleet, through its sheer weight of numbers, found manoeuvring difficult and became disorganised. Fundamental lessons on how to wage war at sea when outnumbered were learnt, and from that point, naval warfare became a vital and integrated part of creating empires. As a result, maritime security became another factor for leaders of cities, states and empires to reflect upon.

Early Beginnings

The maritime domain, however, was not all about warfare and conquest. The Phoenicians had shown the importance of maritime trade, as they had created a trading empire that extended across the length of the Mediterranean Sea, connecting Tyre with Antioch, Carthage, Tingis (Tangier) and Gades (Cadiz).

By the beginning of the first millennium, a series of trading networks had been established linking the eastern end of the Atlantic Ocean, over mainland Africa and through the Mediterranean Sea, across the Arabian Peninsula to Persia, India and onto the Han Empire in China. These trading routes carried goods by land and by sea. The potential for sea trading routes was being realised. The maritime trading routes in the Indian Ocean enabled links to be created between the Roman Mediterranean Sea, East Africa, the Persian Gulf, India and Taprobane (Sri Lanka) onwards to the East Indies.[5] Whilst Greek ships focused upon the coast, the lateen-rigged dhows used the seasonal wind patterns of the monsoon winds—so well known today by Somali pirates—to move beyond the traditional coastal patterns of trading to establish major trading routes across the Indian Ocean.

The discovery of the sea route through the Malacca Straits in the eighth century was a notable development in the ever-expanding network of trade routes. The journey from the Persian Gulf to Hanoi could take 120 days. Using the trade winds the Arabs would travel eastwards in November to return to the west in the summer. They exported iron, wool, incense and bullion in return for silks and spices. This trade route is significant, given the potential for emerging trade routes through the Arctic Circle as a result of climate change. As the ice coverage continues to retreat, new trading routes will open from the Eastern seaboard of the United States to Japan and China, cutting thousands of miles from the journey.

During the first millennium, the maritime domain could be characterised by its uses as a food source and an environment in which to move armies and trade. During this period, three societies excelled as navigators and explorers: these were the Vikings, the Arabs and the Polynesians. The Viking longship enabled the Scandinavians to range from the rivers of Russia, through the Baltic Sea, across the Atlantic Ocean to Iceland, to the east coast of what we now regard as North America. The Arabs were already accomplished seafarers exploiting the trade routes across the Indian Ocean to the East Indies.

Arguably the most prolific users of the maritime domain in this period were the Polynesians. Their seafaring exploits are significant, if for no other reason than for the sheer scale of the distances they travelled at sea. Hugging the coastline was simply not an option in the vast expanses of the Pacific Ocean. From their early beginnings in the period before 1500 BCE, where migrations from New Guinea through the Coral Sea have been traced to Fiji, several different further waves of migrations occurred in the periods from 1500 to 1000 BCE, where the leap from Fiji to the Samoa Islands was made, through the period 1000 BCE to 1 BCE when the Carolinas Islands and the Marquesas Islands where inhabited, to the major movements that resulted in the colonisation of New Zealand, the Hawaiian Islands and Tahiti in the first and second millennium. By 1200 CE, the Polynesians had discovered nearly all of the islands in the Pacific Ocean using boats based on designs such as twin-hulled canoes up to 30 metres in length.

The development of trading links and the application of sea power in this period was by no means confined to the emergent Western nations. Levathes documents the rise of Chinese naval power between 1405 and 1433 at a time when the Emperor Zhu Di ordered the construction of an ocean-going fleet totalling nearly 1600 vessels.[6] This was a significant departure for China that had, until that point, relied on Confucian attitudes of maintaining China as self-sufficient and isolated. Today, as China's economic growth spreads its influence again across the maritime environment, isolationism is simply not possible.

One hundred years before Columbus embarked upon his journey to the New World, fleets of giant junks carried out major expeditions into the South China Sea and beyond, across the Indian Ocean, to establish trading routes to replenish the Chinese treasury, which had been depleted by years of civil war. This expansionist period was to come to an abrupt end as China was beset by poor harvests, famine, epidemics and rebellions. Emperor Zhu Di was forced to re-evaluate his priorities and the age of Chinese maritime ascendency over the South China Sea and the wider regional areas passed, as the fleet was allowed to decay; by 1500 it was a capital crime to build ocean-going vessels. This was a setback in Chinese naval capability that is only now being addressed as China seeks to develop a blue-water navy to protect its increasingly important SLOC.

Whilst trade routes blossomed and new discoveries were made, unexpected problems also arose as the world started to become connected by trading patterns. The spread of bubonic plague is one example. In the fourteenth century, maritime trade routes carried the disease over global distances from China to Europe through the Arabian Peninsula, arriving in Marseille in 1347, London and Mecca in 1348, Edinburgh in 1350 and Aden in 1351. The rapid spread of the plague and the foothold it established quickly across Europe provide contemporary insights for those concerned with the use of the seas to smuggle modern biological and other deadly forms of weapons and pandemics for nefarious purposes.

From its earliest beginnings in the ancient civilisations of Egypt, Greece and Rome, the need to secure the coastline and its immediate marine environment focused upon the potential for invasion and occupation from forces moved by a combination of land and sea. The nature of maritime security in the period leading up to and including the first millennium was defined by having a navy, and being able to use military power to defeat other navies and remove the threats posed by other nation states. Such freedom of the seas has often been termed 'command of the sea'. The notion of being able to command the sea in anything other than a localised sense lacks credence. The situation off the Horn of Africa provides daily testament to the problems of command of the sea. At best, a coalition of warships can contain an area of the sea and make it difficult for pirates to conduct their activities, occasionally disrupting them when they set out to sea. But to achieve a state of control over the sea, when other naval forces seek to compete for that position, is extremely difficult. In time, China's attempts to create a modern-day state of hegemony over the South China Sea will no doubt be a cause for many of these arguments to be replayed. Mahan was clear in his analysis: true command of the sea can only be achieved when a decisive battle occurs and one side in the conflict loses. In the second and third decades of the twenty-first century the potential for China and India to act out such a scenario as they compete over the Indian Ocean is not a flight of fancy. The lessons learnt by the earliest civilisations still apply today, albeit in a slightly different sense.

Sea Power up to the end of the Seventeenth Century

In the second millennium, countries that mastered naval power to defend their coastlines also grew increasingly aware of their ability to project power overseas. States were able to range far and wide and impose their own civilisation upon others, such as the Spanish and Portuguese in Latin America, and the British in North America. Pirates, operating sometimes under a letter of marque from a state, roamed the oceans to disrupt the use of the marine environment for trade, and to plunder the riches from occupations of foreign lands. The seventeenth century saw lengthy wars between emerging naval powers, such as the naval wars with the Dutch between 1603 and 1688, and then Spain and France in the eighteenth century.

In the period from 1350 to 1800 the power of the British Royal Navy fluctuated in response to dynamic shifts in national strategic priorities. Throughout the fourteenth century England had no standing navy. At that time, England had a focus upon land warfare and its navy was configured to provide logistics and support to military operations in Europe, and to suppress the occasional bouts of internecine warfare that erupted in and around the British Isles. This local focus required that both naval and merchant vessels were seconded into service. This mix of the merchant and military is an abiding model that also showed its utility in the Falkland Islands campaign, in which cruise liners such as the *QE2* and the *Canberra*, and vessels such as the *Atlantic Conveyer* were brought into service.

The sizeable operations mounted in Europe swallowed up the resources available to the national treasury and resulted in periods of time when investments in naval capacity were almost non-existent. It was King Henry VIII who, borrowing an idea from Scotland's James IV, started to build a navy that could operate over extended ranges. The vision of an empire was born as English maritime prowess started the process that led to its eventual, albeit temporary, command of the seas. Elizabeth I used the legacy given to her by her father to defeat the Spanish Armada in 1588.

The period of naval history between 1500 and 1650 has been studied in depth by Glete.[7] His work provides a detailed study of the development of naval power in the period, highlighting the impact of warfare upon the maritime domain. This was the period when the maritime domain and sea trading routes became important as the discoveries of the navigators of the time, such as Magellan, opened up the international dimensions of moving trade by sea, and the building of empires began to be realised.

Glete charts the development of maritime power, noting technical developments in naval warfare and the consequent limitations on sea-based warfare, before the developments of the large battle fleets of the middle of the seventeenth century. He also aligns the development of naval power from its initial employment by traders, whose sole aim was to protect their rapidly developing SLOC, to the development of the navies employed by states as the idea of the nation state emerged after the signing of the Treaty of Westphalia in 1648. The transition from the mercantile state to the nation state was a hugely important development, and presaged the emergence of nation state navies that could protect SLOC on the international stage, moving away from the focus on the local and regional SLOC that had been so important to the mercantile empires of the Mediterranean Sea. It is perhaps worth pausing for a second to ponder on the parallels that might emerge as today's transnational actors, like Al-Qaeda, move into the maritime domain. Will they be reminiscent of the mercantile navies? Arguably, the activities of transnational criminal organisations that smuggle people and drugs are latter-day variants of the mercantile navies of places such as Venice.

This change coincided with the development of new approaches to the design of naval vessels, as the old galleys used for protecting the mercantile trading networks of the Mediterranean Sea could not be adapted for the harsher environments of the world's oceans. Glete makes clear the nature of maritime warfare in the fifteenth century and its reliance upon what we today refer to as 'amphibious operations'. The majority of maritime operations were focussed upon attacks carried out along coastlines against an adversary's fortresses. Glete specifically documents the events surrounding the Battle of Zonchio in 1499, referring to it as a decisive battle and a turning point for Venetian naval power. For some historians, the outcome of the Battle of Zonchio was more important than that of the Battle of Lepanto in 1571, which some commentators believe to be the most significant naval engagement since the Battle of Actium in the Ionian Sea in 31 BC.

In the latter part of the fifteenth century, Venice had established a preeminent position in the Mediterranean Sea, despite its obvious geographic limitations, being located at the end of the Adriatic Sea and being vulnerable to attacks by the Ottoman Empire to the east. In 1489, it added Cyprus to its empire and in 1945 its navy helped the French in their invasion of Naples. Venice relied on its ability to project power through the Adriatic and Ionian Sea into the wider Mediterranean Sea. When the Ottoman Empire defeated the Venetian Navy at Zonchio in 1499, it was a watershed for naval power in the region, and Venice became increasingly unable to protect its SLOC. Glete notes that whilst Venice retained a strong commercial position in the aftermath of this battle, it could no longer control the SLOC outside the Adriatic by naval force, which severely hampered its trading status.

Glete observes the impact of the rapid emergence of sea-borne trade over this period, as greater volumes of more diverse products were carried over ever-greater ranges. This combination of circumstances saw this period as one in history from which, it can be argued, the trading links we know today have been built. But he also notes the decline of empires and the period when the Mediterranean Sea and its trading networks, centred on places such as Venice, became less influential. Glete sees the early decades of the sixteenth century as being a turning point at which the old mercantile empires and centres of power started their terminal decline. Younger empires based upon exploiting the discoveries of the Americas and the emergent trading links to India, China and the Middle East offered expanded horizons and new trading opportunities.

As the new empires emerged, so did the threats to trading routes. Piracy, sometimes legitimised by buccaneers operating under a letter of marque, emerged to disrupt developing trading routes. Whilst the nature of the goods that move by sea today is very different, the issues with protecting SLOC and ensuring the safe delivery of goods to their destination, without disruption, is as relevant now as it was the in the period between 1500 and 1650.

The history of the period analysed by Glete is replete with civil wars, and culminates in the Thirty Years War between 1618 and 1648. At this time there was a nexus between commercial and political interests that lay behind much of the motivation for the application of maritime power; this arguably drove forward the development of new technologies in one of the earliest forms of an arms race. Commercial imperatives to expand and protect trading routes and establish empires lay behind some of the most important developments in naval technology that were to result in the development of new warships in the latter part of the seventeenth century and on into the eighteenth century. This was a time when the oceans saw an unprecedented increase in levels of shipping and trade, with obvious implications for maritime security.

Maritime Power in the Eighteenth and Nineteenth Centuries

Naval planners would have viewed the issues of maritime security in the eighteenth and nineteenth centuries through quite a narrow lens. Their priorities would have been focussed upon denying a potential adversary the ability to invade or to disrupt the SLOC that gave economic vibrancy to the state along with associated political clout. It was vital to secure the state and stop the enemy from invading the shores. For island nations, such as the United Kingdom, the natural barrier of the English Channel has often been crucial to the continuance of the state. Arguably, the use of fire ships by the Royal Navy to disrupt the Spanish Armada, whilst it was anchored off the coast at Gravelines, was an example of acting pre-emptively to destroy an attempted invasion before it got too close to the shoreline. Blockading was another strategy employed by the Royal Navy, although it had its limitations in terms of resupply. These were ways of achieving a form of maritime security and disabling an adversary, which are reflective of an approach to maritime security that can be traced back further.

Building upon the initial trading routes in Europe, such as those operated by the Hanseatic Trade League in the twelfth, thirteenth and fourteenth centuries, new clipper boats started to follow in the wake of explorers like Dias, Columbus, Vasco de Gama, Magellan, Frobisher and Cook and open up new trading routes globally. The formation of the East India Company on 1 January 1600, under a royal charter that initially provided for a fifteen-year licence to trade in the East Indies, was the harbinger of the first steps towards what we know today as globalisation, and the worldwide trading environment that inextricably links the economies of the world.

Increasing competition over trade routes inevitably led to conflict. The end of the twelve-year truce between Spain and the Netherlands in 1621 is an example of how an increasingly powerful and global trading fleet, was able to threaten Spanish hegemony over trading routes. Skills in shipbuilding and navigation, along with an aggressive approach to opening up new markets and a strong economy, enabled the Dutch to expand their shipping routes to unprecedented levels, dominating the route from Brazil to Europe and helping place Amsterdam at the centre of Europe's insurance market. In 1641, the Portuguese lost the key port of Malacca to the Dutch, who had been blockading it for six years. In this period, the Dutch also captured other Portuguese colonies from the Persian Gulf to Japan, gaining control of the lucrative trade in cloves, nutmegs, cinnamon and pepper.

The Dutch, however, did clash with other emerging trading nations. In October 1651, relations between the Dutch and the English dipped when the English Parliament approved the legislation that challenged Dutch mercantile supremacy. In what was regarded as a thinly disguised attack upon the position of Amsterdam as a leading mercantile power, the Navigation Act required that only English ships could import goods from Asia, Africa and America. It came at a time when the English economy was suffering from the impact of three years of harvest failures and the effects of plague. This forced the Parliament into introducing an element of protectionism into previously unregulated trading arrangements.

Rodger provides a history of the issues of safeguarding the sea from 660 to 1649 from a British perspective.[8] Richard Harding has chronicled the development of naval tactics in the period between 1650 and 1830 in his book, *Seapower and Naval Warfare.*[9] He considers the importance of seapower at a time when the expansion of sea trade was developing at a frenetic pace. He also charts the development of key trading routes and the emergence of the battlefleet as a key instrument of maritime security and the application of naval power. Harding notes that it is hardly surprising that some of the largest sea battles in history, in purely numerical terms, took place in the North Sea during the period of the Anglo-Dutch Wars; here engagements could involve over 150 warships, some of which were merchantmen adapted for warfare, which fought alongside dedicated warships. The chaos of those confrontations precluded the developments of sophisticated naval tactics. Damaged ships that survived the encounters would be repaired and sent back to sea as quickly as possible.

The outcomes of the battles however were important strategically as each side vied for control over important trading routes, such as the English Channel. Sea battles would be conducted to contest the passage of a single convoy. On 30 November 1652, the Dutch Admiral de Ruyter defeated the English off the coast of Dungeness, allowing him to escort a convoy into Dutch waters that had assembled near La Rochelle. Subsequent English naval victories at the Gabbard in 1653 and Scheveningen in 1653 closed the English Channel and forced the Dutch to discuss terms. Similar events in 1666 and 1673, when the Dutch Navy was unable to defeat the English Navy in the English Channel, constrained Dutch commerce. The ability of the English Navy to control the area around the Straits of Dover hampered Dutch commercial expansion. This outcome demonstrated that sea control could be established in a vital maritime area, albeit on a temporary basis, if resources permitted.

The importance of controlling important SLOC was clear, as the Dutch needed access to international trading routes for their active mercantile activities to be successful. The choke point, the English Channel, was clearly something worth fighting over in the first instance. Despite the outcomes of these battles, the limitations of maritime power to deliver security over longer distances rapidly became apparent. Harding notes that the ability of navies to control the SLOC beyond any distance from their own harbours, such as those along the south and east coast of England, was only to develop slowly; logistical problems provided one constraint on the application of naval power over far wider areas. Sustaining any level of significant naval presence remotely was a difficult thing to achieve.

With threats in the Mediterranean Sea from Barbary Corsairs, naval squadrons had to operate using Italian ports alongside Cadiz and Gibraltar for victuals and supplies. Harding notes that in 1694, during the Nine Years War (1688–1697), William III overwintered a squadron of ships in the Mediterranean Sea to support his Spanish allies and opines that this was the beginning of an attempt to maintain a permanent force in the area; an effort that the captures of Gibraltar and Minorca in 1704 and 1708 were to help, as they reduced their dependency upon allies for access to anchorages. This idea of maintaining a permanent presence overseas is something that has many parallels with contemporary French and American naval strategy of being based upon key locations around the world. In the first decade of the twenty-first century, American, British, Australian and other naval forces expended a great deal of effort in the Persian Gulf in what, arguably, were presence patrols designed to show a long-term commitment to the region.

Wider Historical Perspectives

Naval historians often use slightly different starting points for their analyses of this period. Rodger provides his analysis from a starting point of 1649 and the period of the Anglo-Dutch Wars, through to the Treaty of Paris in 1815. Padfield takes a specific look at the outcomes from major naval campaigns in the period 1788–1851, and the ways in which they have shaped the international maritime environment we have today.[10]

Documenting both the drama of the battles themselves and the impact they had, he develops an insightful commentary on the key moments in the period, chronicling events from the French Revolution through to the naval battles of Cape St. Vincent, the Nile, Copenhagen and Trafalgar, before considering the implications of the American War in 1812, Napoleon's dénouement at Waterloo, and his subsequent nemesis at St. Helena. The choice of ending his analysis in 1851 is an interesting one, coinciding with the Great Exhibition held that year in Hyde Park in London.

It was, many commentators feel, the point at which Britain held a position as the supreme world power, extending its influence across the maritime domain through all of the major trading routes. Through its exercise of sea power Britain had created a maritime environment that enjoyed a level of security that today's mariners would envy. The United States, however, was gradually developing its maritime capabilities, starting out on its way to becoming the preeminent force that it is today, as the world's only maritime superpower.[11] This situation, however, may be contested as the twenty-first century develops.

Clearly threats still existed to SLOC, and confrontations with slave traders were a key aspect of combating a form of criminality that endures even today, albeit in the slightly modified form of providing passage to economic migrants. Isolated pockets of slave trading, especially in young people and women, still exist today, but its scale is not like that which blighted the west coast of Africa in the eighteenth century.

Today maritime security is often spoken of in the context of a broader national security strategy. Harding notes that the idea of some overarching maritime strategy being in place, that shapes the approaches to the application of sea power, initially appeared in the middle of the eighteenth century.[12] He re-examines the idea of sea power during the period of sail-powered navies. His aim is to consider the nature of the relationship between the battleship and the exercise of sea power as a whole. He lays out the history of this relationship, providing a valuable discussion that details the emergence of the form of sea power that the naval strategist Alfred Thayer Mahan took up in his work towards the end of the nineteenth century, and his advocacy of the merits of the overwhelmingly powerful battle fleet.

Roy and Lesley Adkins provide an equally illuminating commentary on the period that complements Padfield's own analysis of 2003.[13] Adkins and Adkins chose to analyse a similar period in naval history and concluded, that by the time of Waterloo, the Royal Navy controlled the world's sea lanes. This is an important statement in the context of this book. The word 'control' can be seen from a number of vantage points.

At one end of a spectrum it could mean that nothing could happen on the world's oceans without the Royal Navy's knowledge, which is not representative of the prevailing situation; at the other, it could mean that no other naval power was able to challenge the Royal Navy's authority over the seas, a more representative viewpoint of the situation. The debate surrounding the degree of control is what ultimately led Alfred Mahan and William Corbett to devise their somewhat different takes on the nature of the control of the oceans.

Hore analyses the history of the Royal Navy over a different period, namely that of the 400 years from the time of the Tudors to the end of the Second World War.[14] In this work, he develops some very different perspectives, using material from the National Maritime Museum that provides rare insights into the lives of seafarers of the period. Hore also provides a very technical viewpoint on the development of sea power, documenting developments in gunnery, copper-sheathed hulls and the emergence of the great ironclad dreadnoughts that fought in the Battle of Jutland.

For Nelson, maritime security was afforded through tactics such as blockading and direct engagement with the enemy, such as in the Battle of the Nile or Trafalgar. Nelson's task was to secure the United Kingdom by operating upstream and disabling the threat far away from the English Channel. In his mind, the term maritime security had a strategic perspective. Every instance in which he could meet and defeat the French in battle at sea would make his homeland safer. During the First World War, when U-Boats made their appearance in the sea lanes off the Western Approaches, maritime security took on a new mantle as the United Kingdom's opponents started sinking vessels carrying supplies. This was not a blockade of a specific harbour, although German mine-laying added its own dimension to the overall problems during the Battle of the Atlantic, but an attempt to constrict and suffocate sea lanes of communications using surface and subsurface naval units.

Had the Cold War ever erupted into a direct confrontation of forces, one of its focal points would have inevitably been a rerun of the Battle of the Atlantic, with Soviet submarines trying to disrupt the movement of reinforcements to European and NATO naval vessels trying to fend off attacks from the air, through the Iceland-Greenland-Faroes gaps, and by conducting anti-submarine warfare operations against Soviet submarines.

Throughout the First World War, the German Navy and the Royal Navy vied with each other to dominate the North Sea. Intelligence became a vital asset in trying to track the sorties mounted against the eastern coastal towns, such as Yarmouth. The German Navy could choose when and where to mount attacks. The attacks could occur on a random basis, offering little insight into any strategic purpose that might otherwise reveal intent and be subject to detailed analysis. It would appear the attacks were carried out more to be a nuisance, and today might be regarded as part of a reconnaissance campaign, designed to alarm the local population and to highlight the limitations of the Royal Navy. In order to stream south and bring the German Navy to an engagement, the Royal Navy needed intelligence forewarning of their departure from the safety of the Jade.

The Battle of Jutland, whilst in itself inconclusive and its outcome the subject of much empirical debate, did ensure that the North Sea was ceded to the Royal Navy. The concept of a fleet as part of a strategy to achieve maritime security was reaffirmed and the writings of Alfred Thomas Mahan validated. It seemed like the Mahanian approach to naval strategy had endured the rigours of the First World War, and it emerged as the dominant approach to naval warfare.

In the past, maritime security would have been seen through quite a narrow lens, dominated with concerns about piracy, slavery and projecting naval power around the world to safeguard vital sea lanes of communications, the latter being a notable achievement of the Royal Navy during the time of the British Empire. Events occurring a long way from home mattered to the overall economy and wellbeing of the United Kingdom. Writers such as Corbett and Mahan theorised on the nature of control of the seas and what that meant at the end of the nineteenth century. With over 70 per cent of our planet covered by oceans, the idea of controlling the sea is difficult to envisage, even at a comparatively local level. In the Gulf of Aden the difficulties of establishing control over what might appear on maps to be quite a small area of the world's oceans is apparent. Pirates and those engaged in criminal activities are provided a great deal of manoeuvring room.

In recent history, the security of the United Kingdom came down to the threat of action by the Royal Navy. In the Second World War, Operation Sea Lion threatened to subordinate the United Kingdom to the Third Reich. Maritime security became synonymous with national security and survival. If the Royal Air Force had failed to secure the victory it achieved in the Battle of Britain, the very survival of the United Kingdom would have rested on the shoulders of the Royal Navy. The outcome would have been far from certain.

The concept of maritime security advocated by Mahan, however, had its limitations despite its apparent durability. During the Second World War, coastal convoys plying their trade along the eastern coastline of the United Kingdom came under repeated attacks from E-Boats that launched random raids to disrupt the passage of vital supplies from the north to the south of Britain. Today, this tactic would be seen as a form of asymmetric warfare, avoiding the classic set-piece naval battle. The fleet-in-being did not provide a deterrent against the rapid attack tactics used by the German E-Boats: it was too static and deployed to the rear of the maritime environment, reducing the threat from German submarines. This was, and remains, a major failing of the concept. The current United States tactics of forward deployment into areas such as the Persian Gulf develop the concept of a fleet-in-being to a new level where it is placed in the way of harm. The potential for the modern day equivalent of the E-Boats in the Iranian Navy to be a threat to the major combat units of the United States Navy has been the subject of a lot of debate and discussion. Swarming tactics are notoriously difficult to defeat, especially if attacks are coordinated between surface vessels and shore-based anti-ship missiles. The mere presence of the Royal Navy at Scapa Flow did not deter the determined crews that mounted attacks along the eastern seaboard of the United Kingdom. Echoes of this can be found in the tactics developed by the Sea Tigers of Sri Lanka as they sought to engage, overwhelm and destroy units of the Sri Lankan Navy; tactics that have also been adopted by the Iranian Navy, and to a lesser extent by transnational groups such as Hamas and Hezbollah.

Legal Definitions of Maritime Security

Having considered some key aspects of the historical development of maritime security from the viewpoint of the instrument of military power, it is important to also briefly review developments in the legal frameworks that govern the use of the sea. It is worthwhile, for example, considering what is meant by the term maritime domain, any analysis of which must be undertaken against the legal backdrop of international agreements.

The United Nations Convention on the Law of the Sea (UNCLOS) was designed to replace the concept of freedom of the seas developed in the seventeenth century. The Third United Nations Convention on the Law of the Sea in 1982 (UNCLOS III) provided the framework that introduced the EEZ. In contrast to previous efforts at defining the legal frameworks concerning the use of the sea, it was based upon a consensus process rather than majority voting. This may explain why the convention was so long in its development, after initial discussions in 1973, which marked the start of the Third United Nation Conference on the Law of the Sea.

UNCLOS III replaced several previous treaties, such as UNCLOS I, which was initially published after deliberations that lasted at the United Nations from 1956 to 1958. It came into force on 16 November 1994 when Guyana ratified the treaty. UNCLOS III also replaced and brought clarity to the older 'freedom of the seas' concept which dated from the seventeenth century, from the pamphlet published by Hugo Grotius in 1609; the time, when to all intents and purposes, the Dutch gained their freedom from Spain with the signing of the twelve year truce. This was called *Mare Liberum* (the Free Sea) and it was based upon the idea that the sea was international territory and all nations should be free to use it for trade.

At this time[15] Dutch naval power had developed and was supporting the growth in its international trade beyond its immediate European partners towards the Mediterranean Sea, the Americas and the South Pacific. This situation did not endure for long as the Golden Age of the Dutch Republic was short-lived, but at the time it contributed towards enforcing the concepts that emerged from this scholarly work. The ideas outlined in this pamphlet were challenged by William Welwod, a Scottish jurist. He argued against the ideas published by Grotius in a work *An Abridgment of All Sea-Lawes* in 1613, which elicited a response from Grotius in 1615 entitled *Defensio capitis quinti Maris Liberi oppugnati a Gulielmo Welwodo* (Defence of the Five Free oceans, opposed by William Welwod). The English jurist and philosopher John Selden also contributed to the development of the ideas with his work *Mare clausum* in 1635, where he set out to prove that in practice the sea was as capable of being appropriated as the land. This work was dedicated to King Charles I, and was regarded by many as a form of state paper.

Selden's work had been published sixteen years after it had been written, as it had initially been banned by James I for political reasons.

The delay meant it actually appeared nearly a quarter of a century after the publication of *Mare Liberum* by Hugo Grotius. When it was finally published in 1635, it appeared to be motivated by a desire to challenge the apparent rights of Dutch fishermen in the waters off the coast of England.

The ideas that were to form the foundation of what we know today as UNCLOS III, were further developed by the Dutch jurist Cornelius van Bynkershoek. His work published in 1702 called *De Domino Maris* constrained the definition of national waters to what has been referred to as the 'cannon shot rule' which effectively defined territorial waters as being those which could be defended by a cannon based upon the land. The three-mile limit was born, defining the coastal and territorial waters of states. The rest of the sea, however, was an area to be used as nation states saw fit. It provided an opaque environment in which criminality could be nurtured and could thrive. One outcome of that was the development of the international slave trade, which has echoes today in the ways in which economic migrants willingly seek to move to other countries;[16] this is the exact opposite of being forced into slavery, as in the nineteenth century.

Paul Reynolds, writing for the BBC, has sought a solution to piracy that draws on this period of history, looking at the Royal Navy's interventions against the African slave trade.[17] In 1841, Lord Palmerston was quoted as saying that 'taking a wasps' nest [...] is more effective than catching the wasps one-by-one'. Citing the escapades of a British Naval Officer, Joseph Denman, he notes the proactive stance taken by Denman towards disrupting the slave trade, such as pre-emptive raids upon settlements and blockading rivers. This was regarded by some as operating on the borders of the law itself, if not beyond. In time, Denman's actions were to be vindicated as the Royal Navy led operations between 1820 and 1870 that seized nearly 1,600 ships and released 150,000 slaves. In his analysis, Reynolds contrasts the somewhat liberal interpretations of international law that existed at the time with the hesitancy and prevarication that dominates contemporary responses to piracy.

Today, legal considerations about the use of force in the maritime domain are often a matter for the United Nations. Operations off the Horn of Africa are mandated under Security Council Resolution 1846 (2008) which provides the legal framework for member states to conduct operations that deliver food supplies under the auspices of the World

Food Programme (WFP) to the people of Somalia, and the efforts to achieve an international response to the problems of piracy in the area.

This development was a reaction to a report issued by the International Maritime Bureau (IMB) in January 2009 that cited an 11 per cent increase in incidences of piracy at sea in 2008, with 111 recorded off the coast of Somalia, with an increase of 200 per cent in the Gulf of Aden, earning the pirates involved an estimated $30 million in the year in ransom payments. An international response was clearly required and the United Nations is the obvious vehicle for nation-states to come together to develop solutions to this problem, in accordance with internationally accepted laws. These do place constraints upon the operations that are taking place in the Indian Ocean and Gulf of Aden, as pirates are often initially arrested and then either released, or in some cases, moved to Kenya where a legal process has been developed to take them through the courts. The approach of the international community to implementing these sanctions against the pirates is not consistent and it does not send out a clear message that can alter their behaviour. Dangers exist if the current legal frameworks are not revised. Piracy and other forms of criminal behaviour will inevitably increase. With other pressures over the exploitation of dwindling resources, the potential for the maritime environment to descend into anarchy is not impossible. It is clear that the long-standing arrangement with respect to the freedom of the seas needs to be revised. In a globalised and inter-connected world an anarchic sea is not desirable. It needs to be governed.

3

THE MARITIME ENVIRONMENT

The combination of the enormous scope, variety and room for manoeuvre offered by the physical and geographical realities of the (earth's) maritime environment [...] presents a sobering and uncomfortable reality [...] What compounds this reality further is that the commercial milieu that simultaneously affords [...] the ability to deploy, finance operations, tactical concealment, logistical fluidity and wealth of targets of opportunity—the commercial maritime industry—is itself numerically vast, complex, deliberately opaque and in a permanent state of flux.

Rupert Herbert-Burns, 2005
Lloyds of London

Background

At the start of the twenty-first century over 90 per cent of the world's goods move by sea. It is the highway that allows the world's economy to operate. Anything that interferes with the operation of this highway, or the sea lanes of communications as they are often known, can have major impacts upon the livelihoods of people all over world. Insurance premiums can fluctuate and the cost of moving goods can increase if longer sea routes have to be taken, with longer journeys adding to the contribution the maritime domain makes to increasing levels of pollution in the atmosphere.[1] A secure marine environment, where goods can be moved between trading partners without fear of disruption or harassment, is a vital ingredient of a successful and vibrant global economy.

What constitutes a secure marine environment? Certainly the ability to mount operations to save seafarers from difficulties when, for example, the weather or a mechanical failure threatens to overwhelm a vessel, or where basic human error creates situations in which people's lives are placed at risk. A measure of the security in the marine environment is the ability to mobilise resources to help save lives in such situations. This is, however, only one yardstick.

A secure maritime environment is also one in which criminal activities, in whatever form they take, are reduced to a minimum. The freedom of the sea appeals to criminal groups and to transnational terrorist organisations. They can use the vastness of the ocean to avoid being detected, to conduct activities that move contraband across oceans and seas and establish a presence on a wider basis to exploit new markets overseas, using entry points to countries that have weak or failing governments.[2] Similar advantages apply to those wishing to fish illegally and also hijack or rob those using the sea for pleasure or the movement of economic goods. Maritime security also means that countries can harness the resources within their internationally agreed maritime boundaries, such as oil and gas reserves. Maritime security is therefore a multi-dimensional concept, as we have already shown, and it has local, regional and global connotations.

Achieving the goal of a secure maritime environment is not easy. The sheer size of the oceans and the lengths of national coastlines complicate the delivery of security; it is worth recalling that over 30,000 containers a day arrive in American ports. Terrorists and criminals have a lot of room in which to manoeuvre. The lack of transparency on ship ownership can also hinder efforts to understand and profile potential threats from vessels entering and leaving territorial waters. This is compounded by what has been described as a fluid approach to crewing by owners and operators of commercial vessels. The development of a comprehensive understanding of the maritime environment not only requires knowledge of the current location of vessels, but also where they have been, what they are carrying, and information on the registration and biometric identity of crew members. Preventing terrorist attacks and focussing law enforcement efforts at specific aspects of criminality is always helped by the earliest identification of threats, allowing the appropriate interdiction by security forces that are selected for the mission in question.

For countries seeking to secure their maritime borders, difficult trade-offs have to be made for the capability to provide that secure environment. These considerations need to be made as part of developing a national maritime strategy. This would look at the coupling that exists between the national interest and the marine environment and can be significant for some countries. Its focus would cover the need to:

- Protect sea lanes of communications bringing good or tourists into ports and harbours.
- Protect national resources within the Exclusive Economic Zone (EEZ),[3] such as fish, oil, gas and mineral deposits from illegal exploitation.
- Deter smuggling of people, weapons and goods through exploiting coastlines that are not policed.
- Develop tourism and to protect the marine environment from pollution.
- Ensure vessels can transit or use natural anchorages in coastal waters without fear of harassment or robbery.
- Protect national boundaries when they come under threat of invasion or attack from other nation-states.
- Protect seafarers in the course of their duties should they get into difficulties.
- Ensure that the impact of natural disasters, such as the Indian Ocean Tsunami, can be minimised through the deployment of early warning systems.

Maritime Domain Awareness

The key to deploying national assets effectively to create maritime security is MDA. This idea of domain awareness applies above and below the water and covers the brown, green and blue-water environments that interact across the land-sea boundary. Knowing what goes on in the areas of the world's oceans and seas that are of national interest is important. However, achieving a high level of maritime domain awareness is currently unrealistic. The coastlines and areas of the oceans cover too large an area to monitor satisfactorily using contemporary technologies, where persistence of observation is difficult to achieve. Developing the right circumstances in which a secure maritime environment can be created is extremely difficult.

Until technologies offer radically different solutions, the answer, limited though it may be, lies in integrating the various elements that can provide insights and indications of patterns of illegal behaviour, proving that areas of the sea are being used for criminal activities. This is the intelligence-led approach and is indicative of how nation states are currently responding to a need to deploy limited resources effectively in large areas of sea covering current and potentially extended forms of the EEZ.

Building MDA becomes a matter of identifying all of the potential sources, such as the deployment of the AIS, satellite-based reconnaissance, local people who know local waters (such as fishermen and yachtsmen), coastguard, gendarmerie and naval units (both sea and air-based) that might contribute in a concerted effort to patrol and gain information on what is happening on the sea and around the coastlines of a nation state. The combination of local fishermen, equipped with mobile phones, and an effective infrastructure can allow maritime domain awareness to be formed, albeit not in real-time unless, considerable resources are deployed. In some parts of Africa, at present, this is simply not affordable. Local economies cannot sustain the levels of investment, and overseas aid packages are often directed at other priorities. However, the ubiquitous spread of mobile phone networks does provide a basic capability which provides a starting point. Africa is a continent that is celebrated for its innovation and resilience when faced by hardship and environmental challenges. Providing simple reporting networks using mobile phones and short-range radio communications systems carefully distributed along the coast can allow local people to monitor and report on any encroachment from people conducting illegal fishing to central authorities. They can then deploy their limited coastguard facilities quickly into areas where reports of illegal activity have been provided through these local networks.

It is important that central governments in those countries employ and maintain the capabilities they have been given as part of overseas aid packages, developing indigenous support facilities. Eritrea is one country that has shown how this can be achieved, with help from an Australian company which established a boat building and repair facility that allows local manufacture of patrol boats and even a small export business to be developed.

Similar efforts by the Malayan, Singaporean and Indonesian governments to crack down on piracy in the Malacca Strait,[4] continues to demonstrate the importance of SLOC to national and regional economies[5] such as those in Southeast Asia. Bradford has explored[6] the potential for regional cooperation in Southeast Asia to further develop, initially providing an analysis of its extent at the end of the Cold War, when the area was regarded as a relatively stable area. Bradford moves on to chronicle the efforts made in the region, both through bilateral and multilateral initiatives to foster maritime security, and reduce the potential for state-on-state conflicts; he specifically quotes the first communiqué from the 1992 Association of South East Asian Nations (ASEAN), which covered a security matter which emphasised the necessity to resolve all sovereignty and jurisdictional issues pertaining to the South China Sea by peaceful means. This led to a series of South China Sea workshops aimed at reducing regional tensions over matters such as the Spratley and Paracel Islands. Multilateral cooperation, as Bradford notes, can have its problems, as progress can be limited by the least supportive partner. Nevertheless, this is a model that shows just what can be achieved as a result of carefully planned and targeted regional cooperation.

In this situation, a blend of bilateral and multilateral agreements provides an approach that allows a wider catchment of nations to be involved from a strategic viewpoint, and for practical tactical measures to be implemented at the bilateral level to combat criminality and other threats. This mix of approaches offers a potential model for other regions where long-standing disputes concerning the definition of the EEZ[7] might otherwise hamper efforts in creating a secure maritime environment and create the conditions where piracy, terrorism and criminality can thrive exploiting the gaps in the security architectures.

In November 2004, sixteen countries, the ASEAN members plus China, South Korea, Japan, India and Sri Lanka, concluded the Regional Cooperation Agreement on Combating Piracy and Armed Robbery against Ships (ReCAAP) initiative. Bradford notes in his analysis that while ReCAAP is important, it alone would not eradicate Asian piracy; other more specific measures would be needed. The cooperation between Singapore, Indonesia and Malaysia provided a practical framework through which action could be taken to tackle piracy in the Malacca Strait. Robbery, however, remains an enduring problem.

The positive developments in the area are clearly a result of inter-state cooperation. The Japanese have also participated and assisted the anti-piracy effort through its coastguard agency.[8] This assistance eschews the images of Japanese warships projecting excessive military power. Images of the Second World War are still too vivid for many people to accept more than a Japanese civilian presence in the region. Regional cooperation does have its limits despite the obvious shared concerns over the protection of the SLOC, and disputes over the extent of EEZ also create difficulties.

Piracy is also a major factor off the coast of Nigeria. Equally important though perhaps less heralded efforts are also going on to build capacity in Africa through the joint US and European Africa Partnership Station (APS). The initial focus of these efforts is upon the Gulf of Guinea and the Mediterranean sea with NATO warships trying to disrupt the smuggling of weapons of mass destruction. The PSI is another example of multi-national cooperation aimed at the specific threat of the proliferation of weapons of mass destruction or WMD. All of these efforts seek to deny the freedom of the seas to those involved in terrorism and criminality and bring increasing order to what had the potential to be a chaotic environment.

The maritime domain plays an important role in transnational crime. Links across the South Atlantic Ocean see narcotics moving from Latin America to the west coast of Africa. Economic migrants routinely use maritime channels to try and get from places such as Sub-Saharan Africa to Europe. The Canary Islands and the Mediterranean Sea are examples of locations from where people try to leave the coast of North Africa. Australia has problems with economic migrants trying to cross the South East Indian Ocean and the Timor Sea from Indonesia.[9] The Red Sea and the Caribbean Sea are also important routes for people seeking the economic vibrancy of Saudi Arabia and the United States.

In addition to the activities of transnational criminals and terrorists another major threat to maritime security arises from Illegal, Unregulated and Unreported (IUU) fishing. For the people of coastal states, survival is often closely linked to artisanal fishing. In many countries where local geography and climate do not provide for the sustainable development of agriculture, fishing is literally a matter of life and death. In the absence of a suitable deterrent fishing trawlers from countries across the world can move into an area, such as off the west coast of Africa, and take this means of subsistence away from the local domestic markets.

Anecdotal evidence suggests that artisanal fishermen in many countries of Africa now take significantly longer time at sea to find fish. Unregulated exploitation of this resourse has a direct impact on the artisanal fishing activities and denudes stocks. This activity also impacts the revenues that can be earned by countries by regulating the fish take and issuing licences to commercial fishermen. Estimates about the impact on African economies vary but the overall value, in terms of lost revenue, is believed to be close to $1 billion a year. For many countries this is a loss of a vital national asset.

The oceans are also areas of concern and have the potential to become the places where major confrontations between blue-water navies occur, over disputes concerning energy security and attempts to disrupt and dislocate important SLOC in a time of crisis. Vice Admiral Mihir Roy has explored the issues in a paper entitled 'Maritime Security in South West Asia'[10] that focuses upon the Indian Ocean, charting its history and highlighting its current importance as a major area of maritime trade. In the paper, Admiral Roy notes that the region is responsible for 65 per cent of the world's known oil reserves in what he describes as ten littoral zones. This high density is responsible for the growing concerns in the region over the possibility of energy security acting as a catalyst for confrontation on the high seas. The build up of the Indian Navy,[11] the Chinese Navy and other regional powers' naval forces presages a form of maritime arms race in the area.[12] The rapid acquisition of submarines by the navies of Malaya, Vietnam, India, China and Singapore illustrates a focus on sea denial operations. The next Battle of the Atlantic may well be the Battle of the Indian Ocean as states compete to secure their SLOC.

Admiral Roy's analysis acknowledges that maritime security is multi-faceted and multi-dimensional involving both military and non-military issues and argues that Tokyo, New Delhi and Washington are in many ways natural allies whose common purpose is to see that threats to the SLOC are addressed through regional and international cooperation. Noting the events of 11 September as a watershed in international security, he cites threats from arms trafficking, narco-terrorism,[13] fishing, the exploitation of minerals from the sea bed and offshore oil and gas resources, illegal immigration and concerns over the vulnerability of SLOC as being the main source of problems for the Indian Ocean, commenting that SLOC are the arteries of a region and serve as an umbilical cord for the country.

Admiral Roy argues that India's interests in the Indian Ocean cannot be compartmentalised, positing that they are complex and include subjects such as energy security and the issues of multi-ethnic societies where mixed communities can have an impact on the ability of states to act. He believes that regional security measures, including those that encourage transparency and help build confidence are important.[14] However, at the same time, India is also acting to increase its own position in the Indian Ocean should such measures fail to materialise. In August 2009, India announced it would be stepping up its cooperation with the Maldives Islands to protect the archipelago from terrorism and to counter China's increasing presence in the Indian Ocean.[15]

This analysis has been supported in other paper published by Rear Admiral Chopra that considers the maritime dimension of energy security in the Indian Ocean.[16] He argues that the Indian Ocean is the most militarised water body in the world. This is quite a shift that has occurred from the naval dispositions at the height of the Cold War with NATO forces being forward deployed to try and control the Soviet Navy's access to the sea. Chopra specifically raises the issues of protecting SLOC in the area noting that in 2004 around fifty tankers visited Indian ports on a daily basis with a potential for the numbers to rise to between 150 and 200 daily visits in 2020. He recognises the impact this may have on the levels of traffic passing through the region and the ability for interdiction by state or non-state actors, noting obvious Indian concerns about the intentions of China and the People's Liberation Army Navy (PLAN). In documenting the ambitious plans for the development of the PLAN, Admiral Chopra believes that China is adopting the strategy of *tao guang yang hui* (conceal one's talent, arouse minimum concern and suspicion). This creates problems for those tasked with analysing China's intent. What for them is a cultural approach to their maritime security is for Western analysts a 'lack of transparency' and a deliberate attempt to deceive and mask their intentions. China's approach to defence and security still draws a lot from the teachings of Sun Tzu. Achieving a capability by stealth is one of his most important dictums. Breaking-out when a potential adversary has little or no ability to respond goes to the core of Chinese cultural thinking. It allows conditions to be created when potential conflicts can be resolved without a shot being fired. It is, as Sun Tzu advocated, the clever way to resolve confrontations. Trying to second guess China's aspirations is difficult as direct observation of their plans is difficult. Assessments have to rely on indicators which China would find hard to disguise, such as its increasing investment in the PLAN.

Admiral Chopra notes that after China became a net importer of oil in 1973, the Director of the Chinese Navy General Staff Logistics

Department, Zao Nanqi, announced that 'we can no longer accept the Indian Ocean as an ocean only of the Indians'. Admiral Chopra writes that in his view, it will not be long before the Chinese Navy adopts the 'creeping strategy' of one of its illustrious naval leaders, Admiral Cheng Ho, by progressively but innocuously extending its reach through cooperation with countries that ring the Indian Ocean.

China's strategy in the Indian Ocean is based upon what is called 'the String of Pearls' set against a stated policy of 'peaceful development'. The phrase 'String of Pearls' denotes the creation of important links across the region in terms of access to port facilities, and other forms of regional cooperation that provides a series of nodes that could be used as forward bases for operations to protect their SLOC should circumstances require the deployment of the Chinese Navy to protect the SLOC. Urmila Venugopalan, writing in *Jane's Intelligence Review*, opines that while China's strategy of creating maritime links across the Indian Ocean is clear, its motivation is probably more closely linked with the application of soft power in contrast to having specific capabilities that might allow greater freedom of manoeuvre for China's emerging naval forces.[17] China's approach is understandable given the current reliance it has on seaborne routes for its energy supplies. China imports 95 per cent of its oil supply by sea; 80 per cent of which moves through the Malacca Strait. Links with various countries in Africa and other locations such as Venezuela are designed to guarantee China's oil supplies, and are part of a comprehensive effort to ensure China's energy security.[18]

Pehrson has provided a detailed analysis of this strategy from a United States viewpoint, highlighting the current difficulties that exist in the area where the potential for an arms race in the Indian Ocean remains high, as countries compete for regional hegemony and China embarks upon a major upgrade of its military forces.[19] He also addresses the issues that arise from China's willingness to maintain relationships with so-called rogue states, and explores the need to develop confidence building measures and the need to develop transparency as part of developing mutual trust. In a particularly insightful analysis, Pehrson also addresses areas where the US and China's strategic objectives are both convergent and divergent, exploring the implications of this for future US engagement with China.

It is clear from the analysis offered by Pehrson that China is trying to reduce its dependency on these routes through creating land-based connections with the emerging oil producing areas of Kazakhstan and Turkmenistan. However, this is difficult, as western China has a poor infrastructure and the distances are daunting and there are difficulties in some areas that are threatened with a developing insurgency.

It is clear that for the foreseeable future, China's economic well-being depends upon the defence of its SLOC and that this simply cannot be carried out by a navy that is purely based in Chinese waters. Overseas bases, the development and deployment of a carrier task force, and places for re-supply and power projection are vital; hence China's 'string of pearls' strategy, which is trying to reach out over the Indian Ocean Region (IOR) to countries such as Myanmar, Mauritius, the Maldives, Sri Lanka, the Seychelles and Pakistan.[20] Each of these is envisaged as an individual pearl in the string that allows China to forward base naval units to escort its energy supplies through the Indian Ocean and avoid any interference in those SLOC by potential adversaries, such as India. In participating in the international effort off the Horn of Africa, PLAN is developing tactical skills and insights[21] that will be invaluable should it need to project maritime forces into the Indian Ocean to protect its own SLOC in a time of crisis, which may involve China in a confrontation with India as part of an attempt to establish hegemony over the IOR.

Maritime Terrorism: Delivered from the Sea in Mumbai

Admiral Roy's insightful analysis of the situation in the Indian Ocean was compiled before the terrorist attack on Mumbai and its significance for Indian National Security. The images of Mumbai and the violence perpetuated on an unsuspecting population in over sixty-two hours of specifically targeted attacks in a major international financial centre, in which a reported 171 people died, are easily recalled. A new dimension was added to the definition of maritime terrorism after Mumbai, which until that point had been focussed upon attacks at sea. Perhaps the most important aspect of the Mumbai operation, was the rapid way in which the security forces response became dislocated and the apparent ease with which the terrorists were able to maintain the tempo of their operations and media coverage.

The attack on the rail terminus is a specific instance where the terrorists took a taxi to the terminal, started randomly shooting at passengers and then moved on to one of the local hospitals; trying to stay one step ahead of the response of the security services to isolate and contain the area in which the terrorists had initially started their operation. Couple this with the apparent spontaneous outbreak of events in other parts of the city, some quite specifically targeted at certain ethnic groups, and it is easy to see why it took the Indian security authorities time to get the situation under control. Meanwhile, the media served up a series of images of mayhem at various locations around the city, which were all designed to shape public perceptions and reactions.

While not as dramatic as the scenes of 11 September 2001, they nevertheless had the capacity to leave an indelible print upon the public consciousness. In the National Intelligence Estimate (NIE) published on 12 February 2009, the United States government posited that: 'we assess Al-Qaeda continues to pursue plans for Homeland attacks and is likely focussing on prominent political, economic and infrastructure targets designed to produce mass casualties, visually dramatic destruction, significant economic aftershocks and fear amongst the population'. It is clear that attacks such as Mumbai were in the mindset of the author as the words were drafted.

Terrorism moved to a new level of sophistication and drama in November 2008. Visually dramatic destruction was seen to be a new aspect of terrorism; drawing upon the scenes of the Munich Olympics in 1972 and the Iranian hostage siege in London, so dramatically ended by the Special Air Services.

The attack on the Sri Lankan cricket team in Lahore in Pakistan on 3 March 2009 was also clearly designed to attract media attention.[22] It took place directly outside a television station and was the first international attack upon athletes since the massacre at Munich. The images of the fourteen gunmen walking around shooting at the buses carrying the cricketers, killing six security guards and injuring seven players and officials, provided a spectacle that gave the perception that the attacks were not opposed, with little resistance from local Pakistani guards tasked with protecting the sportsmen. The attack has had a long-term impact on the ability of Pakistan to be involved in hosting sporting events. Media coverage and its associated impact upon the people are a routine part of terrorism, but the sporting dimension was indeed a throw back to Munich and 1972.

The Evolution of Maritime Terrorism

Mumbai was different in one particular way. Terrorism arrived, unannounced, from the sea. The terrorists hijacked a local fishing vessel and used Rubber Inflatable Boats (RIB) to arrive ashore with little more than a passing glance from local people. This form of maritime terrorism was already seen in the actions of the Tamil Tigers and their Sea Tiger maritime arm in Sri Lanka and the actions of the combined Hamas/a-Aqsa Martyr's Brigade team when they attacked the Israeli port of Ashdod in 2004. Maritime terrorism was already an established problem with organisations such as Al-Qaeda urging their followers to become involved in opening up this new flank of their global jihad.

The list of maritime terrorism events is growing, albeit quite slowly in comparison with the land-based attacks that are often splashed across the media from places such as Iraq, seemingly every day. The USS *Cole* incident in 2000, the *Limberg* incident in 2002 and the *SuperFerry 14* incident in the Philippines in 2004 are a subset of that catalogue of events. These events, and the growing body of evidence that the maritime domain is increasingly becoming a place of manoeuvre for terrorists and criminals, brings to the fore the issue of how to secure such an environment. This becomes of even greater importance with threats being issued in June and July 2010 to close the Bab al-Mandab by terrorist groups based in Somalia and Yemen, and the alleged attack on the Japanese tanker *M.Star* in July 2010 in the Straits of Hormuz. The freedom with which Somali pirates are now ranging into the southern parts of the Red Sea and to the north of Hanish Island is important. It is not difficult for a pirate to be replaced by a terrorist. Whilst none of these events had immediate impact upon oil prices, another event in fairly quick order in either of the locations could see international oil prices spike very quickly with all sorts of economic consequences. Given Al-Qaeda's desire to attack the Western world at its weakest points and the inherent vulnerabilities that exist at all the world's main sea choke points it would be a brave person that would predict the end to events like the *Limburg* and the attack on the *USS Cole*.

Maritime security is very much in vogue at the start of the twenty-first century. But it does have a problem in the mindset of the public. Land-based terrorism, and the sheer scale of events in Iraq where scores of people frequently die in major attacks, is much more readily delivered to the public eye. It used to be said that 'terrorists want a lot of people watching, not a lot of people dead'. Today, that point of view has developed slightly into a desire to achieve both large numbers of casualties and many people watching; ideally being terrorised by what they see unfolding over a long duration on their television screens in what is often close-to saturation coverage.

The maritime domain, through its sheer size, can be perceived as being remote. In the public eye, attacks taking place on the land assume immediacy and urgency that events taking place in the sea cannot quite match up to. Coverage of maritime events is often cursory; images of a burning tanker or of a holed warship have less impact upon the public. The event lacks the kind of longevity that interests the media. The impact of terrorism at sea is arguably less when it comes to media coverage.

The remoteness of the maritime environment creates a problem for those trying to ensure that it does get the resources and attention that is required. After all, Mumbai showed that the threat is very real. In a review published in 2007, the United States Coastguard alluded to the difficulties that need to be overcome to create a consistent approach to maritime security.[23] It quoted the maritime domain as being:

> One of the least governed regions left on the earth. Many millions of square miles of ocean are a global commons under no man's jurisdiction [...] much of the ocean is only lightly governed and its maritime borders are generally less restricted and are freely accessible to transit with mechanism for detection and investigation.

This viewpoint of course strictly applies in the blue-water ocean where surveillance is minimal and vessels can be manoeuvred with little in the way of restrictions. As the shoreline approaches, some constraints do get imposed upon that freedom and things become more regulated. But the point made is a fair one and highlights the problems faced in the maritime security world. The nature of the threats posed to people using the maritime environment is becoming more diverse. One example of the way in which organised crime is able to manoeuvre to counter the efforts of maritime security agencies is the development of mini-submarines in the jungles of South America that are then used to smuggle drugs across the Gulf of Mexico. Just as the maritime security and their law enforcement partners were starting to press the criminals through greater cooperation on the land, the above-water and airborne environments, successfully detecting and neutralising drug shipments, the criminals started developing mini-submarines and went below the surface. While these vessels are cheap, and hardly provide good living conditions for the crew, they are able to move large quantities of drugs on a single-use mission.

These new tactical developments are also becoming commonplace as terrorists develop sea-based IED that can be dispersed into waterways, threatening key sea lanes. The threat by Islamist extremists in Somalia and Yemen in the early part of 2010 to block the Bab al-Mandab Strait could well be carried out using relatively simple sea-based IED designs that double for what state-based militaries would deploy as mines. Given the ease with which such criminal and terrorist groups can pick up and apply these technologies it is not difficult to see why the maritime environment could be descending into anarchy.

The Aftermath of 11 September 2001

Writing in the aftermath of the terrorist attacks of 11 September 2001, Michael Greenberg and his colleagues from the RAND Corporation looked at the potential for Maritime Terrorism.[24] Highlighting the huge wave of optimism that was associated with the end of the Cold War, stating 'it was widely assumed that the international system was on the threshold of unprecedented peace and stability', they provide an important context for the expectations that had been set in the late 1990s.

The bi-polar world of two major superpower blocks was to be replaced by a multi-lateral globalised world in which global economies would grow, and issues such as poverty would now become a focal point of politicians. Western liberal thinking had won the Cold War and was now on the march. For some, however, the very idea of Western liberal ideology invading their world was too much to bear. A stand had to be taken. The problem was how to take that stand when the only remaining superpower in the world had such military might and was so powerful. A new means of conducting war had to be found. As a result a new era of a much more devastating form of terrorism was born. The new forms of warfare that have emerged are fought asymmetrically in recognition that terrorists and insurgents do not have the capabilities to resist major military powers and their coalitions in a straight physical confrontation. The new forms of warfare are conducted as much in the chat rooms, blogs and media channels (where they directly influence public opinion) as they are on the ground. Part of this sophisticated form of messaging is the steady drum beat of casualties and people injured by IEDs.

Greenberg and his colleagues go on to recognise the false dawn that occurred stating 'that the initial euphoria evoked by the end of the Cold War has been replaced by growing recognition that global stability has not been achieved and has, in fact, been decisively undermined by transnational security challenges'. This applies to the land and the sea. Their analysis considers a number of facets of a world in which maritime terrorism poses a significant risk. Highlighting the specific attractions to a transnational terror group such as Al-Qaeda, which needs to move on from the spectacular attack mounted in the US, they discuss the potential for cruise liners to be targeted. They observed that not only do cruise ships cater for large numbers of people who are confined to a single geographic space, they are also iconic in nature, reflecting the type of explicit Western materialism, affluence and discretionary spending to which Bin Laden-inspired terrorists are opposed. In many ways a cruise liner can be thought of as a skyscraper on the sea; current designs can host close to 4,000 passengers and crew members.[25] Evidence obtained by intelligence officials in Sauid Arabia from an Al-Qaeda suspect, Abd al-Rahim al-Nashiri, when he was arrested in the United Arab Emirates, pointed to an interest in cruise liners and their sailing dates.

Almost all cruise liners' sailing times are set and published well in advance, easing the planning issues associated with any attack. Terrorists could choose to seize a vessel whilst underway at sea or in a major port. Facilities such as those provided by Google Earth, provide a wealth of information to terrorists about specific locations. After the attack on Mumbai there was, and remains, considerable speculation about the terrorists planning their attack remotely in Pakistan using Google Earth, and not actually having visited the target area, to avoid the risk of compromising the operation. In an era where the emphasis is upon visually dramatic destruction, the attack upon the *Seaborne Spirit* off the coast of Somalia by pirates in November 2005 generated little more than a passing interest in the issues that would have arisen for the welfare of the passengers and crew, had they been taken hostage.

The story that has emerged of Abd al-Rahim al-Nashiri, is one of an exemplar of a contemporary terrorist leader, with his focus on the maritime domain. Accounts suggest he was originally tasked with attacking a Western oil tanker off the coast of Yemen in 1998 in a private meeting with the leader of Al-Qaeda. That original objective was modified to target a United States warship in the Port of Aden. In January 2000, an attack upon the USS *The Sullivans* ended in failure when the attackers' speedboat sank under the weight of the explosives it was carrying. After being urged to try again, the successful attack on the USS *Cole* occurred in October 2000. Even though Abd al-Rahim al-Nashiri was reportedly in Afghanistan at the time of the attack, it is clear that he was the mastermind behind its execution.

When he was arrested, it emerged that his latest planning focussed upon an effort to crash a small plane onto the deck of a Western naval vessel based in Port Rashid in the United Arab Emirates, which he hoped to see carried out in November or December 2002. Reports suggested that he also planned to target warships in the Straits of Hormuz and that he had ambitions to carry out attacks against Western vessels in the Strait of Gibraltar, and the Port of Dubai and against land-based targets in countries such as Morocco, Qatar and Saudi Arabia—all countries with close ties to the west.

Case Studies in Maritime Security: The Wider Viewpoint

Maritime security, however, also addresses a wider set of issues. Competition for natural resources is an important consideration in a number of areas around the world. The definition of the extent of the continental shelf is a key issue for countries trying to boost their economies by harnessing the potential of the subterranean areas of their coastline.[26] Maritime security can also look at conservation issues such as biosecurity, as species can be transported by sea, having a devastating impact upon local indigenous populations.

The question is how to put in place an infrastructure along the coastline that protects it from all of these possible dangers. Sometimes countries can do this unilaterally; other times they require coordinated efforts on a bilateral or multilateral basis. This brings a very variable approach to maritime security that creates weaknesses that can be exploited by those with criminal intent, such as in the case of fisheries exploitation. Policing such activities is an important aspect of maritime security with developing an indigenous capability to do that often being an important local political concern.

This book draws insights from a range of core case studies. Each of these has been selected to try and provide a different perspective on the problem of creating secure maritime environments. They cover diverse geographical areas such as the United States, the United Arab Emirates,[27] Canada,[28] Venezuela, the Arctic and Antarctic, Brazil, Eritrea[29] and Chile. A specific case study is provided that looks at the French approach to maritime security, given its wide ranging international links and the need to protect overseas bases and use them to help develop ways to enhance the security of SLOC.[30] Multi-national disputes over the ownership of key areas such as the Spratley Islands, Hans Island[31] and the Lomonosov Ridge, add nuanced understanding and a wider perspective.

The case studies also cover thematic subject areas pertinent to maritime security and maritime security operations or MSO. The emergence of asymmetric approaches to maritime conflict, including swarming attacks and Water-Borne Improvised Explosive Devices (WBIED), are particularly challenging. One of the case studies looks at the implications of smuggling WMD. These geographic and thematic viewpoints are complemented by case studies that look at the ways various countries such as India and Kenya are developing solutions through multiple-tiered architectures.[32] The presence of enhanced EEZ, arising from opportunities to extend boundaries out to 350 nm from the original 200 nm, will challenge many already struggling to deliver a secure environment in their territorial waters, let alone the currently defined EEZ.

Sea Power and MSO

Sea Power is that form of national strength which enables its possessor to send his armies and commerce across stretches of the sea and ocean which lie between his country or the countries of his allies, and those territories to which he needs access in war; and to prevent his enemy from doing the same.

Sir Herbert Richmond
(cited in Paul Kennedy, *The Rise and Fall of British Naval Mastery*)

Given that MSO emerge from the military viewpoint, their relationship with the term 'sea power' is crucial, as this is the means by which governments exercise control over parts of the maritime environment (coastal and riverine zones and their Exclusive Economic Zones, from which they harness natural resources that are important to their economies).

Sir Herbert Richmond's definition of sea power cited above comes from a very narrow viewpoint. It is of his time and reflective of the world in the eighteenth century. Sea power was seen in terms of invasion and of creating and maintaining empires. Today our challenge is a little different. Sea power still retains that military dimension, despite the increasing recognition that military power is only a subset of a wider definition of power that includes economic and political levers alongside the military element.

The United States and its allies used sea power (or perhaps more correctly, military power applied from manoeuvring in the maritime domain) to achieve initial campaign success in Iraq in the Second Gulf War in 2003, and also in the First Gulf War in 1991. The United Kingdom's military forces applied sea power to recover the Falkland Islands and to intervene in Sierra Leone. Australia and its allies applied sea power in East Timor when the situation deteriorated in that country and Israel used a limited form of sea power in the naval bombardment of the Gaza Strip in 2009.

Maritime manoeuvres were an important aspect of the ability to initially conduct the air-land battle, and to land amphibious forces that gained a foothold in key flanking areas of the main thrust from Kuwait in 2003. The battle rapidly moved from the maritime domain to the land, but that could not have occurred without the support of the naval units, and their cruise missiles, employed in the initial onslaught. This balance between naval and land forces existed in the First Gulf War as the potential for a direct frontal assault by marines into Kuwait was part of an elaborate deception plan designed to dilute the concentrations of Iraqi forces.

In the course of the First Gulf War, one shore based missile battery did fire two Silkworm missiles at the naval task force units off the coast of Kuwait. A salvo of two Sea Dart missiles, launched from HMS *Gloucester* (D96) brought down one of the Silkworm missiles which appeared to have penetrated the chaff screen and was seeking to engage a target. This single example, and the threats posed by sea mines to the coalition task force, provides a microcosm of the spectrum of threats faced at the start of the twenty-first century by naval units engaged in the projection of sea power against an adversary, or in trying to set the conditions for security and stability.

Maritime Security: The Asymmetric Dimension

For the coalition naval commanders involved in both the First and Second Gulf Wars, the military viewpoint of maritime security would have featured in their planning before, during and after the operation. A particular concern in the Second Gulf War would have been the added complication of dealing with the application of asymmetric warfare, vividly illustrated by the attack on the USS *Cole* in 2000. With so many naval units assembled in some quite narrow areas in the Persian Gulf, the potential for a renegade Iranian Unit, or some other terrorist cell from within Saudi Arabia, to mount an attack on the task force had to be kept in mind. There have been a number of close calls in which the Iranians have conducted aggressive manoeuvres against United States warships that have shown restraint in what are difficult situations, where a threat may manifest itself at very short notice. Such deliberate provocation is not difficult for organisations that operate just below the surface of government authority, using the cover of plausible deniability. Often those in charge of such groups do not value the lives of those who they put into harms way; they relish the publicity and international reaction of the media providing coverage of an event that often fits into a ninety-second media 'package' and does not report the context and overall situation prevailing at the time. Public perceptions are always easy to shape if one side is seen to have acted hastily, no matter how unreasonable that reaction is given the wider prevailing situation. Swarming tactics, developed by the Sea Tigers units of the Tamil Tigers in Sri Lanka, are a new dimension to that emerging threat, alongside simple submarines and underwater swimmers.

Asymmetric warfare has evolved since the Second World War as the world has become polarised by those countries with huge military capability, and those states and organisations who wish to press their cause using military means, such as transnational terrorist groups. Colonel Thomas Hammes in his book, *The Sling and the Stone*, drew on the clash between David and Goliath as a metaphor for asymmetric warfare.[33] Much of his analysis is currently being played out in Afghanistan where lessons could immediately be drawn from the insurgency in Iraq.

Charting the development of what he termed the 'Fourth Generation War' back to the communist insurgency led by Mao Zedong and its subsequent emergence in Vietnam, the Sandinista refinement of the model to the *Intifada* clashes between the Palestinian and eventually the Israel military forces, Colonel Hammes observes a very uncertain world. 'War', Colonel Hammes concludes, 'like all human endeavours is constantly changing'. Advocating flexibility in response, he goes on to posit that the unexpected is woven into every generation of war and it would be foolish to think that we would be exempt. Given the changing nature of the combat operations in Afghanistan, and the agility with which organisations such as Al-Qaeda have harnessed the power of the media and the Internet to change their business model and enable a worldwide franchise of associated organisations, his advice seems prescient and insightful.

Through careful analysis of the historical perspectives provided in the book, he shows how asymmetric warfare has already evolved, and he deduces that further evolution of this form of warfare is likely. The pace of change is likely to accelerate as technology and the media provide the means whereby people in one part of the world can rapidly learn from others—this is the nature of transnational asymmetric warfare. Whilst Hammes focused on the land environment, his ideas and thoughts apply equally well to the maritime world. Criminals and terrorist organisations tend not to have the rigid structures that governments employ to manage their resources. Terrorists and criminals move seamlessly through all domains, showing agility and flexibility as they seek to achieve their various goals.

Sea power is now being exercised against a very different and evolving threat from adversaries who value the media impact and profile that comes from successfully attacking a major warship, or in the case of the tanker the *Limburg*, a merchant vessel, using very unsophisticated means, the very essence of asymmetric warfare.

The ability to manoeuvre by sea is not solely restricted to those with massive naval firepower, as the residents of Mumbai discovered to their cost, along with those hijacked off the coast of the Gulf of Aden. The maritime domain, in contrast to land-based operations, where terrain can often be quite restrictive, offers great advantages to those able and wishing to use it to create a surprise.

In the immediate aftermath of the Second Gulf War, the concerns over maritime security turned to economic considerations. Protecting the two main Iraqi oil terminals, through which the majority of their national income is derived, has become hugely important. Economic considerations have displaced the purely military form of sea power envisaged by Sir Herbert Richmond. The task of protecting the Al Basrah and Khawr Al Amaya oil terminals has fallen to a coalition Task Force 158.[34]

The diversity of the issues involved in MSO can be exemplified by making reference to the evolving mobile aspects of the TBM capability that is now available from the sea. One facet of MSO that is quite specific to Southeast Asia is the protection that can be afforded by Aegis Class Guided Missile destroyers as they are equipped with missiles that can shoot down a Short or Medium Range Ballistic Missile (S/M RBM).

With North Korea posturing over its situation and routinely conducting mass launches of Ballistic Missiles (BMs), with some trajectories overflying Japan and heading towards Hawaii, concerns exist about how best to create the kind of anti-ballistic missile system originally envisaged by President Reagan in his 'Star Wars' Programme (Strategic Defence Initiative). This contrasts the delivery of terrorism from the sea in Mumbai with the delivery of security from the sea in the form of a ballistic missile shield that can protect major city centres and their populations. For countries such as South Korea and Japan, who have readily mobilised defence capabilities, operating in international waters offers a new dimension to their national security. One way to visualise this is to think of the concept of the ink spots of security, developed as part of the counterinsurgency (COIN) doctrine, in three dimensions instead of two, as the vertical element is threatened by ballistic missiles. The ink spot is then the missile engagement zone that can be protected against a specific ballistic missile threat from the sea.

Maritime Security Operations

MSO are designed to deliver a secure maritime environment. A valid question, however, is where is that secure maritime environment created? Achieving that across the marine environment is difficult. Locally around a specific port it is possible to achieve a long-term presence. But as operations move beyond the littoral into the deeper ocean, the sheer scale of the problem becomes daunting.

The British Naval historian, Julian Corbett, writing against a backdrop of Carl von Clausewitz's well-known work, *On War*, attempted to look at the issues of maritime warfare in the context of what was being written about land battle. Corbett signed up to the principle of the primacy of politics in war advocated by Clausewitz. In his writings, however, Corbett recognised major differences in the two domains. One of these was the issue of the SLOC.

Corbett's writings were focussed upon the wider issue of maritime strategy and not naval warfare per se. He would have found it stimulating to look at MSO today through the lens of his original thinking. In his definitive work, *Principles of Naval Strategy*, Corbett recognised a fundamental truism: that command of the sea was a relative and not an absolute state that could be achieved. Today, command of the sea, as much as can be achieved off the coast of Somalia when faced by a pirate threat that is agile and responsive, using the marine environment to manoeuvre over an area of 2 million nm^2, is hugely difficult.

What can be achieved, ephemerally, is sea control over a specific area. This is what Corbett focussed on. A comprehensive maritime strategy must include missions, tactics and the capability to deliver sea power into specific areas to achieve some form of effect. MSO are an element of a comprehensive maritime strategy that allows a country to mount a variety of forms of naval interventions. A Versatile Maritime Force (VMF) provides the agility and flexibility to perform such activities, moving seamlessly from one form of operation to another, should the situation require an adaptable response.

As a term, 'MSO' is used to define the activities of contemporary naval forces designed to 'combat terrorism and other illegal activities, such as hijacking, piracy and human trafficking'.[35] This understanding of MSO lacks nuance. The Royal Navy provides a slightly different perspective that recognises the counter terrorism aspect of the activity, but takes a wider definition, stating, 'MSO set the conditions for security and stability in the marine environment and complement the counter terrorism and security efforts of regional nations'. This focal point on counter terrorism is further developed with the sentence, 'MSO deny illegal use of the marine environment as a venue for attack or to transport personnel, weapons or other material'. This definition reflects a slightly more nuanced viewpoint, and at least illustrates the concept of illegal use of the marine environment, but it still tends to focus, unsurprisingly for a navy viewpoint, on the military perceptions of threats. A specific example will illustrate some of the issues faced when delivering a secure maritime environment.

At the end of the Gulf War, the coalition recognised the importance of the two main oil-exporting terminals in southern Iraq. They were hugely vulnerable to a terrorist attack. Task Force 158 was established to place a naval presence in the area to disrupt and interdict threats to the terminals which exported the main bulk of Iraqi crude oil on which Iraq's economic recovery would depend. Task Force 158 was created to conduct MSO in a restricted area of the Persian Gulf until an Iraqi Navy presence could be trained and established in the area. At the time of writing, the Iraqi Navy is gradually taking over responsibility for the protection of the terminals as new patrol boats are delivered and naval crews finish their training activities. The challenge to protect the terminals is a difficult one.

The area in which they patrol is frequently occupied by several hundred fishing dhows. Discerning those who have malevolent intent from those engaged in fishing as a livelihood is difficult. Patterns of behaviour become an important tool in the armoury of those seeking to provide security to such an area. A valid question to ask is, what is a threatening pattern of behaviour? The crew of the USS *Cole* did not believe that the speedboat heading towards them with people waving, posed a threat. It was not believed to be a departure from a known mode of behaviour. Surely people were just being curious and friendly. Discerning the intent of the suicide bombers aboard the speedboat was hugely difficult because of this, but seventeen United States servicemen died because of that failure to understand the nature of the threat.

Task Force 158 personnel have to develop their own perceptions of situations that may appear to rapidly pose a threat. Dhows can act erratically and move towards the 3 km exclusion zone. Hailing on radio systems is often ineffective. Positioning naval units between the path of the dhow and the oil terminals becomes a matter of skilled seamanship and quick reactions. Some captains of dhows operating in the area can become distracted and appear to be acting in a threatening manner. Difficult decisions often have to be made quickly as a situation evolves. It is far better to act earlier to ensure that their intentions are clear from the outset, than to wait and have to react at short notice.

In such situations, captains of warships have to act decisively and yet in a measured and proportioned way. Increasing speed, making noises and manoeuvring are all obvious elements of an escalating response that could see warning shots being fired as the situation develops. In the end, the Captain may have to resort to the application of naval firepower and sink a threatening vessel. Given the potential for making mistakes and for a backlash to occur, these choices are hugely difficult ones to make and do not allow much time for conversations with military headquarters or to receive political guidance.

The potential for a direct attempt to disrupt the Iraqi economy was illustrated in April 2004, when Iraqi oil terminals were attacked by suicide bombers aboard three dhows which exploded when boarding parties were sent to investigate their behaviour. One dhow flipped over a raiding craft and the other two exploded about 50 yards from the Al Basrah terminal when other intercept teams fired on them. The attack caused the loss of an estimated one million barrels of oil production, at a cost of $28 million to the Iraqi economy and resulted in the death of a member of the United States Coastguard, with four other United States servicemen wounded. The attack was claimed by Abu Musab Al Zarqawi, the Jordanian terrorist who gained notoriety in Iraq for his attempts to ferment civil war in the aftermath of the initial combat operations.

A Wider Perspective on MSO

This understanding of MSO provides a somewhat narrow viewpoint. Establishing a baseline for a comprehensive definition of maritime security and MSO is therefore far from straightforward. In writing his book, *The Maritime Dimension of International Security*, Peter Chalk addresses the implications of the vast and unregulated space of the oceans, making specific recommendations on measures to improve maritime security. He also explores the complications that may arise if groups engaged in a range of criminal activities, such as piracy and terrorism, start to cooperate.

Citing little evidence to justify such an assertion at present, Chalk does, however, leave that possibility open. One lesson that can be learnt from recent experiences in Iraq and ongoing operations in Afghanistan is that despite efforts to disrupt and disable their capabilities, transnational actors such as Al-Qaeda show a remarkable resilience and ability to adapt their approaches.

From an initially fairly centralised model, it can be argued that Al-Qaeda has completely decentralised its operations, creating a franchise of its brand that anyone can take up and support. Given such agility, supported and aided by personal contacts and those recruited through the ubiquity of the Internet, it would be wise not to rule out such a nexus appearing in time. Al-Qaeda has also shown that it is able to move from the land to the sea, as the attacks on the USS *Cole* and the MV *Limberg* illustrate. Despite what might appear to be actions that are in contradiction to their hard-line religious beliefs, Al-Qaeda has shown a high degree of pragmatism when faced by concerted action from the international community, involving itself in drug smuggling activities in locations such as Guinea Bissau. Where religious beliefs come into conflict with the survival of the organisation, Al-Qaeda has shown itself able to find convenient reasoning in its interpretation of religious texts to justify its actions to its followers. In this respect the organisation has shown some ability to manoeuvre in its ideology, which is its key source of strength.

The pressures that Al-Qaeda has been under in Iraq, combined with the United States' troop surge in Afghanistan at the start of the Obama administration, and the efforts by the Pakistani Government to disrupt the operations of terrorist groups operating in areas close to the border with Afghanistan, could well lead to an increase in terrorist attacks at sea, as Al-Qaeda moves to maintain its operational relevance. Whilst the events in Mumbai have yet to be directly tied to Al-Qaeda, it does appear that the evidence shows links with organisations that have made no secret of their shared objectives with the transnational group. There has been, and remains, a clear and present danger to major shipping routes around the world from further acts of terrorism.

The activities in the maritime arena of major transnational groups, such as Al-Qaeda, have been explored in depth by Michael Richardson in his work, *A Time Bomb for Global Trade: Maritime-related Terrorism in an Age of Weapons of Mass Destruction*. His book seeks to answer some important questions concerning the potential for organisations, such as Al-Qaeda, to use the global maritime trading network to deliver some form of device either to a port, or to a major trading route or maritime choke point.[36] He explores the implications of this in areas such as the 16.74-mile long Bosphorus and Turkish Straits, through which 50,000 vessels pass a year, of which 5,500 are oil tankers.

The Strait has an average width of 0.81 nm, and the Straits of Istanbul have many turns that have to be negotiated requiring ships to alter course twelve times in the bends and a great deal of ferry traffic crosses the waterway. At its narrowest point, it is 698 metres wide at Kandilli Point, at which a 45° turn has to be carried out. This is the largest outlet for Russian crude oil supplies (estimated at 2.4 million barrels a day in 2006; which was slightly reduced on previous analysis) and is perhaps one of the easiest choke points to consider blockading, although the impact of such an attack might well be reduced as other outlets are created, in the form of overland pipelines that provide some resilience, should an attempt be made to block the Bosphorus Strait.

Richardson goes on to discuss the 18 mile wide Bab el-Mandeb Strait (3.3 million barrels of oil a day) and the Malacca and Singapore Straits, which carry an estimated 10 million barrels of oil a day in forty-five tankers that pass through a Strait which, at its narrowest point, is 1.7 miles wide in the Phillips Channel.

Ghosh explores the maritime security challenges in South Asia and the Indian Ocean, highlighting the spiralling demand for energy from India, China and Japan as being the major driver in the region for the development of methods that can secure the SLOC and ensure freedom of passage through the choke points.[37] The Indian Ocean is home to a number of important SLOC and maritime choke points. The Strait of Hormuz recorded a transit volume of 15.4 million barrels of oil per day in 1998, rising to 16.5–17 million barrels a day in 2008,[38] and its closure would have potentially catastrophic implications for the world's economies.

Ghosh offers the viewpoint that the best approach to SLOC security lies in extensive cooperation. This can arise in several different ways, with some building confidence and helping to avoid potential confrontations arising as a result of mutual suspicion. In these situations, transparency and the development of agreed confidence-building measures are paramount to diffuse tensions that may arise from incorrectly assessing the intentions of a potential adversary. It is not difficult to recall the events prior to the start of the First World War, where two huge military machines created a situation where a single event could push them into war. Where military forces grow, and misconceptions arise, there is always the potential for a flashpoint to trigger a conflict. In such situations, military manoeuvres have their own momentum; something President Kennedy fought hard to avoid throughout the Cuban Missile Crisis. For some time now, China has been considered by many nations in the region as not being straight about its planned naval growth and concerns exist about the potential for a naval arms race to develop, with India and China vying to establish hegemony over the region. Through transparency in such matters, trust can be developed and a balance of power established that is mutually acceptable.

While an act of terrorism aimed at restricting major flows of crude oil through these vital seaways would have major implications for the world's economy, an attack of a similar magnitude on the Straits of Hormuz would be catastrophic. The maritime choke points of the world, through which so much important shipping passes, are an attractive location for terrorists to act and therefore need to have special attention paid to them for developing a comprehensive maritime strategy. MSO in these areas are crucial for deterring and disrupting any potential attack that would have the ability to suffocate an international economy already suffering from the ravages of a deep recession. It is crucial that competent local maritime security forces be trained and deployed to act, in the protection of their own interests. The efforts in the southern part of the Persian Gulf to provide support to the Gulf States and the Saudis are important counterweights to the increasing threat from Iran. The potential for confrontation to break out in the Persian Gulf is never far away. There are too many unresolved disputes over territorial rights in the area that could create the spark that could ignite a conflict.

For some, a definition could readily materialise from an analysis of a typical week of reporting by the Office of National Intelligence (ONI) and their *Worldwide Threat to Shipping* reports as they inform its readership about pirate activity off the coast of Somalia in the Gulf of Aden and the Indian Ocean. In one week alone, thirty-eight reports[39] of suspicious approaches or actual attacks were recorded by the ONI reports in these areas. This would, however, provide a somewhat narrow perspective, but it would show the key role played by criminality in threatening maritime security. To complicate matters, criminal organisations now also understand the freedom offered by manoeuvring in the maritime domain. Organised crime gangs are quite willing to exploit the plight of economic migrants, who desire to travel to foreign lands to escape poverty, to move drug shipments. Criminality at sea is not all semi-spontaneous and opportunistic; it is well organised and coordinated.

It would be easy to see why some analysts might view maritime security purely through a lens that is modulated by the current focus on piracy off the coast of Somalia and into the Indian Ocean, and its potential links with maritime terrorism.[40] The daily coverage of the problems in these areas might well lend strength to the arguments and focus it has received. To do so, however, would be to deny the emerging nature of the threats in South America and the enduring nature of the problems in Nigeria and in Southeast Asia.[41]

If there is any lesson to be learnt from a maritime security perspective about the problems in the Gulf of Aden area it is that, despite the international community's coordinated efforts to place naval vessels in the area covering over 2 million square miles of sea,[42] it is difficult when pirates enjoy the freedom of the longest coastline in Africa (Somalia has a coastline of 3025 km) from which to launch their attacks at a time and place of their choosing.

The extension of their operating space in the early part of 2009, partly in reaction to the deployment of the warships from a 'coalition of the willing' that includes nations as diverse as Iran, the United States, the United Kingdom and South Korea, is a testament to the problems the pirates have created in making the Gulf of Aden so insecure. Operating from mother vessels, the pirates have reinforced the inherent agility that is offered in the maritime domain. With close to 23,000 vessels transiting the area each year, avoiding the much longer route around the Cape of Good Hope, any form of insecurity in the area would be a major concern on a global scale.

The space for manoeuvre enjoyed by the pirates, only really constrained to any degree by weather conditions in the area, provides a major problem for the international community and their efforts to stem the rising tide of incidents in the area. The focus of the international community at present is plain to see, but this does not mean that maritime security can only been seen from this and other allied viewpoints from a limited number of known locations around the world plagued by piracy.

A detailed review of the ONI reports paints a clearer picture of a much wider range of threats to shipping that helps us gain greater insight into the definition of maritime security. These reports also contain reports of hijackings off the coast of Vietnam, pirate attacks off the Peruvian coast, attempted boardings, kidnapping and hostage-taking from vessels in Nigerian waters and off the coast of Cameroon, and robberies of vessels under way, in port, and at anchor in places like Thailand, Bangladesh and Tanzania. These reports highlight the global nature, enduring characteristics and diversity of the problems associated with maritime security.

History bedevils the exercise of clearly articulating what maritime security is all about with definitions that are clearly of their time and are blurred by far wider considerations. How does, for example, maritime security relate to terms such as sea power? Surely there is some connection? For writers such as Captain Mahan, well known for his seminal works in the field, even the definition of the term sea power was difficult. Paul Kennedy writing in his book, *The Rise and Fall of British Naval Mastery*, highlights how, at the beginning of his studies, Mahan did not want to define sea power, preferring instead to 'show its nature by historical studies'. Kennedy uses the previously cited quotation from Sir Herbert Richmond to provide what he refers to as the 'first working definition' of sea power. Whilst this does not define maritime security, it certainly provides a component of its definition. History provides us with some background.

International Perspectives on Maritime Security

It is not difficult to see how defining maritime security can be as difficult as it has proven to be, to even try and gain a consensus on the meaning of the word 'terrorism'. For any student of terrorism, just simply finding a set of words that actually define what the term means, that are nuanced and yet simple, is hard. Maritime security falls into a similar area. One of the problems is the perspective of the person attempting to derive the definition. If you are an Indian Naval official trying to deal with the aftermath of events in Mumbai in November 2008, your definition of maritime security may well be a little different from that of the Captain of the USS *Cole*, or any other warship passing through dangerous and narrowly confined waters, such as the Straits of Gibraltar. The government of Brazil, with their newly acquired offshore oil resources, may well have a different take on maritime security from the government of Chile, whose position as a major supplier of fish is vital to the economy. In this regard, the geography of the situation matters.

Canada provides an excellent example of a country faced with a rapidly changing situation with respect to its coastal waters. Its reaction to these changes, and the priority it accords to the maritime security of its local waters, will go a long way towards defining how the international landscape for maritime security will unfold in the coming decades. Canada's maritime security challenges mirror many of those being faced by other countries around the world as the competition for energy resources increases.

The recent shrink in the Arctic icecap is seen by many commentators to be yet another indication of climate change. Whether the current situation will continue, or the diminishing coverage of Arctic sea ice will stabilise, is the subject of debate. What is not in doubt is that the recent trend, if continued, is opening up a range of possibilities and potential disputes over subterranean resources previously thought not to be exploitable. The Lomonosov Ridge is now a place well known in the media by the extensive coverage it has received in the press. Places that were once only names known to the few are suddenly catapulted into the public eye. The potential for confrontation over the ownership of the Continental Shelf and the natural resources believed to lie below the ocean will increase. In the South China Sea, the competition over the Spratley Islands continues to engage countries such as the Philippines, Malaysia, Vietnam, China and Taiwan in what is a mirror image of the disputes that exist over the Lomonosov Ridge.

Maritime security does, however, also have some other dimensions. The potential for the sea to carry WMD preoccupied the Bush administration in the wake of the terrorist attacks in 2001. The potential for the attacks on New York and Washington to simply be a platform for an even deadlier form of terrorism, has caused many to have disturbed nights. The image of a mushroom cloud hanging over New York haunts many involved in maritime security. With so much of the world's trade carried by container ships and arriving just-in-time, the notion of creating a comprehensive defence against the smuggling of WMD, or their precursors, is difficult.

Measures have been introduced to establish standards around the world for the handling of shipments. Lessons have been learnt from the tightening of airport security around the world that occurred in the wake of the terrorist attacks in the 1970s and 1980s. Terror seemed to filter down to the weakest link. In the twenty-first century that remains its aim. Strengthening all of the potential weakest links is extremely hard. It has been said many times, but the terrorists only have to succeed once. The Proliferation Security Initiative (PSI) is one element of the response put in place by the Bush administration to this threat. Initially it did not get many takers and there were those who questioned its legality. After North Korea conducted its second nuclear test in May 2009, the South Korean government, who had previously been reluctant to participate, quickly signed up and deployed naval units in international waters to intercept any attempt by the North Korean regime to smuggle nuclear materials to other states.

In many countries around the world, the viewpoint of maritime security can become quite focused on the problems of economic migrants. The Red Sea and Persian Gulf are areas where specific activities occur, as people desperate to escape poverty move from countries in Sub-Saharan Africa across the Red Sea to Yemen, as the gateway to Saudi Arabia, with its opportunities for work and large migrant populations. The United States is a destination many seek to reach from places such as Haiti, crossing the Caribbean Sea.[43] Europe is also a favoured destination for people, who try to reach the Canary Islands from across the Atlantic Ocean or the shoreline of France or Italy from the North African coast, such as Libya. Many of these people die attempting to cross waters that are often treacherous and unpredictable. Some are even made to swim or are simply cast into the water by those that organise the journey. The criminal gangs are quite ruthless in exploiting these vulnerable people. When boats become swamped and call for help, they can stretch the search and rescue efforts of nearby states and passing vessels who feel it is their duty to pick up survivors, and can often end up becoming political pawns, such as in the case of several Vietnamese boat people and the vessel's Captain who saved their lives.

Maritime security, therefore, has many dimensions and should be seen through a military and criminal perspective. Both of these perspectives now appreciate the value of goods moved by sea, the profit that can be obtained from piracy, and the space for manoeuvre afforded in the maritime domain. The sheer scale of flexibility that appeals to those with criminal intent creates huge problems for those trying to set the conditions in which a secure maritime environment can be created.

Criminal Use of the Maritime Domain

Today's definition of maritime security at the start of the twenty-first century, if indeed it is possible to provide such a clear understanding of what is an increasingly complex and inter-linked set of issues, is characterised by a far wider range of considerations. However, enduring elements remain. Coastal waters still need to be protected from the threat of invasion. In many parts of the world, that threat is not of another state landing its military forces on a particular shoreline; instead, it arises from the widespread use of unguarded coastal waters by those engaged in criminal behaviour.

While contemporary history puts a lot of focus on the problems associated with piracy off the coast of Somalia, it is other countries, such as Mozambique, that also suffer from a lack of maritime security. Illegal fishing from Asian countries uses the lack of an indigenous naval capacity to exploit the 2470 km of its coastal waters. The impact of this illegal fishing is immediately damaging to the local population, and also causes long-term harm as sensitive eco-systems are damaged through the ways that fisheries are exploited.

Other parts of the African coastline are also exploited for other forms of criminal gain. Smuggling people is a particular feature of the west coast of Africa. The Canary Islands are a route into Europe and people leave states along the west coast of Africa hoping to reach the islands across dangerous seas. Coastguard authorities in the Caribbean can sometimes feel overrun by the sheer scale of the problems, with vessels only equipped to take a few tens of people, sailing with several hundred people aboard. The risks involved far outweigh the potential to have a new life in the United States. The smuggling of people also occurs across the Mediterranean Sea from the north coast of Africa, from countries such as Tunisia and Morocco. These routes are also well known for the smuggling of drugs such as hashish.

Where effective coastguard cooperation denies smugglers specific routes, criminal gangs show remarkable resilience and adaptability. In the Gulf of Mexico, cocaine smugglers have developed mini-submarines that are capable of diving and evading increasingly sophisticated surface activity by coastguard and military patrols, such as those mounted by the Dutch, United States and British naval units operating in the area. Where coordination between Spanish, French and British authorities have created greater challenges for smugglers seeking to bring cocaine from the Caribbean area to Europe across the Atlantic Ocean, the smugglers have moved south into the Western African coastline regions, to exploit the vulnerabilities that exist in various administrations in the area, such as Guinea Bissau, Ghana and Sierra Leone. Lawless areas attract criminality. They fill the gaps where effective governance fails to provide secure maritime and land-based borders. Where the governance of states is weak, criminal entities can profit from corrupting local officials or war lords to ensure the smooth passage of drugs through various overland routes[44] to the North African coastline through Mauritania, Mali and Algeria and from there on into Europe.

4

THREATS TO MARITIME SECURITY

The security, prosperity and vital interests of the United States are increasingly coupled to those of other nations. Our national interests are best served by fostering a peaceful global system comprised of interdependent networks of trade, finance, information, law, people and governance.

Opening remarks of the document:
A Cooperative Strategy for 21st Century Seapower

Overview

The risks to all of those who make use of the maritime environment are kaleidoscopic, covering a broad spectrum of threats, and are likely to be enduring.[1] Terrorism is a single dimension of this complex array of threats that is regularly mutating and changing its point of focus, with terrorists often acting opportunistically to gain publicity, and to use the leverage of the media to influence target audiences around the world. Terrorists know very well that the attitudes and beliefs of people in these target audiences can be shaped by events. It is possible to suggest that people are usually biased towards these events, implying that the media coverage can fuel existing stereotypes and attitudes.

The Israeli military intervention of the Gaza-bound air convoy in June 2010 provided a great deal of media coverage for the Israelis, much of which was negative. The incident shows how difficult it is in the twenty-first century to enforce a security perimeter that has both land and sea dimensions in the presence of the media. With the potential for terrorist groups to place people aboard such ships to act as agent provocateurs, it is highly likely that any intervention is going to produce some negative publicity.

Russell offers a number of insights, drawing from recent history, on the development of maritime security concerning the Middle East.[2] He cites a variety of indicators of the extent to which terrorist groups are thinking about mounting attacks in the maritime environment. He notes the interest shown by terrorists in a range of maritime-related targets. He also cites a number of attacks, such as those that occurred in November 2003 in Istanbul, the targeting of Israeli cruise ships in the port of Antalya and the attack upon the United States naval vessels the *Ashland* and the *Kearsage* whilst they were docked in Aqaba, as evidence of the continuing threat from maritime-related terrorism. Attacks against shore-based facilities should also not be forgotten as events in Turkey in May 2010 illustrate, when militants opened rocket-fire on the Turkish naval base in the southern city of Iskenderun.

In June 2002, Moroccan authorities uncovered an Al-Qaeda plot to target military shipping transiting the Straits of Gibraltar and, in the same year, the Saudi authorities arrested a group of extremists who were planning an attack upon the world's largest offshore oil terminal at Ras Tanura. The economic aftershocks and strategic implications of a successful attack can only be imagined. These are a set of examples of a much wider problem associated with terrorist attacks that are aimed at the oil and gas industries, that have been catalogued by Steinhäusler et al.[3]

It would be very wrong, however, to see the threats to maritime security through the narrow lens of maritime terrorism. In a single week in August 2009, incidents that illustrate the nature of the international problems associated with the maritime domain were reported off the coast of Puerto Rico, where a boat carrying thirty-five Dominican migrants was seized when trying to use the island as a staging post to reach the United States.

The piracy off the coast of Somalia is also an enduring problem, and the nature of the threat posed to human life should not be ignored, both during the attack itself and during periods when the hostages are threatened during captivity. On 11 August, Somali pirates released the German freighter, *Hansa Stavanger*, after it had been held for four months and a $2.7 million ransom was paid; the crews' tales of their treatment provide a harrowing example of what it is like to be held captive for a lengthy period of time by people whose drug-induced behaviour can become erratic. The Captain of the vessel estimated that there were always around thirty pirates aboard the vessel whilst it was being held near Harardhere.

The problems in the Gulf of Aden have naturally provided a focus for the international community, as it is a major trading route and SLOC. They have also provided some valuable insights as to the nature of threats that face SLOC. The international response in deploying warships to the region provides a measure of the concern felt over the threat of piracy, even though the *Sirius Star* remains the one major oil tanker to have been seized in this area. By the middle of 2009, the pirates had operated on a mainly opportunistic basis, looking to seize vessels that were vulnerable.

The pirates appeared to be relying on the idea that capturing significant quantities of vessels and getting large numbers of relatively small ransom payments would be enough to maintain their new lifestyles. The trends in piracy have seen too many people drawn into the activity for it to suddenly disappear, and earnings from piracy will be reduced by the overall lowering of the numbers of successful attacks that have been undertaken. In the meantime, in the absence of any political progress towards developing a solution in Somalia, the coalition will have to maintain its forces at an estimated cost of $500 million a year.

This pattern may be about to change, as the international community's warships have challenged the ease with which pirates seize vessels through marshalling vessels into convoys and developing other tactics to reduce the chances of a successful hijack. The successful development of such tactics may cause the pirates, who had originally responded by widening their areas of attack, to adopt a more selective approach—picking out quite specific vessels and extracting larger ransoms for those carrying important commodities, such as oil.

The collective experiences of the international community in trying to police the area will no doubt be of use in informing the countries that are looking towards the future concerning their evolving approaches to energy security. The Gulf of Aden is providing a laboratory for approaches to maritime security, and not all the answers arising from the experiences are positive ones. One of those lessons is that if the pattern of the world's shipping does change in the coming decades, the threats to the emergent SLOC may also challenge the international community. Somalia is by no means the only state from which criminals, pirates and the disaffected may chose to launch attacks and hijack vessels; a number of other vulnerable locations exist around the world. The terrorist group Jemaah Islamiyah appears to have regrouped at the start of 2010, and is likely to start attacking vessels operating in the Malacca Straits. The Singapore Shipping Association has been quoted on 2 March 2010 as saying, that it had received an advisory from the Singapore Navy Information Fusion Centre about 'an indication that a terrorist group is planning attacks on oil tankers in the Malacca Strait'. It added: 'This does not preclude possible attacks on other large vessels with dangerous cargo'. The Navy Centre's advisory reportedly said: 'The terrorists' intent is probably to achieve widespread publicity and showcase that it remains a viable group'. It reminded shipping operators that the militants could use smaller vessels such as dinghies and speedboats to attack oil tankers. It recommended that ships should 'strengthen their onboard security measures and adopt community reporting to increase awareness and strengthen the safety of all seafarers', according to the Association.

It is clear that Malaya remains an important conduit for terrorists operating in the region of Southeast Asia. The coastal regions of Sumatra are poorly protected and terrorist groups operating there have a number of areas in which to manoeuvre. The islands along the coastline such as the Aruah, Sinaboi, Rupat Bengkalis and Karimunbesar Islands provide excellent sanctuaries for those wishing to launch piracy or terrorism attacks in the area.

At the same time, off the coast of North Korea, the threat of ballistic missiles[4] to countries in the region was being countered by a TBM capability deployed at sea on board warships, and the United Arab Emirates seized a vessel carrying arms from North Korea to Iran.[5] In related incidents, vessels have also been seized moving arms from Iran to Hezbollah through the Red Sea; the *Mahan-1* arrested by the Yemenis on 26 October 2009 is one example. Iran is a country that is clearly involved in smuggling weapons by sea, alongside North Korea and a number of other countries. The potential for these routes to be used to smuggle more deadly materials is a constant concern. In January 2010, the Yemenis announced that they would be creating the first regional centre dedicated to fighting piracy, and it would be established in the first quarter of 2010 to help coordinate efforts to fight piracy in the region.

In 1998, the USS *Samuel B. Roberts* (FFG-58) was severely damaged by an M-08 Iranian mine as it participated in 'Operation Earnest Will', the plot to escort reflagged Kuwaiti oil tankers during the Iran-Iraq War. The mine blew a 15-foot hole in the side of the vessel, flooding the machine room and knocking the two gas turbines from their mounts. Ten sailors were treated for injuries sustained whilst trying to save the ship. Four days later the United States military retaliated, mounting 'Operation Praying Mantis', which involved the largest American surface action engagement since the end of the Second World War, destroying Iranian oil platforms, an Iranian Frigate and three fast patrol boats. With Iran known to be involved in the proliferation of weapon technologies for transnational terrorist movements, such as Hezbollah, the potential for improvised mine technologies to appear in other parts of the world's sea lanes should not be dismissed too lightly.

In between those polarised threats, from the smuggling of people for criminal purposes, to the threat of using ballistic missiles for a pre-emptive strike against South Korea and/or Japan ahead of the declaration of war, a vast array of other incidents were happening all over the world. Gunmen attacked the cruise liner *Aqua Expeditions*[6] off the coast of Peru; a tug *en route* from Vietnam to Singapore repelled an attempted boarding in the South China Sea; a South Korean naval vessel rescued a Bahamian commercial ship off the coast of Somalia seizing seven pirates; the Indian Navy and Coastguard seized a Thai vessel carrying sugar off the coast of the Andaman and Nicobar islands; and ships were scouring the seas for the *Arctic Sea* that had mysteriously disappeared. Whilst this is only a picture of a series of maritime events that occurred at one particular time, it provides a graphic illustration of the gradual erosion of the freedom of the seas and gives some supportive evidence to the assertion in this book of a growing anarchic environment in the maritime domain.

For the Israeli Navy, the term maritime security has a focus on groups smuggling arms to the Gaza Strip by sea, and its consequences.[7] During the Yom Kippur War of 1973, the Egyptian Navy blockaded the Israeli port of Eilat, preventing vital oil supplies from reaching Israel during the conflict. During the 2006 conflict with Hezbollah, an Israeli Anti-Air Warfare destroyer (*Saar 5*) was attacked and damaged by an Iranian missile fired from the coast of the Lebanon. Transnational terrorism certainly has a long reach.

For some time, the Israelis have been aware of a complex, multi-modal route through which Hamas was able to obtain weapons from Iran. Shipments originated from the southern Iranian port of Bandar-e Abbas, which were then shipped to the Yemen, and then across the Red Sea into Sudan, before they made their final journey by land through Egypt into the Gaza Strip. Israeli maritime and air units have conducted a number of operations designed to deter and disrupt this supply route, acting upstream to prevent the weapons from reaching their destination. As part of an increasingly vigilant approach being adopted by the Israeli Navy to these weapon-smuggling operations, its Dolphin-class attacker submarine has been deployed for the first time into the Red Sea via the Suez Canal. The ability to base the submarine in the Red Sea is a covert intelligence collection asset, to monitor the movement of suspicious vessels in the area.

At the start of the twenty-first century, transnational terrorism and those engaged in international criminal activities are challenging the basis of maritime security. Along with the attacks on the USS *Cole* and the MV *Limburg*, and the recent supposed attack upon the *M.Star* in the Straits of Hormuz, the events in Mumbai provided another watershed in the development of threats to the maritime environment. By moving from the sea to the shore, the terrorists are able to gain more purchase for their messages, from the immediacy of the media coverage. This has caused many nation states with coastal waters to reflect upon what might be possible in this era of the ubiquitous terrorist.[8] In Singapore, with its lack of strategic depth, maritime security is focussed upon the forward projection of maritime power upstream, where the threat originates. For Singapore, the protection of its SLOC is vital as it depends upon those for its economic prosperity.[9]

Problems with economic migrants[10] in particular areas, such as in the Caribbean Sea, can be illustrated by the large-scale SAR operation that had to be mounted involving international partners off the coast of the Turks and Caicos Islands. On the night of 26 July, a Haitian sloop went aground on a reef off the coast of West Caicos with over 200 people aboard. Due to the multinational SAR effort, 125 people were rescued. The area around the Turks and Caicos Islands is a known smuggling route and one used by Haitians desperate to gain access to the United States by making the thirty-six hour crossing from Haiti. The local police force in the Turks and Caicos Islands operates a number of launches, and a spotter plane is airborne every day patrolling the known routes used by the smugglers. Close cooperation with the United States Coastguard service is vital, as the area provides an important point for interception of smugglers moving people across to Puerto Rico. Across the world there are a number of known people-smuggling routes.[11]

This one incident is an indicator of a much wider problem that exists in many areas of the world, and highlights the need for all coastal states to be able to maintain a SAR capability as part of developing a comprehensive approach to maritime security.[12] Table 4.1 documents a contemporary list of maritime disasters that have occurred since 1980. The loss of these vessels is attributed to a variety of problems, such as the weather and mechanical failures.

Table 4.1: Contemporary Examples of Maritime Disasters.

Vessel Name	*Date of Accident*	*Death Toll*	*Comments*
MV *Derbyshire*	9 September 1980	44	Sank during Typhoon Orchid
MV *Doña Paz*	20 December 1987	4341	Collided with an oil tanker in the Philippines
MS *Scandinavian Star*	7 April 1990	158	Caught fire *en route* between Denmark and Norway
MV *Estonia*	28 September 1994	1000	Failure of the bow visor door in rough seas in the Baltic Sea
MV *Princess of the Orient*	18 September 1998	150	Capsized in Typhoon Vicky
Le Joola	26 September 2002	1863	Capsized in rough seas off the coast of Senegal
Al Salam Boccaccio 98	3 February 2006	1020	Sank in the Red Sea *en route* to Safaga, Egypt
MV *Princes of the Stars*	21 June 2008	814	Sank in Typhoon Fengshen off the Philippines
MV *Princess Ashika*	5 August 2009	85	Sank quickly off the coast of Tonga

Australia[13] is experiencing similar problems with a new wave of economic migrants from Indonesia,[14] replacing the Vietnamese boat-people migrations at the end of the twentieth century. Reports suggest that desperate people trying to leave war-torn Somalia[15] are trying to move across the Red Sea into the Yemen and on to Saudi Arabia.[16]

Indonesia is one country that is planning significant upgrades to its maritime capabilities, to improve its ability to react to local disasters, and also to increase protection of its extensive borders. Priority is being given to the procurement of extra patrol and landing ships to help increase protection of its borders. Indonesia has been highly active in the efforts to suppress piracy in the Malacca Strait. But new routes are opening up for people smuggling from Central Asia to countries such as Australia, and patrolling such areas provides one level of response to deterring the activities of the organised crime gangs involved.

Countries' motivations for monitoring their coastal zones will vary. Some will, by necessity, be very myopic in nature. Mexico is a good example, as it wishes to deter drug smugglers who use its borders as a staging post to the United States. Criminals enjoy a certain freedom of action in areas such as the Gulf of Mexico; although on occasions when they are caught red-handed, their arrest can make good television.[17] Once certain smuggling routes are closed, others open up. The capture of $200 million of cocaine on a makeshift submarine, which was stopped by the Coastguard 280 km off the coast of Guatemala, is an example of the ways in which organised crime syndicates manoeuvre along vulnerable coastlines. Four Colombians and one Mexican were aboard the vessel with what was reported to be ten tonnes of cocaine. The move to land narcotics in Guatemala is a direct response to a clampdown upon the Mexican cartels ordered by Mexico's President Felipe Calderon who deployed an additional 45,000 troops to fight the trade in narcotics since he came to power in December 2006.

The Mexican Government is also planning new budgets to conduct MSO and has allocated $1.2 billion to the Mexican Navy Secretariat to enable it to purchase additional Oaxaca-class patrol vessels, the fifth and sixth in class, and two helicopters. Five new coastal patrol vessels will also be procured to operate alongside short-range 16 metre coastal intercept and rapid reaction crafts. Four dedicated maritime patrol aircrafts are also being purchased. These are significant investments being made to protect the maritime environment in and around the shores of Mexico and reflect the concerns the government has about the links between the narcotics gangs and criminality.

Criminal gangs' attempts to smuggle cocaine into Western Europe use the space for manoeuvre in the sea to make passage around Ireland and the top of Scotland into the North Sea, delivering their goods *en route* through little fishing vessels that come out to meet the so-called mother vessel. Increased vigilance by the United Kingdom border agencies has seen this route becoming less important as the routes have moved south to the vulnerable coastlines of West Africa in areas such as Guinea-Bissau. Whilst such trends in smuggling patterns are clearly discernable, criminals do still try to use the freedom afforded by the sea to take the shorter routes directly into the United Kingdom. The arrest on 12 September 2009 of the 35ft yacht, *Ronin*, off the coast of Cornwall in South West England, is an example of the enduring nature of the problem. It had £10 million of cocaine aboard and had been *en route* from the Caribbean.

Eritrea wishes to protect its environment, which has huge potential for development for tourism. Chile has defined its own plan, named the *Presencial Sea* in the Pacific,[18] over which it has a moral responsibility to act, and which covers more than its legally agreed EEZ. Countries such as Brazil,[19] Angola and Venezuela[20] are concerned about potential threats to offshore energy resources and local disputes over ownership of coastal islands and waters.[21]

For smaller and poorer countries such as Guinea-Bissau, their limited capacity to develop a picture of the maritime domain creates a magnet for those seeking to move drugs from South America through West Africa into Europe. The poor levels of maritime security create openings for transnational criminals and potentially for those involved in terrorism. As drugs pour into a country, they inevitably lead to increased local consumption and to the threat of a downward spiral to a failed state. Securing the maritime domain from such threats is crucial to state survival and development.

It seems that maritime security is a term that has meaning in the context of the time and place in which it is considered. History provides a great many insights. When, on 22 April 1778, John Paul Jones led thirty men from the USS *Ranger* in an attack on the port of Whitehaven in England during the War of Independence, he probably did not realise that some two centuries later his achievement and surprise in launching a raid from the sea would be mimicked by terrorists attacking Mumbai. The sheer scale of the ocean challenges the development of maritime security. Someone intent on attacking a coastline is afforded a great deal of room for manoeuvre to select where and when to mount an operation.

For some countries, such as Russia, China, the United States, France, Japan and the United Kingdom, the term has a global dimension, with the need to protect sea lanes on the international stage; hence the willingness of countries to become part of a coalition of the willing to protect shipping in the Gulf of Aden. Norway announced its decision to participate in European Union activities in July 2009 and dispatched its brand new Frigate, the *Fridtjof Nansen*, to work alongside the other cooperating nations.[22] Given Norway's obvious concerns about the resurgence of the Russian Naval and Air Force activities around its coastline,[23] its decision to join Operation Atalanta is one that provided valuable training in multinational coalition operations; something with which it may need to be familiar, if tensions around the Arctic Circle develop further. The dispute over the sovereignty of the Lomonosov Ridge could cause a future confrontation in the Arctic Circle.

For others, such as countries in Africa, the Middle East and some in the Far East, the notion of maritime security is seen, perhaps parochially, as more regionally or locally focussed. The protection of their own coastlines, and their potential for fisheries and natural resources, and preventing their use by criminals are the primary concern.[24] Tunisia is one country that is investing for an indigenous capability to develop patrol boats through manufacturing a 14-metre patrol boat at Bizerta at a cost of $380,000. The Tunisian Navy is a coastal defence force that uses a mix of patrol boats and fast attack crafts built in China, France and Germany to protect its 1,148 km coastline by interdicting the activities of organised crime gangs involved in smuggling people and narcotics. Malta is also a Mediterranean country that has recently taken delivery of two inshore patrol crafts to work alongside its existing fleet of patrol boats. The new boats will be used for border protection and surveillance activities, alongside SAR duties.

There are occasions when the global and local perspectives coalesce, with tensions arising in particular locations. Giant factory ships exploiting fisheries off the coast of Africa originate from across the globe and can indiscriminately plunder valuable fishing stocks from the coast of Africa, with serious consequences for the local population. Regional pressures can also arise, such as those associated with economic migrants leaving the shores of Western Africa around the Gulf of Guinea, seeking to reach the Canary Islands and a new life in Europe.[25]

In the wake of the terrorist attacks on 11 September 2001, new perspectives emerged on maritime security. The oceans were to become another layer in the defence of the United States from attacks mounted by transnational terrorists. New initiatives, such as the 'Megaports Initiative', have sought to strengthen security at ports around the world that are significantly involved in major trading routes. This is one of a host of measures being taken to improve maritime security around the world, such as the CSI and C-TPAT initiatives.

State-on-state warfare has appeared to diminish in its priority for Western liberal societies. They no longer feel specifically threatened after the end of the Cold War, but transnational threats from terrorists and criminal gangs provide an enduring problem. The potential for state-on-state confrontation still exists. Harnessing natural resources that are available in coastal waters in areas such as the Arctic Ocean has already raised concerns that with the impact of climate change and the melting of the polar ice caps, new state-on-state confrontations may arise.[26]

Russia has certainly upped the ante in this regard with its claim on the Lomonosov Ridge, which according to reports from the United States Geological Survey (USGS), has three times as much untapped natural gas as oil, and holds an estimated 13 per cent of the world's undiscovered oil and 30 per cent of the undiscovered natural gas. At a time when energy security is a growing issue, these potential reserves are an obvious potential flash point, as several countries lay claim to the seabed in the area.[27]

The Context of the Threat

The term 'maritime security' is also hugely contextually dependent. For mariners faced by huge storms at sea and machinery failures, the context is one that has a specific focus upon their survival, and the need for nation states and the international community to mount rescue operations to save their lives.

However, for the Captain of a major warship, the context of the threat may be defined by the intentions of a small boat seemingly moving quickly across the sea towards his ship. In some waters, the potential for boats to swarm over a target vessel, providing the distraction for a suicide boat to deliver the coup de grace, is another cause of concern. On 1 July 2009, the MV *Yohteisan* reported four fast, grey, craft harassing vessels operating in the Straits of Hormuz, echoing the events during which Iranian vessels made similar passes near United States Warships in January 2008.

Iran's ambitions to protect itself by threatening any naval operations planned within the Persian Gulf were illustrated by Aryan when he quoted the Commander of the Navy of the Islamic Republic of Iran Military (IRIM) as stating that 'if necessary we can prevent any enemy ship from entering the Persian Gulf'[28] and clearly portrayed the regional ambitions of Iran by elaborating further 'the mastery of the Islamic Republic is reaching the Indian Ocean'. This is hardly diplomatic language likely to endear the Iranians to any of their neighbours within the Persian Gulf or to those in the Indian Ocean and the Arabian Sea.[29]

Iranian intentions, with respect to conducting asymmetric forms of attack in the Persian Gulf, are also brought into sharp focus by their development of a number of mini-submarines under the Qadir-class programme.[30] Up to ten vessels are thought to be in development as part of an indigenous activity that has all the hallmarks of another form of asymmetric warfare, which will operate alongside the other Iranian submarine programmes involving the production of the Nahang- and Qaeem-class boats again using indigenous capabilities. The existence of the Nahang-class of submarines was first reported in April 2006, noting that they were 25 metres long and designed for the shallow waters of the Persian Gulf with a potential to act as host crafts from which swimmer delivery vehicles could be launched. The Qaeem-class are reported to be 1,000 tonne coastal submarines capable of carrying torpedoes and mines. The Iranians also have three Russian-built Kilo-class submarines that were originally procured in the latter part of the twentieth century, and whose serviceability might be questionable. Through developing their own capabilities, they reduce the implications of international sanctions aimed at constraining the country's nuclear programme.

The tactics developed by the Tamil Tigers to attack the Sri Lankan Navy and cargo vessels operating in Sri Lankan waters[31] are thoroughly exportable,[32] including their development of what can be described as stealth; something that it is too easy to assume is only available to nation states as it requires access to technology. This is far from the case, as pirates off the coast of Somalia have shown, and the Iranian Navy continues to illustrate, with the development of low visibility small boats that can quickly emerge and target major naval units. Delaying detection time, along with the presentation of multiple targets, can threaten to overwhelm the defensive capabilities of naval units.

Using outlets such as the various services that are available on the Internet, terrorist groups can quickly learn strategies from the new tactics developed by terrorist groups who are responding to their own local constraints; in the case of the Tamil Tigers, they needed to move by sea due to the constraints placed on their location on land.

The subject of maritime terrorism and its implications has been explored in detail by Alexander and Richardson. They take an unconventional look at maritime security and explore the measures to mitigate its impact.[33] Cataloguing the history of maritime terrorism, the authors explore the tactics of terrorists in general and consider how they have been applied in the maritime domain. With the proliferation of technologies involved in terrorism, from Iraq to Afghanistan, such as the use of shaped charges in creating more deadly IED, this book acknowledges the potential for tactics developed on the land to be exported to the maritime environment.

They argue that the ability to move cargos safely by sea is at the heart of the US economy and critical to military operations. But experience has proven that US shipping is not as secure as one might wish. They conclude that the threat of maritime terrorism to their infrastructure is palpable. Contemporary history and the recent debate concerning US port security clearly demonstrates that the maritime industry, including the merchant marines, shipbuilding industries, and the United States Navy, is vulnerable to terrorist attacks and that it would be wise to maintain a high level of alert, given the potential implications of a successful attack on the United States economy.

Guarding port facilities, profiling seafarers and monitoring the patterns of behaviour of certain vessels are all parts of the equation that seeks to create a secure environment in which goods can be moved safely at sea.[34] There are shades of the measures that are in place at airports to ensure the safe movement of passengers and goods by air, as in an extreme situation, terrorists could hijack a ship with the aim of using it as a guided weapon to attack a port facility. While evidence has emerged of occasions when terrorists have briefly hijacked vessels, tied up the crew and appeared to conduct some manoeuvres, the reporting has been questioned by some commentators. Irrespective of the truth of the reports, the potential for people to train on simulators or to plan a cyber attack against a vessel using insider information should not be dismissed too lightly. In this increasingly connected world, the idea of cyber terrorists taking control of a large supertanker from some remote and inaccessible location in the world and steering the vessel into a major coastal facility should not be consigned to the realm of science fiction.

Davis explores the potential collision course that is emerging between maritime terrorism and the global maritime transportation system.[35] His analysis of the potential risks to the maritime environment is forensic, in that he places the emergent tactics of terrorism under the magnifying glass, analysing the threats to a diverse range of vessels and looking beyond maritime shipping per se. Using the example of the 95,000 miles of coastline of the United States and the associated 3.5 million square miles of its EEZ, he provides a perspective on the land-sea boundary and the threats that could yet emerge from maritime terrorism, and also documents terrorist methodologies, such as money laundering, that help them sustain their operations.

Writing from the viewpoint of a retired United States Coastguard Maritime Investigator and Intelligence Officer, he brings a practical viewpoint to the range of opportunities open to terrorist groups to attack the maritime infrastructure, pointing out areas where defined boundaries between the land and sea environments are perhaps unclear. He balks at the notion that the oft-quoted examples of the USS *Cole* and the *Limburg* represent the likely end-point of maritime terrorism, drawing attention to the threat from fast boats and sea skimmers, and the potential for terrorists to target passenger ferries capable of carrying between 500–750 people, quoting specific case studies in some detail. Citing the case of Ahmed Ressam in December 1999, Davis shows how terrorists are capable of using multi-modal transport to try and bypass border checks. Boarding the Motor Vessel Coho ferry in Victoria, British Columbia, Ressam was questioned by Customs Inspectors and panicked. The officials discover nitro-glycerine and timing devices in his car, which were destined for an attack on Los Angeles Airport.

In parts of the Gulf of Mexico, maritime security can be seen from a slightly different point of view, with a focus on guaranteeing the security of the offshore industry and intercepting those that are involved in smuggling people and drugs into the United States. The development of mini-submarines to carry drugs highlights just how agile criminal groups are becoming at using particular technologies that are now being adapted for smuggling operations. The use of jet-skis, fast boats and submarines, and the potential threats that might arise from swimmers in the water mining vessels show the various ways in which this threat can evolve and illustrate its polymorphous nature. Naylor et al. explore the specific implications of the threat to maritime tankers, with 55 per cent of the United States crude supply being imported alongside significant quantities of Liquefied Natural Gas (LNG) and aviation fuel. The authors draw attention to the vulnerability of a number of key areas in the maritime environment, and dissect the types of threats to tankers and the implications of a successful attack.[36]

Maritime security in the Asia-Pacific region has been discussed by Ho and Raymond. Drawing upon the collective expertise of a number of internationally recognised authorities in the field, they address the issue through a three-step approach. Firstly, they look at the regional maritime environment. Clearly at the time of writing, the world economic downturn was difficult to forecast and their analysis may, on reflection, have been a little optimistic. However the division of the trade patterns is still reflective of the major routes that are active in the Asia-Pacific Rim. Secondly, the analysis moves on to look at the specific challenges facing the maritime community, with boundary and territorial disputes in the South China Sea being examined alongside what they call the 'spectre of terrorism', and the forced modernisation programmes of a number of local navies in the area. In conclusion, the authors develop some ideas for maritime initiatives to build cooperative approaches to securing the maritime environment, whilst also exploring the implications of the proliferation security initiative or PSI.

The Legacy of Mumbai

However, maritime security is not all about the threats at sea launched from within the sea scope. Mumbai changed that understanding, and added in the dimension of threats being launched from the sea against the land. While amphibious operators will already understand the issues associated with this paradigm change, the world is a different place after Mumbai.

Mumbai added a new element into the equation, and its impact is being profoundly felt across the world as governments take a long hard look at their maritime strategies. Launching threats against the land was a feature of the approach taken by the Tamil Tigers; using the power of maritime manoeuvre to attack key targets in Sri Lanka. Arguably, the Tamil Tigers have been at the forefront of the development of asymmetric warfare, with the use of suicide terrorism and the development of the Sea Tigers and their Black Sea Tigers divisions.[37] The Sea Tigers developed entirely new concepts for fighting an insurgency based around the deployment of WBIED and swarming attacks.

In his excellent book, *Beating Goliath: Why Insurgencies Win*, Jeffrey Record examines why the weak are able to defeat the Leviathans or Goliaths of the world. A key conclusion that he draws is that insurgencies often rely heavily on external assistance to maintain the tempo of their operations. Record states in his analysis that 'indeed, the presence or absence of external assistance may be the single most important determinant of insurgent war outcomes'. Contemporary case studies highlight the enduring power of his arguments concerning the common elements of various different insurgencies in China, Indonesia, Malaysia and Oman.

In Afghanistan, the support from across the border in Pakistan to the Taliban is clear. In Vietnam, the North supported the insurgents in the South. The insurgency in Iraq in the wake of the Second Gulf War relied on support from those willing to die being shipped down the so-called 'rat lines' from the Syrian border to Baghdad. Record's conclusions apply to the Tamil Tigers. They relied upon external support, but it was delivered by basing their arms and supplies at sea. They used the freedom of the seas to operate a fleet of their own merchant vessels that would operate a long way away from the Tamil Tigers' base in northern Sri Lanka on the Jaffna peninsula, and run in to rendezvous with fishing vessels to offload supplies that were landed on the beach.

When the Sri Lankan Navy was itself able to project power on a regional basis across the Indian ocean to find the merchant fleet and destroy it. They did this in a series of operations lasting over a year, and the end game for the Tamil Tigers was being written, which ultimately led to their defeat in 2009. Without that external assistance, they were no longer able to sustain their campaign.

Intriguingly, as the authors of an entirely new approach to insurgency warfare, it is interesting to speculate whether the Tamil Tigers' defeat means the end of their campaign for a free Tamil homeland. Taking their innovation a step further, it is not difficult to imagine parts of the eastern coast of India across the narrows of the Palk Strait from a sanctuary in Tamil Nadu becoming a remote sanctuary from which Tamils launch attacks on Sri Lanka. This will be a question for the Tamils, who still believe that the cause is worth fighting for and that the campaign should be sustained. The Tamil Tigers used various means to gain financial support for their campaign and leveraged money from an extensive diaspora located across the world. The potential to continue the struggle exists, and a new dimension of an insurgency being supported from a sanctuary based across the sea is possible. Whilst novel, however, this is not an entirely new concept.

Aside from the tunnels that exist from the Gaza Strip into Egypt, similar efforts are made by many Palestinian fishermen who are drawn into arms-smuggling and other sea-based acts of terror (note the associated dedicated Case Study on Israeli naval capabilities and threats). Israeli gunboats tried to create a secure environment off the coast of the Gaza Strip and continuously harass Palestinian fishermen, many of whom are simply trying to support their families. Agreements that have been made appear to be arbitrarily torn up and discarded, as the definition of where the fishermen are allowed to operate is changed.

A Kaleidoscope of Dangers

It is tempting to ask oneself, given the vastness of the oceans, and the room for manoeuvre that exists for criminals and those people and organisations intent on conflict or acts of terrorism, is anywhere safe? A multitude of threats now appear to threaten the passage of vessels going about their lawful passage at sea, with the ever-present danger that the geographic spread of these threats could be increased; hence the view that this has all the hallmarks of an anarchic environment.

The pirates off Somalia have shown ingenuity and agility in moving their attacks out into the Indian Ocean,[38] with one attack mounted over 1,000 nm from the coastline and other attacks ranging far to the north of the Seychelles.[39] Using a mother craft, such as the vessel *Win Far 161* (a previously hijacked fishing vessel), the pirates can extend their range, launching skiffs from the host vessel.[40] They have also become more sophisticated and better armed, with their activities appearing to be more coordinated, both within a group and between groups, also mounting attacks at night[41] and in a spate of attacks over a short period.[42] This is no longer an isolated series of attacks mounted apparently at random by individuals in an uncoordinated approach, as the development of tactics involving pirate action groups illustrates. Given this increasing sophistication, the potential for the pirates to spread their activities to the north into the Red Sea off the coast of Eritrea, and south into the Mozambique Channel, should not be lost on those considering the future trajectory of the threat.[43]

The pattern of attacks off the coast of Somalia has changed from largely taking place during daylight hours to being spread out over longer periods of time, using factors such as the haze that develops from the land as a result of the combination of sun and sandstorms, to create a difficult backdrop against which to detect the skiffs that approach at speeds of up to 26 knots (48 km/hour). They are often painted blue or white to help the boats merge into the background amongst the sea swells and their construction from wood and fibreglass makes them virtually invisible to radar systems. The skiffs also carry High Frequency and Ultra High Frequency radio sets and Thurayia-type satellite phones to maintain contact with their handlers. They also hide amongst boats that are moving economic migrants across the Gulf of Aden to the Yemen. The detection of the pirates is also hampered by the fact that the fishermen in the local area carry weapons for their own protection; the mere presence of weapons is not sufficient to declare a skiff as a pirate vessel. Attacks are often mounted by varying numbers of boats, sometimes involving quite large numbers. On 25 September 2008, a so-called 'wolf pack' of more than fifty pirates seized the Ukrainian-owned MV *Faina*, which was carrying a cargo of thirty-three T-72 tanks.

It seems that hardly a day goes by without a report being published in the media that has some connection with the issue of maritime security, and the hijacking of the *Arctic Sea* indicates a potential escalation of the threat. As reports circulating at the time indicated that the original attack may have been mounted off the coast of Sweden, before the vessel was moved through the North Sea, along the English Channel and out into the Atlantic Ocean where it had reportedly disappeared. The implications for this are profound. This alleged hijack took place apparently several thousand kilometres away from where the vessel was taken, off the Cape Verde Islands. Terrorists considering the potential of the sea to mount attacks against major harbour facilities would have taken clear note of the ease with which the *Arctic Sea* moved through one of the busiest sea lanes in the world without being challenged.[44] The implications of this incident, when combined with the Mumbai terrorist attack, presage an entirely new dimension to maritime security. One important lesson that needs to be learnt from the *Arctic Sea* incident is the lack of communication between many important government agencies in the area concerning what they, as individual agencies, knew. Had the purpose of the *Arctic Sea* been more deadly, such as launching an attack along the southern coast of the United Kingdom, a subsequent enquiry would have had a field day with the classic problem of agencies failing to connect the dots.

The rich and the famous are not immune to the issue, and those with luxury yachts can also be robbed and hijacked. The potential for such yachts to be hijacked was all too graphically illustrated by the capture of the yacht *Tanit* and its subsequent release when it was stormed by French Special Forces on 4 April 2009, resulting in the death of one of the crew members.[45] This threat has led many wealthy yacht owners to hire security guards and equip the vessels with modern technologies to defeat potential attacks, such as the L-RAD, a long range acoustic device that is also being installed on cruise liners. With a price tag of $1 million per square metre, some super yachts are attractive targets, as events in the Mediterranean Sea off the coast of Corsica in 2008 and Naples in 2009 have shown, as local criminal gangs have turned to the sea to rob high-profile vessels.

While it is easy to become preoccupied with specific high-profile instances of hijackings and piracy alongside the ever increasing potential for terrorism to be displaced from the land to the sea, the wider issues of maritime security, including natural disasters and the sheer power of the sea to overwhelm vessels, should not be forgotten.

Writers, such as Langewiesche, have provided a broad commentary on what he refers to as the chaos and crime that currently exists on the world's oceans, some of which threatens the 43,000 ships that carry the bulk of the trade that supports the global economy.[46] His vivid account of the sinking of the ferry *Estonia* in 1994, and the loss of the general-purpose tanker the *Kristal*, illustrates that the sea itself can be a threat to maritime security. Combinations of extreme weather conditions and failings in mechanical design and machinery can create situations where seafarers' lives are placed at risk.

Stewart provides a detailed analysis of the ways in which organised crime uses the freedom of the seas to conduct its activities, using a number of quite specific instances of the work of criminals at sea.[47] His work ranges from topics as diverse as terrorism and the threats to national infrastructure, to piracy. He specifically offers some in-depth analysis into the world of the Chinese Triads. This illustrates the wider nature of criminal activity at sea, and the broader implications that has for maritime security, such as the implications that phantom ships have, when vessels are hijacked and renamed and to all intents and purposes disappear, the crew being killed or forced to work to stay alive.

For anyone who has been involved in such acts of criminality, their view on the subject of maritime security might well be slightly different to those who have not experienced the fear that can arise when encountering people whose lifestyle and existence is motivated by criminal profiteering. In too many areas of the world's oceans at the start of the twenty-first century, the lack of an effective infrastructure for the policing and deterring of criminal activities creates a fundamental lack of security for mariners who are threatened by an increasingly technologically aware and capable adversary. Concerted action in this regard must become a priority for nation states and regional and international cooperation. As ever, where one specific issue, such as the piracy off the coast of Somalia, dominates the headlines, it usually means that a number of other problems are still present but have dropped just below the metaphorical radar of politicians. In a media-driven age, in which political leaders are often forced into reacting to specific events, time rarely provides them with the space in which to reflect in any detail on the wider nature of the threats facing the maritime environment.

Economic Migration

Nations such as the United States, Canada, Australia and many European countries have specific geographic challenges to manage threats from illegal immigrants, drugs smuggling and disputes over territorial boundaries being among a list of problem areas that need to be addressed at the local, regional and international level.

It is difficult to estimate the number of economic migrants that die each year when trying to flee oppression and war to reach what they perceive to be a 'promised land'. The United Nations tries to make assessments based upon a range of information sources that they can access, but which are often difficult to obtain and may not be an accurate record.

In the period between May and July 2009, they estimated that 11,000 people tried to leave Africa for the Yemen during the monsoon season. This is significantly up on previous years' estimates of around 4,000 people attempting the journey in 2008, and only 200 in 2007. The problem is clearly on the increase. Many of the migrants are Somalis driven from their homeland by the fighting. They are often crammed into small boats, with little food and water, making a perilous thirty-hour crossing to the Yemen. Over 1,000 were reported to have drowned in 2008. Anecdotal evidence suggests that on some occasions people were forced into the water by ruthless criminals who had little regard for their lives.[48]

There are areas of the Italian coastline where the bodies of Sub-Saharan African migrants regularly wash up. The criminal gangs use the vastness of the oceans to ply their trade in human misery. The plight of such migrants, while being motivated for different reasons, does have some links in history to the slave trade.

Australia is an interesting example. Its strategic position is important, and creates a dilemma for the Australian authorities. The historic flow of refugees to Australia from the conflict in Vietnam has been stemmed, in part due to Vietnam's rapid transformation to having a market economy. The uncertain situation in places such as Sri Lanka and Afghanistan is now a cause for people to try and leave, using routes that include Indonesia. On 11 October 2009, Indonesian naval vessels intercepted the KM *Jaya Lestari* in the Sunda Strait, as it was transporting 260 illegal Sri Lankan immigrants to Australia. This is by no means an isolated incident with routine reporting highlighting the frequency of such efforts to place people ashore in Australia. Although the number of immigrants travelling by boat is relatively small, with estimates suggesting it amounts to 1.5 per cent of the 190,000 immigrants a year arriving in Australia, its coverage stirs strong reactions from the local people. This is a lucrative business, and Sri Lankan and Afghan refugees see hope for a new life in Australia and are willing to take the risks. In recognition of this issue, the Australian Prime Minister Julia Gillard proposed plans in July 2010 to create a regional hub for processing refugees, or what the Australian Government calls 'irregular maritime arrivals' on East Timor.

The issue of boat-people coming from Afghanistan and Sri Lanka became an important election issue in August 2010, and the two main political parties ought to gain political capital from their relative positions on the issue, recognising the concerns being raised by the electorate. The issue of illegal immigration also received a great deal of media coverage in Canada in August 2010, as a boatload of nearly 500 Sri Lankan refugees arrived off the coast of British Columbia having chosen to make their passage across the Pacific Ocean rather than try to land in Australia. Concerns were raised that the boat contained some people who were part of the leadership of the Tamil Tigers who were fleeing from Sri Lanka after the collapse of their safe haven in the northern part of the country. Passengers had paid a reported $48,000 to secure a spot on the MV *Sun Sea*. Illegal immigration is a huge business with large rewards. Reports surfacing at the time suggested that some of the money had been donated by the 300,000 strong diaspora already living in Canada.

Australia is clearly one destination for such economic migrants. There are other major trading routes from Sub-Saharan Africa, through the west and north coasts of the continent into Europe. The Red Sea is another location where the smuggling of people is rife, and the Indian Ocean and the Caribbean Sea also have their routes for people drawn by the thought of earning a living in Saudi Arabia or the United States. These channels are used to earn transnational criminal groups large sums of money. It is believed that the trade in international migrants is now the fastest growing element in international criminality, and has a value of several billion dollars a year. It provides them with additional room to manoeuvre over and above that which they achieve through their land-based routes.

Illegal Fishing and the Threat to Coastal Populations

The problems with creating a secure maritime environment manifest themselves in a variety of different forms and are protean in nature. The threats are also polymorphous, with their appearance subtly varying across local situations. Each country with a coastline can experience a different mix of threats and situations depending upon their local geography, the demographics of their population, economic development, climate and bathymetry. These various factors modulate the nature of the threats posed to coastal states[49] and create a framework in which the threats to states that are in danger of failing can be analysed.

The development of many coastal African nations is bedevilled by the scourge of illegal fishing. Their economic development is hampered by criminal gangs and warlords who use tribal affiliations to fragment communities and prevent the development of national approaches to security and nation building. Failed states offer opportunities for criminal gangs and terrorist organisations to manoeuvre, and establish operating bases from which they can continue their activities. Archipelagos also provide locations for temporary forward-bases from which pirates can launch attacks. It would be natural for pirates to take the respite that can be found from the rigours of being at sea on small, isolated islands on the periphery of the Seychelles and the Dahlak Archipelago in the Red Sea. This would enable pirate action groups to conduct refuelling and resupply activities, possibly rendezvousing with a mother ship based in the area. The support to double the size of the Seychelles Coastguard being provided by the United Arab Emirates and India is an important step and will provide new helicopters, five new patrol boats and a new maritime patrol aircraft alongside a major investment in a new base at Mahe. This will also act as a hub for a chain of coastal radars that will provide maritime domain awareness of activities in the coastal region.

Some nation states have lingering disputes with other nations concerning boundaries and access to coastal waters and harbours, such as Bolivia and Ethiopia, which can turn into flash points and cause conflict. These boundary problems can extend into deeper waters, and create arguments over the ownership of the continental shelf. The Spratley and Paracel Islands in the South China Sea sit alongside the Lomonosov Ridge in the Arctic Ocean as potential flash points for future confrontations over the ownership of their potential resources. The sheer geographic scale of the Spratley Islands, and the list of countries that border the area, make them a real cause for concern as they also lie on a major trading route. With its recent rise to being the world's foremost consumer of energy supplies, alongside its position as the world's second most important economy, China is keen to stake its claims on the Paracel Islands, which is part of the Spratly Island area in the South China Sea where vast oil and gas reserves are believed to lie under the ocean floor. One of the reasons driving the Chinese to expand their naval forces is to be able to project power into this area, and to maintain a presence to deter others with claims on the seabed in this region, such as Vietnam, Malaya and Indonesia. This explains, in part, why the Chinese have embarked upon a massive expansion of their naval capabilities. They have a strong need to create a carrier task force to project further than their usual focus on their coastal waters, and a need to be able to manoeuvre that task force through various chains of islands occupied by the Japanese.

Today, maritime security can also be seen through a broad lens that looks at a spectrum of threats from transnational criminals and terrorists to those causing pollution, rising sea levels as an artefact of climate change and natural disasters, such as the Tsunami in December 2004. This range of threats makes the delivery of maritime security that much harder at the start of the twenty-first century. It places challenges on governments as to how they should respond. The recent investment in early warning systems to alert populations on the coast of the potential for another Tsunami is one encouraging development. Resorts in places which are vulnerable, such as the Seychelles and Maldives Islands in the Indian Ocean, now have Tsunami assembly points to which people will be temporarily located until the danger passes. This has been a regional response to a maritime security problem.

Some initiatives are obviously better taken on the international stage where coordinated action to establish standards and appropriate legal frameworks are important building blocks upon which efforts to achieve a secure maritime environment can be based. PSI is an example of an international response to the threat of the proliferation of WMD.

The International Ship and Port Facility Security (ISPS) Code is one such example of the United States offering help on a global basis to countries wishing to establish operating procedures so they are seen as having taken the necessary measures to secure their port facilities.[50] The threat to port facilities is convoluted, as the suicide attacks carried out by the al-Aqsa Martyr's Brigade on the Israeli port of Ashdod in 2004 highlights, where ten people were killed and twenty injured in an attack on 14 March. The port of Ashdod is a key economic centre for Israel, and a location where cruise liners and other vessels come alongside to discharge cargos. The attack was clearly designed to send a signal to users of the port concerning its apparent lack of security.

Piracy: A Global Phenomenon?

The fact of the matter is that despite the media being drawn to events off the coast of Somalia and out into the wider panorama of the Indian Ocean, as pirates spread their wings into deeper waters, the oceans of the world are still quite safe. It is a question of where you look and your perspective. If you are a Nigerian fisherman seeking to go and catch fish to feed your family, with the risk of running into pirates operating in the Gulf of Guinea, then you are likely to regularly consider the security, or lack of it, in the local area.[51]

If you are a merchant seaman operating in the Malacca Strait, and streaming at speed through the area to minimise the possibility of being hijacked by pirates who will seize your vessel and cast you adrift, your viewpoint may be similar but subtly different. Cruise liners, the traditional bastions of rest and relaxation, have had their scary moments in the Indian Ocean to the north of the Seychelles Islands.[52] Passengers have experienced what it is like to be shot at by pirates who are anxious to seize their vessel. The ransom payments just might get a little more interesting if you have 3,000 passengers to show off to the media.

Piracy is not limited to the coast of Africa. Murphy provides a detailed insight into the extent of piracy in 2006, showing it as a global phenomenon. The pattern of attacks recorded in 2006 show several areas where a very small number of attacks have occurred and a small number of focal points at which significant levels of attacks (on average close to one a month) occur. Areas such as the coastal waters of Bangladesh and Myanmar, Tanzania, Angola, Peru and Venezuela stand out from the traditional areas with which piracy is associated.

Murphy's analysis provides a detailed and contemporary understanding of the nature of piracy and explores a potentially emerging nexus between piracy, terrorism and the growing levels of criminality in the maritime environment. The potential for these three forms of criminality to merge and cooperate has been a long-standing concern of Western security services.

In the Al Anbar Province in Iraq, their actions and inflexibility led them to be removed when local tribal leaders reached a tipping point. The ideological inflexibility of Islamic extremists and their unwillingness to compromise on their narrow interpretation of Sharia law, ultimately cost them their position in Iraq. Prosaically, their approach leads to their own demise and they seem unable to be flexible and adjust their position. Frequently this situation prevails, with the likelihood of some grand union of terrorism and criminality occurring remaining unlikely; albeit local cooperation and support may well occur where pragmatism overcomes ideology.

Tomberlin provides a different perspective on this point, arguing that the connections between terrorism and piracy are, in fact, more deeply rooted.[53] Making connections with the Barbary Wars launched by the United States in the Mediterranean Sea in the nineteenth century, the first time the United States projected maritime power on a global scale, he highlights the tripling of reported piracy attacks off the coasts of Nigeria, Somalia and the Strait of Malacca in the last decade, at the start of the twenty-first century. Arguably, since writing his thoughts on this, the situation on a worldwide basis has deteriorated dramatically, with incidences of piracy doubling in the first half of 2009.[54] The International Maritime Bureau (IMB) reported the number of piracy attacks as growing up to 240, from the 114 reported in the same six months in 2008.[55] They also reported signs of an increasing geographic spread of the incidents of piracy, with attacks being reported in the southern Red Sea, and further out into the Indian Ocean and along the Omani coastline, which has seen a recent surge in pirate attacks. Monsoon weather still modulates the levels of attacks, with none reported in June 2009, and difficult weather conditions causing a resumption of widespread piracy in the area unlikely until late August 2009. However, pirates are showing increasing agility and awareness of local sea conditions, and can mobilise quickly if the weather moderates and attempted boarding operations can resume.[56]

The solution in Somalia clearly lies on the land, but it must be in the hands of local people who can unite across the fault lines of tribal and clan history to seek a new and federal Somalia.[57] It is difficult to see this happening in the short-term. In the absence of a united political settlement on the land, the maritime environment will continue to foster the conditions in which piracy prevails. The problem is that it may now have got such a foothold in the local economies, with an ever-widening group of people now dependent upon the ransoms being paid, that it may now be endemic.[58]

Murphy also argues that with signs of political progress being made in places such as Iraq, and with the real sense of progress in that country being tangible, although fragile, the maritime environment has particular attractions for terrorists and criminals organisations that clearly do not respect state boundaries. He explores the conditions that cause piracy and terrorism to develop, citing factors such as legal and jurisdictional weakness; favourable geography; the presence of conflict and disorder; the potential for reward; and the cultural acceptability of choosing to become involved in piracy. Of these, the weakest point, and the one that has perhaps had the most short-term impact, has been the cultural acceptability.

Roggio highlights the impact of the cultural aspect of piracy as he shows the effect of the imposition of Sharia Law upon the local population by the Islamic Courts[59] in central and southern Somalia. During this period, the levels of pirate attacks rapidly declined as their leaders declared piracy to be un-Islamic. This is important as it highlights a paradox. Despite the obvious encouragement of the Islamic Courts by Osama Bin Laden, as chronicled by Roggio, the benefits of their rule were clear with regard to local stability and the ability of people to repair what they could of their daily lives. When the Ethiopians intervened to replace the Islamic Courts, fearing that their ideas and links with transnational terrorism would spread, the situation rapidly deteriorated, creating a fear of insecurity; a re-emergence of the warlords as tribal allegiances took control to impose some semblance of law and order upon local populations, and the levels of piracy increased quickly. This return to higher levels of piracy can hardly be seen to be a serendipitous outcome.

The impact of this uncertainty is illustrated in the Case Study on Somalia. The events in 2006 and up until 2009, show the lasting legacy that can occur when the balance between political stability on land, lawlessness and crime can divide already segmented societies along tribal and clan lines, exposing old fault lines in their structures and igniting long-standing inter-tribal tensions. Osman and Souaré provide a detailed analysis of the tortured history of Somalia,[60] illustrating the difficulties that the international community faces in trying to encourage a solution on the land that will have an impact upon the maritime environment.

Local, Regional and International Perspectives

It would be understandable if most commentators tended to view the issue of maritime security through a highly localised lens. Countries such as Eritrea, with all their economic pressures, tend to see the world through the here and now. Getting through the short-term is important. But when you lack natural resources and have little bargaining power on the world stage, it is important to think about what assets you do have and how they might be used to create maritime security. Eritrea's approach to maritime security is arguably quite unique for a country that has only recently gained its independence.

The government in Eritrea clearly recognises the importance of the natural heritage of its local reef systems and the need to develop fisheries on a sustainable basis. The catches in the area are believed to be well below those that might be economically sustainable and of use to the population living on the coastline. The war with Ethiopia created problems, and Eritrea's success has denied Ethiopia an indigenous route to the sea. Surrounded on all sides by countries that it believes mean to harm it, the Eritrean Government has reached out and created relationships with a number of partners who make, on the surface, quite strange bedfellows. Open source reporting, of which the Eritrean authorities consistently deny the authority, suggests that the Government has close links with both Israel and Iran; not a natural trinity by any stretch of the imagination.

The pragmatism of their position is clearly based upon forging links with whoever needs to use the strategic location of Eritrea as an advantage. What Eritrea offers both Israel and Iran is 'operational depth' concerning their own maritime activities. This operational depth comes from an ability to base forces away from the homeland so that they might operate upstream of the threats they perceive. For the Israelis, it's the Iranian arms shipments through Eritrea and the Sudan reaching Egypt. In a similar vein, Iran gets to use its relationships with Eritrea to base intelligence collection assets at the Port of Assab and monitor shipping movements in the Red Sea. Despite the denials issued by senior officials in the Eritrean Government, the idea does not appear far-fetched to anyone looking at how Eritrea can help itself both locally and tactically concerning its situation, by offering assistance and its territory to others seeking to play a wider regional role. The basing of American forces at Diego Garcia in the Indian Ocean is an example of a similar use of territory, but on this occasion for the purpose of manoeuvring on the international and strategic stage.

French maritime policy provides an interesting perspective on this aspect of maritime security. With territories and dependencies based across the world, the French Government has specific challenges when creating its approach to maritime security. The recent increasingly close ties between France and NATO seem to herald a new post-Gaullist era, where the French military is being reintegrated into the wider military operations of NATO. French maritime power extends on the international stage.

Maritime Security in the Persian Gulf

The Persian Gulf continues to represent one of the most strategically vital areas in the world, with seventeen million barrels of oil passing out through the Strait of Hormuz daily, representing one fifth of worldwide trade. This makes the apparent terrorist attack on the Japanese tanker the *M.Star* in the Straits of Hormuz on 28 July 2010 all the more concerning. The Strait of Hormuz itself is one of the most crucial chokepoints in the world, and has an average width of just 34 miles. Fariborz Haghshenass does not overestimate its importance when he calls it 'one of the most important bodies of water on earth'.[61] The region has proved to be a central focus of US foreign policy efforts as the world's hegemonic power has recognised the need to defend its interests in the region, because 16 per cent of its imported oil flows out of the Gulf's waters. Today, with the Iranian nuclear programme the focus of intense political manoeuvring and pre-emptive action, the Gulf's significance has only increased, making it the crux of the brewing confrontations between Iran, the United States and the Gulf States who fear the ascension of their Persian neighbour.

There have been several noteworthy incidents that have placed the Islamic Republic in Western nations' sights. In January 2008, five suspected Iranian speedboats harassed a US patrol in the Strait of Hormuz. The US forces were merely seconds away from firing after one of the Iranian speedboats told them that, 'I am coming at you. You will explode in a couple of minutes'.[62] Moreover, Pentagon spokesman Bryan Whitman highlighted that on several occasions, the speedboats dropped 'box-like objects' in an attempt to confuse the US forces and possibly escalate the situation.[63] On 23 March 2007, Iran seized fifteen British sailors whom they claimed had violated their territorial waters. An international furore erupted, and after almost two weeks the captives were released and returned home. The latter of these examples highlights how ownership and territory is an important aspect concerning security in the Gulf. Iran's territorial waters continue to appear contentious as this confrontation highlights, and further concerns arise given that they continue to exert ownership claims over the Shaat al-Arab waterway, the border between Iraq and Iran, and the three islands that they seized from the UAE in 1971: Abu Musa, Lesser Tunb and Greater Tunb. Moreover, a diplomatic row with Bahrain led to the latter expelling all Iranian vessels from their territorial waters. The catalyst that caused this row was that an adviser to the Supreme Ayatollah Ali Khamenei, Ali Akbar Nateq Noori, stated a belief that Bahrain belongs to Iran as its fourteenth province, a view that many in the Islamic Republic continue to preach. Bahrain suspended talks concerning a gas deal as a result, reaffirming its Arab identity as it positioned itself on the Arabian side of the Gulf.

Iran has repeatedly threatened to 'shut' the Strait of Hormuz should it be placed under significant duress. However, their dependence upon oil to sustain their economy has always hindered such a prospect. Petroleum accounts for 80 per cent of Iranian export income, and arguably this enormous dependence upon such a resource is one motivation for their nuclear programme, for were they to wean themselves off their reliance on non-renewable energy sources, then their threats to disrupt traffic flowing out of Hormuz would have to be taken seriously. Furthermore, Iran has recently buried large numbers of Silkworm missiles deep along the Strait, that allow it to make good on its threat at very short notice. As former CIA Agent Robert Baer notes, it would prove near impossible for a pre-emptive strike to neutralise their threat, or rather, to be confident that it had done so.

One should make no mistake that the Gulf is an economic centre of gravity in the world, and therefore all focus within the region should be set within this framework. For example, energy infrastructure has always been a key target for belligerents looking to disrupt the region. In 2004, a suicide attack on an offshore facility in the southern city of Basra killed three US sailors and wounded a further four. Iraq's two offshore oil installations are essential to their economic capacity and have been defended by coalition forces. After receiving considerable help from the Australian Navy and the Royal Navy, Iraq is now ready to assume control of its own defences of the two main oil terminals in the Persian Gulf. A number of Royal Navy personnel have remained in Iraq to continue to train and build up the Iraqi forces, so that they can maintain security in the region while the coalition presence decreases. At the Iraqi base of Umm Qasr, Coalition Naval Training Teams (CNTTs) are continuing their work, although their presence is dependent upon a memorandum of understanding, which is yet to be ratified by the Iraqi parliament.[64]

The United States Fifth Fleet, however, is currently stationed at Bahrain, and they conduct numerous operations that relate to the Areas of Responsibility (AOR) as dictated by the US Central Command

(USCENTCOM). The Gulf represents just one of these waterways, with further Combined Task Force operations occurring in places such as the Gulf of Aden, where piracy continues to interrupt merchant shipping in the region. The US forces have no intention of surrendering their forward presence in the region any time soon, as reiterated by senior commanders at USCENTCOM. This places their forces regularly within range of Iranian assets, as the January 2008 incident demonstrates.

While there are fears that a nuclear Iran could spur an unconventional arms race across the Middle East, Iranian naval manoeuvres have led to a 'balance of power' being further cemented in the region. The Gulf Co-operation Council is positioning itself against Iran in the region, fearful of the latter's military superiority. The Council has begun plans to further integrate its military systems. Saudi Arabia has responded to the threat posed by Iran's three Kilo-class submarines by purchasing three La-Fayette frigates from France. An article, published in the Wall Street Journal in 2006, highlighted how a nuclear Iran would 'force the US Navy out of its shallow waters'. Iran is further investing in asymmetrical capabilities designed to further the opinions of Saddam Hussein in Kuwait in 1990 and Osama Bin Laden in Afghanistan, following 9/11, that the US is incapable of sustaining casualties. They have sought advanced weaponry that further supports this, for example, by purchasing a variety of 'smart' mines capable of inflicting great damage on US forces. Their emphasis on asymmetric approaches is clearly evident in the fact that the Iranian Revolutionary Guards Corps Naval Division (IRGCN) is allocated 20,000 personnel, who traditionally operate in small dynamic units on Fast Attack Crafts, whereas the regular navy has just 18,000. Kamal has reported on the activities of the group known as the Al Azhar Engineers Organisation[65] who, he reports, were planning attacks upon oil tankers that were in transit through the Suez Canal in order to obstruct navigation in the canal.

5

MARITIME STRATEGY

Strategy: *A plan of action designed to achieve a long-term or overall aim*
Decisive: *Settling an issue; producing a definitive result*
Manoeuvre: *A movement or series of moves requiring skill and care*

Oxford English Dictionary, Second Edition, 2003

Defining Maritime Strategy

A secure maritime environment can be created, but the process is helped immeasurably if this is not on the basis of ad hoc measures. Framing maritime security in the context of a national maritime strategy, with any overtones and links to allied national defence and security strategies, provides the necessary setting and procures analysis from which decisions that have some provenance can be taken. This is especially important when the nature of war is being polarised to the so-called high-end operations, which in a maritime sense would involve major blue-sea combat operations where a large naval force confronts another, and the low-end naval operations which do not involve combat activity in the same sense. This has led to the suggestion that in order to flexibly swing between these two ends of the spectrum of naval operations, some form of hybrid concept has to evolve to be doctrinal, where elements of a force can either be joined to face the high-end threat or operate as effective units dispersed over large areas of the sea.

This kind of consideration does not apply to many navies. The United States is one of the few that can legitimately develop a doctrinal approach to naval warfare based upon such a strategy. The Royal Navy and many other Western navies are struggling to maintain the levels of maritime force that might allow them to operate in anything other than in a coalition with partners, or deploying single units into specific trouble spots should major combat operations be required. The United States Naval War College was charged to work with the Johns Hopkins Institute to develop a new strategy for the application of maritime power by the United States Navy. The document, *A Cooperative Strategy for 21st Century Seapower*, is the result of that effort, and was guided and shaped by other documents, such as the *National Security Strategy* and the *National Strategy for Maritime Security*.

It represents a contemporary perspective on the utility of naval power from the perspective of the United States being the world's only superpower, highlighting what could be achieved.[1] It is underpinned by eight supporting plans. These address topics such as the development of domain awareness, the development of an integrated intelligence approach designed to build the basis of improved MDA through cooperation with international partners, and the maritime infrastructure recovery plan which would be activated in the wake of a specific terrorist incident. Concerning maritime security, it makes specific commitments to naval forces being postured where they can exercise some degree of command of the sea, in areas where the United States' interest requires that it should be established. The strategy makes a specific note of the rapidly developing diesel submarine threat,[2] remarking 'there are many challenges to our ability to exercise sea control, perhaps none as significant as the growing numbers of nations operating submarines, both advanced diesel-electric and nuclear propelled'. The proliferation of the submarine threat is clearly a source of some concern and takes an important place, amongst other priorities, in the development of the maritime strategy. Despite the end of the Cold War, retaining a viable anti-submarine warfare capability to defeat any submarine threat to SLOC must be a feature of any short, medium and long-term naval procurement strategy.

However, despite the levels of investment available, even the United States has to make tough choices between competing demands for investment that aim to provide a versatile response, and that can apply maritime power to the threats posed by transnational criminals and terrorists, while also being able to confront potentially unforeseen state and non-state adversaries that might arise in the future.[3] The United States Navy

Chief of Naval Operations, Admiral Gary Roughead, summed up the situation when he noted

> The maritime strategy gets back to the essence of what the Navy does. Our Navy provides for the safety, the security and the prosperity of our country. And our Navy is a global Navy. It's a Navy that's a deterrent force. It's a Navy that can control the sea, and it's a Navy that can project power when we're called upon.

In defining the approach being taken by the United States Secretary of Defence, Robert Gates, he has stated that 'the defining principle of the Pentagon's new National Defence Strategy is balance'. He went on to add that 'the Department of Defence must set priorities and consider inescapable trade-offs and opportunity costs'. The strategy strives for balance, prevailing in current conflicts while trying to prepare for other contingencies. It tries to select the correct balance between institutionalising current counter-insurgency operations into defence doctrine while attempting to retain an ability to engage and defeat adversaries in conventional situations (with the Americans' traditional advantage of technological differentiation). It also tries to retain the cultural traits of the US military that have enabled it to harness its people so effectively in past conflicts, while letting go of those traits that hamper its development.

These are difficult choices to make, and perhaps the hardest concerns the balance between fighting and indoctrinating asymmetric warfare, and yet trying to maintain a focus on a potential conventional war in the future. The problem is that the metaphorical genie of asymmetric warfare, so hidden by a lack of media coverage in places like Oman and Malaysia, is now well and truly out of the bottle after Iraq and Afghanistan, and it is possible that we may never see a return to so-called conventional warfare ever again, as state and non-state actors resort to a variety of asymmetric forms of warfare, including cyber warfare. From the viewpoint of the maritime domain, the development of asymmetric warfare has followed a number of paths, some with historical precedents, which are likely to result in those tactics being institutionalised into the doctrines and tactics of our adversaries; be those nation states, transnational crime gangs or terrorist groups.

In shaping a contemporary maritime strategy, it is important to reflect on lessons that might be drawn from history. Freidman explores this subject in detail in the context of the post Cold War world, setting out why naval strategy differs markedly from other forms of military strategy.[4] His analysis underlines how vital it is to understand that those historical insights are derived from a very different setting and situation, and therefore attempts to apply them to contemporary situations must too be carried out with care. Despite the passing of time and the changing nature of the international security landscape, his arguments still hold true.

There are some enduring aspects of the maritime environment that continue to shape the way that maritime power can be applied, despite the obvious developments in technology and the changing world situation. It is therefore important when looking at contemporary approaches to maritime security, to delve into the insights that have been documented by respected and often quoted authors on the subject. Foremost amongst those today is Professor Geoffrey Till, who explored many of the issues associated with this subject in his wide-ranging treatise *Seapower*, which drew on a number of historical and contemporary examples to illustrate the meaning and application of maritime power.[5]

Arguably Alfred Thayer Mahan (1840–1914) and Sir Julian Stafford Corbett (1854–1922) are two of the most influential writers on the subject of maritime strategy and the application of sea power. Their writings were published at a time of great change, as the age of sail was giving way to that of the more mechanised era of steam, the emergence of the threat of submarines, and the earliest days of naval aviation.

New technologies are always emerging that might invalidate and challenge accepted doctrines and approaches. However, despite dramatic technological advances in the interwar period, German and Japanese naval planners became avid readers of the work of Alfred Mahan. The surprise attack on Pearl Harbour reflects his ideas, as the Japanese Navy launched a massive strike aimed at gaining control of the Pacific Ocean. During the Second World War, it seemed that Corbett's writings had become largely ignored even though it is fair to say that he accepted Mahan's notion of the decisive battle, but it was only one way to achieve control of the sea and Corbett felt that such a condition might be transitory.

The war focussed the planner's attention on the destruction of the enemy and having major decisive battles such as Midway and Coral Sea, and arguably the destruction of the *Bismarck* and the attack on Taranto and the Battle of Matapan—each of these was decisive in its own right. At the start of the twenty-first century, it is interesting to ask—against the contemporary backdrop of insecurity with its overtones in piracy, criminality and terrorism—if the writings of these two strategists are still applicable.

Maritime Strategy and Maritime Security

Both Mahan and Corbett were hugely indebted to Sir John Knox Laughton (1830–1915), who was perhaps the preeminent naval historian of the time and amongst the first to recognise that the strategy and tactics of the land warfare environment did not necessarily correlate directly with the conduct of warfare in the maritime domain. Wars at the time, such as the Battle of Leipzig, were fought with half a million combatants over a period of four successive days, and were undertaken on a continental stage and scale. The history of empires depended on their outcome in battle, and a single battle had a high likelihood of changing the political landscape.[6]

The observations of Sir John Laughton were nuanced and astute, and born of a man who had served in the naval campaigns in the Baltic and the Far East. The sea was a very different environment, over which, as Corbett was subsequently to suggest, you could not gain absolute control. Clearly any sense of control of the sea would be hugely dependent on the scale of the area over which control was being exercised, and the duration for which the situation had to be maintained. The practical limitations of controlling the sea today are apparent off the Horn of Africa. If Corbett were alive today, he would recognise the problems encountered by the multinational naval presence off the coast of Somalia and the manoeuvring of pirates out into the wider Indian Ocean. These are the ideas and tactics that have strong echoes in the writings of Corbett. So has the pendulum swung towards Corbett today? Or does Mahan still have something to offer to those involved in developing contemporary naval strategy?

A clearly developed and articulated maritime strategy defines the means of achieving maritime security. This security can be delivered by a strategy that is laid out with an appropriate doctrine. These shape equipment procurement programmes, and ultimately deliver a versatile maritime force that is suited to contemporary maritime operations. The problem is that when this is undertaken, there is always a price tag. However starting logically and linearly like this does have its problems, as governments will always have a limit to the level of national investments that they are prepared to make for their maritime security. Ambitions laid out in strategic documents may require some serious costs to be calculated before it can be known whether or not they are affordable. This can lead to maritime strategy being documented in a somewhat ambiguous way, open to a variety of different interpretations.

One example of this is the degree to which a strategy can define maritime security for a nation state as being: something that ends at the edge of territorial waters; the EEZ; the protection of vital SLOC; the wider deployment of maritime forces upstream to disrupt and deter transnational criminals and terrorists;[7] or the ability to project expeditionary operations ashore in defence of a nation's self interests. As a state moves through these levels of capability, the costs increase dramatically, especially at the point where opposed expeditionary operations by amphibious forces are being considered for use against a capable adversary. The crux in the investment curve appears at the point where a nation state decides it is going to develop and deploy a highly capable and versatile blue-water navy, and provides political leaders with the ability to project maritime power across the globe at a time and place of their choosing.

Maritime strategy defines the areas of the sea thought to be important to national interests and those where threats might emerge. Get it wrong and you can have strategic surprises, like the attacks made on Mumbai that were launched from the sea. The terrorists used the manoeuvring room provided by the sea to position themselves and enter Mumbai through the back door. The compression being experienced by transnational terrorist groups such as Al-Qaeda in the land domain, due to the ongoing military operations in Iraq, Afghanistan and Pakistan does allow them either to stay and fight, or to change the locations of their operations by using the sea to transport people and weapons to new locations. The Yemen is emerging as an obvious focal point for this, but destinations that cover the area from the Maghreb and the Sahel in Africa to the outer reaches of the Philippines Islands are equally as interesting. Dispersion of the core Al-Qaeda team in order to link up with its franchises in these various areas would make sense, and would be a further evolution of the way that Al-Qaeda has shown agility when adapting to the constraints placed on its operating capabilities. Corbett would understand this kind of reaction by Al-Qaeda. He would also understand the role the sea could play in facilitating the realignment of the organisation—dispersing its leadership using the unguarded sea as a means for moving its key leadership. Corbett's view that the sea is not an area over which you can establish permanent control, tallies with terrorist thinking and their subsequent use of that environment.

The maritime domain has attractions for terrorist groups, and the high-profile attacks on the USS *Cole* and the MV *Limberg* confirm their interest in such tactics, which is still the case today.[8] In developing a maritime strategy, therefore, governments the world over have to reflect on the threats to their national interests that exist in their local waters, the immediate littoral, and into the global maritime domain. Chile, for example, with its concept of the 'Presencial Sea' is leading the debate on widening the traditional remit of maritime security by embracing areas those of the Pacific Ocean which it has a moral responsibility to protect, despite having no recognised international jurisdiction over those areas. This enlarged area is far bigger than the internationally agreed EEZ.

One approach to maritime security could be to draw upon the model of 'clear, build and hold' being established in Afghanistan. The concept is to build local security from what are referred to as 'ink spots'. These are areas from which insurgents are cleared and where local security forces are brought in to provide security. Whilst the vastness of the sea poses challenges for such an approach, the efforts to provide security in major choke points around the world could be thought of as 'ink spots'. In many of these areas, local forces are providing increased levels of security for the vital shipping lanes. Clearing out the pirates and criminals from the sea is difficult as they have a great deal of room in which to manoeuvre, but recent tactical innovations by NATO off the coast of Somalia, using maritime patrol aircraft and forward based amphibious forces to interdict pirates before they even get to sea, are providing some respite for the maritime task force.

Long-term solutions depend on the encouraging developments in Puntland and Somaliland, where local coastguard forces are being trained to bring security to their own area, which will take time. But the notion that local areas could be cleared of pirates could apply to several of the piracy hot spots that exist around the world, and the lessons from the counter-piracy efforts in the Malacca Strait suggest that regional solutions are possible, even if the geography of the area assists in shaping the reduction in pirate activity. Local 'ink spots' could well be an element of a future approach to maritime security, but the geography of the coastline and nearby seas would modulate their effectiveness.

In Eritrea, for example, this would focus on the need to protect the coral reef and its local coastal waters, as they have considerable potential to develop tourism. This is quite a limited perspective, but nonetheless hugely important to the Eritrean government. Eritrea, however, lacks many allies and is a very poor country.[9] The Eritrean government has therefore developed a strategy of the indigenous development of its naval capabilities, alongside gaining donations of vessels from countries with which it has established friendly relations. It has developed its own local shipyard in Assab that builds patrol vessels that are capable of monitoring its coastline and deterring criminal behaviour. This is a joint venture with an Australian company that already builds around 45–60 vessels a year for local and overseas use. The use of those assets in the interests of the nation delivers maritime security through the application of a doctrine that has been created for the naval force, which focuses on the protection of the marine environment and the sustainable development of its coastlines; these have considerable potential to be developed for tourism if the supporting infrastructure can be built without having a major impact on the environment.

Countries in Africa, such as Eritrea, face increasing threats from criminal behaviour in their coastal waters. IUU fishing depletes local stocks and creates problems for local people. Smuggling also creates insecurity as people, drugs and weapons are moved by sea in areas where a limited naval presence can be achieved. These activities create real hardship for local people. For countries such as Kenya, with its limited naval capacity, manoeuvring and using local intelligence information, such as that provided by fishermen, is crucial to enforcing some form of security in their coastal waters. Developing medium-term intelligence in likely areas where criminals or other groups might be active, would allow patrols to be mounted to target specific threats. When resources are limited, making good use of them becomes important. Corbett would have understood the development of this maritime strategy against such a backdrop, as he would recognise the changing dynamic of sea control being temporarily achieved in some localised areas.

With criminals and others illegally fishing, the Mahanian notion of a decisive battle appears to have little relevance. The arrest of a major fishing vessel or the capture of boats containing economic migrants can achieve high profile coverage in the media, but do little to deter the activities of criminal organisations, the leaders of which often stay insulated and remote from their foot soldiers on the ground who risk arrest.

Given these current localised views of maritime security and strategies that have a sub-regional focus, one may be tempted to suggest that

Mahanian thinking is in terminal decline, and only the writings of Corbett are worthy of contemporary study. This, however, would be to do a great disservice to the originality and clarity of the thought of Alfred Thayer Mahan.

The Enduring Influence of Mahan

Today, it is not difficult to see that Mahan still influences thinking on the application of naval power; Chinese, Indian and Russian naval commanders clearly still think along these lines as they seek to develop a fully fledged blue-water naval capability. In this respect, the ideas of Mahan have proven durable over a century.

This thinking, however, is still conditioned to a large extent by an implied understanding of the threat of a major war between particular protagonists that have large naval capabilities and who might threaten each others' trading routes or areas seen to be part of national territory that are resource-rich. Certainly in the future, the potential for conflicts to arise over areas of the sea such as the Lomonosov Ridge or the Spratley Islands in the South China Sea could well see small skirmishes being replaced by combat between major naval units. Such an outcome, that also draws in maritime forces from other nations into a wider destructive battle, could not be ruled out.

There are, however, many commentators who like to think of such a postulated outcome as being unlikely and the result of scaremongering by writers who are concerned by the apparent demise of sea power, and who believe that such navies are no longer required. One line to take (to use the language of the spin doctors of today), is that this mode of thinking is a thing of the past.

Maritime security, they argue, is not about major wars. These have been consigned to history. The future is about protecting coastlines from the activities of criminals or terrorists to avoid Mumbai-style attacks launched from the sea. In a world where warfare should be the exception not the rule, disputes over SLOC and access to key energy resources will be solved through sensible discussion and negotiation. Such reasoning is based upon a gross denial of history, coupled with a large dose of wishful thinking, and a form of naïvety that borders on dangerous.

Today, China is reaching out across the globe to create relationships with countries in South America and Africa that can help to guarantee its future needs for energy supplies. The need for energy security (the notion of guaranteed access to oil and gas from trading partners overseas) is at the heart of Chinese foreign policy, and dictates a lot of the work they are currently involved in across Africa. Protecting the sea lanes that will deliver those supplies to China across the Pacific, Atlantic and Indian Oceans, is a key reason for the emergence of a blue-water capability for the Chinese Navy. Much of their commercial traffic has to pass areas that an emergent Indian Navy could harass in a time of tension. The planned investment in submarines by many navies in this area, is a warning of their emerging doctrinal intent and possible plans to use such platforms not only for the relatively benign task of intelligence collection, but also, as in the case of hostilities, to sink the ships of adversaries.

Establishing secure sea lanes in the Indian Ocean for energy security may well challenge the Chinese Navy, as it seeks to avoid Indian hegemony over the Indian Ocean.[10] The need to protect SLOC may well, on its own, lead to a conventional arms race, as countries build up their maritime forces to fulfil their own specific needs and distort the local equilibriums that may have been established. The potential for China and India to rapidly build up their naval capabilities in the next decade could be a major source of instability in the Indian Ocean, and have effects on a much wider international stage.

In a world where dwindling energy supplies create the potential for major confrontations to occur that might escalate into conflict, navies can and may be drawn into major naval exchanges. Maritime security is directly linked to energy security in many places around the world, including Brazil with its huge reserves of oil offshore. Efforts by the United States to assist countries in the Gulf of Guinea to develop their own indigenous capabilities for maritime security, providing equipment such as vessels, radar systems and communications networks to help develop MDA, are aimed at providing security within the Gulf of Guinea, being strategically important as a supplier of oil to the United States. Energy security is a key factor in the development of maritime security. The hijacking of the *Sirius Star* in the Gulf of Aden clearly demonstrated the link between maritime security and energy security.

Where the sea is anarchic, economic consequences can and do occur. In this respect, Corbett would have understood the need to establish sea control in certain key areas of an EEZ that are economically vital, such as offshore energy production sites. Where a threat to those facilities is longstanding, it may require patrol patterns that are permanent, such as those provided by Task Force 158 in the Persian Gulf.[11] Corbett would also have recognised the importance of coalition efforts to protect energy supplies, establishing sea control in what is, after all, quite a restricted area, measuring only a few kilometres around the terminals. While on paper this may sound straightforward, with a frigate being able to readily protect a sea area measured in a few tens of kilometres that is defined as a no-entry area, the density of local fishing vessels (where, on occasions, several hundred may be in the local area) creates huge problems for MDA and for enforcing a cordon. Developing insights into long-term patterns of behaviour is crucial if abnormal activities are to be discovered in enough time to prevent an attack.

Another important point is that the current situation in the world, which many commentators believe to be unrepresentative of the more likely medium-term situation, is likely to change. Energy security will have an impact on the way the global economy functions. New regional power blocks could emerge. An alignment between India, Taiwan and Vietnam could prove to be very interesting and a threat to China's ability to protect its sea lanes. In an uncertain world, where such relationships can develop around mutual assistance and trading, it is hard to dismiss situations as being unlikely. Only long-term environmental scanning can pick up such trends, and give clues as to future political and economic alignments. The sheer economic potential of China, if sustained, will make some of its neighbours fearful of its perceived aims to impose a form of regional hegemony over South East Asia. The reaction to this is likely to be the formation of new partnerships based on a form of mutual interest, to deny the Chinese that overarching ability to intimidate and, if necessary, coerce their neighbours.

Witnessing the events off the coast of Somalia, where many of the world's navies are currently assembled for the sole purpose of protecting a major sea lane from acts of piracy, it is not difficult to see the significance of how national interests can extend beyond traditional national maritime boundaries. For China, as one example, there is a crucial connection between energy security and maritime security that goes far beyond the boundaries of its EEZ.

Projecting power across the oceans is a part of a country achieving its own maritime security. Countries such as Iran, South Korea, Japan, Russia and others have all sent naval units to the area, which is far outside their national jurisdiction. It provides an indication of the increasing blue-water viewpoint of these countries. Protecting sea lanes of communication is of national importance, and the ideas expressed by Mahan still find resonance in the opinions of those who undertake an objective assessment of the world today, in contrast to those who view the world through somewhat rose-tinted spectacles.

The Contemporary Value of Mahan's Analysis

At the core of Mahan's ideas was the concept of a decisive battle; one that would resolve the issue of who had control of the sea and by implication the freedom to use their SLOC as they saw fit. His ideas contained echoes of the military thinking of Clausewitz and his views on total war. Mahan published *The Influence of Seapower upon History, 1660–1783*, which is still regarded as a classic in 1890. Mahan's ideas were heavily influenced by the outcomes of the eighteenth century naval wars between France and Britain. One of his key assertions was that a fleet should not be divided; only by the concentration of force could victory be guaranteed. Once the enemy had been engaged and destroyed in a set piece battle, the command of the sea would pass to the victor.

In his work, *From Mahan to Pearl Harbor*, Professor Sado Asada from the Doshisha University in Kyoto, Japan, concludes that the 'ghost of Mahan hung over Japanese Naval Commanders'. This thinking was certainly understood by the Japanese and Russian Commanders who fought in the Battle of Tsushima Strait on 27–28 May 1905. In this battle, the Japanese Admiral Heihachiro Togo defeated the Russian Fleet in what some historians regard as the greatest naval battle at the time since the Battle of Trafalgar. It was the largest and only major naval engagement fought by pre-Dreadnought battleships, and produced a decisive outcome for the Japanese Navy.

For a moment, it is appropriate to consider the word 'decisive'. Without wishing to delve into major semantic arguments, it is worth reflecting on what the word means from a contemporary perspective. Mahan certainly would have understood the definition provided by the Oxford English Dictionary. For him, the set piece battle would decide an issue, once and for all. A definitive result would arise, albeit for one moment in time, of a varying duration. Certainly Admiral Sir John Jellicoe would have understood what was at stake when he sailed from Scapa Flow on the eve of the Battle of Jutland. Admiral Beatty, Admiral Jellicoe's subordinate, would have harboured no doubts as to the importance of the coming battle, as he was a devotee of Mahan.

The Battle of Jutland is a major feature of British maritime history. The intelligence that was available from 'Room 40' in the Admiralty, where they believed, from intercepting signals traffic, that the German High Seas Fleet was preparing a sortie, was invaluable to enabling the Royal Navy to put to sea in time. This ended the frustrations experienced when the Germans would sortie at short notice to bombard the east coast, which created the impression that the Royal Navy was incapable of bringing the German fleet to an engagement. To many along the east coast of England during the early part of the First World War, it must have seemed as though it was the Germans who held control of the North Sea and not the Royal Navy. For the local people, whose appreciation of the nuances of naval strategy might be quite limited, it is possible to imagine the cry 'where the hell is the Royal Navy' ringing out, as another naval bombardment occurred, apparently unopposed.

Clearly, gaining control of the sea in various ways can be achieved through a number of means. Historically, sailing vessels could blockade major enemy ports to restrict the movement of an adversary's fleet. There are many examples where such a close blockade was used to good effect, such as the blockade of the French coast during 1759, which crippled the French Atlantic dockyards.[12] But, as the era of sail turned to steam, duration at sea became an issue for the coal-fired ironclads, and the idea of retaining a blockade at sea over a prolonged period of time had to change. A decisive battle became all the more attractive as it would remove the enemy's fleet from the equation once and for all, and allow the victor to establish trade and other communication routes in the knowledge that the maritime environment was safe from interference from potential adversaries.

The impact of the major sea battles of the Second World War certainly suggests that Mahan's ideas were still very much in the philosophy of military planners as the war drew to a close, having withstood the test of time. The Battle of Midway is one example of a decisive battle that, arguably, shaped the outcome of the war in the Pacific. The Battle of the Coral Sea, while perhaps not as decisive as Midway, created the conditions that can ultimately be seen as having shaped the battle's outcome. It was the first major sea battle in which neither sides' ships directly fired at one another as the battle was conducted by air power launched from sea platforms. Intelligence again played a vital role in the prelude to the battle.

Had the United States carriers been at Pearl Harbour on 7 December 1941, an equal, but quite different, outcome may have been feasible. Midway is one of a number of sea battles that were instrumental to shaping the outcome of the war. Many of those battles can be said to have had a decisive effect on the local, tactical, and operational considerations. At the end of the Second World War, the ideas expressed by Mahan sixty years earlier still had purchase in the opinions of naval commanders in many parts of the world. Were he still alive at the end of the Second World War, Alfred Thayer Mahan would feel very much a part of the fabric of naval academic thinking.

What would Julian Corbett make of MSO?

The gradual elucidation of the theory of war, it must be remembered, has almost entirely been the work of soldiers [...] a moment's consideration will reveal how far-reaching the differences are [...] Firstly there is the idea of concentration of force [...] overthrowing the enemy's main strength by bringing to bear upon it the utmost accumulation of weight and energy with your means.

Extracted from *Principles of Maritime Strategy* by Julian Corbett

When he was alive, Julian Corbett courted controversy with his analysis of maritime strategy, which departed from what, at the time, was the conventional wisdom, the idea that war at sea was broadly similar to conflict in the land environment. It is possible to argue that, as the various forms of asymmetric warfare being conducted by insurgents in countries such as Iraq and Afghanistan move from the land to the maritime environment, Corbett's words still apply today. His rejection of the central tenet of the established naval maritime strategy, the 'concentration' of force,[13] was deemed by some in the Admiralty to be worthy of the charge of high treason. His viewpoint was shaped by his readings of Clausewitz, and particularly his definitive work, *On War*.

Writing about what he describes as Julian Corbett's 'heuristic point of departure', Michael Handel argues that Julian Corbett was inspired by the writings of Clausewitz and his preoccupation with the Napoleonic thesis of warfare, noting the role of the 'decisive battle'.[14] Corbett was not convinced that this argument played directly into the maritime domain. His intellectual rejection of force-concentration in favour of a more agile approach has echoes in the thinking of Sun Tzu, even though little evidence exists of Corbett being influenced by the ideas of a man who is perhaps the most famous philosopher on the subject of warfare.

Amongst his many thoughts documented in *The Art of Warfare*, Sun Tzu positively argues for the concept of splitting a force. Sun Tzu prefers subtlety. His approach is to deceive and distract an adversary, and to win without actually engaging in combat. This is fundamentally at odds with the thinking of those who advocate force concentration.

Any study of major maritime battles, such as Jutland, or the events that led to the sinking of the Bismarck, would find it hard to refute the need to concentrate force. Naval commanders in the First World War, quite simply, lost the war in an afternoon because of a decisive naval defeat. The concentration of force was vital in order to bring the enemy into a decisive battle. Salami slicing begins, because selecting sections of the enemy at a time and place where sudden numerical superiority could be achieved, was not going to happen. The Battle of Jutland was, as people have often remarked, a close-run thing.

Its effect, to use the contemporary language of 'effects-based warfare', was to negate the impact made by the German Navy for the remainder of the First World War. In purely numerical terms however, superior German gunnery and firepower created much for Royal Navy leaders—such as Admiral Jellicoe and Beatty—to ponder in the aftermath of the battle. In more recent times, the Royal Navy concentrated the majority of its fighting units in the Falkland Islands as it tried to shape the maritime environment and create the right conditions for a successful amphibious assault to reclaim the islands. History is, therefore, punctuated with examples of force concentration. Moreover, some contemporary examples seem to illustrate the durability of this argument.

Naval forces were concentrated in the Middle East for the First and Second Gulf Wars. In the Balkans, naval units were similarly massed in the Adriatic. In the wake of the terrorist attacks on the United States in 2001, naval units supporting the initial operations of Special Forces and intelligence agencies in their efforts to support the Northern Alliance in Afghanistan, certainly massed in the Indian Ocean and the Arabian Sea. Contemporary maritime operations, designed to deliver firepower over the horizon in support of ground-based operations, do lead to force concentrations. The issue here, however, is that these contemporary examples of the use of maritime power have not been against equally matched naval forces. The Battle of Jutland and some major engagements in the Second World War, such as the Battle of Leyte Gulf and Midway, are arguably the last of their kind, when a naval force met an opposing naval force on what might be described as equal terms.

So are we seeing, through the passage of time, a re-emergence of the thinking of Julian Corbett? Do his ideas, born out of a need to study the wider implications of maritime strategy, now have a greater relevance? What would he think of MSO if he were alive today?

In using the work of Clausewitz as a point of departure for the development of his own ideas, it could be said that Corbett has anticipated the nature of the warfare that is emerging at the start of the twenty-first century. In rejecting the notion of the decisive battle, with all of its bloodshed and inevitable outcome, it can be argued that Corbett was paving the way for operations that seek a more proportionate use of force, balancing kinetic with non-kinetic operations. Today's military strategists seek a more palatable form of warfare that is a departure from the kinds of encounters that have occurred in history. A revolution within military affairs is the goal where technology provides the commander with the battle-winning edge, as the enemy's dispositions and intentions are fully appreciated.

Warfare of such a bloody nature is difficult to conduct in the twenty-first century in the face of a curious media and saturation coverage. Historically, warfare has been witnessed by the participants, and has rarely made it into the sitting rooms of the public. The Vietnam War has often been cited as the first time the horrors of war were displayed in the court of public opinion. The harsh reality of war was very different from the stereotypical images of warfare that were emerging from Hollywood. Maintaining a justification for such war, in what appeared to be a world away from their homeland in a very different time-zone and culture, was hard to achieve. Confronting the spread of communism in such a direct way was too much to bear for a nation still scarred by the Second World War and the Korean War. Populations tire of conflict[15] and circumstances that change the landscape sufficiently for efforts at reconciliation to commence. The issue for many conflicts today is that of how to create the conditions on the ground which enable that process to be speeded up, meaning that conflicts can be brought to a resolution more quickly.

Political leaders continue to struggle with this wider engagement with the public as they try to justify going to war. The problems of war coverage have become so difficult to manage that military authorities are now seeking to exclude the media from covering operations. Operation Cast Lead, the Israeli incursion into Gaza in January 2009, was based on an attempt to dominate the media by excluding them from being on the ground. Contemporary Western liberal societies do not, it appears, have much stomach for the fight. For some, the images of the Second World War are still too vivid in people's minds.

Contemporary warfare is often conducted against insurgents in far-off places. The immediacy of the threat to the homeland seems diluted. The Russian Navy is, after all, not sailing up the River Thames or landing amphibious units in northern Norway. Populations will allow the build-up of forces as the conflict gets closer to home, as the threat seems more tangible. Many also believe the era of state-on-state warfare to be consigned to history, and that the world is about to move on from such military confrontations. The end of the Cold War was supposed to presage such a change. Sadly, history is not fulfilling those expectations. If anything, the world is a more complex and uncertain place. In his major policy speech in Prague on 5 April 2009, President Obama highlighted what he termed 'a strange turn of history'. He noted that 'the threat of nuclear war has gone down, but the risk of nuclear attack has gone up'. He was clearly referring to the issue of the proliferation of WMD, and the potential for such technologies to be used again, but perhaps not in the context of a traditional state-on-state conflict.

Russian and Chinese naval planning, and that of the Indian and United States navies, does not seem to support that analysis. The opportunities for major sea battles to occur again in the future may well present themselves to future naval leaders. Today's focus, and that for the foreseeable future, however, remains on expeditionary warfare, and projecting military power in support of peace keeping, humanitarian relief operations and stabilisation operations aimed at addressing the issues of failed states. This is not an era of the application of a decisive battle, in the sense of the Battle of Jutland,[16] but rather a series of individual confrontations and skirmishes that lead to the gradual attrition of forces.

The language of force concentration still applies in Afghanistan, but it is applied differently. It has all the advantages of using contemporary technologies to apply that force in ways that aim to have specific and localised effects. Using network-enabled technologies, commanders can bring together their decisive firepower to a single location. Ground forces in Afghanistan rely on an ability to coordinate their operations with fast air, close air support and artillery. A concentration of force occurs on a daily basis in Afghanistan, but it rarely leads to a decisive battle in the sense advocated by Clausewitz. It is arguable that decisive confrontations do occur, for example the battle to recapture Musa Qal'ah in Helmand Province in November 2007 which was certainly a major set-back for the Taliban, but it is hard to argue, from this current understanding of history, that it was a decisive battle in the overall campaign.

While these historical and occasional contemporary examples illustrate some of the enduring characteristics of war and seem to support the ideas of von Clausewitz, albeit a modern form of warfare, Corbett's rejection of the decisive naval battle does still resonate today. Corbett cited the maritime domain as the only place where a major military formation could be withdrawn from the battlefield beyond the reach of friendly forces. The withdrawal of the Argentinean Navy in the wake of the sinking of the *Belgrano* provides a contemporary example. Although the notion of an air force would have been alien to Corbett, the withdrawal of the Iraqi Air Force from Iran at the end of the Iran-Iraq War had a similar impact. Both examples sought to preserve its capability for future use.

Off the Horn of Africa, the countries in the coalition that are tackling piracy have a major problem in delivering maritime security in the medium and long-term. The deployment of warships can only ever be a short-term measure. Efforts have to be made to create the conditions on the ground for the Somalis to take control of the situation and to police their own coastline. Initial efforts to establish a Coastguard Service are making some limited progress with the support of the international community. The situation, however, remains fragile. One lesson to be learnt that emerges from this situation is the need for navies to be able to project soft power ashore, to influence the local populations. This requires the availability of dedicated intelligence resources to map the atmospherics[17] that exist in the local population, and to identify the key leaders who might be able to provide security, even if it is only in small enclaves to start with, from which larger conurbations of security can be built. Somalia has many problems and it is unlikely that there will be a solution to the problem of piracy that will appear quickly. The ability to project soft power from the warships off the coast of Somalia, onto the shore and thus to have a positive impact is a challenge, and will require the development of new capabilities for gaining insights into the complex and often anarchic societal structures that exist in some parts of the world.

An Alternative Viewpoint

Such notions have very Clausewitzian origins and a clear application in the latter part of the nineteenth and early twentieth century. However, today, the notion of a decisive battle (or engagement) may have changed. In a globalised world in which politicians are increasingly being held to account over their actions, it is important to add to the equation the question of viewpoint: who sees the battle as having been decisive? The implied meaning of this naval strategy is that a decisive outcome is one that is clear to an enemy's commander. He knows when the game is up.

Admiral Yamamoto was clearly concerned, in the aftermath of Pearl Harbour, that while he had achieved a great victory on the day, all he had done was to stir a slumbering giant from its sleep and provoked an awesome response that harnessed the industrial might of the United States in a concerted national effort to redress the wrong that had been done there. Whilst similar language has been used to describe the 11 September attacks as a Pearl Harbour event, the situation is different; the adversaries are less easily discriminated against on the battlefield as they fight an asymmetric form of warfare, seeking to drain public support and open fault lines between the nations cooperating in the operations.[18]

But in a twenty-first century context, a wider range of audiences and opinions have to be considered. Their views matter on whether something has been decisive or not, as this shapes the way in which politicians of democracies have to operate. Public opinion can be fickle, difficult to understand and dynamic in the way it which it evolves. It is not necessarily rational. Arguments of cause and effect do not apply because the language of spin has been so discredited. The point is that many different interest groups and audiences may look at the outcome of a specific naval engagement and may each have their own take on the decisiveness of the outcome.

Although Mahan's idea of the decisive battle was greatly shaping maritime strategy through the First World War, the intervening years, and the Second World War, it appears that the arguments put forward by Corbett have found less favour. Industrial warfare, on a global scale, seemed to be the only backdrop against which Mahan's ideas and concepts could be appreciated. It suited the time, and provided a robust intellectual backdrop for the development of tactical innovations that arose from the introduction of new technologies.

These advances gave the commander, at the tactical level, subtle advantages. But the heart of maritime strategy was still governed by the idea of seeking out the enemy's fleet, or certainly its iconic vessels such as the *Bismarck* or the *Graf Spee*, and engaging them in a heated battle to the death. Glory or the ignominy of failure awaited the outcome.

Latterly, the sinking of the Argentinean Cruiser the *General Belgrano* during the Falklands conflict, can also be said to have been an example of Mahanian thinking. The moment when the vessel was lost was a decisive one for the Argentinean Navy. It moved from a strategy based on strategic offense, where its aim was to meet and engage the Royal Navy in a decisive battle, where the loss of one of the two carriers in the Task Force was deemed to be sufficient to make the Royal Navy withdraw, to a plan of a fleet-in-being, and the adoption of a strategic defensive posture. The loss of the cruiser was a major blow for the Argentinean Navy, and they could not risk the loss of any more of its main combat units. In contrast, the Royal Navy moved on to mount the amphibious landing at San Carlos Water, and ejected the Argentinean military forces from the Islands.

Today, the United States Navy, because of its sheer size and global presence, cannot necessarily seek a decisive engagement with another navy, as an equally equipped navy does not currently exist. Certainly there are indications that in the coming decade the Russian, Chinese and possibly Indian navies will embark on programmes that may well deliver significant blue-water capabilities, such as carrier strike groups.

Those who wish to consign the idea of naval warfare to history may argue that the Russians have ambitious vision, but lack the ability to fulfil this, as they have an industrial infrastructure that is ill suited to the development of a large-scale navy. They might also suggest that the Indian Navy could struggle to deliver on its vision; its track record to date is not one that stands up to scrutiny of its approach to procurement.

The Chinese, however, do have the economic growth and capacity to field a new navy. For them it is a question of time. A repeat of the Battle of Jutland or the clash between the Russian and Japanese fleets in the Tsushima Strait will not happen soon though, as the emergence of the Chinese, Indian and Russian navies takes shape. This suggests, for the moment, that the pendulum may have swung towards the ideas about maritime strategy that were articulated by Corbett, and that Mahanian ideas are not currently de rigueur. That, however, given the planned investment by the Russian, Chinese and Indian Navies in major blue-water fleets, is unlikely to be a situation that remains unchanged.

The third decade of the twenty-first century is one in which a combination of issues related to energy security, and the emergence of a number of blue-water fleets to rival the dominance of the United States and NATO fleets, may well provide a period of vulnerability where, ironically, 100 years on from the Second World War, tensions could well cause major confrontations to take place at sea that echo some of the major battles that occurred in the Pacific and Atlantic Oceans. Based upon current trends, there is a real danger that history could repeat itself. Navies that are not currently investing to protect the vital SLOC to ensure that their national needs for energy are maintained, may well find themselves increasingly marginalised as the world's maritime domain becomes polarised by the presence of a number of major blue-water navies.[19]

While such naval battles may echo the Second World War, including the use of asymmetric forms of warfare that recall images of the kamikaze attacks on major United States warships, the advent of new technologies are likely to change some of the dynamics of the battle; although perhaps more for efficient use of time than for geographic dispersal. There will, however, remain those major confrontations of battle fleets that can be dated back to the sixteenth century, which have decisive outcomes.

Corbett and Manoeuvre in the Maritime Domain

Corbett's departure from Mahan came because he placed less emphasis upon the idea of a decisive battle as a way of gaining sea control, which he regarded as a temporary phenomenon and not sustainable. Better to choose a time and place to apply sea power than to try to eliminate one's adversaries in a single major battle. At the time, he angered many in the higher ranks of the British Royal Navy, who regarded such thinking as close to heresy, and believed that by offering such views he had shamed the heroism of Nelson and his cohorts.

Corbett was an advocate of manoeuverist theory. He looked carefully at the differences between the land and naval environments that created the backdrop to war in the nineteenth century. His concern was that too much of the doctrine of land battle had been brought across into the maritime domain. Corbett developed a viewpoint based on the ideas of manoeuvring for tactical advantage, which he saw as being more easily conducted at sea. He developed an approach that could be thought of as 'the art of naval warfare', whereby through manoeuvre one could gain the upper hand. Commanders in the days of sail knew the importance of the weather gauge in establishing an advantage over an adversary. Today, similar advantages can be gained by commanders who can apply the information derived from the particular processes that achieve maritime domain awareness. Those who know where to target limited assets, benefit from using the power of that information to place units at places where there are likely to be more effective. This harnesses the force multiplier effect of information, and enables commanders to manoeuvre their forces appropriately. While Corbett was born in an era before the impact of the contemporary technologies that we take for granted, today he would have readily understood this form of manoeuvre.

Manoeuvre, however, does not simply have to take place at sea. Governments have room for manoeuvre in the way that they equip their forces and set out the strategy. It is valid to manoeuvre in the procurement of that equipment as well as in its deployment. This is not a traditional interpretation of Corbett's logic, but it does provide an extension to his main principle. For those who perceive no immediate threat of invasion, there may be a priority for the development of a maritime constabulary force, modelled perhaps along the lines of the French Gendarmerie. A mix of OPVs and fast, responsive, inshore patrol crafts would provide a rapid reaction capability.

The approach being adopted by Kenya towards its navy and its integration with elements of its air force, demonstrates some agility in the way its maritime force is being configured. Its two main frigates were sent away to an Italian shipyard to be maintained and have their missile systems removed. The vessels, originally built by Vosper Thornycroft and entered service in 1987, were designated as Guided Missile Patrol Craft. The reconfiguration of the vessels, with the removal of their Surface-to-Surface Missile (SSM) systems, effectively converted the vessels into an OPV configuration. These can operate alongside the two Shupavu-class patrol craft that entered service in 1998, providing a force of four OPVs to patrol Kenya's EEZ, and providing protection for the vital SLOCs that take cruise ships and vessels carrying economic materials into Mombasa.

Kenya's long-running saga over the procurement of the survey vessel *Jasiri*, will also eventually add an additional element to the maritime capabilities in the area, and will be capable of patrolling for longer durations and also conducting survey operations which are vital for harnessing any offshore oil, gas and mineral reserves that might exist off the Kenyan coastline. Inshore protection of the littoral zone, ports and harbour facilities is being provided by six vessels donated by the United States, which will work alongside the installation of shore-based radar systems that can monitor the movement of vessels in the area.

When operational in 2010, this capability will provide the Kenyan government with an effective capability to deliver maritime security within its coastal waters. From an African standpoint, this will be an effective maritime security force that is able to provide policing of its coastal waters. The United States is also participating, through the APS initiative, in the on-going development of the indigenous capacity of the Kenyan Navy through port visits, and conducting joint exercises across a range of activities designed to build its skills and capabilities to manage and provide security within its own maritime environment.

Corbett's Wider Thinking on Maritime Strategy

Corbett, however, did not go on to develop a general theory of naval warfare. His focus was on naval strategy and the meaning that naval power gave to the power that could be exerted by a nation. The Armilla Patrol, for example, showed how the Royal Navy could project power into the Persian Gulf to protect vital SLOCs, escorting British flagged vessels through a war zone. Corbett also challenged the notion of concentration that was allied with the concept of a decisive battle. He observed that the principle of concentration had become 'a kind of shibboleth' that had done more harm than good. In what was a marked contrast, Corbett felt that concentration caused an adversary to avoid battle, and instead moved to attack places that were poorly defended. He argued that concentration had a huge weakness in that it also provided an adversary with an idea of where your forces were located: they were hard to hide. The very act of concentration, Corbett argued, created an asymmetric response from the adversary who would avoid that all-important decisive battle.

The form of flexibility and focus on the enemy as advocated by Corbett seems well suited to the kind of routine maritime security operations that are conducted by the Royal Navy today in areas such as the North and South Atlantic, off the west coast of Africa, to nation states there that are seeking to build naval capacity, off the Cape Verde Islands, the Gulf of Aden, operations in the Mediterranean Sea to disrupt terrorism, and in the Persian Gulf to protect Iraq's vital oil terminals.

In the majority of these cases, the adversary is clearly identified, and the deployment is aimed at disrupting their ability to continue criminal activities, such as piracy and smuggling. This is the selective application of naval power to protect major SLOC, and to deter and disrupt criminal behaviour on the high seas. It shows the inherent flexibility that naval power affords political leaders. It is an application of naval power that Corbett's thinking would reflect. In these days of increasing fiscal strictures on all military budgets, the real problem is that ships can only be in one place at a time. This limits the ability of navies to deploy vessels in large numbers, and a mixed solution that uses unmanned surveillance drones coupled with fast response vessels and platforms widens additional firepower. This coupled with indigenous helicopter capabilities may provide a workable solution. Enforcing maritime security may well require the development not only of OPVs, with their obvious area capability, but also a lower-end constabulary capability that can be launched alongside the helicopter to arrest and search a suspect vessel. Ideally, this would be mixed with a new kind of medium-scale helicopter platform that could deploy several helicopters to cater for the activities of several pirate action groups in one area at the same time. The mix of maritime platforms that need to be employed in future MSO should be carefully addressed, and lessons learnt from the operations off the Horn of Africa.

The Military Utility Curve and Contemporary Maritime Doctrine

Today, one should consider the utility of naval power from the perspective of the contribution it can make to contemporary military operations. Some commentators refer to this as the 'Utility of Military Power' curve. This plots the freedom of political choice along a vertical axis, against the level of military commitment on the horizontal axis. By owning naval forces, political leaders gain some freedom of choice as to where and when to intervene in potential trouble spots around the world.

The curve itself can be thought of as bell-shaped, with its peak at the point of military intervention. Contemporary doctrine sees wars moving from a situation where they can be prevented, through a stage of intervention, to post-conflict stabilisation. The limit to national power is at the point of intervention, when forces are committed. Prior to that, the curve builds from a low point, where actions are designed to prevent a conflict from occurring. After the limit of national power has been reached, the curve rapidly descends to a low point where political choice is highly restricted. The situation in Afghanistan is a contemporary example.

'Operation Palliser' mounted by the Royal Navy in Sierra Leone in the spring of 2000, when the country was in danger of descending into civil war, is an example of the utility of naval power.[20] Arguably, Operation Palliser halted the break down of Sierra Leone and all of its associated consequences. The short duration of the intervention prevented a descent into the kind of chaos and anarchy that now creates so many problems in Somalia.

The operation launched by the Royal Navy to evacuate civilians from the conflict in the Lebanon ('Operation Highbrow') is another example of military power being used for high political leverage on the international stage. The maritime domain retains that flexibility, as the curve ascends towards the point of intervention. Coercion, embargo and mere presence can deter war and the build up of weapons beforehand. It also offers political leaders some degree of choice, ahead of launching a full-scale intervention operation. A threat of a rising scale of escalation can determine the resolve of a potential adversary to go to war. Options for negotiated solutions can remain on the table.

When intervention becomes necessary, the maritime domain provides an excellent location from which to mount subsequent operations. Despite Afghanistan being a country with no coastal waters, the Royal Navy played a crucial part in the initial operations designed to secure the country in the wake of the events of 11 September 2001. Intervention launched from the sea affords excellent room for manoeuvre and provides a launch pad from which amphibious and air operations can be mounted in support of military activities on the ground. This can comprise the insertion of large-scale forces or the use of Special Forces to achieve specific highly targeted objectives. Arguably, the use of Special Forces and members of the intelligence agencies was an innovative deployment, where the maritime domain contributed to the provision of close air support, and helped minimise the footprint on the ground.

Once major combat operations are over, the freedom of political choice rapidly decreases, as the aim is to build an indigenous capacity to govern and to return the country to its own leadership and political system. External political choice becomes constrained as the local population seeks to take back control, and political leaders in the warfighting coalition begin to discuss an exit strategy. The danger is that an enduring military presence is perceived as an occupation; this was certainly a factor of the reaction of the Sunni population in Iraq, and something that fanned the flames of the insurgency and led to the coining of the term 'hybrid warfare'. In this situation, the maritime domain can again provide flexibility, as the need to reduce the footprint and yet maintain a presence in the area becomes crucial. This inherent flexibility that the application of naval power offers, is something that Corbett truly comprehended, and is reflective of his wider approach to maritime strategy.

Contemporary Perspectives

Historically, maritime security could be characterised by fighting in what today is known as an upstream environment, away from the homeland, imposing naval blockades and engaging in pitched naval confrontations in near and far-off lands. The state's coastline, and its associated national integrity, was defended by a standing navy that was maintained close to home, and by projecting power over long distances.

The definition of what constitutes maritime security clearly changes over time, and is highly contextually dependent. Sir Herbert Richmond's definition of sea power, cited above, is an example. Written by a person who was a close friend of Sir Julian Corbett, his discussion of sea power in the language of armies, warfare and enemies provides a somewhat narrow interpretation of the subject that was of its time in the early years of the nineteenth century, and echoes terms that would be well understood by the military commanders of bygone eras.

The Cuban Missile Crisis of 1962 provides another lens through which to look at sea power. The United States imposed an embargo on Russian ship movements into Cuban waters. President Kennedy announced the embargo in a speech on the crisis on 22 October 1962, when he stated that 'a strict quarantine on all military equipment under shipment to Cuba is being initiated'.

The use of the term 'quarantine' is interesting. It applies only to military equipment being shipped into an area; other goods are allowed to pass unhindered. A blockade, in contrast, stops all vessels destined for a specific location. It can be considered as an act of war. The vessels would be challenged and boarded in international waters and this posed problems for the United States, who sought to portray the Russians as the aggressors and the United States as the threatened party.

In defining the area as under quarantine, the United States was seeking to apply sea power selectively, and not to ratchet up the ante quickly. Throughout the crisis, President Kennedy sought to maintain some semblance of political control over events, despite the urgings of some senior military commanders to get engaged in a scenario reminiscent of the film *Dr Strangelove*.

To make such a claim credible, the resources of maritime patrol aircraft, satellite-based surveillance and surface ships and submarines would have to be drawn together to scour the waters of the Atlantic for vessels underway to Cuba. The ocean is, and remains, a large place even when all of that surveillance power is available to a state.

Operations off the coast of Somalia attest to the enduring nature of this problem. Sea power can only be applied where the right conditions can be created for its application. Vessels must be sent to specific locations, and not roam the seas in an apparent attempt to locate vessels seeking to break the blockade, or to attack other ships going about their lawful use of the sea.

At the start of the twenty-first century, this language and tone of 'quarantine' still has some meaning and relevance, concerning, for example, the naval elements of the invasion of the Falkland Islands in 1982, Iraq in 1991 and 2003, where the maritime domain played an important part. Here, sea power can be seen in terms of dominating an area and ensuring that one's own operations in that area are not contested. Sea power is, by its nature, applied temporarily in an area to ensure that one's own forces are capable of carrying out their operations, and when challenged, can defeat any enemy that threatens those activities, such as through the deployment of mines or the use of asymmetric forms of warfare being developed by the Iranian Navy and practised by the Tamil Tigers.

It is not difficult for the reader to rapidly appreciate that sea power has traditionally been seen in terms of warfare, and the need to invade and hold foreign territories whilst defeating any attempt at resistance. While it is hugely difficult to envisage a future for mankind that avoids the classic state-on-state conflict in the future, to rule it out would be to ignore the lessons of history, economic pressures, the widening application of Western liberal ideas of democracy, and the desire to eliminate poverty may create the conditions for the evolution of the application of sea power.

Norman Freeman in his work *Seapower as Strategy: Navies and National Inerests*[21], envisages the United States Navy as the foremost instrument of United States diplomacy. Outlining arguments that are based on an emerging consensus concerning the importance of sea power, he widens the debate about what can be achieved by sea power, highlighting the increasing importance of manoeuvring in the maritime domain on MSO.[22]

Through a consideration of these emerging types of confrontation, we gain greater insights into the definition of twenty-first century maritime security and the challenges that will exist in the coming decades, as the combination of energy security and the impact of climate change create tensions in the international landscape, particularly as resources such as water and food become scarce in several areas of the world. These problems will be enhanced by the presence of transnational criminal and terrorist groups who seek to exploit weak states, finding locations from which they can train and maintain their activities.

MSO missions have several definitions that often reflect views held by specific state administrations. Whilst these definitions are often locally expressed in terms of military doctrine, a consensus is emerging as to their nature and objectives. They include, for example, humanitarian relief, peace keeping and peace making[23] operations envisaged in the Petersberg Tasks, that were incorporated within the European Security and Defence Policy of the European Union, having first been formulated in June 1992. This provides the basis of operations being undertaken by European nation states in countries such as Afghanistan, and those conducted by Australian forces in East Timor in 1999, where naval support was a crucial factor in determining the outcome.

The twentieth century saw a number of wars conducted in which power blocs, such as NATO, imposed their collective will on other countries. The confrontations that took place in the Balkans are one example of when power was projected into the land environment from the maritime domain. Warships operating in the Adriatic enjoyed the freedom of the seas to carry out operations in support of the peace keeping and peace enforcement activities that were mounted by coalition forces. The maritime domain was also denied to the belligerents, as blockades were imposed on the movement of goods or supplies by sea.

A valid question to ask, therefore, is what are the components of maritime security at the start of the twenty-first century? A supplementary question of equal validity, is to ask to what extent is what we are seeing today transient and of our time?

The ability to project 'naval power' in the maritime domain is clearly an *element* of achieving maritime security. What constitutes naval power in this respect is something that will be a feature of the analysis presented in this book. In simple terms, naval power might be seen as a measure of the number and military capability of vessels available to patrol a specific maritime domain of interest to a country.[24] These maritime domains of interest can span coastal waters and riverine areas.

In today's world of complex definitions of what constitutes the immediate boundary of a coastline, with 200 nm being the boundary of the EEZ, nation states need to be able to exert authority over an area that is often vital to their national interests, for fisheries, tourism, oil and gas exploration and exploitation, and vital SLOC. Surely protecting a coastline requires some ability to patrol and protect the maritime domain?[25]

While naval power is indeed, in part, a measure of a country's ability to place a vessel into its maritime domain, there is also a key question concerning how best to use those resources. Power, it is argued, is not only the ability to project capabilities, but is critically derived from being informed 'where to apply that maritime capacity to achieve maximum effect and impact'. Power, therefore, is derived from a fusion of the capability to physically place a vessel, with its indigenous firepower and the ability to undertake Vessel Board, Search and Seizure (VBSS) activities, at a specific location.[26]

To achieve this, states need the capability to develop their MDA. It implies that a state is capable of forming a picture of who and what is using its maritime domain, and have an assessment of their intent. Over time, this data builds into an historical record of patterns of behaviour that provide warnings and indicators of particular activities that might threaten the state's interests.[27]

Maritime power, therefore, is not solely measured in terms of naval power and numbers of vessels. It also comprises an ability to harness information, often drawn from a range of sources, which enables unusual patterns of behaviour to be analysed and detected, in order that the vessels employed to project that power can be deployed effectively.

The sources of the material that develop information about the background pattern of activity in a state's maritime domain are varied. The problem is that over time, the picture can become anodyne. Little things that often matter can be missed. Hindsight is a great thing, and often explains nuanced behaviour that at the time appeared innocuous. Local fishermen, for example, often know what is regarded as a typical pattern of activity by local vessels. This can be modulated by seasonal or short-term weather conditions, such as the Monsoons.

Some behaviour is routine, such as the departure of ferries that use specific crossings. Ferry captains and their watch crews also develop an understanding of the maritime background through traversing an area frequently. Local Coastguard authorities or those seeking to police a state's maritime domain against exploitation by criminals involved in a range of smuggling activities, also use an awareness of the patterns of behaviour to detect the unusual. HM Customs and Excise and allied agencies operating in the coastal waters of the United Kingdom are often interested in the lone vessel sailing along the coast appearing to avoid known fishing grounds and other locations, from which they may be sighted or reported.

Where local sailing clubs venture out, skippers can also often see something that they regard as unusual. Automatic Identification Systems or AISs provide an ability to monitor activity in the immediate costal zones of larger vessels.[28] Increasingly, through donations from countries such as the United States, and where countries have made their own investments, AISs are being deployed on a worldwide basis, improving the MDA capabilities to develop a picture of what is happening at key choke points, such as the Malacca Straits, and also to pick up patterns of movements of major vessels. This is a start, but by no means completes the picture, and underscores the need for the OPVs that participate in policing coastal waters to have the capability to show the integrated maritime picture aboard, to assist naval commanders in their decision making.

Final Analysis

It is hard to conclude in the final analysis, from the arguments presented in this chapter, that the ideas of Mahan and Corbett are not relevant today; it is a question of where they are applied in the development of specific types of maritime strategy. While the concepts developed by Corbett perhaps find more relevance in the activities of nations with local and regional criminal behaviour, Mahanian thinking still resonates with those interested in projecting military power at the continental level.

Although there are some who advocate that warfare is a thing of the past, others see it as an enduring human trait. It would be a person with a uniquely narrow viewpoint and little knowledge of history who would argue that major fleet combat action in a blue-water environment will never occur again. For those who believe it is best to use the adage 'never say never', Mahanian thinking still provides founding principles on which to base naval strategy.

In contrast, for those who are developing strategy at a local level, such as many of the poorest countries in the world in Africa, Corbett's thinking will resonate. The notion of a decisive battle is not for them, but rather ideas about manoeuvring and using the intelligence gained from local fishermen to gain a tactical advantage and to understand the criminal's patterns of behaviour.

Whilst time may have passed somewhat since they developed their ideas, the thoughts of both Mahan and Corbett still have resonances today for those developing maritime strategy and using it to deliver maritime security. In an ever more uncertain world, historical insights do matter and are important. In this light, the thoughts of Mahan and Corbett and their links to John Knox Laughton will remain key elements of the syllabi of naval colleges for the foreseeable future. There is no greater testimony than this to their originality and the durability of their ideas.

6

DELIVERING MARITIME SECURITY IN THE TWENTY-FIRST CENTURY

The underlying issue is that neither AIS nor any other silver bullet will achieve maritime domain awareness Maritime Domain Awareness requires all manner of sensors, databases, data sharing, decision aids, displays etc.

Commander Steven Boraz, US Navy, 2009

Delivering a secure maritime environment is challenging,[1] and a far from easy task in a world whose security environment is punctuated with so much uncertainty.[2] At the start of the twenty-first century, predicting the way that contemporary threats may evolve is far from easy. The potential for catastrophic convergences to occur, when totally unexpected outcomes arise from the conjunction of people, technology and location, has never been greater. This uncertain situation is made more difficult with facilities like the Internet enabling such convergences to happen in the virtual, as well as real, world.

This uncertainty is why senior naval planners in many parts of the world have added the concept of hybrid naval warfare to their lexicons. Admiral Roughead makes frequent references to it in his speeches as the United States Chief of Naval Operations. Being versatile and able to change rapidly from high-end operations (which may well involve a high degree of force concentration) to the kind of low-end maritime operations which will tend to be geographically dispersed, is important;

it is where naval forces offer huge flexibility to defence planners. Admiral Roughead speaks of his naval forces being 'out and about', using a somewhat simple vernacular to describe the difficult balancing act of deployment of forces across the globe. In his speeches, he makes the hugely important point that the position of the United States Navy is forward deployed and this is vital to be able to mobilise and concentrate forces at short notice if a political crisis requires the presence of naval forces. To gain the maximum flexibility of any naval force, it must be able to be mobilised into the areas where threats are emerging, to act as a means of deterring escalation and where that fails, projecting both hard and soft power.

The first step in the approach should be to arrange what is already known about the maritime domain into a picture that allows some form of maritime domain awareness to be created; Boraz argues this point saying that, maritime domain awareness 'is where it all begins',[3] and observes that 'maritime domain awareness is considerably more than white shipping'. His paper tackles several myths about maritime domain awareness, such as those that suggest that AIS is the answer, and that it can be carried out in an entirely unclassified manner, fusing together information that is already available on many separate computer systems. This allows the creation of what can be called a 'pattern of life' around the coastline that indicates what might be thought of as normal behaviour. Once this has been established, departures from it may become indicators of criminal or terrorist activity that threaten a nation's coastal zone and its assets.

Whilst a great deal of the maritime picture can be pieced together from open sources, there are many important contributions that can also come from strategic intelligence collection assets.[4] These can often produce nuanced levels of understanding and warnings that allow intelligence analysts to focus their attention on specific areas. Boraz also makes the hugely important point that naval intelligence skills have been allowed to atrophy after the end of the Cold War. The seemingly diminished threat level led to this neglect of important intelligence analysis skills, and as a result the skill base withered on the vine.

It is clear that this now needs to be built up again quickly, as the post-Cold War threats have become clear and their protean nature requires new forms of intelligence analysis skills. Boraz concludes by making an important observation, that 'maritime domain awareness is neither tracks on a screen, systems that monitor white shipping or something that maritime security forces have always done'. He makes it clear that this is a new discipline, and one that requires new and more rounded forms of thinking that can understand complex social networks, demographics, economic and political linkages and the impact of natural disasters on the world's population.

Maritime security means being able to detect ships that are discharging pollutants that will have a detrimental effect on the environment, mitigating the impacts of natural phenomena such as tsunami, hurricanes and bad weather, and rescuing those involved, and preventing and disrupting criminal or terrorist uses of the sea. It is a multidimensional problem, with particular concerns being raised in the United States[5] over what measures could be taken to monitor the activities of smaller leisure craft, and the lessons learnt from Mumbai for the protection of major coastal resorts along the 150,000 km of the United States' maritime borders.[6]

Countries such as the United States, South Korea and Singapore have all been investing in new facilities and capabilities to defend their coastal waters. The United States introduced the Maritime Security Response Team (MSRT) in 2004, which they see as being a critical part of an early response to a potential threat, with a particular emphasis on reacting quickly to a WMD threat. The South Koreans have the *Cheonghae* anti-piracy unit, deploying warships off the coast of Somalia, and the Singaporeans have invested in a new fleet of ten *Shark* patrol-craft at a cost of $17 million each, which are designed to provide a fast response to deal with anyone intruding in their territorial waters. In the first half of 2009, the Singaporeans stopped 143 suspicious vessels carrying smugglers and illegal immigrants, arrested fifty-five people and seized seven boats with contraband worth close to $1 million, in eighteen operations.

In the United Kingdom, greater efforts to coordinate responses to potential criminal or terrorist behaviour in the maritime environment are, in part, being driven by plans for the 2012 Olympic Games. Command and Control facilities are operational twenty-four hours a day, covering key areas of the coastline, and working with various assets that can be swiftly deployed as intelligence information becomes available. Cooperation with European nations in the English Channel and North Sea areas continues to develop quickly.

The first dimension to delivering maritime security concerns the need to be able to safeguard human life, however it may be threatened.[7] Flooding, tidal waves and hurricanes all need to be detected and tracked. Global meteorological forecasting is improving, and the dissemination of information concerning natural phenomena, such as tsunamis, has improved measurably since the tragedy of December 2004. The loss of over 250,000 people in a single event provided a lesson that needed to be learnt, and quickly. All states have an obligation to protect their citizens, who may be affected by a coastal tidal surge or other forms of extreme weather conditions. Alongside this, states need to understand the underlying hydrographic structures that constrain the movement of vessels in their coastal waters.

The sheer challenge that can emerge, however, was aptly illustrated by Hurricane Katrina, and the impact it had on the southern states of America. When nature unleashes the full forces at its disposal, even the world's only recognised superpower can struggle. It was for many, a levelling and humbling experience. Forecasting and predicting the paths of such events, and the scale of damage that will inevitably follow in their wake, is still an area of fundamental research.

Mitigating the impact on coastal communities requires forecasting of improved accuracy, so that appropriate measures can be put in place. Being able to reduce the levels of casualties and losses associated with such extreme events in coastal regions is one measure of an overall holistic approach to maritime security. Saving lives that are put at risk at sea, when seafarers find themselves in danger, is another key measure of the ability of a state to protect its coastal waters and its user community, be that for leisure or commercial use.

Maritime security does have a dimension that involves keeping navigation charts up to date, especially in areas where the dynamics of tidal patterns and local currents can quickly change the locations of sand banks. This is often an area where fruitful international collaboration can take place between trading partners. However, at a time when ownership of the continental shelf is increasingly a major focus for countries determined to claim and exploit increasingly sparse mineral and energy supplies, the need for countries to have access to their own survey vessels that can map the local size of the continental shelf is a relatively new dimension to maritime security, with its associated potential for confrontation to occur over ownership of key pieces of the sea bed.[8] The decision by the Russian Government to deploy two new research vessels is indicative of the growing importance of this aspect of maritime domain awareness,[9] that of the geology of the subterranean seabed.

The problems associated with securing the maritime environment against its use by criminals, terrorists or state-based forces intent on confrontation is an entirely different matter, and one of a very different order of magnitude. Criminals have a great deal of space to exploit and are adept at shifting the focal point of their activities when states uncover and disrupt specific supply routes and entry-points. They know how to utilise that room, and have demonstrated agility in stretching maritime security operations. The challenges posed to the international community off the Horn of Africa illustrate the ease with which people equipped with very limited resources, can create real issues for billion-dollar warships, built for a very different purpose.

The Gulf of Mexico is another area where criminals use the freedom of the sea to move drugs both on the surface and innovatively, using small mini-submarines. Given the scale of the problem and the vast area to be monitored, the Mexican Ministry of the Navy has decided to purchase an unmanned aerial system[10] to provide surveillance over the area in order to counter narcotics, weapons and people-smuggling in the area. This will operate from the La Pesca Naval Sector in the state of Tamaulipas at the northern end of the Gulf of Mexico.[11] The adoption of this system will replace a number of light aircraft that are currently employed for these coastal monitoring duties.

The challenges to creating a secure maritime environment are manifestly difficult and encompass:

- Creating an *effective* legal framework in which transnational criminals, terrorists and pirates can be arrested and prosecuted for their actions; the international community must be capable of enacting the full range of sanctions where it sees fit. Measures already taken, such as the PSI and the various initiatives to secure the contents of goods being moved by sea, such as the CSI, are important and necessary first steps.
- Retaining the ability, within that legal framework, to make use of an *escalating* level of force, from warning shots across the bows of vessels suspected of being involved in criminal activity, to an exchange of fire, should that be deemed necessary. When United States Special Forces and French Special Forces intervened in two piracy situations that ultimate sanction they employed—the deployment of military force—cannot and should not be ruled out in future.
- Projecting amphibious forces into areas where terrorists might be sheltering, to disrupt their activities and destroy their bases.[12]

- Providing, as an indigenous part of any maritime response, a capability to project *soft* power from the sea to the land, in terms of radio broadcasts and other forms of mass media communication to disrupt and deter those engaged in criminal behaviour.
- Ensuring that future naval forces are created in a *balanced* way, that is able to support constabulary missions alongside the major expeditionary roles that are currently envisaged by many departments of defence, against a range of increasingly novel conventional and asymmetric threats. The enduring flexibility of maritime power allows for ships, such as fleet auxiliaries, to vary their roles. One model from history that may be worth revisiting is the rapid adaptation of vessels into temporary aircraft carriers that were deployed in the Battle of the Atlantic. Air surveillance and the ability to bring firepower to bear quickly, are likely to remain important. Having more helicopters on such platforms, in areas like the Horn of Africa, would provide greater agility to the maritime task force as it tries to cover an ever-increasing area of sea. There are, however, limitations. When faced with a threat from smugglers using fast boats, having an embarked air capability is important, and provides flexibility. Having vessels that can counter the kind of swarming tactics employed by the Tamil Tigers and now adopted by the Iranian Navy, is important. Rate of fire, detection of the threat over the horizon and maintaining multiple arcs of fire are important capabilities.
- Looking to vary tactics that use the forward-basing of amphibious forces at sea and are capable of interdicting threats as soon as they cross the land-sea boundary. This was a tactic employed by Dutch marines, and their accompanying Maltese Vessel Protection Detachment in the middle of 2010, as they were deployed just off the coast of Somalia to disrupt the pirates as they first departed from their land bases. The Royal Naval Ship *Johan de Witt*, provided the sea-base for the landing craft that were used to provide the presence patrols off the coastline of Somalia, where they also acted as an intelligence, surveillance and reconnaissance platform.
- Addressing the threat from sub-surface craft, be they engaged in smuggling drugs along the coast of Mexico, or a hostile submarine trying to attack a naval task force. Anti-Submarine Warfare equipment that is capable of operating against a range of marine environments, such as blue-water and the complexities of the littoral, are required to oper-

ate alongside maritime air reconnaissance aircraft that is equipped with sonobuoys and torpedoes.

- Addressing the threat from ballistic missiles to surface ships, naval task forces and countries in the local area.
- Addressing the threat from mines, which continue to have the ability to create major problems in shipping lanes, as seen during the operations of the Armilla Patrol in the Persian Gulf, and the lessons from that are unlikely to be forgotten by countries that are keenly studying various asymmetric ways of defeating what, on paper, is a technological, networked and superior force. Developments off the Gaza Strip in the early part of 2010 presage the deployment of simple floating IED as mines in other parts of the world by terrorist groups.
- Addressing the threat from swimmers in the water or those using simple sub-surface vessels that were popular in the Second World War, and also have been developed by the Sea Tigers to penetrate into port areas to target specific ships and installations.
- Maintaining persistence of surveillance over an area, in order to overcome the limitations of surface-based observations. Any versatile maritime force needs land-based and indigenous air assets that can maintain surveillance over an area, and detect small, fast-moving boats that might be engaged in criminal activity. It is this need for persistence that is critical for providing an effective response to the surface threats. It provides warning time for potential terrorist attacks, and can help steer surface-based responses to intercept those engaged in smuggling. Persistence also provides the kind of background patterns of behaviour from which unusual activity can be delineated.
- Creating a networked force that is able to share local sensor data across a wide range of partners operating in a combined operation. The United States' effort to create a global interoperable communications infrastructure based on CENTRIX, is clearly a major step towards achieving an interoperable, international, versatile maritime force. This capability allows coalitions of the willing to form rapidly, and share information within specific domains focussed upon particular regions of operation.
- Creating an effective infrastructure whereby a picture of what is happening in the maritime domain can be assembled and analysed by those with access to other major databases, such as various shipping registers, that enable a picture of maritime activity in various at-risk

areas to be developed. The concept of a national data centre, which may exist virtually as well as physically, is an important building block upon which nation states with coastlines and EEZ to protect can assemble their maritime domain awareness both above and below the surface. The deployment of the versatile maritime force depends on the information and cues that emerge from the analysis work undertaken in the centre.

Principles

Creating a secure maritime environment is clearly a complex task. No single element of the components presented above provides the answer. A range of measures have to be adopted that are appropriate to specific circumstances and reflective of local concerns and priorities.

The case studies that are presented in this text highlight the local, regional and global implications for trying to secure the maritime environment. The definition of maritime security provided at the outset appears able to withstand the rigours of a detailed analysis, as it contains some quite specific elements. The first is the bedrock of the respect for international law. While that may not be perfect and is subject to varying interpretations, the global application of those laws, such as UNCLOS, is an important starting point for any worldwide approach to creating a secure maritime environment.

The second element of the definition emphasised the importance of the right of navigation. This is another founding principle, that users of the sea should have the right to go where they please, subject to obvious restrictions on safe passage that arise from local guidelines and bathymetry. The sea is the highway of the global economy, and the impact of major disruption to the free passage of goods has already been clear, as ship owners decide not to risk the Gulf of Aden and take the longer route from the Indian to the Atlantic Ocean via the tip of South Africa.

For commercial operators, who supply the economies of the world through a tried and tested 'hub-and-spoke' distribution system that is centred on a key number of mega ports, any delays or additional costs have to be passed on to the consumer. At a time when the global economy is already weak, any additional factors can have a detrimental effect on an international basis. Additional insurance premiums and operating costs for vessel owners arise because the Gulf of Aden is perceived as a high risk area, although in practice quite a small percentage of vessels are actually hijacked.

In the short term, the efforts by the coalition warships operating in the Gulf of Aden are having an effect, although hijackings are continuing,[13] for example, the seizure of the 4,800 tonne Liberian-owned cargo ship the MV *Rim* on 4 February 2010. This incident followed a spate of hijackings in the beginning of January 2010, when four vessels were seized, including the British-flagged *Asian Glory* and the Singaporean-flagged *Pramoni*—a chemical tanker with a crew of twenty-four.

Through coordinating their responses, using the air elements selectively, and placing warships on known routes used by the pirates to leave the shore, the task forces are presenting an agile response to the pirates.[14] Escorting convoys is important, forming groups to move at a similar speed is all well and good, but many vessels cannot readily be marshalled in this way, having differing structural designs and operating speeds.

Convoys alone are not the answer; they need to be conducted as part of a wider approach that seeks to disrupt the activities of the pirates.[15] At the start of 2010, the pirates had reportedly received a sum of $7 million for the release of the Greek-flagged oil tanker the *Maren Centaurus*, which had been hijacked in November 2009 to the north-east of the Seychelles islands. This vessel was the second largest hijacked at the time. The payment of the ransom was the cue for an outbreak of fighting on the land and at sea between two groups of pirates who wished to secure the ransom payment, which was a worrying development. The payment for the release of the *Maren Centaurus* contrasts with the reported $3 million ransom paid for the release of the *Sirius Star* in January 2009.

In the case of the attack on 3 February 2010 on the MV *Ariella*, a 32,442 dwt bulk carrier in the Gulf of Aden, the swift response of a team of special forces aboard a nearby Danish warship is an important development as, up until this point, maritime forces had been reluctant to intervene once a ship had been hijacked. In this case, the twenty-five crew members withdrew to a citadel on the vessel, having issued an alarm call, and waited for a response. Fortunately, the Danish warship was close by and responded quickly, driving off the pirates. This response may not be one that can always be carried out, as the ability to respond depends upon a range of factors, such as the proximity of the warship to the scene of a hijacking.

New technologies may also provide novel solutions, as the potential for weapons that can cut an engine remotely are being discussed; disabling the pirates' engines would be an interesting capability, and not one that is readily countered by shielding. Laser dazzling devices are also being developed[16] that are claimed to have a range of 1,000 yards. Technology may yet tip the balance towards the coalition forces. However, it would be foolish to write off the pirates who have shown agility and an ability to manoeuvre in order to stretch the operations of the coalition warships by moving out further into the Indian Ocean, with a move into the Red Sea off the coast of Eritrea being a real possibility.

The final solution to the piracy problems off the coast of Somalia lies on the land, not in maintaining a coalition of warships operating to protect a vital SLOCs from people armed with little more than an AK-47 and a few RPGs. The potential for this form of activity to spread further using other states that are unable to govern their coastal waters, is a real and important driving force that underpins the joint US and EU APS work. Attempts are being made to reconstruct a viable and effective Coastguard service in Somalia and the government of the Philippines has made an offer to assist with the training of the personnel involved.[17]

Developing an indigenous capability to patrol and secure national coastal and territorial waters will be an important aspect of reducing the threat from the spread of piracy. The potential for several African countries to become locations from which copy-cat models of the piracy in Somalia develops, is a real and pressing concern. The conditions that helped piracy develop in Somalia are not unique to that country. The potential for it to spread is very real, and should be a major concern for the international community.

It is a true reflection of the global nature of the world's economy that this relatively small and simple threat, comprising of up to 5,000 people in Somalia who are actively involved in piracy, can create such a significant impact on the global economy, and can result in over a dozen nation states basing warships in the region in a coalition of the willing. The ongoing burden of maintaining that presence, which appears to have little chance of changing in the short-term (the rewards are simply too large for people living at subsistence levels to ignore), drains national exchequers at a time when financial stringency is creating real problems for national economies across the world.

The Degree of Maritime Security

The level of maritime security that can be achieved by a nation state can be seen as the ability to:

- Protect its own EEZ and land from criminals, those engaged in illegal fishing and exploitation of natural resources, terrorists and activities by potential aggressors.
- Protect SLOCs beyond the state's EEZ to protect trade that is of vital interest to the state, such as cruise liners and vessels carrying vital trade and supplies.
- Disrupt the activities of transnational criminals and terrorists who use the room for manoeuvre afforded by the world's oceans to undertake their activities.
- The ability to project expeditionary maritime power *upstream* to the source of a potential threat, to intercept the threat before it reaches either the SLOCs or the state's EEZ.

This book is focussed on the delivery of maritime security, and not the projection of naval maritime power per se, although where examples can be drawn from the application of naval power, these have been discussed using examples from history. We shall therefore address the first two aspects of this ability to provide maritime security. That said, it is vital that the issue of the international legality of some actions being undertaken in the field should be addressed.

We shall refer in this analysis to the *degree* of maritime security that can be achieved. This reflects the percentage of activities that exploit the maritime environment illegally, or for other covert activities that will be detected, in time, for meaningful action to be taken against the threat. This suggests that it will not be perfect. The aim is to achieve a level that causes those who wish to exploit the maritime domain to expect that a percentage of their activities will be visible and detectable, and hence subject to interception. This is a practical and somewhat pragmatic view, although developments in unmanned air vehicle technologies may, one day, provide a higher degree of capability than can currently be achieved.

Mexico is one of a number of countries exploring the potential of this technology to improve its MDA. It is likely that other countries with significant areas of EEZ to cover and who have major challenges from criminal activities and illegal fishing, may well also adopt such technologies in the future. Australia and Canada are good examples of countries with advanced plans to integrate this kind of technology, and Indonesia would be a country that would benefit from the deployment of those technologies. Canada has pioneered the RADARSAT satellite-based monitoring system to help it monitor its large coastal areas, and unmanned vehicles would provide a complementary capability to that delivered by RADARSAT. The European Union has developed a similar capability for monitoring its coastal borders in conjunction with the European Space Agency (ESA), with data being passed to the relevant authorities within thirty to sixty minutes of the overpass of the satellite.[18] Whilst satellite-based observations provide a source that can see wider areas, the current coverage of those systems, such as ERS-2 and ENVISAT, and the limitations that apply to sensor-duty cycles, do hamper the areas that can be covered. RADARSAT has the advantage of being in an orbital configuration that provides a greater revisit time over the Canadian EEZ, and hence overcomes some of the limitations that the ESA service will experience in the Mediterranean Sea.

There are also major challenges to be overcome in detecting vessels of a smaller size, such as those used to smuggle economic migrants, as the radar returns from the sea can be complex, and exhibit noise-like characteristics. Discerning the signal indicating the presence of a small boat is not an easy task, and requires favourable viewing conditions. However, while point targets are difficult to detect, research has shown that oil spills and illegal discharges of ballast can be detected under a range of sea states and conditions. The potential for satellites to contribute to monitoring illegal pollution has been clearly demonstrated. The wakes produced by vessels also form a dispersed target, and can be detected by satellite radar sensor systems when the vessels are of a particular size and the sea state conditions do not provide too high a level of background noise. Despite their obvious advantages in being able to look down from above on the maritime environment satellite-based sensor systems, while offering some potential to help create MDA, they do not provide a fully reliable source of information that is routinely available.

Gaining intelligence is one thing, taking action based on its findings is another. For effective measures to be put in place, robust and reliable communication infrastructures must be available to underpin maritime security activities. Cooperation in regions, such as that which occurs in the North Sea between British and European partners, is hugely important. But the communications infrastructure needs to be available 24/7, and be available over several different forms of carrier. Reliance on one specific form of communication, some of which can be monitored by criminals and potential terrorists, is not a secure solution.

Command and Control centres also have to be manned 24/7, to process and deploy the assets to areas that are thought to be at risk from short-term or medium-to-longer term activities. Where resources permit, taking time to study the geography of the coastlines and to profile the risks of certain areas being used for illicit activity, also helps focus activities in the maritime security arena.

As operations off the Horn of Africa have shown, the sea is a large place that affords those engaged in criminal behaviour with a lot of room in which to manoeuvre. Even using maritime patrol aircraft, with their duration and basing issues, does not provide a perfect solution. Admiral Mullen, the United States Chairman of the Joint Chiefs of Staff, was quoted in August 2009 as saying that it would require a force of 100 naval vessels to provide complete protection for vessels in-transit through the Gulf of Aden and into the Indian Ocean.[19] Quite clearly, that is not going to be available to any of the naval commanders operating in the area. It would require a huge investment of naval assets from across the world, let alone the ships that would have to be working prior to deployment, and those that are heading home having completed their patrol duties. The idea of an international coalition response in areas where maritime security is now part of the landscape of international politics, and will remain an important part of the international community's response to specific threats to vital SLOC.

The degree of maritime security that can be achieved, given limited resources, is a function of many variables. A less than comprehensive list is provided in Table 6.1. This is designed to highlight the numbers of variables involved. It provides, to a first order, an indication of some of the variables that would be needed to model the ways in which maritime security could be achieved in a country, from the starting-point of trying to deter the criminal behaviour. Of all the parameters listed, the speed of the threat is arguably the most important, as it ranges from a slow fishing boat with its nets in the water to fast boats that are built especially to try to outrun customs cutters, and determines the mathematics of the probability of intercepts occurring. The nature of the threat is also an important parameter, as this will also determine if it can be detected.

Table 6.1: Variables Involved in Achieving Maritime Security in a State's EEZ and SLOC[20]

Element	*Comment*
Speed of the Threat	The speed of the threat varies from sub-surface craft, to fishing boats with their nets in the water, to fast boats designed to avoid customs and anti–terrorism patrols.
Nature of the Threat	This encompasses the potential for mines to be laid, or threatened to be deployed, in key SLOC from a small fishing vessel, Vessel Borne Improvised Explosive Devices (VBIED), sub-surface craft, surface craft of varying capabilities, including hovercraft for operation in river delta areas.
Length of Coastline/Size of EEZ	This has a straightforward linear impact on the resources required to create a secure maritime environment and also covers the size of the EEZ.
Environmental Conditions	This can have a major impact on the threat; for example the impact of the Monsoon winds on the activities of the pirates in the Gulf of Aden. It can also hamper the detection of the threat as sensors range can be impaired by varying environmental conditions.
Ports and their locations	Determines the ranges and areas that can be covered from the ports and any forward operating bases used temporarily. This can be a complex relationship as the ports are unlikely to be linearly located along the coastline due to geographic and bathymetric constraints.
Specific Focus Areas	Areas within the EEZ that are a matter of specific priority, such as approaches to Ports, environmentally sensitive areas, offshore energy production facilities etc. These may require a specific level of protection if a particular threat emerges.
Number of Vessels	This is not a reflection of simply state-owned assets, it is about leveraging any vessel operating in the EEZ that can act as a sensor system to detect illegal activity and report it; such as through a confidential free reporting phone number that can be used by boat owners, fishermen, those

	engaged in re-supply operations to offshore platforms etc. In other words harness all of the passing traffic (both state owned and privately owned) in a national effort to protect the EEZ and its natural resources. This is not going to scale linearly as some vessels will naturally congregate in certain areas that will have a higher density of coverage in an area, such as known fishing grounds. Such a scheme however allows other state assets to focus in the areas that might be exploited by criminals. There is a gearing effect of harmonising the detection capability of all vessels operating in an EEZ that helps create a directed response to coverage and development of the MDA. Consideration should be given to strengthening international maritime law in this regard.
Aircraft, Helicopters, UMA and Satellite	The numbers and types of aircraft and helicopters that are used to provide coverage of the EEZ, sometimes directed by specific intelligence information, is an important element of the overall equation.
Responsiveness	The degree to which assets can be held at high states of readiness, less than one hour's notice to move, to respond to specific opportunities to intercept threats that are detected in the EEZ.
Duration[21]	The range, sea-time, sea-state limitations and other meteorological factors that can inhibit patrol duration. This is a function of the various platforms involved. This would also include the time-to-reach a patrol area when deployed forward of the EEZ to protect a SLOC.
Patrol Patterns	The way in which the surface and airborne assets are used to provide coverage of the EEZ. These can be: Directed (as a result of specific intelligence or known seasonal patterns of behaviour arising from MDA analysis) • Random Sweep • By-Area [to guarantee coverage of offshore assets] • Barrier [to provide a line in the sea that a threat cannot penetrate]

Shore-Based Assets	Coastal radar systems, Coastguard Services and AIS facilities that can monitor specific vessels on passage.
Networking Capabilities	The ability to link up various platforms and create a fused picture of the maritime environment as well as link to regional partners, such as the connections formed by Malaysia, Singapore and Indonesia in the Malacca Strait.
National Fusion Node	A location(s) where information developed from the various sources is networked, fused and analysed for short-term and long-term insights into the uses of the maritime domain.

The economics of the levels of investment needed to provide this level of protection is a matter for another text, as the implications of a lack of security from an economic viewpoint could be catastrophic. Al Qaeda estimated the cost of the 11 September attacks to the American economy at $1 trillion. Relatively simple additional measures taken at airports where the attackers boarded would have cost considerably less than this, and be easy to justify in the minds of state treasuries.

Unfortunately, that is not the way it works. Risk assessments are conducted to inform investment decisions. Often these risk assessments are made from quite narrowly focused perspectives. Holistic approaches need to be developed that allow a more strategic approach to be developed. It is axiomatic that clearing up after an event, be it a terrorist action or the emergence of a long-term security threat, costs more than preventing its outbreak.

Looking at the long-term costs of policing the waters off the Horn of Africa, it is possible to opine that some form of more direct intervention to help the Somali fishermen avoid the initial confrontation with foreign fishing fleets that led to the escalation into piracy, might have been, with hindsight, a better option. APS is certainly based on that viewpoint, and shows that lessons have been learnt. The issue is to sustain the engagement over an appropriate period of time, and not take the view that a short-term fix is bound to guarantee a long-term solution. Up-front investments are that much harder to justify, as it is always difficult to say what might have happened if the capabilities had not been introduced. From a maritime security perspective, moving to a more holistic approach for risk analysis seems to be a sensible step.

One aspect of such an approach would also be to spend time reflecting in detail on the development of what might be called the 'business model of the adversary'. What is it that makes them carry out their actions that lead to insecurity in the maritime environment? Where can we find pressure-points or fault lines in that business model that allow efforts to create a secure maritime environment to be successful, whilst minimising the resources deployed? Mathematical models of the interaction between the parties can be developed, that allow greater insights to be gained into the knowledge of where it is best to apply the military instrument of power.

It is suggested that this degree of maritime security might vary from 2.5 per cent (a medium level of search rates for inbound containers into a country that would be fully opened and checked), to a figure of 25 per cent; meaning that one in four boats conducting illegal fishing or involved in smuggling is caught and prosecuted. Higher levels of security are unlikely to be possible, given current technology limitations and the inevitable gaps that will appear in the coverage and generation of the MDA.

What would be ideal is a figure that seriously deters criminal and related activities within the EEZ, such as 50 per cent, as this would prove difficult for business models that rely on certain parts of the routes being cheap to operate. What is needed is to place sufficient resources into an area to disrupt the business model being used by those engaged in illegal activities. This requires cross-institutional action to develop examples of the business models operated by criminals in order to identify the pressure-points that can be exploited.

If, for example, loss rates in smuggling reached 50 per cent for commodities such as narcotics, it would have a bearing on the business model used by such criminals and would have a deterring effect. Some may be tempted to laugh at such a suggestion, but until the detailed analysis of the business models is complete, the actual levels of deterrence that can be achieved cannot be accurately determined. Those engaged in illegal fishing or dumping toxic waste at sea might also be deterred by the levels of security that would be a by-product of increased vigilance over the EEZ. Pressure applied in the maritime arena would create some movement from criminal gangs as they would have to diversify, though the unintended consequences of this might be difficult to imagine at present.

The currency of the MDA (a reflection of how up-to-date the picture is at any time) is a product of 'persistence'. This is the ability to watch over the EEZ and develop a near-real-time update of the various vessels operating in it, and be able to draw from enough sources of information to classify each of those vessels as a potential threat, and then ensure its arrest and prosecution. This will depend on the *responsiveness* of the forces deployed to make such arrests, as they are on notice-to-move to get airborne or sail to intercept the threat.

Intelligence sources that are reliable and accurate can improve this degree of security, but this will often be on a temporary basis as organised criminality, for instance, has proven itself adept at changing smuggling routes when seizures increase. The move to the use of small-scale submarines off the coast of Mexico is just one example of that flexibility.

Soft Power: An Instrument of Maritime Security?

History often illustrates the nature of the relationship between the application of hard power, naval forces and maritime security. Meeting kinetic power with a higher degree of force applied at a greater tempo or with more refined tactics, has always been a way to apply the maritime strategy as outlined by Alfred Mahan. The decisive battle was the route to success and maritime security. Off the coast of Somalia, Indonesia, Nigeria, Sierra Leone[22] and some of the shores of Central and Latin America today, it is difficult to envisage with whom a naval commander could engage in a decisive battle. Asymmetry means that you never quite get to fight the opposition in one place where he can be defeated, and the Iranian Navy clearly understands this concept. Mao Zedong understood this, harnessing his forces for what he saw as the ultimate third phase of a guerrilla war, when the balance of forces and the willpower of the population would shift toward the insurgents.

In the absence of an ability to apply hard power in a decisive way, it is important to reflect on how a balance might be struck using soft power to persuade and cajole, instead of trying to coerce a change in behaviour.[23]

Clearly warships are a manifestation of kinetic power, but their use can also be documented in the media and local reporting within Somalia, to deter those who may wish to become involved in piracy. To do that effectively, there is a huge need to have some effective sanctions in place that deter involvement in the activity. Currently, the benefits and rewards[24] outweigh the sanctions.[25] To change people's behaviour, that calculus must be altered in people's minds.

The problem with this is that expeditionary operations, moving upstream to tackle the danger before it reaches the homeland, are now the basis of policy for many governments who wish to intercept threats but also protect SLOC. However, to do that effectively, the doctrine also needs to develop in respect to the indigenous naval intelligence and psychological operations capabilities that are afloat and close to the danger area. To make progress, the right balance between the application of hard and soft power off the coast of Somalia needs to be developed. In this respect, at the moment the development of the doctrine required is not keeping pace with the overall strategy. The skills needed to exploit messaging and creating a narrative and appropriate dialogue with local people to deter their criminality are not coming together in a coordinated way.

In part, the United Nations food supplies that are delivered by ships into Mogadishu are a part of the application of soft power. Preventing these from falling into the hands of warlords and criminals who might otherwise use the goods to raise capital from already impoverished people, is important. It is a basic product of soft power to deliver urgently needed humanitarian relief.

Unfortunately, given the scale of the breakdown of society within Somalia, what happens to those food supplies once they reach land is a matter that often cannot be directly controlled. They still may get stored in warehouses and used as bargaining chips in wider disputes between the so-called community and gang leaders. Part of any narrative that is developed to try to reach beyond the warlords and gang leaders into the population at large, has to emphasise that the military forces cooperating off the coast of Somalia are working every day to deliver supplies into the main port. Those efforts may often go unrecognised in large parts of Somalia, and the people may not be the direct beneficiaries of the efforts being made. This is a form of sea-blindness that impacts the target audiences by making them believe that NATO, the European Union and other nations involved, wish to influence and change their behaviour.

Changing the behaviour of the local population in war-torn states that are on the brink of collapse is far from easy. The United States military, for one, has a history of trying to help Somalia, having tried to help out before when famine threatened the population. The Hollywood portrayal of the Battle of Mogadishu, *Black Hawk Down*, is deeply ingrained in the political psyche of the United States' collective memory. This is one facet of a much wider set of problems that surround the nature of interventions in potential conflict zones in the future.

The British historian Eric Hobsbawm, explored a wider aspect of this in a series of essays looking at the issues that arose from the union of globalisation, democracy and terrorism.[26] His incisive analysis draws attention to one of the difficulties associated with the application of soft power. Countries with a history of colonialism may well reject influence-based activities as a form of post-colonial interference in their affairs. Where interventions do occur, there can be distortions to the local economy that arise, prejudicing against indigenous economic development. Hobsbawm speaks of the 'parasitic impact' of an occupation on local economies. Clearly such impacts can be reduced, such as through the kind of engagement undertaken by APS in Africa, where the footprint on the ground is significantly reduced through the use of sea-basing ideas, which is gaining acceptance as a way of reducing some of the unintended consequences of land-centric interventions.

Despite all the warnings for Somalia having the potential to be another Afghanistan, the chances of another international effort to bring security to the country remain remote, as African nations struggle to impose security on a highly factionalised and ethnically divided population.[27]

To apply soft power, it is vital to create a detailed map of the societal landscape and to understand key factors about the customs, creeds and social norms that underlie the way in which societies operate. Many of these societies feel ill at ease if they break with the social norms of behaviour that have governed their lives since antiquity. Their values and belief systems, and their rights of passage celebrations, are often a testimony to their important place in society. Flouting those norms and behaving in ways that appear to be at odds with accepted social behaviour causes tensions.

In Iraq, the 'Awakening Councils' were developed because the population in the Al Anbar Province felt uneasy about the way in which local insurgents and foreign fighters were imposing their views and interpretations of Sharia law upon an increasingly wary local population, and they often saw justice meted out in increasingly violent ways. The interpretations of the insurgents, notably the foreign fighters, seemed to clash with the traditional values and belief systems upon which their societies depend. When these values and social norms became challenged, the local population reached a tipping point and rejected the ideology of the insurgents, and drove them out of their societies. It is often a paradox that the great strength such insurgencies draw from their ideology is also a major source of weakness and inflexibility. This situation hampered Al-Qaeda's initial attempts to establish a foothold in Somalia, as it failed to grasp the nuanced differences between its Salafist-based doctrine and interpretation of Sharia law, and the greater emphasis on the Sufi-based school of Islam that is prominent in Somalia. This created a backlash from the local people in Somalia that was reminiscent of the tribal dynamics in Iraq at the time of the emergence of the Awakening Councils. These tensions, or fault lines in the societal landscape, need to be exploited.

General Petraeus, in his actions soon after assuming command of the international task force in Afghanistan in July 2010, has indicated that this is an approach that will be central to his way of thinking concerning the evolution of the mission to bring secure and stable government to that worn-torn country. Enabling local tribal forces, which in Afghanistan are called the *Arbakai*, appears to be central to creating fault lines with the insurgents.

If progress is to be made in Somalia and in other potential problem areas in the future, soft power has to be applied in ways that resonate with the local population. To develop the understanding required to create connectivity with the local population, a systematic approach must be taken to build a clear understanding of the way local customs, creeds and traditions modulate the way societies work. Through this, possible leverage can be identified at an operational and tactical level that can be utilised within an overall strategic approach to communications that sets out a dialogue with those who need to change their behaviour. This comprises a theme (narrative) and a series of orchestrated messages that deliver profound content, which the population will find hard to reject or ignore.

Maritime forces can play a hugely important role in helping create the conditions in which this engagement can occur. Intelligence collection, using surface-based platforms and assets at sea, can provide insights into the prevailing atmospherics within the community. Human intelligence sources (HUMINT) can also play an important role in showing where fault lines exist that might be exploitable through the developing dialogue. It is generally accepted that progress is made in such campaigns by trying to separate the population from those engaged in the illegal activity. This means that the population must engage in a dialogue where its own values and belief systems are centre stage, calling on them to apply their customs and traditions, and highlight any obvious discrepancies that may arise.

During their brief reign before the Ethiopian military intervention, the Islamic Courts pressed down hard on piracy and that did change people's behaviour. There were clear echoes of the situation in Al Anbar, as Islamic Courts handed out their own extreme interpretations of Sharia law, creating some resentment amongst the local population. This often takes time to develop, as initially the insurgents' crackdown on criminality does often create, albeit temporarily, a period of calm. Local people, tired of what has been an endless period of conflict, initially tolerate the privations that arise from the application of Sharia law. In time, as extremes develop, their tolerance of this can become significantly reduced and rebellion can occur when a tipping-point is reached. The aim of those trying to create these conditions in Somalia, is to help that process along through the development of a dialogue and the application of specific messaging to targeted populations where exploitable fault lines have been identified.

Ship-based broadcast platforms can be an element of getting the message across, using local dialects to reach specific communities. In military circles, this is often wrapped-up in what are called 'psychological operations' or PSYOPS, an instrument of military power that has often been misunderstood, and has associated with it a number of connotations that are unhelpful, such as its association with brainwashing. It is clear that naval task forces require an indigenous capability to develop material that will send messages to local criminal groups to try to change their behaviour.

The skills and expertise required for this needs to go alongside the capacity to build the MDA and also link that to what is happening on the land where the threat originates. Where, for example, pirates or smugglers are captured, their interrogation is an ideal opportunity for the employment of mobile biometric sensors to be used, to capture information that may provide insights into the patterns of behaviour. Links between the criminals and local criminal groups can be established, sometimes through the membership signatures that people wear or have tattooed onto their bodies. Gang culture has a strong element of identity, and intelligence information can be derived from such sources. Over time, the material collected will allow patterns to be established for those engaged in the operations at sea that can then be translated into programmes of action on land. Ultimately, a large percentage of solutions to the problem of maritime security will arise in actions taken on land, as this is the place from which threats originate.

Reachback[28] is also an important capability. This enables resources to be balanced between being deployed forward in the front-line of operations with assets, such as strategic intelligence collection assets, that operate from the homeland. With effective networking it is possible to create virtual assessment teams that can bring together people with particular expertise in the homeland, such as deep knowledge of the ethnic and anthropological past of specific tribal groups, with the team collecting material and trying to understand its context. Often the access to such expertise has been fleeting, during study days before deployments, and not when material becomes available in the teams. Opportunities are missed to identify potentially crucial points in a campaign, as the interpretation of specific intelligence material lacks insights that can be gained from academics and those who have been deployed on previous operations.

Creating an infrastructure that enables the collective knowledge of groups in the homeland to be harnessed by those on operations is one of the most important challenges for military operations that are being conducted against complex ethnic and tribal backdrops.[29] The ability to pull people into temporary assessment groups that can collectively form the assessment is an aspect of the analysis of intelligence information that, at present, is not being fully exploited, as the practice is following a conventional doctrine of how to approach intelligence analysis. New approaches are required that see the development of a new doctrine that can fully exploit the potential of reach-back.

International Cooperation

One encouraging feature of the international response to the problem of piracy in the Gulf of Aden has been the nature of the cooperation that has occurred between states. The work that is going on in the Gulf of Aden and in the Indian Ocean, involving countries such as the Seychelles Islands, is an important model for the future. No nation state or even a superpower such as the United States, can guarantee to protect all of the vital SLOC that are so important to the global economy.

The Chinese, Indian and Russian Governments clearly appreciate this dilemma, and are building blue-water navies that will enable them to project power globally and on a sustained basis, so as to protect their SLOC and deter any neighbours that might covet what they regard as their national resources. The maritime strategy that underpins the creation of such blue-water navies is reminiscent of the thinking that prevailed at the end of the nineteenth century, when Mahan and Corbett were developing their ideas and approaches to the application of maritime power.

Some of the navies involved have a history of cooperation. The European Union and NATO elements of the maritime force have worked with each other for many years. Standing maritime forces have been an element of the NATO historical response to the Cold War.

Since the end of the Cold War, their roles have changed, and the development of the PSI shows a specific response to a threat from the proliferation of WMD. The PSI model provides a basis for even greater cooperation between navies and coastguards, aimed at disrupting other criminal behaviour that uses coastal waters and the high seas for their illicit activities. While, in this regard, the international legal framework has yet to catch up with the nature of the increasing threat, in time, frameworks will be put in place that will provide greater flexibility than currently exists for dealing with transnational criminal gangs and groups involved in criminality. Warden analysed the challenges posed by the introduction of the PSI, and concluded that the development of a multinational trusted network for information sharing was a major element of any overall solution.[30]

Cooperation between Europe and several countries in North Africa over the need to combat the trade in economic migrants is also important. This regional initiative involved cooperation between coastguard and naval units and intelligence-sharing, to help stem the tide of migrants that risk their lives and try to gain entry through the Canary Islands, Cape Verde and across the Mediterranean Sea into Italy and France. These journeys are hazardous and many economic migrants do not arrive, perishing at sea.

National Strategies for Maritime Security

Cooperation between navies and coastguards is a necessary part of a future approach to delivering maritime security. However, this does not provide nation states with an excuse to shift their responsibilities to other nation states and regional initiatives. Each nation state with a coastline needs to take its own initiative to contribute to the overall development of maritime security. Deterring illegal fishing off the coast of Africa is important, if the model of piracy is not to be repeated elsewhere, which would create havoc for the international trading system.

Countries with coastal waters need to develop their own individual maritime strategies for protecting their natural resources, securing freedom of navigation and ensuring that they disrupt local criminal behaviour. Developing a *comprehensive* maritime strategy requires the maritime domain of each nation state to be considered by their political leaders as an integral part of the national economy, not just as an afterthought. Too many nation states believe that the land is the focus of their development, and that the sea plays a somewhat incidental part in their lives. This comprehensive approach will need to impact on the infrastructure that will need to be in place in order to provide a secure maritime environment. This will be governed largely by the perceived threats to the maritime waters. It will comprise of:

- A maritime information centre that can develop short, medium and long-term analysis of the uses of the maritime environment and associated risks.
- Communications and sensor-based infrastructure to support the development of real-time maritime domain awareness based on sustained maritime patrols that achieve high degrees of persistence and presence.
- Multi-agency and multi-organisational liaison and information exchange.
- Specific security initiatives that reflect concerns over the vulnerability of particular parts of the critical national infrastructure, such as oil refineries, port facilities, sites of special environmental concern and major tourist centres; all of which may have specific threats in a local context.

Sea blindness not only effects major trading nations who take the sea for granted and fail to invest properly in the development of maritime security. Establishing priorities and understanding the impact of the sea on the economy through tourism, the exploitation of natural resources, ensuring channels to harbours do not become silted up and impassable, and deterring potential aggression from neighbours or regional powers whose own political aims may lack transparency, allows for the strategy to be articulated in the form of a series of investments in infrastructure and equipment.

One important debate is the degree to which naval units in the future will be able to retain a presence in various potential trouble spots around the world. For each ship deployed, there are those in refit and maintenance, and others working up to the deployment, and those whose time at sea has just come to an end. Various rules of thumb exist, but one accepted ratio is that for each vessel a navy keeps at sea, between two and three are in the background being prepared in some way for future deployments. This ratio is hugely important, as it is used to shape the requirements for future procurements of ships, and it often comes under a great deal of political scrutiny by various national treasury officials. Looking at how best to create a presence in likely trouble spots is therefore an issue of some discussion.[31] Johnson explores the various cases for three models: minimal presence, periodic presence and continuous presence, and their ramifications for the contemporary backdrop of the international landscape in the Middle East.[32]

Creating a secure maritime environment requires the development of MDA that is both accurate and timely. Deploying resources, which will often be stretched thinly over potentially large areas, will require countries to create national initiatives, and to cooperate in regional initiatives aimed at exchanging information for mutual benefit. A national maritime information centre is a basic building block upon which nation states can develop the necessary awareness of what is happening in their maritime domains. This need not be an expensive venture.

The United Kingdom's maritime doctrine is based on the idea[33] of a Versatile Maritime Force (VMF). The idea is that the Royal Navy is configured with a variety of platforms and vessels that are capable of being adapted to other roles, should the need arise, and for those platforms to be deployed on a global scale. For specialist vessels, such as minesweepers, this might be difficult to achieve, as their characteristics tend to reflect the nature of their primary role. While this distinct nature of mine warfare is a contemporary viewpoint, in time, platforms will be developed that have multi-mission capabilities, where modules are used to configure the vessels for a specific patrol or activity.

The Royal Navy has illustrated what it means by the creation of a VMF through its use of different platforms in a number of roles, and by showing an ability to mass a naval formation quickly to undertake major evacuation operations, such as Operation Palliser and Operation Highbrow.

The use of Royal Fleet Auxiliaries in the Caribbean Sea to arrest those involved in drugs and people smuggling, whilst always being ready to react to any natural disaster, is another example of a VMF in action. The Royal Navy, like many of its counterparts, also shows agility in becoming integrated within multinational coalition task forces that have specific missions, such as those carried out as part of the PSI activities. In an era in which the threat of a ballistic missile strike is increasing, one facet of that versatility will be the degree to which new platforms, such as Daring class destroyers, can be adapted and upgraded in their service life to counter the threat from countries such as Iran, North Korea and Syria.

Maritime Domain Awareness

Given the sheer size of the maritime domain, covering 70 per cent of the Earth's surface, developing the previously discussed concept of MDA, is clearly going to be challenging. Tools such as the Automatic Identification Systems (AISs) and associated shore-based maritime radar systems, located on offshore platforms and vessels at sea, all contribute small pieces of what is a huge jigsaw puzzle that needs to be assembled in a maritime information centre.

Today, many of those ground-based systems provide quite limited and localised pictures, their views being restricted by a combination of weather conditions and the ubiquitous horizon. A great majority of the maritime environment remains unobserved. It is important to maximise the opportunities to monitor vessels when they enter areas where sensor systems can track and explore issues such as their point of departure, the name of the ship's master, crew details, ownership, cargo manifest information and any previous history associated with the vessel's activities that may raise suspicions. Ports, known fishing grounds (where vessels congregate) and maritime choke points (such as the Straits of Gibraltar) that place specific constrictions on the flow of vessels, such as where traffic separation schemes are to be followed, represent locations where information can be collected on vessels that might help build up a picture of their activities.

Of particular concern are the so-called 'ghost ships'. These are vessels that are hijacked, their crews sometimes put overboard into the sea and to an uncertain future, and then renamed to ply the seas for alternative purposes. Persistent reports of the existence of an Al-Qaeda merchant fleet suggests that Al-Qaeda, mindful of the increasing efforts in building border security for air passengers arriving in countries, is turning to the room for manoeuvre afforded by the sea to move people and money to its franchised and associated groups. Hijacked vessels can be readily renamed and painted, even their external features changed and disguised, to portray them as legitimate vessels going about their lawful business when, in fact, their cargoes have a more sinister intent.

Maritime choke points around the world, where vessels have to call in on radio, are obvious locations for material to be collected and analysed.

Over time, patterns of behaviour can be assembled that provide indications of what are the routine voyages of vessels, helping to identify the activities that might be regarded as unworthy of further investigation. For some countries, such as the United States, these data collection points help build up pictures of vessels that might need that extra moment of attention before they are allowed to cross into local territorial waters.

This is a defence-in-depth strategy, which sees the various choke points around the world as an opportunity to collect information that might be indicative of which vessels are engaged in criminality. They also present important locations where, if it was required, amphibious landings could be carried out to defend those choke points, if access to them was in danger of being denied.[34] The better the MDA, the greater the chances of targeting the 3 per cent of searches conducted of inbound cargo containers more effectively.

The National Maritime Information Centre

At the most basic level, the national maritime information centre should be able to garner information and intelligence material supplied by a range of actors and organisations, and plot that information in ways that allow short, medium and long-term trends to be developed, indicating the patterns of behaviour (warnings and indicators) of other nation states who appear to pose a threat, or of those involved in the criminal exploitation of the sea.

The increasing coverage of mobile phone networks in many coastal areas around the world provides an important infrastructure upon which an informal reporting network can be built. Freephone numbers can be operated by national governments to allow people, such as local fishermen, to report any concerns they have about potentially illegal fishing activity that is threatening their livelihoods. This initial building block is one that would allow a national maritime information centre to assemble pictures of activity in national territorial waters, which would help coastguard and military units to be deployed with optimum effect. Several African nations whose economies could not withstand a significant initial investment in a sophisticated, technologically-based solution to developing MDA, could gain from the existing investments in mobile phone networks, which have become a ubiquitous measure of national development as a nation state.

Many countries have had a highly fragmented approach to maritime security, such as the United Kingdom and India. Countries across the world have a lot to learn from the integrated approach to maritime security adopted by the French Government, which is based on the deployment of permanent maritime forces in key locations around the world.

Multi-agency and multi-organisational cooperation (involving non-governmental organisations such as those from the voluntary sector and those involved in leisure industries) is vital if national waters are to be protected, and if a comprehensive analysis of activity in coastal waters is to be assembled. Where one agency is aware of a pattern of behaviour, it is important that this is shared, in order that the most comprehensive understanding of the maritime domain is created. Agencies often take quite a parochial view on information that is operating against their own legal frameworks, and discharge their responsibilities in keeping with their own specific local context. This creates a narrow perspective whereby one agency may be unable to appreciate the significance of a piece of information to another agency.

Liaison officials, based at a national maritime information centre, can act as a conduit and filter for information that may have far wider implications for maritime security. They provide an important source of knowledge and expertise that can ensure that the information received in the centre is analysed from the widest possible viewpoints. With technological development, liaisons can occur through the application of contemporary networking facilities, such as video-conferencing and the use of secure chat-room software. This, however, may be beyond some states, which may initially struggle to create an infrastructure that is very sophisticated.

States that seek to help those that are trying to develop their indigenous capacity may choose to base their personnel within indigenous centres for limited periods of time, to assist with the training and development of staff. This can be an important and tangible form of assistance that is not necessarily costly.

National maritime information centres should be the source of national expertise on the patterns of use for coastal waters, sharing that information with neighbouring states to build mutual confidence and trust where boundary disputes have the potential to spill over into conflict. Where the continental shelf is being exploited for oil and gas reserves, the centres would hold information on the nature of the infrastructure involved in that process, such as oil and gas platforms and their operators. As part of a more comprehensive solution, any radar sensors about the platform or camera-based systems for local security could also be linked into the maritime centres.

Where nation states can afford to invest in a slightly more sophisticated infrastructure, or be helped by donations from other states seeking to help their indigenous development, the procurement of coastal radar systems, associated communications infrastructure and the installation of AIS capability is another level of their ability. The Yemen is a good example of such a development, and the plans announced by the Indian government in the wake of Mumbai illustrate a comprehensive approach to multi-agency cooperation. This is a model that, inevitably, other countries will follow. While that increases the coverage of coastal zones, it still only addresses part of the problem of monitoring the maritime domain. The announcement by the Yemini Coastguard that it is building a base in the Bab al-Mandab which will be located on Miyoun Island, is operationally important in terms of protection of the shipping using the area, through which an estimated three million barrels of oil a day pass, but is also of strategic significance. It sends out a clear message to the international community that the government of Yemen will be involved in the counter-piracy and criminal activities that go on in the area. The announcement in June 2010 came at an important point, as the pirates hijacked the MV *Motivator* on 4 July 2010 as it was en route through the southern Red Sea carrying lubricant oil. Previously, the MV *Golden Blessing* was hijacked in the eastern end of the Gulf of Aden on 28 June 2010, 133 nm to the north of Bossaso and 85 nm to the south east of Al Mukalla, in an area where the wind speeds and wave heights are reduced during the monsoon by the lee effect of the Horn of Africa. In both cases, the pirates used local knowledge of the weather conditions to prey upon vulnerable vessels operating in rather restricted areas.

Unmanned Air Vehicles and Persistence

With so much of the world's oceans not under routine surveillance, the potential for unmanned air vehicles to become a vital part of the international community's armoury is creating a plethora of solutions that are capable of carrying a variety of sensor platforms.[35] Space-based sensor systems can provide some coverage of areas that are seen to be at risk.

The Canadian Radarsat programme has delivered an operational capability that provides information concerning the extent of the ice and its thickness, the movement of large ships and the potential to detect illegal discharges of pollutants.

The orbiting characteristic of the satellite provides good coverage over the northern waters of Canada with its steerable antenna. The coverage and duty cycle of the sensor systems places constraints on its use elsewhere. With orbital limitations and current technology limiting the ability of space-based sensor systems to contribute a great deal to the real-time monitoring of the Horn of Africa, for example, the potential for high-altitude, long duration platforms that are capable of remaining airborne for over twenty-four hours to play a role in contributing to MDA cannot be overlooked.[36]

The potential for these platforms to provide persistent coverage over large tracts of the ocean will be something that plays on the minds of many governments with large EEZ to protect.[37] Countries such as Australia have long had an interest in the potential for unmanned air vehicles to help monitor their 60,000 km coastal waters and EEZ. The nature of the problem facing countries like Australia was illustrated on 3 October 2003, when what has been reported as the 'longest pursuit in maritime history', came to an end[38] with the Uruguayan fishing vessel the *Viarsa 1* being escorted into Australian coastal waters after an eight-week effort by the Australian Fisheries protection vessel the *Southern Supporter* and an international collaborative effort involving the South African Navy and the Royal Navy fisheries protection ship the *Dorada*, which had also been deployed from its normal patrol pattern in the area off the Falkland Islands. The flotilla of vessels that had been assembled to track and detain the boat eventually cornered and arrested the *Viarsa 1* and her crew after a pursuit lasting twenty-one days, covering a distance of 3,900 nm (7,200 km). This was an international effort to capture a vessel that was found to contain 85 tonnes of toothfish that had been illegally taken in Australian waters.

The Australian Government's *Project Air 7000* had set out to purchase a fleet of the High Altitude Long Endurance (HALE) platforms for maritime surveillance missions, and the Australian Government considered, and then rejected, joining the United States Broad-Area Surveillance (BAMS) programme. The original aim was to operate the unmanned vehicles alongside the new P-8A maritime patrol craft, and to use those to deploy surface craft to intercept vessels entering Australian Waters. The idea of creating a mixed fleet of manned and unmanned air vehicles that would patrol the coastal waters and associated EEZ is unlikely to be a solution that is unique to countries such as Australia, Canada and the United States. Other countries with significant EEZ to patrol will also eventually wish to deploy the technologies.

The use of these drones to monitor the maritime environment is actively being explored by a number of major research programmes. A number of issues have to be addressed:

- The mix of the sensor suite on the platforms, in some locations electro-optical sensor systems can be hampered by local climate conditions in detecting targets. Radar-based sensor systems can have their detection capabilities reduced by the sea state, making their use in the monsoon season, arguably, of limited value. The kinds of targets against which the drones from the Seychelles are operating, readily blend into the background.
- The launch point of the platforms, local security arrangements to protect them on the ground, and the time it would take to transit to the deployment area. Land-based platforms have some inherent advantages, but being able to launch persistent coverage over an area as part of an organic capability within a naval task force would offer important benefits.
- The time-on-task of the platforms and their energy sources; some high altitude platforms use solar panels on their wings to generate energy for the sensor systems offering great flexibility and increased duration.
- The weight of the payloads that can be carried and the impact this has on duration and areas that can be covered.
- The competition that arises over the use of the platforms, as often missions exceed the capacity of the drones themselves and their sensor suite. Managing the inevitable clashes over priorities is hugely important.

All of these various issues have to be considered in a range of trade-off studies, as no single specific platform addresses all of the issues. The trade-offs involve looking at the capacity of the sensor systems to scan a wider area in order to detect a surface threat, and then be able to focus on specific threats when they have been detected and track their activities. The sensor suite needs to be capable of operating both in a surveillance mode, where new targets may be detected, or in a track mode to hand-off particular potential threats to surface vessels and their organic air elements, such as helicopters, that can be deployed to place eyes on the target before any specific measures to disrupt, deter or destroy the threat are carried out.

The balance between the wider areas of surveillance, detection and resolution of the target against what can be a noisy backdrop of the sea and the problems of false alarms (when systems detect targets that are not real but a surface phenomenon that has the appearance of a target), are a constant source of challenges to sensor system designers. Constraints emerging from the limitations that inevitably arise from what is technologically feasible then have to be translated into the configuration of the platform, and the trade-offs there concerning the altitude at which it can fly, its duration and other related parameters. Once all of these trade-offs have been considered, a number of platforms will inevitably arise.

Some of these will be capable of acting as organic air components of surface vessels, providing real-time links from the platform to local, networked ships in a task group where the analysis and command decisions concerning the threat can be addressed. These are tactical assets under the command of the local task force commander. They will probably have a limited duration, and may be deployed in quite specific situations. It is likely that any overarching maritime security solution will employ a mix of such sensor systems and platforms, with each providing its own specific insights into the uses of the maritime domain. Land-based platforms, capable of operating over large areas of the sea, will operate in tandem with organically-based platforms that are deployed to focus on a specific area, perhaps operating in conjunction with a helicopter or manned vehicle that acts as a master controller and deploying the unmanned platforms according to the emerging threat picture.

Versatile Maritime Force

To enable illegal activities and threats to the national infrastructure to be addressed, coastguard and naval units need to be operational in order to respond in time, or patrol with sufficient duration, to provide a credible presence at sea and to inter-operate with both manned and unmanned air vehicles.

The increasing procurement of OPVs of varying sizes, that are capable of remaining on station in a wide range of sea states, is an indication of the importance attached to deterring illegal activities in coastal waters. The larger OPVs provide specific capabilities for countries with large EEZ and territorial waters to protect, such as Chile, Brazil and Canada.

In recognition of the growing potential of the North West Passage, and the impact of climate change on the Arctic ice cap, Canada has embarked on a programme to purchase between six and eight new OPVs that will be especially able to operate in the variable conditions of the Arctic Ocean. Studies undertaken by the Canadian Government evaluated a number of options and the decision to build the new Polar-class of OPV was announced in July 2008 by the Canadian Prime Minister. These will operate alongside two unmanned aerial vehicle squadrons, which will provide surveillance in the region complementing that already provided by the national satellite system, Radarsat.

Many shipyards across the world are now producing a plethora of OPVs of varying shapes, sizes and sea handling capabilities. Duration at sea, the ability to move quickly to an area within a country's EEZ and then project maritime force through patrol boats to conduct vessel search and boarding drills are important elements. Just as the pirates use mother craft to project their capabilities from the southern part of the Red Sea, through the Gulf of Aden out into the Indian Ocean and along the Omani coastline, OPVs can be used to project their capabilities for search and rescue, and to interdict criminals and those engaged in illegal fishing. Many of the larger classes of OPV have organic air elements and, in time, will also deploy unmanned vehicles to provide all-round surveillance of an area.

Countries such as Algeria, who have serious concerns about terrorist and criminal activity in their coastal waters,[39] are looking to obtain larger versions of OPV. Malaysia, Malta and Oman are also actively engaged in obtaining various versions of this class of versatile vessel, which some are now referring to as a 'constabulary ship' and others as 'corvettes'.[40]

The last of the six Kedah-class corvettes for the Royal Malaysian Navy's Next Generation Patrol Vessel (NGPV) programme was launched in Malaysia in July 2009. These first six vessels are part of a longer-term plan to eventually deploy eighteen vessels[41] to protect the Malaysian coastline and contribute to local maritime security initiatives, including search and rescue, anti-pollution, oil clean-up operations and more general offshore patrol activities.

The organic air component of these vessels was originally to be a general purpose helicopter, but as the programme has progressed this has been changed to a full anti-submarine warfare capability. That decision is not difficult to understand given the nature of the local maritime environment and the range of potential sub-surface threats that the Royal Malaysian Navy might face in the next thirty years. These vessels provide the Royal Malaysian Navy with another component of what might be referred to as a versatile maritime force that can also:

- Counter and deter any threats from mining operations that might close important sea lanes in its vicinity.
- Project maritime power upstream of Malaysia to interdict surface and sub-surface threats before they reach the immediate vicinity of Malaysia using a range of surface combatants, such as its guided-missile patrol craft, small submarine forces and frigates.
- Project amphibious forces, should that be needed, to counter piracy or terrorist activities in the local area.

Delivering maritime security, in whatever form is needed to address specific local concerns, will need an international framework of cooperation that draws together maritime forces that have a variety of capabilities. The vision of the 1,000-Ship Navy drawn up by the United States was conceptually brilliant from a strictly maritime viewpoint, but flawed politically.

In fiscally stringent economic times, the idea of getting nation states to focus on specific areas of the required capability is hardly innovative. It is a pragmatic and necessary way forward to securing the highway on which the world's economy so depends. While the aforementioned idea of the 1,000-Ship Navy floundered on the problem of establishing the United States as the world's only current superpower, in a leadership position—something that it is not difficult to imagine some countries objecting to—the concept may yet still be achieved through a somewhat softer and more gradual approach. The APS initiative is trying to obtain locally appropriate solutions in Africa, whilst minimising the footprint on the ground, with all of its political overtones.

Through the donation of vessels and VTMS capabilities to help build maritime domain awareness, allied with regular support, port visits and training, the APS programme seeks to engage nation states in Africa in a gradual process, whereby their indigenous capabilities are developed to a point where they can provide an increasingly secure maritime environment within their Territorial Waters and EEZ. Developments in the last five years in the Gulf of Guinea[42] are proving to be a model on which the APS' work is trying to build. Through mounting patrols that have some high visibility, and prosecuting those arrested for being involved in criminal activities, the aim is to deter its growth and development. The EU is also trying to develop indigenous solutions to the problems in Somalia by paying to train Somali coastguards in Djibouti.

In theory, these measures sound like a sensible and pragmatic approach, However, where criminal gangs are able to intimidate the vulnerable, there will still be those forced to run the gauntlet of improved maritime security arrangements to carry out the wishes of their criminal leaders. Increasing the maritime security capability at sea is not a silver bullet in its own right; it has to be done in concert with other operations that improve conditions on the land for people who are often living on the edge of hunger and malnutrition.

The key issue in creating the versatile maritime force is, unsurprisingly, the degree of versatility that is required. Major seafaring nations tend to think of versatility as being represented by the multitude of individual missions that maritime forces can undertake. When a naval platform can swing from one role to another, this is generally regarded as being an indication of its versatility and inherent flexibility. In practice, however, limitations do arise when employing naval units that have been designed to operate in one major mission role, but are being used for other. The vision of a sledgehammer used to crack open a nut is never too far away.

That major amphibious platforms, such as the HMS *Ocean* from the Royal Navy, with an embarked air arm can help in the aftermath of a hurricane in the Caribbean, is beyond doubt. As a platform from which to launch counter-narcotics operations, the arguments are less clear. Fast boats travelling at speeds of 50 knots or more can outrun a surface warship, but not its embarked air platform. So the warship needs to be in locations that are known to be major smuggling routes. Then the maritime assets can be directed with some previous knowledge of the patterns of behaviour of the criminals. But when a warship such as HMS *Ocean* has an embarked air arm of several such helicopters, it is not a measure of simply thinking that for each helicopter that is airborne, another drugs smuggler can be locked up. The relationship between organic air and the platforms from which they are projected and ultimately have to return is not straightforward. More helicopters in an area off a single platform can be a force multiplier, and also provide the presence needed to deter and disrupt criminal activities.

Future surface combatants, such as the platform proposed for the Royal Navy, are seen to be capable of rapid re-rolling, but based on a common design and platform. The platforms would be configured to operate in one of a number of different roles such as anti-submarine warfare, anti-air warfare and potentially in the future TMD capabilities, to enable a warship to be part of a flexible and agile task force,[43] protecting it, for example, from attack from ballistic missiles launched by a foreign power or a transnational terrorist or criminal group.

The Israelis found, to their cost, the proliferation of surface-to-surface missiles reaching Hezbollah, and are clearly concerned at the new developments involving the procurement of the Yakhont/Bastion radar-guided anti-ship missile by Syria.[44] The broader lesson to be learnt from this concerning such a rapid increase must not be lost when developing threat estimates. Navies and Coastguard units will operate in increasingly dangerous waters as they try to deliver maritime security both in their own homeland waters and help in others', through foreign aid initiatives and developing indigenous capabilities. As the century wears on, the proliferation of the threat and the diffusion of technologies from state to non-state actors will increase rather than decrease the challenges posed to creating secure maritime environments.

7

CONCLUSION

Securing the maritime environment will require the development of comprehensive approaches that involve nationally-focussed efforts, allied with regional and global initiatives and cooperation.

Many of the issues that we face in the twenty-first century arise because of the high degree of coupling that exists in our world. Many facets of the world's economy are tightly coupled, for instance, and this makes them extremely vulnerable to small-scale disturbances. When pirates threaten seaways because their own livelihoods have been decimated by the activities of foreign fishing fleets, the economic consequences can unleash a vicious circle of interaction that is hugely destabilising. Events can spiral from the local to the regional, and on to the international scale. Imagine what the reaction would be if Iran carried out a threat to blockade the Straits of Hormuz?

The actions of foreign fishing fleets have dramatically upset the balance from the state of equilibrium in which the fishermen of Somalia made a sustainable living from the sea. This dynamic is by no means unique to the coastline of Somalia. As fish resources around the world dwindle, the potential for piracy to spontaneously erupt in other locations is clear. With fishermen finding it increasingly difficult to land their catches, their reaction—to police their own waters and to try and deter whomever they think is responsible—is understandable. Chaos ensues, as the fishermen appear to act spontaneously against those whom they see as being responsible for their plight.

Where instability arises, criminals, and those with other more sinister intentions, do not lurk far behind. If the seas of the world were to become progressively anarchic, it would have serious ramifications for every nation. The present deterioration in the levels of security associated with the maritime environment, whilst localised to a number of hot spots, could easily spread, with disorder and chaos not far behind. It is important that the governments of the world act in a concerted way to tackle this problem and reinforce governance of the seas. President Kennedy argued that 'there are risks and costs to action. But they are far less than the long-range risks of comfortable inaction'; his comments should be heeded by those governments around the world that are unsure about the need to reduce the entropy that is currently affecting the maritime environment. The time to put parochial views to one side has arrived.

History reminds us of the enduring characteristics of the sea, the room for manoeuvre it provides to its users, and how this can be exploited by those associated with criminals or those with malevolent intent. In today's world, as Mumbai reminds us, if you provide the room for manoeuvre, terrorists will rapidly exploit it to deliver their message of fear. The enduring problems with piracy off the coast of Somalia, with all their potential to spread through the adoption of similar tactics in other parts of the world, also serve to show the problems that can exist across the land-sea boundary, when lawlessness and helplessness are rife and threaten people's livelihoods. For those engaged in the legitimate use of the sea, the maritime environment provides an important highway through which to ply their trade and to harness the resources of the sea; any threats to the use of that environment can have dire economic consequences. Julian Corbett was right when he suggested that the maritime environment should not be viewed in isolation from the land environment as the two are closely coupled.

For those who have criminal or evil intent, the sea provides an opaque world that offers a wide range of hiding places from which criminal acts and terrorism can be planned and launched. Since the terrorist attacks on 11 September 2001, the potential for such organisations to use the sea to deliver a nuclear device or other weapon of mass destruction into a port or to a major city on the coastline has rarely been far from the minds of those charged with developing maritime security. The Proliferation Security Initiative (PSI) is one element of an international response to this nightmare scenario. It has engaged the minds of a wide range of countries since September 2001, and provided a framework for a more international response through the participation of increasing numbers of countries within the framework, helping to increase security within the maritime environment and bearing down on the proliferation of WMD. It also has wider implications; PSI is an example of the vision of a 1,000-Ship Navy offered by Admiral Mullen and the coalition operating off the Horn of Africa is another. These are truly international efforts to create a secure maritime domain. The international effort off the Horn of Africa is a laboratory where tests are being carried out to develop approaches to maritime cooperation to protect vital shipping lanes. What is being learnt there will provide insights that, when adapted to a specific local context, can help build an improved security environment at sea. Despite these efforts, challenges remain.

For those agencies engaged in the search for the *Arctic Sea*, where rumours of its involvement in smuggling nuclear materials quickly surfaced in the media, that nightmare may have started to develop a certain sense of reality. In practice, a key lesson from the *Arctic Sea* incident was that agencies, even within a nation state, do need to communicate information about potential threats swiftly to those involved in maritime security operations. It is vital that those who may become involved in conducting operations to arrest or neutralise a threat are given the maximum available information on its nature and composition. Government departments, wherever they may be located across the world, ignore the need to share information at their peril. A failure to join up the dots is not a ready excuse that can be used anymore.

For the Special Forces that stormed the MV *Nisha* on the morning of 21 December 2001 in the English Channel, when it was believed to be carrying WMD, the distance between the fiction of Hollywood and the reality of what they faced that morning narrowed sharply in their minds. Questions do remain, however, over the accuracy of the intelligence that led to the interception of the MV *Nisha*, and the apparent ease with which the *Arctic Sea* was able to sail unhindered along the English Channel, despite reports of its hijacking circulating in intelligence circles. On the surface, it is not difficult to conclude that information was perhaps not being disseminated as quickly as it might have been to those authorities that may have wished to act.

It is the opacity of the environment that provides perhaps the greatest challenge to creating a secure maritime environment. Lifting the veil that hides those with malevolent intentions is a challenge, and one that can only be seriously tackled through a coordinated international response, with specific regional and local initiatives being orchestrated to achieve the greater goal of a secure maritime environment in which acts of pollution, natural disasters and acts of criminality are mitigated or disrupted.

Given the protean nature of the threats and the ability of criminals and terrorist groups to rapidly reconfigure the way they operate, a cornerstone of any response within a secure maritime environment must be to develop an agile and flexible one. If rigid structures are put in place that are highly centralised, then the criminals and terrorists will find fault lines in the inter-agency coordination that they can exploit. This does point to one of the enduring problems in solving piracy off the Horn of Africa, as varied interpretations of United Nations Security Council Resolutions highlight a growing problem, with countries apparently unable to develop an international consensus as to the legal permissibility of certain acts, such as the right of pursuit into existing territorial waters. Agility means delegation and decentralisation of effort, and allowing local people to act on their own initiatives to gain and maintain plans when circumstances present them with opportunities. This also means giving countries the ability to manage their maritime environments using their own forces and capabilities. Initiatives like the African Partnership Station (APS) exhibit all the enduring characteristics of the maritime environment and also provide flexibility to intelligent users, such as the ability to operate whilst minimising the footprint on the ground.

The nature of the maritime environment and the degree of international cooperation that has been achieved off the coast of Somalia makes it an ideal background against which to develop a wider approach to international maritime security. Providing a secure environment in which the nation states of the world can exchange goods and materials is vital for the worldwide economy, especially at a time when the global trading environment is so difficult.

A holistic approach that is based on the development of a comprehensive view of activities occurring within the maritime environment at the local, regional and international level is required, so that risks can be assessed and measures taken to reduce the dangers and police the seas from those who would seek to plunder its resources. The key to any progress in this area is the development of a coherent international approach to developing MDA. It is the bedrock from which security efforts can be targeted at areas that are perceived to be at risk. This holistic view, backed up by a number of specific case studies, has been illustrated in this book. The 'seven dimensions of maritime security' provide a wider-ranging assessment of the issues involved in creating a secure maritime environment and the links that are involved between the individual dimensions.

The approach needs to embrace all the measures in place from the point of origin of the goods, through their transportation over the highway of the sea, to their safe arrival in their port of destination. The safe passage of goods is, however, only one dimension of maritime security. Providing for safe ports and containers that transport goods is important, but not the totality of what maritime security entails. The land environment where the containers carrying goods are loaded and unloaded has to be coupled seamlessly to the maritime environment over which they are transported. As ever, a secure system is only as good as its weakest point, and recent publicly aired concerns in a number of countries over efforts to screen port personnel show that this is a problem that remains difficult to resolve. This is where criminals and terrorists focus their efforts: they identify the weak point and attack it destructively. The crew of the USS *Cole* are unlikely ever to forget that simple maxim.

Regional initiatives, such as cooperation in the Malacca Strait, have clearly demonstrated what can be achieved in terms of significantly reducing piracy. The collaboration in the Malacca Strait provides a good example of what can be achieved, and is a testament to the willingness of the local government to act in a concerted way. They must, however, sustain their efforts. Criminality has a habit of being able to sense a lack of governance. The cooperative efforts off the Horn of Africa are unlikely to achieve similar results in the short-term. The geography of the area helps, as the Malacca Strait is quite a narrow channel. Maritime security measures in the area improved dramatically as the regional states began to cooperate. Similar progress in the Gulf of Aden is hampered by the expanse of the Indian Ocean and the freedom of manoeuvre that this provides the pirates.

The room for manoeuvre afforded to the pirates is simply too large, and they have shown agility in changing and developing their tactics to maintain the momentum and stay ahead of the international task force located in the Gulf of Aden and the Indian Ocean. Attacking at dawn and dusk, and reducing the signature of their boats by painting them in colours that help them blend into the background, are all tactics that the pirates have shown that they can adopt. Concealment, deception and camouflage are not concepts that simply exist in the mindset of Western military strategists. Asymmetric warfare is all about using novel ideas and approaches to defeat a supposedly technically and numerically superior force. That advantage may, however, be changing, as new technologies are considered by shipping operators, including arming ship's crews. This is something that ship owners have been reluctant to do in case this encourages the development of another form of piracy from within the crews themselves. Arming vessels through the employment of dedicated Sea Marshalls, former Special Forces and military personnel whose careers and track records can be rapidly established, offers another solution which countries such as France and Spain have already adopted. It carries with it risks of escalation and of unintended consequences.

Where threats exist, such as in the Persian Gulf or off the coast of North Korea, measures to mitigate those threats need to have a key local dimension that is attuned to the prevailing geographic, economic, political and demographic situation. The recasting of the plan to deploy a BMD system in Europe opens up a new opportunity to highlight the flexibility of maritime forces and the benefits of the freedom of the seas. Aegis-class warships based in the Eastern Mediterranean Sea, off the coast of North Korea, and anywhere else where ballistic missile threats may hamper international relations provides, an excellent counter argument to those trying to make defence cuts who wonder openly about what the future holds for navies. Those who would dispense with navies need to reflect on who is likely to fill the gaps left at sea as they withdraw.

It is quite clear that new ideas are required that introduce elements of the projection of soft power into the ways in which maritime security is achieved. In Somalia, the answer lies on the land and in developing ways of changing the behaviour of specific local communities, each of which has often quite specific agendas. Mapping and understanding the changing nature of these societal landscapes is crucial to making progress, and understanding when and how to apply soft power. Changing ingrained attitudes and behaviour using soft power approaches takes time. It requires perseverance in the face of adversity and is something that is not so easy to achieve in an environment in which the media regularly reminds us, in graphic ways, of the sacrifices that are being made by our servicemen and women in foreign lands. It alone, however, does not provide the answers, as measures taken using soft power need to be seen alongside the threat of kinetic force that can be applied by the presence of the same maritime forces. Being able to swing between the application of soft and hard power quickly is a characteristic of naval power; it is an agility that is built-in, as anyone witnessing the help offered by naval forces in the wake of hurricane disasters will testify. A warship can quickly change from offering humanitarian assistance to moving off in pursuit of those engaged in criminality.

Doctrine associated with the deployment of expeditionary forces needs to keep the pace with the challenges arising from operations such as those being conducted to protect commercial shipping off the coast of Somalia. The ability to reach into the communities that are involved in piracy in this area needs to be developed and levers identified which would enable the behaviour of those communities to be changed.

It is also an area in which developing improved security is vital. The absence of a credible approach to maritime security is a magnet for those seeking to exploit vulnerable countries. Transnational crime and terrorist groups thrive in the absence of security. Achieving a coordinated approach to maritime security is a vital part of securing the international economy. Nation states do have to play their part in creating a secure approach to the highway that the sea provides, in order to participate in and benefit from the globalisation of the world's economy. Whilst legal jurisdiction places constraints on states' ability to act, as witnessed off the coast of Somalia as pirates are captured and then released, steps need to be taken to deter acts of piracy and other forms of criminality that affect local people's livelihoods and well-being.

Mumbai showed just how vulnerable the coastlines of countries can be to a determined terrorist attack. Where terrorists are being pressured on the land through major military operations in Afghanistan and Pakistan, the potential for their activities to be displaced to the sea endures. The maritime domain has been a source of spectacular attacks in the past, and there is little reason to believe that this may not recur in the future. The images of Mumbai should be ingrained in the minds of all those involved in monitoring the security of coastal waters. Identifying areas that are at risk from such attacks is, and will remain, a priority.

Coastal waters can be a huge provider of natural resources and benefits for local people if they are harnessed on a sustainable basis. In time, offshore wind farms may become as important as the platforms used for hunting for oil and gas reserves. Energy security and maritime security will become increasingly linked, as disruption of the sources of reserves and the potential denial of the SLOC through which they move to consumers have the potential to have a major impact on the economy of a country. Projecting maritime power along those sea lanes to maintain their integrity is at the heart of the Chinese 'string of pearls' approach to maritime security.

For local people living along the coastline, potential developments in tourism, and also in fishing, require careful management to sustain the local and national populations; this is clearly recognised by many governments all over the world. For the potential of fisheries to be harnessed on a sustainable basis, infrastructure is required to be in place to store and move the catches to the population centres, as well as the research activities necessary to monitor the health of fish populations. Local variations in water conditions, both seasonally and geographically, need to be understood, in order that fish stocks are managed correctly, and the damaging impacts of pollution and events like 'red tides' are avoided, where harmful algae blooms can arise and kill large populations of fish in a local area. Often this occurs because of a run-off from nitrates that have been used indiscriminately on the land. Environmental policies are needed that help to create the conditions that protect often highly vulnerable marine ecosystems.

Naval and Coastguard forces that can maintain time on station for several weeks and respond rapidly should continue to be developed and deployed, should events occur that demand a national response. States need to develop cooperative measures with their neighbours in order to avoid nearby coastlines becoming sanctuaries from which attacks are launched quickly, and the perpetrators then moving back inside the protection of the territorial waters where maritime security is nonexistent. Cooperation with neighbouring states is vital, and secure means of passing information is an essential pre-requisite for coordinated responses to threats that can emerge quickly and without a great deal of notice. Through such an approach, 'ink spots' where maritime security is being increased will gradually grow and be extended, restoring governance to the seas.

The priority for nation states with coastlines is to create a maritime strategy that reflects the balance they wish to achieve with each of these dimensions. Many states will only be able to initially participate through taking a very narrow and nationally-based view. The development of a national maritime information centre allied with some form of coastguard and naval response capability is the first step. Once created, the value of the information generated can become an asset upon which future investments in maritime infrastructure can be based. Countries that develop their indigenous capabilities with the help of donations need to ensure that they are able to sustain the operations of the systems and equipment that they use. Systems that are poorly maintained do not provide a basis on which to build a robust architecture that secures the maritime environment.

With a maritime strategy in place, and ambitions established, the priority would be to open a national maritime information centre if one does not already exist. For many countries this would not necessarily mean a single location; the centre might benefit from the use of technologies that allow a virtual centre to be created. For other countries whose position is less established, the creation of the national centre enables a focal point for the strategy to be coordinated and further developed. The bedrock of any approach to maritime security is domain awareness and, given the vast size of the oceans, this is difficult. It is vital to get the right balance of staff at the centre with skills in both the maritime domain and in the analysis of intelligence material.

Policing the maritime domain is a matter of states equipping themselves with the elements of what has been referred to as a Versatile Maritime Force or VMF. Local geography, bathymetry and weather conditions will provide some constraints on what can be achieved by deploying such a force. The length of the coastline, the extent of the EEZ and the assessments of the threats that exist will clearly vary greatly. The situation off the coastline of Venezuela is different from that of Angola or Nigeria. Some countries have similar problems, and their responses can be developed from a number of generic building blocks. A layered architecture can be envisaged, where nation states can think of a number of layers through which those involved in terrorism or criminality have to pass in order to be successful in their aims.

The VMF, envisaged as a general purpose solution, operates in up to four physical layers as an integrated architecture that delivers a secure maritime environment. Table 7.1 maps these to the seven dimensions of maritime security. These layers are:

The *outer* layer that sees maritime power deployed upstream to the source of the potential threat, operating beyond the boundaries of the EEZ to intercept and disrupt threats to the homeland.

The *boundary* layer, where maritime forces operate at the outer extent of the national EEZ, conducting survey work on the continental shelf, delineating boundaries and developing insights into the local bathymetry and building up a picture of the use of the maritime domain by those involved in harnessing the resources of the sea, escorting vessels through potentially dangerous waters.

The *intermediate* layer between the immediate territorial waters and the outer reaches of the EEZ, where the ability to maintain a presence is vital to deter and disrupt criminal and potential terrorist activities, respond to maritime accidents and pollution events, and to protect the lives of seafarers undertaking their lawful activities.

The *inner* layer of the immediate littoral zone, and associated riverine areas, where fast reaction patrols need to be mounted to counter criminal activities, provide search and rescue assistance to seafarers at risk, and mitigate threats to the environment.

Table 7.1 provides a description of the contribution that can be made by maritime security for each layer of the maritime security architecture envisaged. Contributions can come from inshore patrol boats, fast patrol boats, OPV, minesweepers, frigates equipped with theatre missile defence capability (to neutralise a ballistic missile threat) and from major combat units. In the case of providing assistance in the wake of a natural disaster, many combat units can be used to act as a logistics hub when vital utilities may be out of operation temporarily in the immediate aftermath of the disaster. Where war does break out, maritime security does also have to provide for the evacuation of non-combatants who might be trapped in the war zone. The events off the coast of Beirut in July 2006 are an example of when maritime force has to be projected into a state-on-state or state-on-transnational group conflict zone in order to evacuate its citizens.

The outer layer is an important collection point for intelligence that can provide important information to direct the surface-based assets in the subsequent layers. Data collected by the various deployed assets, during VBSS procedures, will be passed onto the national fusion nodes for short and medium term analysis to develop any insights that may be gleaned. These help in adapting patrol patterns and structuring use of the forces in more directed activities that give priority to searching specific areas of the sea for threats to maritime security. The immediate littoral and territorial layers will also benefit from maritime domain awareness information derived from AIS and coastal radar systems.

Depending upon the economic resources of the countries involved, the layers can be built up from surface, sub-surface and air-based assets. If all three are present, their effective use depends upon obtaining a detailed and timely picture of the maritime domain. If an air-based platform is used to conduct reconnaissance over an area for a period of time, it is important the surface or sub-surface assets can be deployed to an area where problems are detected. Persistence is an issue. The developments in the field of unmanned aircraft offer a lot of promise and have been recognised by many states with complex coastlines, such as Canada and Mexico.

Developing a comprehensive picture of activity in the maritime environment will need the various elements of the VMF and its organic air assets and other national technical means of intelligence collection to work in harmony. AIS will need to be deployed into areas of the world where coverage is either limited or non-existent. AIS, on their own, are not the answer; they provide only part of the solution. If air traffic control systems can monitor and check on the movement of air traffic the world over, developing the equivalent for the sea should not be beyond our grasp.

National maritime intelligence centres, staffed by a cross-section of people drawn from different parts of the various agencies and charged with responsibilities to protect the maritime environment, must be created and maintained. These centres must be linked up to create the most transparent approach possible to information exchange in local, regional and international contexts. Speed of information exchange is vital, and reporting chains must be flattened out to avoid unnecessary bureaucracy, which creates overheads that might damage effective responses to situations.

Gaps that exist, in what must be a seamless and integrated approach to building MDA, will be exploited by transnational terrorists or criminals. These need to be identified and closed. Resources will restrict the rate at which progress can be made. The manoeuvre room enjoyed by criminals and terrorists needs to be constrained. Persistence is the key to any solution and the development of unmanned aircraft that can remain on station for many hours is an important step. However, both must be backed up by presence on the sea. This is crucial, and is a driver for the designs of many of the OPV that are currently being procured around the world.

This is the challenge for the maritime community and their political leaders at the start of the twenty-first century. There is a very real danger that the maritime environment could become anarchic, with major associated threats to maritime trade and the global economy and implications for national security. An anarchic maritime environment is hardly the basis for increased economic development. Paradoxically, however, it may well provide the basis, through international maritime collaboration, for states to build mutual trust and for that to help reduce concerns that might otherwise have created an opposite effect. It allows them to develop a coherent, collaborative framework that spans national boundaries, and become agile and responsive in the way that they deploy their maritime security forces to deter, disrupt, and if necessary, destroy those that threaten the livelihood and existence of those that use the sea and its coastal waters to support the development of the global economy. It is a challenging task and one that has no immediate solution. But the future of the world's economic development depends upon that effort being successful. Failure, as has been said before, albeit in a different context, is not an option. Preventing the development of an anarchic sea, with all its implications, is in the best interests of all of the countries of the world.

Whilst his observation was set in a very different time and context, the words of President Franklin D. Roosevelt still resonate. 'The point of history at which we stand is full of promise and danger. The world will either move forward toward unity and widely shared prosperity—or it will move apart'. Some of those dangers lie in an unregulated maritime environment that becomes increasingly anarchic. Some of the potential benefits, for all mankind, come in finding ways of making the necessary regulation of that environment beneficial for all of those that depend on the sea for their livelihood and to deny its use to those who would perpetrate acts of evil. There are ways in which we can prevent an anarchic sea. It will take sustained collective willpower on the part of political leaders and communities the world over to ensure it happens.

Table 7.1: The Contribution from the Multi–Layered Architecture to the Seven Dimensions of Maritime Security

Dimension	*Immediate Littoral*	*Territorial Waters*	*EEZ*	*SLOC*
State-on-State	Final defence against invasion from a foreign power or a place to evacuate non-combatants from neighbouring states. Fast Patrol Boats, with guided missiles, to defeat any remnants of an amphibious landing force that has breached the outer layers of the defence architecture and protection of major assets by maritime-based TMD.	Guided missile boats and other maritime assets to defeat any remnants of an enemy force that has broken through the outer layers of the defence architecture. Also protection of key assets using TMD and minesweepers and evacuate non-combatants from neighbouring war zones should state citizens be threatened.	Major combat units, frigates, destroyers and other surface vessels, to deter or destroy any attempt by an adversary to gain access to the EEZ, such as to dispute claims over oil, gas and mineral reserves or to mine those assets to prevent or disrupt their use by the state.	Submarines and major surface combat units to intercept threats to the state's SLOC or EEZ from an adversary conducting blue water combat operations, including forming convoy's and conducting escort duties and evacuating non-combatants.
Trade Protection	Escorting and patrolling of constabulary forces in harbours and nearby to major	Aircraft and maritime forces to provide escorts through potentially disputed	Aircraft and maritime forces to escort vessels travelling through the EEZ that might be	Submarines and major combat units to intercept any threats to the state's SLOC from

	shore-based facilities working alongside VTMS and to deter acts of robbery and related criminal behaviour.	territorial waters or to address threats from piracy or mining operations conducted by a state or non-state adversary.	subject to attack by pirates or face a threat from mines.	an adversary including forming convoy's and conducting escort duties.
Resource Management	Patrolling of the area using inshore patrol boats to intercept illegal fishermen and interdict any threats to renewable and non-renewable energy sources and prosecute any illegal discharges of waste or oil into ecologically sensitive areas.	Patrolling of the area using fast patrol boats to intercept illegal fishermen and interdict any threats to renewable and non-renewable energy sources and prosecute any illegal discharges of waste or oil into ecologically sensitive areas.	Patrolling of the area using fast patrol boats to intercept illegal fishermen and interdict any threats to renewable and non-renewable energy sources and prosecute any illegal discharges of waste or oil into ecologically sensitive areas conducting VBSS procedures.	Not Applicable.
Smuggling	Patrolling using inshore patrol boats to respond to detections of vessels involved in smuggling people, weapons or	Patrolling using patrol boats that can stay at sea for a longer period, including night-time operations, coupled	Patrolling using OPV that can remain at sea for up to thirty days and cover large areas of the EEZ, working in	Manned and unmanned aircraft and surface units to patrol key SLOC and collect intelligence working

	narcotics and conduct VBSS procedures. These boats will typically be capable of operating at sea during the daylight hours. Little immediate role for aircraft, but helicopters can be used to board suspect vessels.	with manned and unmanned aircraft surveillance capabilities to detect and direct constabulary or Gendarmerie forces to intercept.	concert with airborne assets, to deter and disrupt smuggling by conducting VBSS procedures.	alongside submarine platforms that provide an early warning of potential threats and cues constabulary forces.
Terrorism	Patrolling using inshore patrol boats to interdict and deter any terrorist threat and conduct VBSS Procedures. These boats will typically be capable of operating at sea during the daylight hours. Little immediate role for aircraft, but helicopters can be used to board suspect vessels.	Patrolling using patrol boats that can stay at sea for a longer period, including night-time operations, coupled with manned and unmanned aircraft surveillance capabilities to detect and direct constabulary or Gendarmerie forces to intercept.	Patrolling using OPV that can remain at sea for up to thirty days and cover large areas of the EEZ, working in concert with airborne assets, to deter and disrupt terrorism by conducting VBSS procedures.	Manned and unmanned aircraft and surface units to patrol key SLOC and collect intelligence working alongside submarine platforms that provide an early warning to cue maritime response forces.

Disasters	Providing amphibious and major warship relief operations into a disaster area to help with logistics, projecting that capability inland into riverine areas that may be affected by flooding using amphibious craft and helicopters; also providing evacuation for any injured people.	Providing amphibious and major warship relief operations into a disaster area to help with logistics, standing off the coast and projecting supplies ashore using amphibious craft and helicopters. Conducting surveys post event to check any bathymetric changes.	Providing amphibious and major warship relief operations into a disaster area to help with logistics, standing off the coast and projecting supplies ashore using amphibious craft and helicopters. Conducting surveys post event to check any bathymetric changes.	Early warning of threats to SLOC, such as Tsunami alerts or bad weather conditions that might endanger vessels transiting the SLOC.
Oceanography	Monitoring red-tides and other threats to the environment, as a result of run-off from agricultural activities.	Conducting bathymetric surveys of territorial waters to ensure sand bands and other threats to navigation are clearly mapped and recorded.	Mapping extent of the EEZ using survey systems to provide evidence of extent of the Continental Shelf.	Support to submarine operations mapping salinity, thermal and related environmental parameters.

CASE STUDIES ON MARITIME SECURITY

Within this book, a number of case studies are presented in two Annexes to draw out a range of issues associated with creating a secure maritime environment. Each country that has been selected brings its own nuanced element to this with, for example, Canada having the largest coastline to protect, and the emerging threats arising from disputes over the potential natural resources of the Lomonosov Ridge. The case study on Mexico highlights the problems in countering drugs smuggling, and the study of Indonesian coastal waters highlights local problems of maintaining the integrity of the maritime environment when a country is geographically dispersed over a large area. The aim of these case studies is to produce a blended mix, whereby each offers their own unique perspectives to the field of maritime security from a truly global viewpoint. Overlaps and generic elements do appear and that is to be expected. The aim, however, is to try and develop a wider understanding of the spectrum of maritime security issues that face states managing coastlines, including, *inter alia*, constabulary duties and countering a range of what are generic threats from criminal and terrorist activities as well as the broader issues of state-on-state conflicts and disputes allied to energy security and the need to protect SLOC.

At the outset, it is valid to ask ourselves what we believe we mean by the term maritime security. It has many dimensions. It is possible to view maritime security through a somewhat narrow, parochial and topical lens that focuses upon piracy and the issues off the Horn of Africa. That would provide a contemporary viewpoint, but it would lack nuanced appreciation of a range of broader issues. Historically, some might argue that maritime security has to be seen in the context of the threat that arises from inter-state warfare. Despite the assertions of some commentators, it is unlikely that inter-state warfare has suddenly disappeared from the history of mankind. The much-heralded end of the Cold War should provide lessons for analysts making such claims. Threats change and what were seen to be low-level issues, in a globalised and connected world, suddenly become important.

Tensions over the sovereignty of EEZ, such as those that exist over the Spratley Islands, could well provide the source of a future maritime confrontation. Regional security in the Indian Ocean is a particular concern, as issues of how to build trust remain in the face of what appears to be an unrelenting build-up of naval forces by countries such as India and China. Climate change, and the implications for the environment, provide another dimension for maritime security that seeks to ensure that exploitation of the natural resources that are part of the marine environment are developed on a sustainable basis. Protecting the natural environment and harnessing it to develop the economy and tourism are an increasing concern. Eritrea provides an interesting set of perspectives on these challenges from the viewpoint of a developing country where challenges exist in infrastructure and capacity-building that aid environmental protection. This highlights the vital role of scientific analysis of the coastal environments to prominence in developing comprehensive approaches to maritime security. Development work in Australia and New Zealand provides an important model for considering the way scientific research plays into the broader maritime security considerations, such as marine biosecurity and its implications for the aquatic environment.

The challenges facing France, with its need to protect its own coastline from an influx of economic migrants and that of its extensive overseas territories, are also analysed and provide a different perspective. Brazil is also used as a case study, due to its emerging focus upon its continental shelf in the light of significant oil discoveries off the coast of Rio de Janeiro and to the north in the early part of the twenty-first century, catapulting Brazil into a new league as an international oil producer. A Chilean perspective offers insights into what is called the *Presencial Sea* and some wider reflections on the Search and Rescue (SAR) element of maritime security. The Australian case study analyses its plans for deploying new naval assets and looks to its role on the international stage and achieving a balanced approach to maritime security; it also highlights enduring concerns over economic migrants, now referred to as 'irregular migrants'. Concerns in the United States over the potential for a terrorist attack to be mounted from the sea, have led to its defence-in-depth approach based upon increasing international cooperation. The United Kingdom case study provides insights into multi-agency working and the issues when security gaps can occur when organisational frameworks and responsibilities are not clearly defined.

Lessons learnt from the use of the maritime domain by the Sea Tigers, provide insights that complement the specific case study on the attacks mounted from the sea in November 2008 against the Indian city of Mumbai; a source of some concern for countries such as Singapore, with its close proximity to Indonesia, and the threat from local Muslin extremists. Case studies of Guinea-Bissau, Eritrea, Kenya, Somalia and Angola offer contrasts with those of the so-called developed world and offer a particular focus upon criminal activities such as robbery, illegal bunkering, piracy and unauthorised exploitation of important fisheries. Indications of new developments by the pirates operating in the Gulf of Aden using swarming tactics, are noted alongside the extension of their activities into the Indian Ocean.

The case studies do not intend to convey the impression that the named countries are totally focused upon a specific facet of maritime security. There is plenty of evidence to suggest that each country is developing its own localised equivalent of a comprehensive approach given resource constraints, local situations and threats to maritime security. Generic themes, however, do emerge from the analysis concerning environmental protection, the impact of climate change, fisheries, pollution, tourism, exploitation of the resources of the continental shelf, countering terrorism and the threat posed by criminal behaviour, including smuggling of weapons, people and drugs and acts of piracy. The approach adopted by individual states and through regional and international cooperation determines, in the end, how secure their coastal waters can become as they develop ways of cooperating with each other to close the gaps exploited by criminals and terrorists and to deliver a secure maritime environment.

Clearly nothing will ever be perfect and gaps will remain that could be exploited by criminals and those seeking to use the maritime domain to launch terrorist attacks. Through promoting a wider understanding of the complex issues faced by many countries, the hope is that this book can make a contribution to the development of approaches that help states invest in ways that not only have a local impact but also contribute to bilateral and multilateral approaches to improving maritime security, as it is often not possible for one country to succeed alone. In the globalised world of the twenty-first century, such an approach, it is argued, is vital to address the threats faced by the global community at a time when the power of the United States is in decline, and its apparent hegemony in the maritime domain is likely to be challenged as other navies develop blue-water capabilities to protect their SLOC. With over 70 per cent of the world's population living on coastlines, concerns over developing comprehensive approaches to maritime security are an international issue that is enduring in its nature.

CASE STUDIES

National & Regional Case Studies	Comments	Book Reference
Angola: Maritime Threats to Economic Development	Angola is one of a number of countries in the Gulf of Guinea region that has potentially significant offshore natural resources that could deliver economic growth for its citizens.	A1
Australia: Local, Regional or International Player?	Australia has recently published its spending plans for its Navy and faces some interesting issues as a country that cooperates on a regional and international basis. However, it has no obvious immediate local threat until China starts to exert regional influence through the growth of its Navy.	A2
Brazil: Protection of its Continental Shelf	Brazil has some interesting challenges with maritime security, due to the recent oil and gas discoveries and the impending extension of its EEZ.	A3
Canada: Monitoring the World's Longest Coastline	Canada has the longest coastline in the world and faces the impact of melting ice around the Arctic, the opening up of the Northwest Passage (which will have potential pollution implications) and also	A4

	the dispute over the ownership of the Lomonosov Ridge.	
Chile: The Concept of the Presencial Sea	Chile was one of the world's pioneers in the development of the EEZ. Its latest thinking is defined in its definition of the Presencial Sea, which is an area over and above the EEZ in which a sovereign state has certain responsibilities.	A5
China: Protecting Sea Lanes of Communications	The development of the Chinese Navy as a blue-water fleet to protect its Sea Lanes of Communications and imports of oil from its international suppliers.	A6
Eritrea: Protecting the Natural Environment	Eritrea is placing a huge emphasis in its development for the protection of its natural environment along the Red Sea coastline. Its maritime security focus is very much on illegal fishing and ensuring that the tourism potential of its coastline is developed.	A7
France: Protecting Overseas Colonies	France has extensive overseas commitments with former colonies that need maritime security. A balance has to be struck between national protection of the Homeland and the protection of citizens in the former colonies.	A8
Guinea-Bissau: An Absence of Maritime Security	Drugs-smuggling across the Atlantic Ocean from countries such as Brazil—which is a point of departure of cocaine destined for Western Europe—into a failed state and the implications of no effective approach to maritime security.	A9
Indonesia: Maintaining Maritime Integrity	The world's second longest coastline and a large EEZ provide challenges for the government to stop illegal fishing in the area. Indonesia has also been suspicious of Australian intentions in the wake of its	A10

	intervention in East Timor and the Solomon Islands.	
Israel: Projecting Maritime Power Locally and Regionally	Israel's maritime security concerns blend with its overall security position as a sovereign state and the threats it faces. To counter these threats, it has moved upstream to disrupt and deter weapon-smuggling along its own coastline and, where the threat arises, on vessels bringing those weapons from countries such as Iran through staging countries such as the Sudan.	A11
Kenya: Countering Terrorism and Criminal Behaviour across an Extended EEZ	Kenya has just applied to the UN for a large extension to its EEZ. It is a country with a history of terrorist attacks and the presence of terrorist groups on its border with Somalia is a real concern. Protecting its sea lanes of communications bringing tourism vessels into Mombasa is also hugely important economically.	A12
Malacca Strait: Regional Cooperation against Piracy	Securing the marine environment through coordinated international action and the wider implications of maritime choke points, such as the other major oil choke points.	A13
The Maldives: Regional Cooperation	India is cooperating with the Maldives to extend its intelligence collection capabilities in the Indian Ocean, and also to protect the Maldives from piracy and India from indigenous terrorism developed in the Maldives.	A14
Mexico: Where Maritime Security and Criminality Clash	Review of the regional initiative with the United States and several Central American countries to counter drugs-smuggling.	A15

Norway: The Resurgent Threat from the North	The Russian Navy reborn, and the implications of that for Norwegian Coastal Security.	A16
Singapore: Upstream Intervention and Countering Terrorism	This case study looks at Singapore's need to develop a balanced approach to maritime security, which addresses the need to protect SLOC and also its own coastal environment from a potential repeat of a Mumbai-style attack.	A17
Somalia: Building an Indigenous Capability from Small Beginnings	Somalia is associated with piracy in the Gulf of Aden, but it is trying to develop its Coastguard capabilities using indigenous resources. This case study looks at this area and the recent trends in the evolving pattern of piracy attacks.	A18
Sri Lanka: An Insurgency Manoeuvring in the Maritime Domain	The Sea Tigers were the naval component of the Tamil Tigers and the Black Sea Tigers, the element they could use for asymmetric attacks against the Sri Lankan Navy. They also used the marine environment for resupply using merchant vessels.	A19
United Arab Emirates: International Cooperation	The UAE has little physical space in which to work and deter its adversaries. Its position in the Persian Gulf is precarious. The relationship it has forged with France therefore gives it strategic depth to go with its own indigenous capability to protect its waters.	A20
United Kingdom: Multi-Agency Cooperation	The approach to maritime security in the United Kingdom is based upon an intelligence-led approach. This has its weaknesses and therefore needs to be complemented by a multi-agency approach to harness all of the potential sources of insights into the maritime security environment into a coherent viewpoint.	A21

United States: Defence through Multilayered, International Cooperation	The United States has embarked upon a two-prong approach that strengthens its protection of its own coastal waters, whilst also moving upstream to disrupt and deter threats at their point of origin.	A22
Venezuela: Ideological Differences and Tactical Cooperation	Despite its ideological differences with the United States, the Venezuelan authorities still cooperate in the field of counter-narcotics. Disputes also exist with a number of Caribbean Sea Island States over the ownership of Aves Island.	A23

Thematic Case Studies	Comments	Book Reference
Economic Migrants	The maritime security implications (such as the burden on SAR) of the many flows of economic migrants in areas such as the Red Sea, Mediterranean Sea and through the Canary Islands to Spain and Europe.	B1
Arctic and Antarctic Ocean	Contrasting the peaceful research in the Antarctic with the clash over the Lomonosov Ridge in the Arctic Ocean.	B2
Clashes over Definitions of Continental Shelf Boundaries	The Spratley Islands and the disputes between Malaya, Vietnam, China, Taiwan and Indonesia over the boundaries of their continental shelves.	B3
Biosecurity: New Zealand's Aquaculture Industry	The issues for maritime security arising from potential infestations that can arise from the accidental introduction of alien species into an environment, and the impact of harmful algae blooms on aquacultur, with examples from New Zealand, Chile and Norway.	B4

Climate Change and Maritime Security	The wider dimensions of climate change and energy security and the implications for maritime security.	B5
Energy Security	Energy security and the impact on SLOC of increasingly diverse sources of the supply of oil and gas and the impact that will have on established patterns of trade.	B6
Proliferation Security Initiative (PSI)	The aims and objectives of the PSI and why this contributes to maritime security.	B7
Hans Island: Canada and Denmark in Dispute	Disputed ownership and mapping boundaries.	B8
Mumbai Terrorist Attack: A New Paradigm for Maritime Terrorism?	An analysis of the terrorist attacks on Mumbai, and its ramifications on the maritime security arena.	B9
Ballistic Missile Defence: South Korea and Japan	The deployment of a mobile ballistic missile shield in South Korea and Japan to counter the threat from North Korea; an extension of the concept of maritime security which applies in the Persian Gulf and Western Europe after the decision to abandon land-based BMD in Europe and replace it with a sea-based capability.	B10

A1: ANGOLA

MARITIME THREATS TO ECONOMIC DEVELOPMENT

The transportation by sea of the oil produced in our county, the main source of revenues, compels us into also guaranteeing the security of our maritime communications.

Chief of Staff of the Angolan Navy, 11 July 2008

Angola is a country emerging from years of war with a need to focus on economic development and to harness the potential of its offshore industries involved in oil exploration and exploitation, and fisheries. In 2008, its economy was the fastest growing in the world. Currently its ability to form a picture of activities along its 864 nm of coastline or within its 200 nm EEZ, which covers an area of 160,000 square miles (550,000 square kilometres), is limited and hence its offshore industry is very vulnerable to illegal fishing and potential attacks upon oil platforms. The offshore element of Angola accounts for 35 per cent of its total sovereign territory, but generates 95 per cent of the country's external trade. The collapse of the rich coastal fisheries in the area in the middle of the nineteenth century (when foreign fishing fleets seriously depleted the local hake stocks), which was a key source of food for the local population, has the potential to fuel discontent and create the conditions for them to take up piracy. There are similarities with the situation in some coastal regions of Angola to those that exist in Eritrea and Somalia that led to an increasingly organised approach to piracy. There is a danger of the displacement of criminal activities into Angola's coastal waters from countries to its north that currently enjoy the relative lack of maritime security, as the infrastructure of these others countries improves, and starts to deter piracy and smuggling. This aspect is one that represents a potential threat to the nascent and vitally important offshore industry.

Existing maritime domain awareness off the coastline of Angola is patchy and highly fragmented, with the density of coverage varying greatly along the coastline. Fixed and mobile S-band radar systems have been deployed to monitor territorial waters and some of these are also available on offshore platforms. Angolan Navy warships and those visiting from foreign countries to engage in bilateral training exercises do provide some intermediate coverage. Five Spanish-built patrol boats have been refurbished with assistance from North Korea and reentered service in April 2008. They took part in joint exercises with the British warship, HMS *Liverpool*, when it visited Angola in the early part of October 2008. In 2004, the United States Navy spent just ten ship days in the Gulf of Guinea; by 2007 this had increased to 365 ship-days. In other words, the United States Navy was providing a single vessel to the area to help increase maritime domain awareness and to help countries such as Angola develop their own indigenous approach to maritime security through joint training and other exchanges. The United States Navy plans to locate an amphibious ship in the Gulf of Guinea as part of its Global Fleet Station (GFS) initiative.

Angola has announced plans to invest in new naval vessels as part of developing a more responsive naval capability. If these plans reach maturity, they would see the addition of a frigate and a number of new offshore patrol vessels to the fleet, which would be based along the coastline at Luanda, Lobito and Namibe. The addition of the frigate to its fleet would provide a powerful boost that could contribute to regional maritime security developments, which are important, given the increasing overall potential of the Gulf of Guinea as a source of oil, and ongoing concerns about the problems with piracy and criminality off the coastline of Nigeria.

Angola also participates in a number of regional initiatives and data/information exchange programmes designed to deter various forms of criminality and pollution within its coastal waters and those of its neighbours. The government of Angola has signed an agreement with Nigeria, Ghana and South Africa concerning joint naval patrols and the right of hot-pursuit into the coastal waters of neighbouring countries. Joint working has also occurred with the Namibian Navy, with Angolan Navy staff embedded upon Namibian Fisheries patrol vessels. The United States is promoting the idea of regional access to the Maritime Safety and Security Information System (MSSIS) to allow countries in the Gulf of Guinea to access information that covers a worldwide source of material on shipping movements. It would initially be implemented as MSSIS Africa to serve the needs of countries in and around the Gulf of Guinea. Its potential for being extended to others parts of Africa, such as the west coast, to serve the needs of countries such as Kenya and Tanzania, is clear.

Closer integration between the operation of the Navy and the fisheries monitoring organisation within the Angolan government will also arise from the formation of the Maritime Control Unit (MCU) and the associated investment in six Maritime Control Stations. As part of its work through the APS Initiative, the US government has offered the Angolan government a copy of the Regional Maritime Awareness Capability (RMAC) system that has already been successfully installed by Sao Tome. To complete a comprehensive system of coastal monitoring radars would require an additional twenty-four systems to be deployed in order to fully cover Angola's immediate territorial waters, at an estimated cost of $5 million. However, even this capability would have its limitations, as detection ranges for vessels from shore-based radar systems can be reduced significantly depending upon weather conditions. Where oil exploration platforms exist, it would further improve maritime domain awareness if the radar systems on the platforms could be networked into an overall, integrated architecture.

Severe limitations arising from the current poor state of the country's telecommunications infrastructure hamper establishing the form of networks required to link information derived from sensor systems into a central or regional data fusion centre that would be the hub for real-time and analysed maritime information. The launch of ANGOSAT, the first dedicated satellite to serve the needs of Angola, will provide a huge uplift in capability and provide the backbone communications facilities upon which networked solutions can be developed.

A2: AUSTRALIA

LOCAL, REGIONAL OR INTERNATIONAL PLAYER?

Australia could be regarded as being at a crossroads in its development as a state. A reliable partner on the international stage, it is placing its combat troops in the front-line in Iraq and Afghanistan and contributing naval assets in key areas around the world, such as Somalia, and also maintaining a peacekeeping presence in East Timor. It is playing on the regional and international stage and can be said to be punching above its weight militarily; a point illustrated by the deployment of the HMAS *Toowoomba* on 11 September 2009 to join the combined task force operating in the Gulf of Aden.

But dangers also lie closer to home, and from a maritime security viewpoint, a balance has to be maintained between international and regional aspirations and the need to protect the homeland. Times, however, are changing and the historical concerns of the boat people from Vietnam, and the uncertainty over the development of China felt in Australia in the wake of the Korean War, with the potential spread of Communism through insurgencies in Malaya and Indonesia, have passed.

The regional and international dimensions that were so apparent in the middle of the twentieth century have merged seamlessly into a global set of concerns at the start of the twenty-first century. In this globalised world, there are so many interacting agents—such as the emergent nexus between transnational criminality and terrorism—that to try and be isolationist in policy development, as President Bush discovered on 11 September 2001, is fraught with difficulties. Being proactive in contrast to being reactive, appears to be de rigueur, and the challenges faced by Australia in developing a coordinated approach to maritime security do have some echoes in the issues facing the United States—long coastlines, surrounded by large areas of different seas, to name two areas where obvious parallels exist.

Moving upstream towards the threat and trying to disrupt potential adversaries at source is one thing but leaving the back door unguarded is a very different matter, especially with the ever-present issue of China and the potential for Australia to be drawn into a confrontation over Taiwan. Through its overseas military contributions, Australia has played a really important role on the international stage and gained plaudits for the professionalism of its armed forces. However, the changing international landscape continues to pose challenges and the direction in which it is heading complicates planning. The contrasts with the relative certainty of the Cold War have perhaps never been more apparent, and Australia faces some of these challenges acutely, given its geostrategic situation.

With China's seeming relentless drive for economic expansion and its need for oil, the Chinese Navy is being given a blue-water capability to ensure that vital SLOC can be protected from disruption or harassment. It is not difficult to think of how, in a situation of rising tension between China and Taiwan, the United States Navy may seek to restrict the supply of oil to China in the form of an economic blockade that actually imposes restrictions at their sources in Venezuela and at various locations in Africa. That developing blue-water capability of the Chinese Navy is clearly a potential threat to Australia in coming years and something that is influencing contemporary Australian defence planning. It is also, perhaps, a factor in the recent decision to increase the submarine and Anti-Submarine Warfare (ASW) capability of the Australian Navy.

This potential was seemingly tactically acknowledged in the framing of the *Australian Defence White Paper*, which was published in 2009. It outlines ambitious targets for the development of an extended submarine force; a new class of future frigates aimed at increasing the ASW capability; Air Warfare Destroyers with an inventory of cruise missiles that can project military power over the horizon; helicopter and amphibious assault force carriers; and twenty offshore combatant vessels that provide a balanced naval force that can act independently and, should the need arise, lead military coalitions. There are obvious echoes of the military intervention to stabilise East Timor still ringing in the minds of those who shaped the document. The Royal Australian Navy is clearly the main benefactor of the new focus on defence operations which has provided an insightful view of a multipolar world in which the traditional hegemony of the United States Navy will be challenged. The result will be that nation states with long coastlines, such as Australia, would require to be capable of unilateral deployments of forces to meet any threats to the national interest.

Australia has a specific number of problems with its national maritime security, given its location, and the sheer scale of its coastline. The threats of piracy being displaced from the Malacca Strait as a result of successful regional cooperation in the area, the importation of drugs, and the ever-present concerns over international terrorism—highlighted by the attacks in Bali—are all of concern and shape thinking about maritime security in an Australian context. A new wave of boat people are also creating problems, with over twenty-five boats reported to have arrived in Australia this year, exceeding the combined total for the last seven years. With arrests also being made by the Malayan authorities of people preparing to travel to Australia, and also the Indonesian authorities intercepting boats laden with refugees, arrivals of economic migrants reduced from 86 in 1999, to 51 in 2000 and 43 in 2001.

Estimates vary greatly about the actual length of the Australian coastline from 25,760 km to figures exceeding 40,000 km. Of course, it all depends on where you take the measurements and how many islands you add into the calculation. Leaving that debate to one side, the key point is that Australia does have a lengthy coastline that faces many varied challenges, from the loss of natural corals off the coast of the Great Barrier Reef and the economic impact that has on tourism, to the worries over the rise of Chinese naval power and the implications of that for any ambitions China has to establish hegemony over South East Asia. Monitoring this vast area is a major headache. It requires some imaginative solutions combining a range of sensors and platforms, such as the use of High Frequency (HF) search radars that are a focus of the Integrated Marine Observing System (IMOS) programme; they monitor the marine environment and also contribute to a broader scientific understanding of the oceans,. Another element of the Australian maritime security architecture will be eight P8—a maritime patrol aircraft equipped with surface search radar, optical and electronic surveillance systems and an ASW capability. These will operate alongside seven HALE unmanned vehicles and provide the ability to monitor key areas of the coastal waters and

EEZ of Australia directing the Offshore Combatant Vessels to specific areas of concern. The combination of military surveillance activities and the analysis arising from the scientific research being carried out through IMOS provide Australia with a comprehensive and nationally relevant approach to its maritime security needs.

A3: BRAZIL

PROTECTION OF ITS CONTINENTAL SHELF

The dimensions of Brazil—simultaneously continental and maritime; equatorial, tropical and subtropical; sharing extensive land borders with almost all the countries in South America, as well as lengthy coasts; an exclusive economic zone and a continental shelf—endow the Nation with a geostrategic depth and complicates the task of overall defence planning. Brazil's broad demographic and territorial characteristics, as well as the availability of natural resources, set firmly upon its diversified physical geography, generates a variety of scenarios that call for a comprehensive and integrated policy, along with a specific approach for each instance.

Extract from the Brazilian Defence Policy published 1998.

The extract from the Brazilian Defence Policy published in 1998 provides an insight into the geostrategic nature of the position of Brazil and the factors that it has to consider when formulating a defence policy. The coastal waters of Brazil comprise an area of 3,660,995 km^2 and are 7,400 km in length. In 2004, the Brazilian government applied to the United Nations to have the outer boundary of this area extended by adding a further 911,847 km^2 to the area it already claims under Article 76 of UNCLOS. Significant oil discoveries reported 300 km off the coastline of Rio de Janeiro in the Tupi and Jupiter oil fields have made the Brazilian government undertake a major review of its defence policy; the President announced a new version in 2008. These oil discoveries build upon established offshore oil reserves and place Brazil as the eighth largest producer of oil at the end of the first decade of the twenty-first century. The potential for Brazil to rise up in the world rankings, in light of the new finds announced in 2008, is apparent.

The Brazilian situation provides an interesting case study of a country that is rebalancing its focus between the riverine dimension and the coastal aspects of maritime security, as offshore oil exploration has the potential to have a major impact on the growth of the Brazilian economy. After many years of little to no investment in its Navy, the Brazilian government has decided to develop a programme to modernise the navy and to change its focus from being primarily a force dealing with internal security matters to one that can protect the SLOC of Brazil, vital for oil exports, and its expanded EEZ, if this is approved by the United Nations. The Brazilian Navy is also developing close ties with the United States Navy, which has just reformed its Fourth Fleet, which has a focus on the Southern Atlantic Ocean.

In the absence of a clearly defined contemporary threat to the coastal waters of Brazil, the Brazilian government has tended to focus its maritime security efforts on the riverine environment in Brazil, which has over 50,000 km of navigable waterways that provide routes that can be exploited by criminals. The Brazilian Navy is organised into eight naval districts. Its primary concerns have always been criminal activities that exploit the extensive river network to smuggle drugs and conduct illegal logging of the rain forest. Patrolling in the western Amazon region has been a particular focus for the Navy in the area of the Columbian border. A combined force of rapid reaction launches, manned by marines, operates in the area to deter drug smuggling which uses the lengthy coastline of Brazil as a point of departure for cocaine being moved to unstable Sub-Saharan African countries on the eastern coastline of Africa, such as Guinea-Bissau. These patrols also act as a deterrent to guerrilla incursions into Brazil. In October 2008, in a combined service military operation, air force, army and naval units were deployed into the so-called tri-border region where Brazil shares a border with Paraguay and Argentina. This area is known for its long-standing links with international terrorism and involvement in serious crime.

Brazil does retain the ability to project naval force though a blue-water capability, based upon a single aircraft carrier, some submarines and a number of frigates. Brazil has participated in the Organisation of American States (OAS) activities in Haiti, providing marines to help in peacekeeping operations. Minesweeping and inshore patrol vessels add further flexibility into the configuration of the fleet and a number of 1,800-tonne Offshore Patrol Vessels (OPV) are proposed to provide additional capability to patrol the extended EEZ. These vessels will have an operating speed of 20 knots and will be able to patrol up to 6,000 nm at 12 knots and stay at sea for up to twenty days in a sea state six. The Brazilian Navy also plans to introduce an additional twenty-seven 54-metre *Navio Patrulha* patrol ships as part of a modernisation plan that sees the establishment of a Second Fleet that will operate on or near the Amazon River and be procured under the Equipment and Coordination Plan which provides the basis of the new Fleet Renewal plan. Three OPV will be purchased initially and an option will exist on a further two.

A4: CANADA

MONITORING THE WORLD'S LONGEST COASTLINE

Looking back, it is clear that the peace dividend that resulted from the end of the Cold War was relatively short lived.

Canada First Defence Strategy, 2008

Canada has a huge coastal region with an associated EEZ of approximately 2.9 million km^2. Fluctuations in the level of sea ice, with the impact of climate change, are opening up the potential for new sea passages to be used through or close to Canada's EEZ for a number of months of the year. Initially this window might be limited to a few months of the year, but if the rate of retreat of permanent sea ice continues, then estimates show that within a matter of one to two decades, the period when the seas are clear of ice will extend. The potential for vessels to save significant journey times by using the northern routes through Canada's EEZ will be too tempting. Increases in the amount of commercial cargos moved by this route are therefore likely to be significant.

Policing and monitoring those areas will pose a challenge to the Canadian authorities, and in recognition of this, the Canadian government announced some significant investments in its maritime capabilities and ability to project maritime units into these areas were made in July 2007. However, policing the current extent of the Canadian EEZ is only part of the story. The Canadian Government is eyeing a significant extension in its EEZ to give it access to what are believed to be large oil, gas and related natural resources in the Arctic Ocean. The Canadian authorities have until 2013 to submit detailed evidence concerning their claim to extend this area by another 1.5 million km^2 under the provisions of the UNCLOS. The focus of the extended claim is the disputed waters of the Arctic Ocean, where competing submissions concerning the extent of the natural subterranean feature called the Lomonosov Ridge, are the subject of some debate between Norway, Denmark, the United States, Canada and Russia (see the specific Case Study on the Lomonosov Ridge).

Monitoring this huge area of its EEZ, and any potential extension, is not an easy task. The current configuration of the Canadian Navy (referred to as Canadian Forces Maritime Command [MARCOM] is not appropriate for this task. Vessels in its inventory are not suited to maintaining time on station in what are likely to be quite challenging waters. In the Cold War, the Canadian government left the protection of the Arctic Ocean to its allies and did not commit any serious resources to patrolling and establishing a presence in the area. As a direct result of this approach, the current Canadian Navy Frigates, the twelve Halifax-class vessels, and the fleet of Kingston-class maritime coastal defence vessels, are not suited to working in the Arctic Ocean with its challenging environmental operating conditions.

Historically, Canada has had a focus on the North Atlantic and anti-submarine warfare. This was a legacy of the Second World War when the Canadian Navy ended the war as the third-largest navy in the world and controlled the northwest sector of the Atlantic Ocean. This ability to dominate an area of the ocean and to provide safe passage through it for convoys was also an enduring aspect of the Canadian Navy's contribution to the Cold War. The threat posed by Soviet submarines in the Cold War was reminiscent of the U-Boats.

In the twentieth century, Canada's perception of maritime security can be seen through the rather narrow lens of its contribution to NATO and the threat from Soviet submarines operating in and around its coastal waters. At the start of the twenty-first century, that policy stance needed to be reappraised in light of continuing developments in the world economy and Canada's desire to participate fully in international peacekeeping and humanitarian relief operations, such as the supply of food aid to Somalia. That situation has not changed significantly.

The approach being taken by the Canadian government to maritime security at the start of the second millennium is outlined in the Defence Strategy, *Canada First*, published on 12 May 2008. In this document the Canadian government places a new emphasis on security in its own immediate EEZ. The collective impact of climate change and the increasing access to previously difficult-to-exploit resources has changed the situation in the Arctic Sea area. The clue to the new focus of Canada's defence strategy is in the title. Defence of the Homeland is paramount. In July 2007, the Canadian Prime Minister announced that the country would procure between six to eight Polar-class Arctic/Offshore Patrol Vessels (A/OPV), investing an estimated $3 billion in the project. Initially the incoming government had been planning to purchase three new icebreakers, but once they entered office they were persuaded to change their minds and purchase A/OPV. In addition to this, the Canadian government has also decided to invest in a number of other related infrastructure developments, including the development of a new deep water civil/military port near Iqaluit on Baffin Island, purchasing unmanned aircraft and modernising the ten Aurora maritime patrol aircraft to keep them in service until 2020.

However, despite this investment, protecting and monitoring such a large sea area is challenging. The role of the Canadian Navy will cover diplomatic, constabulary and military missions. In recognition of this increasingly national focus for maritime security, Canada has embarked upon the development of satellite-based surveillance of its territorial waters based upon its own indigenous satellite surveillance system, Radarsat. This programme provides a low Earth-orbiting satellite that provides, using its radar sensor system, an ability to scan the oceans for vessels; plot the extent and thickness of sea ice; and detect oil spills and other environmental phenomena. The project has a specific emphasis upon supporting Canada's military forces in responding to threats to its EEZ.

The second satellite in the series was launched in mid-December 2007. As part of the *Polar Epsilon* project, two new satellite ground stations are to be established to help monitor activities in the Arctic Ocean. These will be in place and operational towards the end of 2010, and are located at Aldergrove in British Columbia and Masstown in Nova Scotia. The aim of *Polar Epsilon* is to provide continuous coverage over Canada's Arctic and ocean approaches. The information derived from the ground stations will provide important short and medium-term assessments of where activity is occurring in Canada's coastal waters, and help cue and direct airborne and water-borne assets into areas thought most likely to be at risk. This is all part of a comprehensive strategy that uses satellites to deliver maritime security, in its broadest sense, to the marine waters of Canada and to monitor increases in maritime activity arising from ecotourism, fishing vessels, transpolar shipping, and research and survey vessels charting the waters and exploring for natural resources. In order for Canada to have a comprehensive approach to maritime security, it will need to use its new assets to monitor these activities.

A5: CHILE

THE CONCEPT OF THE PRESENCIAL SEA

Chile has developed the concept of the Presencial Sea and incorporated it in national legislation. The idea is to be attentive to, observe, and be part of the activities that take place on the high seas, to be prepared to defend against any threats that may come from the common space, without weakening the UNCLOS or affecting the freedom that governs common areas.

Rear Admiral Federico Niemann Figari, Chilean Navy
(Published in the Newport Papers, no. 31, 2008)

Geographically, Chile is one of the most interesting countries in the world. The total area of its maritime zones is larger than its landmass. Its coastline is 4,200 km in length and its EEZ covers an area of 4.5 million km^2 including Easter Island, the *Archipiélago Juan Fernández*, and the *Islas de los Desventurados* in the South Eastern Pacific Ocean. Chile has always been in the vanguard of innovative developments in the definition of the jurisdiction of coastal states. In 1947, its unilateral definition of a 200 nm fisher/whaling zone created the foundation for the definition of the EEZ that was encapsulated in the 1982 Law of the Sea Convention. At the start of the twenty-first century, Chile is promoting the idea of the 'Presencial Sea', a controversial concept that gives coastal states special interests in the high seas adjacent to the EEZ, with associated rights to take unilateral actions in respect of enforcing those interests. In 1991, Chile codified the concept of the 'Presencial Sea' into national law and still promotes its thinking on the international stage.

The concept envisages an area that forms a triangle that covers the north and south of Chile, taking in its Antarctic bases out to its western extent on Easter Island, a total area of 26,476,005 km^2. This represents an area that is significantly larger than the internationally defined EEZ and is an area where the Chilean government has stated that it has national responsibilities and commitments, such as providing SAR services. This represents an area that is 500 per cent of the internationally agreed EEZ in which Chile specifically wishes to counter the environmental depredation though illegal fishing. It also seeks to develop a more detailed understanding of the unique oceanographic aspects of the area related to the Humboldt Current and its rich fisheries, which produces one of the most productive marine ecosystems in the world. This is of huge economic benefit to Chile, positioning it consistently amongst the top ten producers of fish and fish-related products in the world.

Chile's long-term motivations for this radical new approach to defining the legal jurisdiction of the sea remain vague but have, at their heart, a real concern for marine ecosystems and the need to develop them upon a sustainable basis, given the importance of fishing to the economy. Despite historical tensions that have arisen from past conflicts, there are now no obvious existing threats to the sovereignty of Chile's EEZ, although claims by the United Kingdom to extend its jurisdiction over their Antarctic Territories may create difficulties in the future. The confrontation with Argentina over the ownership of the Picton, Lennox and Nueva Islands off the southern edge of Tierra del Fuego was resolved by Papal mediation and resulted in the signing of the Treaty of Peace and Friendship in 1984. The enduring legacy of the War of the Pacific, which left Bolivia as a land-locked country, still creates difficulties, and negotiations are exploring how Bolivia might be granted some form of administrative status over a port on the Chilean coast. The depth of feeling over this matter spilled over in Bolivia in 2003 during the natural gas riots.

The War of the Pacific also left a legacy in terms of the relationship with Peru, and localised disputes over fisheries boundaries still remain. Relations between Chile and Peru deteriorated after the Congress in Peru voted to take action to reclaim 38,000 km^2 of maritime territory in November 2005. Chile's retort to this has been based on their view that such matters were resolved in the 1929 Treaty and further confirmed in the 1954 agreement on fishing. In April 2007, Peru took its case to the United Nations and The Hague and formally filed a lawsuit in January 2008. This dispute rumbles on with Chile claiming that Peruvian actions threaten the national sovereignty of Chile.

Chile is a country that depends upon trade. It has been very active in the last two decades, signing trade agreements with a variety of organisations across the world. With 80 per cent of Chile's trade travelling by sea, the protection of the SLOC is clearly an important strategic consideration for the country. Its approach to maritime security is defined in a paper called 'The Three Vectors Strategy'. The three vectors are: The Defence Vector, which covers the defence of the country's sovereignty and maritime interests, ports, coastal zone, EEZ and SLOC, including the southern region and its Antarctic bases, and associated island territories out to Easter Island in the Pacific Ocean; the *International Vector*, through which the Chilean Navy contributes to the maintenance of world order; and the Maritime Vector, which covers Chile's extensive maritime areas.

In 2008, in responding to this strategy, the Chilean Navy will complete a major reconfiguration of its inventory. As part of this process, it will bring into service eight frigates that it has procured from the Royal Netherlands Navy and Royal Navy, alongside two Scorpene submarines. In addition, new maritime patrol craft will enter service alongside a new indigenously developed OPV, of which four will be based in the four major regions into which the Chilean Navy is divided. The OPV will be capable of extended operations at sea over thirty days, over ranges out to 8,600 km, and are equipped with a medium-calibre gun. With planned purchases of eleven Defender-class boats and nineteen Archangel-class patrol boats to provide an inshore capability, the Chilean Navy is developing its own comprehensive approach to delivering maritime security in its coastal waters, which will be based upon an inventory that can project maritime power across the full extent of the *Presencial Sea*.

A6: CHINA

PROTECTING SEA LANES OF COMMUNICATIONS

China's approach to maritime security is being shaped by its need to project naval power on the high seas, in order to ensure that its SLOC remains open during periods of tension or in the event that confrontation turns into conflict. Few commentators doubt China's ability to protect its immediate coastal waters and that any immediate threat to the mainland exists from an outside naval intervention. The long-term issues over Taiwan remain a concern, but are not an immediate source of a threat to the Chinese mainland. An attempt by China to seize or restrict the movement of trade to Taiwan would provoke a potential flash point with the United States Navy and is thought unlikely. However, in the field of international politics, history proves that it is unwise to imply that events might not conspire to create tensions that might lead to confrontations. Whilst many commentators reflect on the potential for 'water-wars' to become a growing part of the international landscape in the twenty-first century, the potential for conflict arising from disputes concerning energy security may be equally likely.

Since the late 1980s, China has embarked upon a major modernisation programme for its Navy, giving it increased status and profile on the world's stage. Its involvement as part of the international task force operating off the Horn of Africa is giving the Chinese Navy valuable experience in developing tactics to protect its SLOC.

This modernisation of the PLAN coincided with the country's shift from being self-sustaining in oil production to becoming a net importer in 1993. In 2004, China imported 100 million tonnes of oil, an increase of 35 per cent on the previous year. Imports are forecast to amount to 65 per cent of the country's oil consumption in 2020, as domestic production slows from its peak of around 200 million tonnes in 2015, as China uses up its estimated 16 billion barrels of reserves. China's rapid economic growth and its significant population create an ever-growing demand for energy, and China has embarked upon a long-term plan to guarantee its energy supplies. China consumed an average of 8 million barrels per day of oil in 2007, and 95 per cent of that travels through the Malacca Strait and 2 per cent through the Straits of Lombok. China is clearly concerned about the movement of such large quantities of oil though the Indian Ocean and through the Malacca Strait, and has embarked upon a series of diplomatic initiatives aimed at securing a strategic position for itself across the Indian Ocean, reaching out to countries such as Sri Lanka, Mauritius, Bangladesh, Myanmar and Pakistan in what is referred to as its 'string of pearls' initiative.

To address the continued demand for energy, China is forging global links with countries in South America, Africa and the Middle East as part of its approach to energy security. Countries such as Angola, Equatorial Guinea and the Sudan have become important sources of oil, counterbalancing the Chinese reliance upon the Middle East and supplies from the Caspian Sea. In the intermediate period, China will eye closer links with Brazil as it develops its offshore oil production capacity and China seeks to diversify its sources. In order for these links to be meaningful, the Chinese Navy must be capable of projecting power into areas where it can guarantee the freedom of the seas for vessels bringing raw material to China. Its deployment of a naval task force into the Indian Ocean and the Gulf of Aden to protect its sea lanes of communication with the Persian Gulf, upon which it is quite reliant, demonstrates the Chinese leadership's intent in this regard. It will use its Navy to protect its sea lanes of communications.

Its interests and claims over the South China Sea—with its proven reserves of 7.7 billion barrels of oil and an estimated total of 28 billion barrels—have, however, similar hallmarks to Russians attempts to claim the Lomonosov Ridge, such as planting a flag on the seabed using a mini-submarine. A clash of naval forces arising from some pre-emptive move with respect to the Spratley or Paracel Islands may be a more realistic scenario, as Taiwan and China both lay claim to vast tracts of the South China Sea. To meet the expectation of future economic growth, energy security must be at the forefront of China's strategic thinking with respect to its perspectives on maritime security. Its Navy must be capable of providing a deterrent to any pre-emptive move on the Spratley Islands or any of the areas to which it lays claim in the South China Sea, which extend to the 200 nm EEZ of the Philippines, Brunei, just south of the Natuna Archipelago (part of Indonesia) and up along the Vietnamese coast encompassing the area from the Paracel Islands to the Gulf of Tonkin, an area of 2.4 million km^2 out of the total area of the South China Sea of 3.5 million km^2. This area is also environmentally significant, as it is believed to hold one third of the world's marine biodiversity.

The Chinese clearly fear the intervention of the United States Navy, through its carrier-groups, in the type of situation that may decisively turn the confrontation in favour of the Taiwanese. The Chinese have conducted a great deal of research looking at the vulnerabilities of such naval battle groups. Lessons that the United States Navy has learnt from its own training and simulation exercises, which have focused upon the implications of operations in the Persian Gulf against an agile adversary employing asymmetric tactics, will not have gone unnoticed in Beijing. In the short-to-medium term, the Chinese Navy has a variety of ways of trying to negate the power of the United States Navy using asymmetric approaches to maritime warfare. The emphasis of the current naval doctrine in China is upon the development of what has been referred to as an *anti-access force*. This is based upon the idea that Chinese naval power can restrict the manoeuvre room of any United States Navy deployment designed to deter a Chinese intervention on Taiwan; this is achieved by delaying its arrival in the area through the projection of submarines, and restricting its operations in and around Taiwan with a combination of land and surface-based missile threats. This is, however, a typically short-term goal to use maritime power to defend its interests should the need arise. The developments of the new Chinese submarine base near Sanya, Hainan is a cause for concern as it is believed that up to twenty nuclear submarines could be based in the facility which is strategically located to enable power to be projected into the Indian and Pacific Oceans.

The Chinese leadership have been making their medium-term objectives for naval development clear through a number of announcements citing the intent to develop at least one, perhaps several, carrier battle groups of their own. Chinese links with Myanmar and the potential for the forward basing of vessels onto the edge of the Indian Ocean, avoiding the potential strictures of the Malacca Strait in a time of heightened tensions, also reflect some careful long-term planning. The developments of the Chinese Navy reflect a clear determination by the Chinese leadership to both establish China as a superpower, which would reflect its economic status, and also be capable of projecting maritime naval power in places of its choosing in defence of its national interests. At the heart of this strategy is the need to provide a secure maritime environment for vital internationally linked SLOC. The development of the PLAN as a blue-water navy will take time and require the deployment of a carrier-based capability to project maritime power beyond the reach of shore-based aviation support.

A7: ERITREA

PROTECTING THE NATURAL ENVIRONMENT

Eritrea has a coastline that is largely untouched by human hands, with little development marring the natural landscape. The coastline is made up of two elements. The first is the 1,151 km along the Red Sea; human occupation of this coastline is sparse and the natural environment provides an important sanctuary for wildlife and an area rich in biodiversity. The second element is the archipelago of Dahlak, which comprises over 350 islands and provides another 1,083 km of coastline, which provides a habitat for over 1,000 species of fish and 220 species of corals. Both areas have huge potential for the development of tourism, which would earn important foreign currency for a country that seeks to develop its economy on a sustainable basis.

As part of developing its Maritime Domain Awareness (MDA), the Eritrean government has invested in creating the *Reference Book*. This is a document that contains analysis of the coastal regions of Eritrea and records demographics of the local population, estimates of the catch landed by artisanal fishermen, scientific assessments of the fish stocks in the region, and related information. This single document provides the basis for the development of a maritime strategy for Eritrea and is an important step.

As part of this strategy, and in the absence of an immediate perceived threat to the maritime waters of Eritrea, the government has given the coastal area of the country 'protected area' status, defining a 100-metre area in which development must be undertaken on a sustainable basis. The Eritrean Navy provides maritime security in this area. Their task is to patrol the coastal waters and ensure that activities conducted within the marine environment are compliant with the government's policy of sustainable development. In the wake of the attack on Mumbai and the desire of international terrorist organisations to attack so-called soft targets—such as the Luxor attack on tourists in Egypt on 17 November 1997 in which over sixty tourists died, and in Bali where over 200 people died in an attack in 2002—any development of tourism by the Eritrean government must be matched by an emphasis upon securing the maritime domain against incursions launched from nearby known terrorist havens such as the Yemen. As the Indians have learnt from the analysis of what happened in Mumbai, this is not an easy task and requires a multi-agency response.

The task of deterring foreign fishing fleets, and a migration of piracy north from the coastline of Somalia, are obvious immediate concerns. The potential for the piracy currently plaguing Somalia to spread north to the coastline of Eritrea is very real. The Somalian piracy has resulted, in part, from foreign fishing vessels plundering the natural fish reserves off the coast of Somalia. Local fishermen initially took people captive to try and deter this activity and found out that they could earn significant sums of money through hijacking fishing vessels and holding the crews to ransom. Extending this to larger vessels became a natural evolution of their activities. With Eritrean waters having largely untapped reserves of fish, the maximum sustainable yield is reported at between 50,000 and 70,000 metric tonnes. As the catch in 2008 was 13,000 metric tonnes, the temptation for unlicensed fishing to occur is clear. Patrolling to ensure that this does not occur is the responsibility of the Eritrean Navy, as part of its wider responsibilities to deliver maritime security.

Today, the Eritrean Navy is partly configured to undertake those tasks. It does, however, have a legacy from its inception at the end of the war of separation with Ethiopia. Disputes over the Hanish Islands and the boundary with Djibouti over the *Ile Doumeira* have required the Eritrean Navy to retain an amphibious landing capability. Resolution of these disputes would allow the Navy to focus upon its primary role of protecting the coastline of the country and allow the development of an indigenous maritime capability, whereby small patrol craft could be built and assembled in Eritrea and provide the country with the capacity to patrol its coastline. Ranging beyond its traditional patrol areas, close to the important ports of Massawa and Asseb, has required harbours and related infrastructure to be built along the coastline. The vessels used by the Eritrean

Navy are not all able to spend several days at sea and therefore patrolling the coastline comprehensively requires access to stopover facilities where vessels can be replenished.

Investment in basic infrastructure, monitoring the environment, the development of indigenous capabilities to built patrol craft and the donation or procurement of vessels that can be on station for several days and cover wider areas, seem likely to form four elements of an overall strategy that will see the Eritrean Navy develop its capacity to patrol its territorial waters in a targeted way, using the material from the *Reference Book* to guide its patrolling patterns and deliver a secure marine environment in which the planned development of economies in the local areas can be successful.

A8: FRANCE

PROTECTING OVERSEAS COLONIES

Knowledge and anticipation represent a new strategic function and have become a priority. In a world characterised by uncertainty and instability, knowledge represents our first line of defence. Knowledge guarantees our autonomy in decision-making and enables France to preserve its strategic initiative.

The French White Paper on Defence and National Security

In an uncertain world where the bipolar nature of superpower politics has been replaced by a series of multipolar complex threats that can emerge with surprising agility, it is understandable that the French government, with their global commitments towards their former colonies, seeks an advantage in knowledge or 'environmental scanning'. Being proactive, in contrast to reactive, clearly provides some strategic leverage in a world where decisions often have to be taken quickly in the eye of the media and its resulting public pressure. President Sarkozy telegraphed major changes in the security policy of France in the White Paper on Defence and National Security published on 17 June 2008. The emphasis in the new defence and national security policy is to be on intelligence and counterterrorism. Citing the potential for a terrorist attack, the President decisively moved French defence and national security policy away from the vision established by President de Gaulle as part of what has become known as the *politique du grandeur*, when he developed an approach based upon France having a strong presence on the foreign stage and an independent foreign policy that allowed France to play a major international role.

The vision of the White Paper is based upon the orientation of the French defence forces towards bilateral and multilateral cooperation. France is now back within the NATO decision-making framework and has focused its efforts in the Indian Ocean, opening a new naval base in the United Arab Emirates. In commenting on this President Sarkozy made it clear that as far as he was concerned, the White Paper represented a *reorientation* rather than a curbing of French ambition. France retains the right and will to intervene if it sees its interests threatened. This was clearly a political statement made to address fears from Gaullists who fear a lack of freedom of manoeuvre, with France reintegrated within the framework of NATO, and its domination by the United States. That said, the election of President Obama has made this change more palatable for many who might otherwise have raised concerns.

In keeping with the emphasis on environmental scanning and being proactive in anticipating threats, the 'French Navy Information File' of 2009 outlined the missions, forces, stages to prepare for the future, and the environment in which French forces will be recruited, trained and operate. Prevention is defined as 'exerting a watchful presence to collect intelligence on potential crisis, to assess the situation and to deal with nascent crisis as early as possible'. This is the hallmark of a proactive approach. Leaving things to being reactive, when terrorist threats can be so varied and unpredictable, is not, in the view of the White Paper, sensible. To deliver maritime security for the homeland of France, certain naval units are prepositioned in locations deemed to be of strategic importance.

Within the framework of the Defence and National Security White Paper, the delivery of maritime security has to be maintained. If anything, its role has increased in the light of the focus on counterterrorism. The French territories extend from French Polynesia and New Caledonia in the Pacific Ocean, to Guiana in South America, the West Indies and Reunion Island in the Indian Ocean, where permanently based patrol and sovereignty ships are located with maritime surveillance aircraft, such as the Guardian and Falcon 50. It is a global commitment alongside its needs to protect its own coastline from the threat of terrorism, illegal immigration and drugs smuggling. But France is also a keen advocate of acting within a European context and often shares its military resources with other countries in joint coalition operations, as well as maintaining forces in places where its national interests are threatened, such as in

Dakar where the French Navy has established a permanent presence in the Gulf of Guinea under Operation Corymbe. This and other operations in the Atlantic Ocean occupy about 30 per cent of the activities of the French Navy, including occasional engagements to target narcotics trafficking from South America to West Africa and illegal immigration from Mauritania as part of Operation Hera III. These are clearly upstream operations aimed at disrupting and deterring smuggling activities. Forward basing of naval forces is one aspect of a comprehensive and proactive response to the perceived threat.

In the Mediterranean theatre of operations, the French Navy is active in providing maritime security operations that aim to disrupt and deter the movement of economic migrants and also drugs from the North African Coastline, through Operation Lévrier in cooperation with the Spanish Navy to target the importation of cannabis. Some of these operations are covered using maritime patrol assets in operations. The French Navy also contributes to the NATO led Operation Active Endeavour in the Eastern Mediterranean and its mission to disrupt the activities of transnational terrorist groups. These deployments, however, only cover part of what has been termed the 'arc of crisis' that extends from the North Atlantic to the Indian Ocean, embracing North Africa, the Mediterranean Sea, the Middle East and South East Asia where the 'risks related to the strategic interests of France and Europe are the highest'.

With facilities in Reunion Island, Djibouti and now the United Arab Emirates, France has a 'string of pearls' with which to influence activities in the region. Whilst force projection remains a key concern of French naval planners, such as Operation Heracles in the Northern Indian Ocean and Operation Corymbe off the Ivory Coast in 2002 and 2004, it is the role of 'maritime safeguard' that is increasingly important. This was illustrated in a speech given on 14 October 2002 by the French Prime Minister when he said, 'our security borders no longer coincide with our geographic boundaries. They extend well beyond and well within, where the terrorist threat dwells'. The idea of 'maritime safeguard' is that it provides an overarching framework for the operations carried out by the French Navy to face potential threats coming from the sea. It forms an element of what is emerging as a comprehensive approach to maritime security, with a global perspective and reach that is able to disrupt and deter threats to French interests wherever they may arise.

A9: GUINEA-BISSAU

AN ABSENCE OF MARITIME SECURITY

Guinea-Bissau is a country whose history has been plagued by political instability and corruption. Its location on the Western side of Africa places it at the nexus of a number of threats from people engaged in criminal behaviour. Increased surveillance designed to reduce the flows of drugs and people along the Iberian Coastline, and to the north by the French and the United Kingdom authorities, has created a displacement of the problem to other locations which cannot provide an effective deterrent.

The 350 km of the Guinea-Bissau coastline is particularly vulnerable; as an impoverished nation, it barely has a navy or fisheries protection capability to call upon to defend its territorial waters. As such, it is currently a back door into Africa through which drugs are moved with relative impunity. The poor state of the economy of Guinea-Bissau, with limited natural resources and little potential for tourism development, adds to the problems faced by its population, many of whom live in subsistence. The lack of a viable national deterrent, coupled with the virtual collapse of state structures and governance in the region—with neighbouring countries suffering their own problems—has enabled a new network of drugs trafficking routes to be established with bases on the West African coastline.

International criminal gangs have proven adept at shifting their supply routes for commodities, drugs, weapons and people, and exploiting weak points in what is emerging as a multilateral cooperation against their activities. Whilst coordination is far from perfect across the world, the increasingly coordinated efforts are placing constraints upon the supply, for example, of drugs from Columbia, through Brazil, across the southern Atlantic Ocean and up to the coast of West Africa. Once landed in West Africa, the supply routes then move across the land up through Senegal, Mauritania and the Western Sahara into places like Morocco and Algeria for onward shipment into Europe. Through displacing the main routes southwards, away from direct landings on the European mainland, the law enforcement authorities are pressurising the business model of the criminals who find the longer routes more expensive. They try and counterbalance this by exploiting routes where the overheads associated with moving the commodities—in terms of bribes and related transport costs—are at a minimum. Locations such as the Cape Verde Islands and the Bijagos Archipelago have historical links with smuggling that date to their colonial periods. This provides an established network of contacts and associated infrastructure from which those wishing to move the axis of the activities to another area can quickly build.

The parlous state of the situation in Guinea-Bissau acts as a magnet to organised criminals, and the seizure by the Royal Navy of cocaine worth £60 million off the coast of West Africa when it boarded a Panamanian-registered vessel *Ster II* off the Canary Islands, provided evidence of the changing nature of these links. This was the fourth such major interception of drugs that had involved the Royal Navy in two months. This operation was a multi-agency effort that comprised Spanish customs officials, working alongside their counterparts in the United Kingdom with *HMS Argyll* and the Royal Fleet Auxiliary supply ship *Fort Austin*, to launch helicopters and boats to secure the shipment on board the Panamanian vessel. The changing nature of the smuggling links prompted the government of United Kingdom to sign an accord with the government of the Cape Verde Islands to increase patrolling in the area by the Royal Navy. Several of the crew seized on the *Ster II* came from Guinea Bissau.

The challenges for Guinea-Bissau in the area of maritime security seem daunting. At present, its Navy is in harbour, and the three fisheries protection vessels that are part of its fleet only able to operate on a highly restricted basis. Its capacity to deter illegal operations in its coastal waters is thus constrained. This is compounded by the geography of the coastline of Guinea-Bissau, which comprises low-lying areas, which can make it prone to flooding, such as that which occurred in 2003 and 2005. Several major rivers draining into the coastal area which has a fractal structure based upon a series of river estuaries (the Corubal, Cacheu, the Mansoa, the Rio Grande de Buba, the Cumbila and the Cacine) and associated mini-deltaic areas that drain a number of very swampy and often quite inaccessible parts, creating problems for policing the region.

Criminal organisations appear to use the offshore Bijagos Archipelago as a stopping-off point for their activities, avoiding bringing vessels in too close to the shoreline. The sparsely inhabited archipelago makes the prefect dropping-off and intermediate storage point for drugs shipped up from South America. Once on the archipelago, the main shipments can be broken down into manageable quantities and moved the 50–100 km to the mainland using fishermen who are anxious to supplement their income. In the absence of any effective law enforcement capability, there is little deterrent to this behaviour.

Guinea-Bissau is a classic case study of a country that is being exploited by many people involved in a variety of criminal undertakings. Stabilising such a country is therefore a challenge. At present, any form of maritime security capability arises from temporary visits that are made by foreign warships from its former colonial partners, Portugal and emergent links with other western European countries. The United States is trying, through the work of the Africa Partnership Station (APS), to develop critical indigenous capacity within the country and foster a sense of national purpose, which will reduce the levels of drugs shipments but also develop capabilities that can also effectively patrol with wider EEZ of Guinea-Bissau. A navy that is capable of patrolling a coastline that is difficult to access may require a mixture of amphibious forces alongside naval elements for maintaining and securing the sea. If any indigenous capability is to be introduced, it will need a mix of riverine, littoral and some nascent blue-water capacity, so that it can mount operations across the full spectrum of the geography of the coastline. Maritime security in Guinea-Bissau needs to start from the basics and build up, and is not a short-term project.

A10: INDONESIA

MAINTAINING MARITIME INTEGRITY

Geographically, Indonesia is located in a strategically important area of the world, astride the Malacca Strait, through which 600 vessels and 11 million barrels of oil a day pass, moving trade through the region. With its 17,508 islands, of which close to 6,000 are inhabited, and a population of over 200 million people, it is one of the most populous countries in the world and has the second longest coastline behind that of Canada. Indonesia's approach to maritime security is defined within its central doctrine, *Wawasan Nusantara*, which stresses the strategic importance of maintaining the integrity and unity of its island and maritime territory. This concept of one nation is challenging when the archipelago is spread over an area of 5.8 million km^2 of which 2.7 million km^2 are territorial waters, and the remaining 3.1 million km^2 are designated as its EEZ. In 2005, the Indonesian government announced its intention to seek an extension to its EEZ out to 350 nm.

In the late 1990s and in the early part of the twenty-first century, Indonesia spent a great deal of time looking inwardly towards threats that arose from the diverse ethnic and religious tensions that punctuate its political and societal landscape. This had implications for the kind of naval force that was developed by the central government, as it had to maintain an amphibious capability to be able to launch security operations through the archipelago when insecurity and insurgencies threatened national unity. More recently, the situation in Indonesia has started to stabilise as separatist movements in Aceh, for example, have accepted proposals for greater autonomy in their regions. This increasing stability has allowed the Indonesian government to look to other priority issues in its maritime sector, such as fisheries. Scientific research suggests that Indonesian waters are capable of sustaining a harvest of 6.2 million metric tonnes of fish a year, the majority of which comes from the territorial waters of Indonesia. The 'precautionary principle' in fisheries management suggests that only 80 per cent of the estimated Total Allowable Catch (TAC) should be landed, suggesting a sustainable harvest of 4.96 million metric tonnes per year. In 2003, records showed that Indonesian fishermen took 4.7 million metric tonnes, an increase of 48 per cent over the catches taken in 1993. This, however, does not produce an accurate assessment of the actual levels of catch, as much of the fish stock is not landed in Indonesia. Estimates suggest that around 700,000 fishing boats operate in Indonesian waters, of which half are not powered. Official figures show that over 2.5 million people are employed in the capture industry, with 2.2 million in aquaculture. 90 per cent of fishing activity is defined as small-scale and artisanal in nature. Very few large commercial fishing boats are locally owned. As the captured part of the marine reserves moves closer to its sustainable levels, the aquaculture element will be further developed.

Whilst arrangements have been put in place to licence commercial fishery exploitation by trawlers operating within the EEZ, concerns remain as to the levels of fish taken by these vessels. Illegal fishing is believed to cost the Indonesian government around $2 billion a year. This is compounded by an uncertain and sometimes confusing approach to regulating fishing conducted by overseas trawlers, such as those from China and Thailand. In March 2007, the Indonesian government announced that, in future, the granting of licences would be conditional upon the owners of the foreign fishing fleets establishing fish processing plants in Indonesia. This was brought into national law through Indonesia Ministerial Decree No. 17/2006. This will ensure that licensed fishing vessels will land their stocks on Indonesian soil first, so that accurate records of exploitation can be maintained. It will also help supply local markets which have not been able to meet demands from the country's burgeoning population. The Ministerial Decree has been accompanied by increased efforts at enforcement. In June 2009, eight fishing vessels were detained on charges of illegal fishing as the Navy started to implement the new legal framework.

The other concern of the Indonesian government is the defence of the archipelago and the potential for regional conflict over energy supplies.

Whilst not specifically contesting the Spratley or Paracel Islands, Indonesia does have energy security concerns. It has over 4 billion barrels of proven oil reserves, which may rise through further exploration to nearly double that figure. Indonesia is the world's leading exporter of natural gas with huge gas deposits, which have the potential to last well into the current century. Its main clients for natural gas are Japan, Taiwan and South Korea. Indonesia also has potentially large-scale mineral deposits that would be of great interest to China and other regional economies; its tin-mining sector is the world's largest.

Indonesia's approach to securing its maritime domain looks inwardly to the problems of illegal fishing and to delivering maritime presence in areas such as the Java Sea, the Banda Sea, the Bali Sea, the Flores Sea and the Arafura Sea. Naval bases are spread from Sabang (95°E) at the western extent of Indonesia, to Jayapura (141°E) in the east. There are very few countries in the world with such a wide geographic spread of territory. This is a challenging area over which to exert control and the Indonesian Navy is spread over twelve naval bases and its maritime arm operates over six air bases. Should Indonesia be threatened with conflict, the objective of the Navy is to mass its forces and deploy quickly upstream to intercept any threat as far away from its EEZ as possible. The issue for Indonesia is that of which direction the threat may emerge from, as it has long held suspicions over the territorial intentions of Australia after its pre-emptive actions in East Timor and the Solomon Islands. Massing naval forces to counter any threat, which might reasonably emerge along an axis from the southeast to the northeast, requires a balanced force that has a mixture of fast patrol boats, warships and an ability to land marines in amphibious deployments should coastal zones become contested. Given the economic strictures that currently plague the Indonesian economy, the much needed and wide-ranging re-equipment of the Navy is unlikely to happen in the short-term. Its recent regional cooperation to deter piracy activities in the Malacca Strait, cooperating with the Malaysian and Singaporean navies, has seen piracy levels in the region fall dramatically. Such regional cooperation is clearly proving successful in delivering some aspects of maritime security. Other concerns remain, and Indonesia faces the difficult task of balancing its naval procurement priorities amongst competing demands to protect the fisheries, still be capable of defending its sovereign territory should it feel threatened, and being able to deliver amphibious operations across the archipelago and to any potential areas where confrontations might occur with other nation states.

A11: ISRAEL

PROJECTING MARITIME POWER LOCALLY AND REGIONALLY

Maritime security through an Israeli lens is clearly focused upon the many threats that Israel faces from its adversaries. The Israeli Navy is at the forefront of delivering maritime security and has a wide range of mission roles. It is truly a multi-mission navy. At a strategic level, maritime security is delivered in the medium-term by having a national triad of nuclear forces that are able to withstand a first strike from a nuclear-armed Iran.

The Israeli Navy also has a capability to project maritime power increasingly upstream from its immediate coastal waters within a regional context. The interception and sinking of an Iranian merchant vessel in the Red Sea in 2009, which was alleged to have been involved in smuggling arms to Hamas in the Gaza Strip, is an example of this ambition. Complex smuggling routes, involving countries such as Iran and the Sudan, provide challenges to locating and disrupting the flow of weapons into the Gaza Strip.

At a local level the Israeli Navy has also to be concerned with trying to regulate the smuggling of weapons into the Gaza Strip, and it mounts patrols using its Fast Attack Craft to try and deter, and where necessary arrest, those involved. This can lead to local confrontations and fuel resentment amongst Palestinian fisherman. On a small number of occasions, local Islamic extremists have turned to suicide tactics and attacked Israeli vessels using similar methods to those employed by the Sea Tigers of Sri Lanka. Whilst no instances of swarming tactics against Israeli vessels have yet been documented, instances of fishing vessels exploding in ways similar to that in a suicide attack have been reported. On 30 March 2009, an unmanned Palestinian fishing boat exploded off the coast of the Gaza Strip in an apparent attack on Israeli patrol boats operating in the area. A previous attack mounted by two Palestinians in 2002 resulted in their deaths, damaged an Israeli patrol vessel and also wounded four Israeli sailors.

The Israeli Navy, therefore, approaches all fishing activity in and around its shores with the view that they could be involved in smuggling, a suicide attack or simply fishing. In examples of is now described as citizen journalism or User Generated Content, the Internet has a number of examples of clashes between the Israeli Navy and local fishermen who are ostensibly going about their day-to-day need to fish to provide for their families. Some of these clashes involve high-speed passes by the Israeli Navy and the use of firearms and water cannon to disrupt the activities of the fishermen. A policy of sea denial seems to be in place concerning the operation of the fishermen who claim that under the Oslo Accords they are allowed to fish out to a distance of 30 km from the shore. The Palestinian fishermen claim that the Israeli Navy is trying to compress them into the immediate 5 km of the littoral zone, restricting the chances that these fishermen could meet up and rendezvous with any merchant-shipping vessel moving in the Mediterranean Sea. In 2008, the Palestinians claimed that twelve fishing vessels have been sunk and over seventy damaged in such clashes. These are examples of the very specific aspects of maritime security that are occurring off the coast of Gaza, as the Israeli Navy tries to impose a naval blockade upon the country as part of its strategy for dealing with the boarder issues of security, and its relationships with the Palestinians. By enforcing the blockade and harassing the local fishermen, the Israeli Navy are playing hardball with the local population. Their actions are clearly based upon what they see as a clear and present danger that is associated with weapon-smuggling operations.

The threat to the Israeli Navy was vividly illustrated when the Israeli Navy Ship (INS) *Hanit*, a corvette, was struck by an Iranian-supplied Noor anti-ship missile (a derivative of the Chinese C-802/YJ-2 *Saccade* radar-guided Anti-Ship Cruise Missile carrying a warhead of about 120 pounds of high explosive) fired by the Islamic Resistance, the armed wing of Hezbollah, on 14 July 2006. Evidence resulting from the subsequent enquiry showed that the presence of such a threat was unknown to the

Israeli Navy, who had many of their sensor systems—such as the ship's automatic missile defence system—disabled despite an apparent warning issued by the Israeli Naval Intelligence organisation.

It is apparent that the Israeli Navy is developing a tiered approach to maritime security with a capability to protect vital SLOC beyond the inner ring, providing security for vessels entering Israeli harbours. At the periphery of these concentric zones, the Israeli Navy retains the right to project maritime power to disrupt threats that it perceives to its sovereignty on a regional basis. This is a scaled-down version of the roles played in the past by the Israeli Secret Service in intercepting weapons and people connected with terrorism that threaten its people or very existence. Israel has always believed that defence starts upstream. This is not a new concept, but one that has been taken on by the Israeli Navy alongside its partners in the Israeli Defence Forces (IDF), such as the Air Force. It was the latter who bombed the Iraqi nuclear plant in Osirak, 18 miles south of Baghdad, on 7 June 1981, and also attacked a Syrian nuclear site on 6 September 2007.

The multi-mission role of the Israeli Navy was further illustrated by its role in Operation Cast Lead, when the IDF mounted an incursion into the Gaza Strip, which lasted from 27 December 2008 until 18 January 2009. During the operation, the Israeli Navy took part in a number of missions designed to thwart attempts to smuggle arms into the Gaza Strip by sea and also to support ground forces. This operation pioneered a number of new approaches to urban warfare, with a high degree of networked elements cooperating in trying to ensure that civilian casualties were minimised. Using the TORC2H situational awareness system, the Israeli Navy was able to join the land battle, providing fire support using the Typhoon weapon system which provides a real-time read out of its flight profile to a target from an electro-optically guided sight.

A12: KENYA

COUNTERING TERRORISM AND CRIMINAL BEHAVIOUR ACROSS AN EXTENDED EEZ

On 6 May 2009, Kenya submitted its claim to extend its current EEZ from 200 nm out to 350 nm. This adds a further 103,000 square kilometres to its EEZ, with all its potential benefits in terms of reaping rewards from the seabed and harnessing new and untapped resources such as petroleum, gas and manganese modules and crusts. The economic importance of succeeding with the bid to extend the EEZ is obvious, but it brings with it some other important considerations, such as how to provide maritime security across the enlarged EEZ.

In the absence of an obvious and enduring maritime threat to its sovereignty, it is reasonable to think that the primary role of the Kenyan Navy is focused on constabulary duties. The main threats to the maritime waters of Kenya arise from criminal activities. Drugs, weapons and people-smuggling, and the ever-present threat of illegal fishing—with its damaging impact upon the local economy—are an enduring problem.

The danger from acts of terrorism that have punctuated the recent history of Kenya, and their potential to occur along the coastline, from where Kenya generates a great deal of revenue from tourism, must also be factored into the equation. Terrorists rarely forget the impact of attacks on soft targets, such as Luxor in Egypt, and Bali. These events, and their related media coverage, do terrorise an international audience. The recent images of Mumbai are simply too raw in the mind to forget the potential for a reoccurrence at one of the major tourist spots along the coastline with long-term implications.

The Kenyan coastline is also host to some important artisanal fisheries upon which local communities depend for a source of protein. Declining catches are affecting nearly 20,000 fishermen along the coastline. The activities of unlicensed fishing vessels operating off the coast of Kenya are having a dramatic knock-on impact upon artisanal fishermen. Anecdotal evidence emerging from local fishermen suggests that some 200 vessels are operating in the vicinity of the country's territorial waters; this is a figure that contrasts markedly with the sixty vessels that are licensed.

This situation is compounded by the burgeoning problem of piracy on its northern borders. Pirates based in Somalia have developed their tactics and extended their range of operations across the Indian Ocean to the Seychelles Islands. The potential for a southern axis to develop, threatening key SLOC to Mombasa, has been demonstrated in the past. As the threat has developed, the Kenyan Navy has largely been a bystander unable to do much directly to intervene, with some of its main units inoperable.

This must be a cause for concern for the Kenyan government. It has taken on a responsibility to prosecute pirates captured by the international task force, in the absence of a recognised and functioning judiciary in Somalia. Kenyan courts are being used by proxy by the international community to prosecute pirates captured by the international maritime force. The potential for an orchestrated backlash against the position of the Kenyan government is all too apparent.

Given current fiscal constraints and economic pressures, with tourism revenues dramatically reduced in 2008, it is unlikely that the size of the Navy could be rapidly increased to cope with the additional burden arising from the extended EEZ. Valid questions, therefore, arise that reflect upon what might be done with its existing capabilities and how new vessels might be obtained from donor countries. How might existing and planned shore-based coastal monitoring assets work in harmony with the Navy to improve maritime security in its coastal waters? Clearly the kind of maritime security regime in which an extended EEZ might be policed should not be a footnote to the application, considered only as an afterthought. It is time for a national strategy to emerge that builds upon existing capabilities.

One model for such an approach to developing a secure zone would be to think of a three-tiered architecture where the Kenyan Navy is able to protect the immediate littoral zone and its associated harbours (the inner region), the territorial waters which cover from 2 nm out to 12 nm (the central region) and the deeper waters of the continental shelf (the outer region) with its potential coverage of a newly defined 350 nm extended EEZ. Other African countries, such as Tanzania, Mozambique and the Gulf of Guinea States, such as Cameroon, Nigeria and Ghana, face similar challenges when it comes to policing their coastal waters.

In Kenya, this capability is currently supported by the string of AISs located along the shoreline; these monitor and detect both violations and criminal activity in the inner region of the maritime security zone, and command a response from the Kenyan Navy. Kenyan Air Force F-5E fighter jets are mobilised to overfly areas where risks are reported. However, fast jets are not readily tailored to the form of specialised mission typical of an airborne maritime patrol aircraft, and time over the target area is often limited. The Kenyan government has been taking informal soundings about converting one of its three DASH-8 troop transport aircraft to give it a maritime patrol capability. No immediate progress on these discussions is believed to have been made, but it is clear that this is a hugely important part of the kind of capability that would be required to police an extended EEZ.

A13: MALACCA STRAIT

REGIONAL COOPERATION AGAINST PIRACY

The Malacca Strait is recognised as one of a number of important maritime choke points that exist across the world that may be vulnerable to some form of attack or disruption. Six of these choke points have added significance as they carry the oil on which the world's economy so depends. The Strait of Hormuz is widely regarded, at present, as being the world's most important choke point, as its carries an estimated 16.5–17 million barrels of oil a day through an area that has several enduring maritime security challenges. Of the other five major oil choke points, such as the Bab el-Mandab, the Turkish Strait (Bosporus), the Suez and Panama Canals, and the Malacca Strait, it is the last of these that is crucial to the economies of South East Asia. It carries over 80 per cent of the oil supplies currently required by China, South Korea and Japan, with 12 million barrels of oil a day and 40 per cent of the world's maritime trade moving through it. Its blockage, even for a short period of time, would have significant worldwide economic implications.

At its narrowest point in the Phillips Channel, the Malacca Strait is 1.7 miles wide. The potential for accidental grounding, oil spills and collisions in bad weather is well recognised by mariners and governments in the region. Its varying width and depth, and the density of traffic moving through the channel provide specific challenges for navigation. It is the busiest strait in the world for international navigation, with over 50,000 vessels a year transiting through it. The authorities that manage this density of journeys use a Traffic Separation Scheme (TSS) to help manage the passages being made by vessels operating in the area, with west-to-east bound vessels operating to the southern side of the channel. If the Malacca Strait were blocked, it is estimated that approximately half the world's fleet of commercial vessels would have to re-route around the Indonesian Archipelago through the Lombok strait (located between the islands of Lombok and Bali) or the Sunda Strait (located between Java and Sumatra).

The navigation measures developed by the coastal states bordering the Malacca Strait date back to a meeting held on 16 November 1971, in which the safety of navigation was agreed as a tripartite effort and an institutional framework was agreed whereby ministerial authority was supported by meetings held by senior government officials and technical expert groups. Since that date, the agreements have been consolidated by follow-on discussions in 1977 and 2005, at which measures relating to addressing major pollution events and improvements to the safety of navigation were agreed. Due to the narrowness of the Strait, these meetings were held against a backdrop of competing ideas over sovereignty of the coastal waters, as even the original definitions of territorial waters dating back to the UNCLOS I agreement were not readily applicable to the geographic landscape of the Malacca Strait.

For centuries the Strait has been one of the most important maritime thoroughfares for developing global commerce, carrying expensive spices from the East to the markets in the West. Given the nature of the cargoes, it was hardly surprising that the area would be vulnerable to the development of piracy, and the area has a history of the problem. That history is difficult to trace specifically, as the term piracy itself has tended to be used to cover a myriad events and people; there has often been the branding of people as pirates because that was a convenient term to use. Records dating to the fifth century CE, which are documented by Adam Young in his book *Contemporary Maritime Piracy in Southeast Asia: History, Causes and Remedies*, notes that the area was infested with pirates and that meeting with them only resulted in death. Similar reports in the eighth and ninth centuries also report the area being inhabited mostly by pirates, and reports dating to the fourteenth century indicate similar issues along the coastline. Young's analysis of the history of piracy in the region considers a number of specific case studies, looking at Bugis, Vietnamese and Chinese pirates alongside the development of Malay piracy, with a particular focus on its development in the nineteenth century. His analysis provides an excellent contextual understanding of contemporary piracy. More recently in 2004, the Strait accounted for 40 per cent of the total of the world's reported piracy attacks, with thirty-eight reported in the year; this was the second highest total after Indonesia, with the area between the island groups off Singapore and in the vicinity of Batam being a known trouble spot. In October 2007, the IMB reported that Indonesia alone continued to be the world's most pirate-prone region, with thirty-seven attacks since the start of the year, and a total of ninety-three during its course. In contrast, the IMB reported seventy-nine attacks in 2005, dropping to fifty in 2006, in the Malacca Strait. In response, India has also provided help in monitoring the Andaman Sea, the area adjacent to the Strait of Malacca, where it is building a Unmanned Aviation Vehicle (UAV) patrol-base on the Andaman and Nicobar Islands.

As the threat from piracy in the twentieth and twenty-first century began to create problems for establishing a secure highway through the Malacca Strait, international efforts started to work towards solutions designed to tackle the problems that emerged with criminal behaviour, such as armed robbery at sea, the local smuggling of goods, people and weapons, and illegal fishing. Initial responses to these threats focused upon a mixture of unilateral, bilateral and tripartite agreements that resulted in increased air and sea patrols, intelligence operations, anti-smuggling operations and measures on the land designed to reduce the threat to shipping passing through the Strait. Other interested parties—users of the Malacca Strait, such as China, Japan and the United States—tried to provide encouragement and support from the sidelines of these meetings. At the start of the twenty-first century, increased cooperation between the littoral states has seen dramatic improvements in maritime security in the region. Whilst this development is clearly welcome, it is difficult to read across specific insights from this regional cooperative effort into measures that might be taken to secure other choke points, as each one has its own specific challenges.

For example, whilst the Straits of Gibraltar are recognised as a maritime choke point, they are not specifically listed as one of the major oil choke points. However, the instability that exists in the Maghreb is a concern and potential terrorist attacks planned for launch against cruise liners, naval vessels and large vessels carrying oil and gas supplies have been detected and disrupted. Constant vigilance in the area is required to ensure the safe passage of major ships through its narrow channel. The issues with the Bab el-Mandab are well documented. Instability off the coast of Somalia has allowed piracy to develop, and the specific problems of trying to protect shipping on passage through the area are difficult, given the larger area over which pirates can mount their attacks. Other major oil choke points such as the Bosporus and the Suez Canal are more likely to suffer from terrorism than attacks on vessels by criminals. Local policing of the situation has an important deterrent effect, but the idea of Chechen separatists hijacking a tanker and blockading the Bosporus cannot be discounted. Whilst the overall disruption to the world's oil supplies would be quite small, with the Bosporus carrying 2.4 million barrels per day by approximately 5,000 tankers a year (around 15 per day transit the area), the fragility of the world's economic situation could see ramifications that might appear on the surface to be disproportionate to the actual impact of the attack. Given this analysis, it is clear that the security of maritime choke points around the world remains a key issue in ensuring a secure maritime environment.

A14: THE MALDIVES

REGIONAL COOPERATION

The archetypical picture postcard image of the Maldives is of a beautiful location where people can rest, relax and get away from the demands of life. The geographic disposition of the atolls could be likened to a string of pearls lying in the Indian Ocean. But it is not in that sense that this case study considers the Maldives. In this analysis, the idea of a 'string of pearls' represents a far grander design aimed at providing ways of securing vital SLOC across the Indian Ocean, and also providing a front-line defence against the potential for the spread of Muslim extremism in the region, based upon a threat that is indigenous to the Maldives. For all their beauty and obvious attraction for tourism, the Maldives Islands possesses a far greater asset that is of particular interest in a time of globalised markets, strategic considerations and vital trading routes—their location.

The economy of the Maldives is hugely dependent upon tourism and has little in the way of natural resources, importing the majority of what it needs in terms of food, apart from harnessing local fisheries. This also makes its population heavily reliant on fishing, which accounts for 15 per cent of the GDP and the livelihood of 30 per cent of the population. The archipelago that makes up the Maldives is made up of 1,190 coral islands that are grouped into twenty-six geographic atolls, of which 202 are inhabited and with a total coastline of 644 km. To police this area the government of the Maldives National Security Service employs a number of fast patrol boats and a staff of around 400 people as the Coastguard. Two of these patrol boats are are Iskandhar-class patrol craft that were commissioned in 1999 and 2002, and the Indian Navy donated a

Trinkat-class vessel after the tsunami in December 2004. The Coastguard are responsible for: protecting the territorial waters of the islands; conducting search, rescue and salvage operations; the enforcement of maritime law; VIP and convoy protection; and coastal surveillance. Drug smuggling is a small but potentially growing area of concern for the Maldives government and the Coastguard is a part of a national effort to restrict its development.

The Maldives are located 644 km to the southwest of Sri Lanka, and occupy a vertical strip of the Indian Ocean that sits astride the main SLOC from the Gulf of Aden through to the South Asian trading areas of Singapore, Japan and China. The total area of the Maldives is 115,350 km^2 (850 km long and 130 km wide). The Maldives claims an EEZ of 859,000 km^2 and the largest natural atoll in the world, Huvadhu Atoll, which has an area of 2,240 km^2 and a lagoon with a depth of 86 metres. None of the islands is more than 3 metres above sea level and they are hugely vulnerable to the potential for sea level rises occurring as a direct result of the onset of climate change, which at present rates of sea-level change could make 80 per cent of the islands uninhabitable within 100 years. The long-term prognosis is not good, and as a warning of what is to come, the capital Male was submerged by flooding in 1987 and the whole country was badly hit by the tsunami in December 2004.

Given the parlous state of the situation in the Maldives, it may seem strange to explore the strategic significance of the islands in respect of their position in the Indian Ocean. However, apart from their obvious attraction as a tourist destination, their other great asset is their location: sitting between the 'eight degree channel' and the 'one and a half degree channel', an important nexus of trading routes that dates back to 2000 BCE involving the Egyptians, Mesopotamians and the peoples from the Indus Valley. The various channels between the islands were seen in history to be potentially dangerous with some being quite broad and deep and others with more complex bathymetry. In 1834–1836, the British Captain Robert Moresby carried out a detailed survey of the island chain and developed the first Hydrographic Survey charts that remained in service until the early 1990s when more accurate material became available from satellite surveys.

The location of the Maldives Islands is crucial from a strategic perspective in the Indian Ocean. It sits at the western end of the economically important Asia trading area, which embraces Japan in the north,

Indonesia in the south, and India and Pakistan in the west. Taken together, this is the world's largest seaborne-trading area, importing 2.5 billion tonnes of cargo in 2005 and exporting 1.6 billion tonnes, 50 per cent more than Western Europe. The Maldives is located at a vital point close to major trading routes and offers the potential for vessels operating from Male to establish a presence in the center of the Indian Ocean. Given the 'string of pearls' strategy being developed by the Chinese, it is not difficult to understand why the Maldives is coveted by a number of countries. China has sought to establish its own naval base in the Maldives on Marao, 40 km to the south of Male in a move that concerns the Indian government.

India is one country that is making great efforts to establish ties with the Maldives. Its interest in the Islands is motivated by a number of factors, one of which is to prevent the Maldives becoming a location from which terrorists could launch an attack similar to the one on Mumbai as the distances are not that different, and in periods between the monsoons the Indian Ocean can be relatively easy to transit in a small craft. The Maldives has a recent history of being a centre for Muslim extremism. While the islands suffered their last terrorist attack in September 2007, injuring twelve tourists from a variety of national backgrounds, there are indications that some young Muslims are prepared to become involved in terrorism, having been indoctrinated in madrasas in Pakistan and Saudi Arabia. Ties with the group thought to be behind the attacks in Mumbai, Lashkar e-Toiba, have also been established. Saudi funding to religious schools in the Maldives has also compounded the situation, tempting more disenfranchised young people to become involved in terrorism.

India, therefore, has an important role to play in the counter-terrorism activities in the Maldives, and evidence has been presented of specific situations when Lashkar e-Toiba planned to use the deserted islands as a warehouse to store arms and ammunition. Reports have also suggested that an attack was planned on the Indian Space Research Organisation (ISRO) facility in Southern India, which had links to specific individuals based in the Maldives. In reaction to these threats, the Indian government has concluded arrangements with the government of the Maldives to base radar stations on all of the twenty-six atolls that make up the island chain. The Indian government has long wished to create a presence on the Maldives island of Gan for its surveillance aircraft and helicopters. The data from the radar sites will be transferred to the Indian Navy's Command Centre at Kochi on the southwest coast. The Indian Coastguard has also offered to provide routine airborne coverage of the uninhabited islands to screen them for any signs that they are possibly in use as terrorist training camps. This is not a baseless concern; despite their obvious beauty and picture-post-card images, the Maldives are clearly coveted by a number of state and non-state actors due to the strategic nature of their location. It is not just the Chinese that see the Maldives as a potentially vital cog or pearl in an extended arc of protection afforded to SLOC. While the Indian government may also share that view, its immediate concerns about the activities of terrorist groups are far more pragmatic and short-term.

A15: MEXICO

WHERE MARITIME SECURITY AND CRIMINALITY CLASH

It is difficult to see the issues of maritime security in Mexico through anything but the lens of criminality and its manifestation in the organisation of drugs and people-smuggling activities in the region. Mexico hardly faces any immediate danger from other states. Its EEZ covers an area of 5,144,295 km^2. It is a major oil exporter to the United States, and therefore shares concerns about the potential for terrorist attacks upon its major offshore exploration and exploitation infrastructure. Mexico does not have any specific territorial disputes with any neighbours in the maritime environment, although there is a history of problems with illegal fishing by Cuban vessels and by other foreign vessels in the Gulf of Mexico. The government of Mexico has moved to assert its claim to sovereignty over Clarion Island with the deployment of a small force of marines. The claim over Clarion Island extends Mexico's Pacific coastal EEZ out to just beyond 114°W and includes the area also covered by the Socorro Islands, where the two EEZ intersect in the area of the Revillagigedo Archipelago. To police this area, the Mexican Navy deploys a mixed force that focuses upon its coastguard duties with its marine infantry elements playing a prominent role in the interdiction of criminal activity in its coastal waters. The particular foci for these operations are the Yucatán Canal and the Mexican Caribbean—where the offshore oil production area of the Campeche Sound is also of strategic concern from an economic viewpoint—and the Isthmus and Gulf of Tehuantepec.

In regional terms, the relationship with the United States is important, as Mexico is one of the primary routes through which cocaine and marijuana moves from Columbia to the United States. Current intelligence estimates show that around 90 per cent of it moving through Mexico with a monetary value that is estimated at around $23 billion a year. The actions of the drugs traffickers have created a situation whereby Mexico is a hub for the movement of cocaine from South America, and it ranks second to the United States as a producer of methamphetamines. Three major drugs cartels control the trafficking of narcotics in Mexico. Routine disputes break out between them as they vie for control of key shipment routes. The operation of the cartels is also complex, as drugs flow north into the United States and weapons and money flow southwards into Mexico. The cartels in Mexico receive most of their weapons from the United States, such as through purchases at gun shows held in the border region. Precursor chemicals used in the production of methamphetamines also flow south from places like Long Beach in California. Mapping the nature of these exchanges is a complex task that requires the deployment of dedicated intelligence assets and resources that are already in demand in trying to counter the illegal movement of people across the border region. Recent trends have seen the cartels making increasing use of simple submarines to move drugs. In 2006, United States Coastguard and Naval officials cited detecting three of these submarines a month. In early 2009, this had increased to ten a month and only one of these was intercepted.

In response to these developments, and the impact they were having upon Mexican society, the government of President Felipe Calderón has embarked upon a major series of internal security operations that are aimed at curbing and disrupting the activities of organised crime groups operating in a number of key areas of Mexico, such as the State of Michoacán, where over 6,500 federal troops where deployed against the criminal cartels in December 2006. This activity had the effect of disrupting the flow of cocaine into the United States at the beginning of 2007. Record seizures by the Mexican Navy also helped increase the pressure on the narcotics traffickers.

In recent times the transnational criminal cartels involved in this activity have started to use novel approaches to smuggling, using submarines alongside the traditional fast boats that journey across the Caribbean and along the coastline of the Gulf of California, from the State of Sinaloa, with its long and difficult-to-monitor coastline. In 2008, several major operations succeeded in intercepting supplies of marijuana at Punta Ahome on the Sonora coast, Altata Bay and El Colorado Bay on the

Sinaloa coastline. These intercepts of major shipments of marijuana illustrate the degree of coordination that is now occurring along this area of the Mexican coastline between its maritime security forces in the region. The Fourth Naval Region has its headquarters at Guaymas, and on 17 May 2008, it coordinated an air-sea-land combined operation to intercept three vessels operating off the coast of Sinaloa, seizing nearly 5 tonnes of marijuana with a street value of over $400,000. The vessels were thought to be heading to Guaymas to offload the drugs for final overland shipment into the United States. The operation involved a C-212 maritime patrol aircraft, a Mi-2 *Hoplite* helicopter, a Durango Class Ocean Patrol Vessel, an Azteca Class Coastal Patrol Vessel and two Polaris Interceptor Craft. The smugglers abandoned their craft and made their escape in the shallows of the Mayo River near Bahiá Yavaros. In a similar event on 16 July 2008, the Mexican Navy seized 5.3 metric tonnes of cocaine with a value of $65–70 million. The level of coordination achieved in these operations is a testament to the development of the TRINOMIO (threefold) concept. This involves the combination of a helicopter, patrol vessel and interceptor craft and has resulted in the seizure of over 55 metric tonnes of cocaine in recent years.

The response to this increasing problem has been for the United States, Mexico, and a number of governments in Central America (including Guatemala, El Salvador, Nicaragua and Costa Rica) to develop the 'Mérida Initiative'. This programme is funded by the United States and provides $1.4 billion in equipment, software and technical assistance to the Mexican authorities over a three-year period. It allows the Mexican government to put more resources into transport helicopters and surveillance planes alongside strengthening infrastructure and allied systems required to target specific criminals groups, such as the Federation and Gulf Cartels, which operate along the Gulf of California and in the Gulf of Mexico. The Central American governments cooperating in the programme are gaining training in anti-gang warfare strategies, alongside communications equipment and allied ports, airport and border security infrastructure as part of an effort to increase border security and to collect and analyse intelligence information that can derived from the new infrastructure.

A16: NORWAY

THE RESURGENT THREAT FROM THE NORTH

Norway's relationship with the maritime domain is as long as its history. The geography and the landscape of the country make the maritime domain hugely important. It is also strategically located, as those planners in the Second World War that sought to occupy Narvik knew. At the height of the Cold War, Norway was in the maritime front line, confronting the threat from the Russian Navy based in Murmansk. Its short, but strategically important border with Russia, close to North Cape, was seen by NATO as being a pivotal location for any opening moves in the maritime domain should war have broken out.

The area off the coast of Norway would have been hugely important in the event of a war. United States and United Kingdom maritime forces, supported by maritime patrol aircraft, would have projected maritime power into the Iceland-Greenland Gap and the Iceland Faroes Gap to ensure the lifeline across the Atlantic Ocean for supplies and reinforcements to reach Europe. The second Battle of the Atlantic was envisaged as one in which Western anti-submarine forces would negate the threat from Russian submarines that had surged to sea ahead of the outbreak of war. One option for naval commanders seeking to protect the convoys, would have been to project maritime power forward into the Norwegian Sea, and on into the so-called bastions, where Russian nuclear submarines would lie in wait ready to unleash their nuclear arsenal upon the West. The Kola Peninsula, with an array of military infrastructure, remains hugely strategically important to Russia, and NATO would have had to have the capacity to place the forces located there under threat of military action. The operations by large-scale naval units in the area would have been designed to improve the 'correlation of forces' on the central front in Germany by opening up a threat to Russia's northern fleet and its bastions off the coast of Murmansk. The Norwegian Navy would have played a pivotal role in those operations. Naval forces operating in these waters needed anti-submarine and anti-aircraft capabilities, one of the main design drivers for the mix of frigates and destroyers procured by the Norwegian Navy at the time.

The end of the Cold War and the dramatic changes to the strategic landscape, such as the rapid demise of the submarine element of the Russian Northern Fleet, could have led to a fundamental reappraisal of Norway's maritime situation. Asymmetric threats to its vital offshore industries would clearly feature in any new estimate of the balance of forces required.

In fact, whilst in the immediate wake of the end of the Cold War—and the rapid demise of the Russian threat—some downsizing of the Norwegian Navy did occur; investments planned at the start of the twenty-first century show that that period of change has been reversed. General Sverre Diesen, Norway's Chief of Defence, noted the impact of climate change and its associated effects in the High North in an interview published in *Jane's Defence Weekly* on 16 September 2009. He noted 'increased access to energy resources, new sea lanes of communications etc.—are extremely interesting and significant issues for the Norwegian armed forces'. His remarks were clearly aimed at the remarkable changes that are occurring in the Arctic Sea and its surrounds as the Arctic Ice sheet retreats, opening up new sea lanes that have huge potential to reduce sea journey times. He also noted that Norway's long-term priority was the procurement of a next generation submarine. This would form an important element of a balanced naval force that could use the submarine for intelligence collection activities, the protection of SLOC and, should it be required, the projection of naval power into the High Arctic region.

One driver for this renewed interest in the Arctic region is the turnaround that is also occurring in Russia as it strives to reestablish itself on the world stage as a superpower. A similar pattern of increased spending is emerging in Russia with the Defence Ministry Budget for 2009 showing 40 per cent of the resources being spent on the Russian Navy. A major element of this spending has been on revitalising the Russian submarine force with the development of the new Borey-class submarines, which are 170 metres long and have a hull diameter of 13 metres. These new vessels will be coming into service from 2010 onwards.

In 2009, the Norwegian government has made a clear choice to take a different path and build up its investment in the Norwegian Navy—something for which it has received criticism in some quarters in NATO. In a departure from what has in the past been regarded as an effort by Scandinavian countries to work to a common agenda, the Norwegian government specifically rejected the line taken by Denmark scrapping its entire submarine force. In 2009, the Norwegian State Secretary, Espen Barth Eide, rejected the NATO comments questioning why Norway needs to invest in new Frigate programmes, such as the Nansen-Class anti-submarine frigates that it is currently commissioning into service alongside investment in the Skjold-class Motor Torpedo Boats. The State Secretary for Defence specifically cited the melting sea ice in the Arctic and the impact that would have upon the regions' geostrategic importance. Three new coastguard vessels of the Barentshav-class are also due to be delivered in 2009—building up the protection of the coastline. In what may be seen to be a very far-reaching strategic investment, the budget for the Norwegian Navy has been increased by 240 million NOK over its previous 3 billion NOK in 2008. The era of downsizing its Navy is over, as the Norwegian government places a high priority on the northern region of its country and its vital oil and gas reserves and places its emphasis on maritime security.

The five Nansen-class anti-submarine warfare frigates have been built by Navantia in Spain, with the first vessel being launched in June 2004. Sea trials in October 2005 started the process of verifying the on-board sensors, weapons, and command and control systems. The main mission of these frigates is anti-submarine warfare. The Norwegian Navy has clearly not forgotten recent history and the lessons of the Swedish Navy when faced by repeated incursions into its territorial waters by submersible vehicles.

The Norwegian government knows that Norway depends upon the sea. It also knows that Russia is becoming increasingly bellicose in its attitude towards energy supplies, and that trouble may well exist around the corner over issues such as the competing claims over the Lomonosov Ridge. The Russian Navy has announced plans to develop and deploy three carrier-based battle groups by the middle of the next decade Whilst these may prove ambitious and the timing may not quite emerge as stated, these announcements are a clear statement of intent. Couple this with the increasing Russian air activity in the area since 2000, with the number of flights made in 2007 equalling the total for the period 1991–2006, and the period of relative calm that descended over Norway's northern border at the end of the Cold War appears to be passing. History may well show that the Norwegian government has taken a hugely important and far-reaching decision over the medium to long-term by increasing the investment in its naval and maritime security capabilities.

A17: SINGAPORE

UPSTREAM INTERVENTION AND COUNTERING TERRORISM

Singapore has established itself at the forefront of the global economy. It depends hugely upon its access to its SLOC in order for it to perform its role as a major hub in the world's trading economy. Its location provides Singapore with a number of major trading advantages, and the large natural anchorage provides a huge and safe location. However, the local geography of Singapore creates problems for its defence from potential aggressors as it lacks strategic depth. As an island state, it would be very difficult to defend Singapore if an aggressor decided to land amphibious forces on the homeland. Defeating the threat at the point of its inception is vital.

To defend Singapore, it is vital that any application of military power occurs upstream at the point of origin of the threat; hence the development and procurement of its new Formidable-class frigates and their associated indigenously developed weapon and command and control systems, and the addition of submarines to the Navy which can also act upstream, potentially blockading any enemy force and preventing their departure from any base or tracking them down at sea. The four Minehunters of the Bedock-class, three of which were built locally, complete the formation of units that can project maritime power and defend the SLOC. This force is part of what are locally known as the third-generation of Singaporean Armed Forces and represent a highly networked force that draws benefits from the ability to interoperate across a multitude of agencies tasked with safeguarding the country. With the commissioning of the fifth and sixth Formidable-class frigates into service in April 2009, some of the major pieces of that capability are now in place awaiting the delivery of their helicopter elements, which will provide organic anti-submarine and anti-surface combat systems. This provides a very agile maritime force that can project and sustain maritime power on a regional, and in some cases, global basis.

Paradoxically, whilst the naval developments have naturally focused upon the defence of the SLOC, it is difficult in the current political climate in the area to suggest that specific neighbours pose a threat to the sovereignty of Singapore. Regional cooperation of maritime forces in the area, with Indonesia and Malaya (instigated in June 2004 with the deployment of seventeen fast patrol boats sourced from the three countries' navy and coastguard forces) is a feature of the prevailing political climate in the region. In September 2005, Thailand joined the security effort and the balance of forces was adjusted. This cooperation resulted in Lloyds removing the Strait of Malacca from its war-risk category in August 2006.

Border disputes are not a focal point of concern, and until recently, the Singapore government has felt able to contribute several warships to major international operations, such as those delivering humanitarian relief, to show it is able to play its part on the international stage. It has shared the benefits of its success as a nation state with others less fortunate, such as the help provided by the Singaporean Navy in the wake of the tsunami in December 2004. Its navy has been the main instrument through which it has been able to make such gestures on the world's stage. The recent fall-off in piracy rates, with no attacks reported in the first half of 2007 in the local area is a reflection of the success of the cooperation being achieved by Singapore and its regional partners. However, it is important to note that the wider maritime security concerns of attacks upon vessels at anchorage, i.e. not to be held for ransom, is still an enduring problem.

The success of the operations of the combined Naval and Coastguard forces in the Strait of Malacca provides a model on which efforts to counter piracy in areas such as the Gulf of Aden should build, despite the obvious local problems of a lack of naval infrastructure on which to build. In April 2009, Singapore started its participation in the operations in the Gulf of Aden as part of Combined Task Force 151.

Today, many commentators would agree that Singapore largely faces threats that arise more from internal tensions in the country, where a Muslim minority often feels undervalued by the majority Chinese population, and from the close ties it has with countries such as the United States, where some of the training of the armed forces of Singapore takes place. The potential for these issues to manifest itself in terrorism is very real, with the close proximity of the home of the extremist group Jemaah Islamiyah, a potential source of a Mumbai-style attack from the sea.

In July 2009, the Singaporean authorities, in a reflection of their concern for the potential for such an attack to occur, conducted a full-scale exercise of their ability to handle a simultaneous attack upon a number of high profile targets in and around the island. Prior to 11 September, the Singaporean Navy was focused upon the development of a blue-water naval capability that could project power upstream to defend its SLOC. In the light of 11 September and the Mumbai attacks in November 2008, the Singaporean authorities have created a Maritime Security Task Force which reports directly to the Chief of the Defence Force whose task it is to coordinate responses, from all concerned agencies, to an attack upon Singapore and its infrastructure. High-profile targets exist both on the land and in the immediate vicinity of the port and its extensive anchorages.

Despite its relative size geographically, Singapore clearly has to develop an approach to maritime security that balances any perceived threat to its SLOC alongside any problems it may have securing its own coastal waters. The close proximity of potential threats is an obvious cause for concern as the potential for a Mumbai-style attack upon key facilities is possible.

A18: SOMALIA

BUILDING AN INDIGENOUS CAPABILITY FROM SMALL BEGINNINGS

It is be tempting to look at the management of the coastal waters of Somalia through the somewhat narrow lens of the piracy that bedevils the Gulf of Aden and the Indian Ocean. Whilst, without doubt, piracy does have its roots in the enduring problems of the internal politics in Somalia, and the associated tribal and kinship-based conflicts, the major cause of the people turning to piracy appears to be the reducing potential for earning an income from fishing. Turning to piracy was, to many, a simple necessity of life. As fishermen, they had the maritime skills and it was merely a question of reapplying these to another purpose. However, there are other factors to be considered, and despite the apparently gloomy picture, some positive moves are occurring that might well improve the maritime security of Somali coastal waters in the near-term. Equally, however, piracy is not the only issue to cause problems in the coastal waters of Somalia, which cover the most area of any nation in Africa.

The fishermen in Somalia have increasingly struggled to eke out a living since the mid 1990s. Foreign fishing vessels are conducting unregulated fishing activity along the coastal waters, and this is having a major impact upon the fish stocks that are usually harvested by the artisanal fishermen. The enduring security issues in Somalia have created a vacuum into which the commercial organisations that exploit fish stocks have moved. In Somali coastal waters, this problem has been exacerbated by the illegal dumping of toxic waste, which is having an additional impact upon the overall health of the fisheries. These problems are at the core of the reasons why fishermen are turning to piracy.

Piracy on its own does not bring in a huge income to all of the parties involved. In 2008, it was estimated that the total income of pirates was around $30 million. This is not an exceptional sum, and it does not get evenly distributed among the people involved. Often warlords operating in the coastal areas take a large part of the earnings and the people at the sharp end of the activities—those risking their lives to hijack the ships—get quite low levels of income. However, those who do benefit from piracy certainly enjoy a lifestyle that would not normally be associated with people living in the region. It does have its attractions, and it is not difficult to persuade people whose livelihoods are threatened to join in the activities.

It has long been a concern of the international community that a nexus was emerging between the piracy in Somalia and international terrorist groups. Whilst undoubtedly contacts exist between the Islamic insurgent groups that are fighting government forces in the central region of Somalia, these links have appeared to date to be tenuous. Suggestions that large sums of money being received by the pirates are being diverted to transnational terrorist groups, such as Al-Qaeda, appear far removed from the real situation on the ground. What is occurring instead, as evidence suggests, is that a nexus is developing between the pirate groups and those involved in other forms of criminality, such as people-smuggling. In what appears to be a bid to confuse the international coalition, the pirates have developed tactics that involve hiding themselves amongst the refugees trying to flee the chaos in Somalia and the economic privations of Ethiopia for a better life in Saudi Arabia. The people-smugglers allow the pirates to blend into the background when coalition warships intercept their activities. The craft carrying the economic migrants act as mother crafts hiding the pirates.

Whilst the problems associated with piracy and people-smuggling in the region are unlikely to evaporate in the near to medium-term, there are encouraging signs in Somalia. In June 2009, the formation of a coastguard for the central coastal areas of Somalia was announced, when over 500 people were recruited to form the force based upon their own local knowledge of the region. Tribal considerations did not apply in the selection of this force; local appreciation of the situation was the foremost consideration. With the Puntland Coastguard providing a limited ability to patrol the northern coastal waters of Somalia and arrest those engaged in illegal fishing, the extension of this capability down the eastern coastline, south of the Horn of Africa, is a positive development. Whilst the impact of the coastguard force may initially be highly localised, the situation that is developing may create some manoeuvre room in which they can extend their activities incrementally.

With pirates extending their activities into the Red Sea and out further along the Omani coast into the Gulf of Oman, and reportedly to the east of the Seychelles Islands into the Indian Ocean, the coastal waters of Somalia are more readily policed by the nascent coastguard force which can focus on the prevention of illegal fishing. The pirates are diluting their effort over greater areas of the Indian Ocean and nearby waters. Whilst patterns of piracy will change, driven in part by considerations of the monsoon winds and the activities of the international task force, any move that makes attacks in the immediate coastal waters of Somalia less likely is welcome, even if it is a brief respite. In what might turn out to be a strange twist, the policing of the coastal waters may become easier as the pirates range out over longer distances, using places like the Seychelles to provide staging-posts to extend the range of their attacks into the deeper waters of the Indian Ocean. This might give the local coastguard some breathing space to extend the zones around the immediate littoral regions of Somalia, and provide some maritime security for local artisanal fishermen who can start to resume their careers and move away from piracy. Given the increasing risks they are taking, this may be a course of action that will create the conditions which undermines piracy in the medium to long-term.

A19: SRI LANKA

AN INSURGENCY MANOEUVRING IN THE MARITIME DOMAIN

The Tamil Tigers provide an interesting case study of a well equipped insurgent group with a nascent Air Force, and a capable naval arm fighting alongside an Army with regular and irregular elements. Suicide terrorism has some of its roots in the Sri Lankan conflict. Asymmetric tactics developed against the backdrop of the campaign in Sri Lanka will be seized upon by other groups with an international agenda, and have the potential to provide a lasting legacy of the insurgency model developed by the Tamil Tigers.

Any analysis, however cursory, by international terrorist groups of the tactics of the pirates off the coast of Somalia, and the difficulties clearly experienced by the international task force operating in the Gulf of Aden and the Indian Ocean, would rapidly lead them to conclude that, as yet, they have not made full use of the maritime dimension of warfare to conduct attacks aimed at terrorising local populations. Add in the lessons from Mumbai, and a powerful set of images emerges that are attractive to groups with a nihilistic perspective on the value of life. The Tamil Tigers, through their Sea Tigers organisation with its Black Sea Tigers suicide teams, provide a very powerful example of what can be achieved by insurgent groups that have a naval capability and who combine these various elements into a doctrine based upon asymmetric forms of warfare.

The maritime activities of the Tamil Tigers have shown another dimension to the issue of maritime security. With their hold on the northern coastline of Sri Lanka ending in May 2009, as the Sri Lankan Army crushed the final armed resistance from the Tamil Tigers, the threat from the Tamil Tiger Navy was also reduced, but perhaps not finally eliminated. Despite statements made by the Tamil Tigers in the immediate aftermath of their defeat and the death of their leader Velupillai Prabhakaran, the potential for disaffected Tamils being excluded from the national reconciliation process outlined by Sri Lanka's President soon after, could provide the basis of a new resistance movement.

They could focus solely upon the maritime domain and build upon their previous expertise for launching attacks from the sea, using mother vessels as the platforms from which to sustain their operations. The defeat of the Tamil Tigers on the land does not totally eliminate the potential for further suicide attacks to be undertaken from the sea in coming years. The Sri Lankan Navy must not let its guard drop, as it seeks to secure Sri Lanka's coastline from Mumbai-like attacks launched from the coastline of India and supported by angry members of diasporas located in places like the United States and Europe.

The Tamil Tigers, through their Sea Tigers Organisation, conducted a range of attacks, both on the Sri Lankan Navy and on the shoreline of Sri Lanka from the sea, despite being largely devastated by the December 2004 tsunami. The Sea Tigers developed asymmetric forms of attack upon Sri Lankan naval vessels, claiming several of them as victims. The Tamil Tigers also started to operate as if they were part of an autonomous state, conducting patrols to protect their coastline. They reportedly chased off Indian fishing vessels that were acting illegally, poaching fish in what were regarded as their coastal waters.

After the setback from the impact of the tsunami, the Tamil Tigers went on a shopping spree for new vessels, using contacts in places like Malaysia, Singapore and Hong Kong. Revised maritime tactics were combined with rapid manoeuvring by surface forces, whilst a vessel containing a suicide bomber was deployed. With several boats attacking in synchronisation, the boat containing the suicide bomber was difficult to detect. These swarm tactics, as they became known, are also practised by the Iranian Navy as it develops its doctrine to counter any potential incursion by the United States Navy into the waters along its coastline. Reports also suggest that in the course of the Israeli incursion into Gaza in January 2009 a fishing vessel exploded in the vicinity of an Israeli Naval unit. This has all the hallmarks of an asymmetric form of attack mirroring the tactics of the Sea Tigers.

The Tamil Tigers showed great agility in their use of a small fleet (rumoured to be less than ten vessels) of ships that brought supplies into northern Sri Lanka. These vessels reportedly made quick visits into the waters off the northern coast and then retreated across the Indian Ocean seeking refuge in distance from the Sri Lankan Navy. As intelligence was developed by the Sri Lankan Navy on these vessels, a series of high profile attacks were mounted, sometimes over several thousand miles of sea, to attack the vessels and attempt to deny supplies to the Tamil Tigers. Their eventual demise as a land-based force occurred quite quickly after these supply ships had been attacked, in one case quite close to the coastal waters of Australia. The Sri Lankan Navy projected power across the Indian Ocean to deny the supplies maintained about what can be thought of as floating warehouses to the land-based forces operating in the northern areas of Sri Lanka.

In the events that led up to the defeat of the Tamils, a major incursion of the Sea Tigers was halted by the Sri Lankan Navy on the 4 April 2009 off the coast of Alampil in the northeast of Sri Lanka where a flotilla of ten Sea Tiger boats, including three suicide craft, were intercepted by the Sri Lankan Navy. This followed on from a previous naval battle on 29–30 March, in which four Sea Tiger boats were destroyed. Whilst the Sea Tigers are clearly finished in their current incarnation, history alone will say if this is the last that the world sees of an insurgency group with a well organised naval element contributing its unique dimension to the overall campaign.

A20: UNITED ARAB EMIRATES

INTERNATIONAL COOPERATION

On 26 May 2009, President Sarkozy of France formally opened a French military base in the United Arab Emirates (UAE). It is France's first permanent base in the Persian Gulf. President Sarkozy agreed the arrangements for the creation of the base in January 2008. The objective of the new base—called 'Peace Camp'—is to provide tangible support to the UAE should a regional conflict break out. The aim is to have a deterrent effect upon any potential aggressor and is a clear move towards an upstream or proactive stance on maritime security, mirroring the developments in the area adopted by the United States.

The UAE is a federation of seven states. It arose from the Trucial States, which had been created after they had achieved independence from the United Kingdom in 1971. The creation of the UAE was in part motivated by a desire for the states—which maintain a high degree of independence—to work together over matters where collaboration was seen to be mutually beneficial. Given the presence and apparent ambitions of Iran, this seems like a sensible reaction. This form of local relationship and burden-sharing provides an enhanced capability. However, given the sheer scale of Iranian military power and its development of asymmetric approaches to warfare, this alone might be insufficient to guarantee the safety of the area and its hugely important oil supplies. Despite multilateral agreements and the economic power enjoyed by the UAE, they lack the strategic depth to engage in a protracted confrontation.

The relationship between Iran and its neighbours across the Straits of Hormuz continues to be defined by a number of regional issues affecting security and mutual confidence. One of these is the dispute over ownership of the islands of Abu Musa and the Greater and Lesser Tunb, which are located in the middle of the strategically important Straits of Hormuz, an oil lifeline to Western economies. In the immediate run-up to the Trucial States achieving independence, Iranian marines mounted the first-ever hovercraft assault on the islands on 30 November 1971, seizing them from a small Arab force, which provided some token resistance. Efforts at creating a bilateral solution failed in 1992, whereupon the UAE sought resolution from the International Court of Justice. Iran refused to join in this process, stating that the islands had always been a part of Iran and that they had no intention of discussing their sovereignty as they were integral part of Iranian territory and administered as part of the Iranian province of Hormozgan; this is a relationship the Iranians chart back to the fourteenth century, when the islands were a part of the dominions of the Kings of Hormuz.

The dispute, however, has not been resolved, and on 30 April 2009 the Gulf Cooperation Council and the European Union both declared that peaceful means to resolve the dispute should be found, and highlighted specific enduring concerns over claims made by Iran over the territorial sovereignty of Bahrain, which is also the location of a major United States naval base in the area. The approach to maritime security in this area is, therefore, crucial for the UAE. Iran's history, contemporary military might, its obvious interest in nuclear weapons, the dispute over the islands and the fact that 40 per cent of the world's oil moves through the Straits of Hormuz, create a heady cocktail with the potential for confrontation never far away.

In reaction to this enduring threat, the UAE has not only created the joint military base with France, but it has embarked upon a major build-up of its own naval forces. In an article with *Jane's* published on 27 May 2009, the Commander of the UAE Naval Forces explicitly stated that the build up was 'not directed at a specific enemy'. It is difficult not to conclude that this is a form of diplomatic language designed to prevent the inflammation of an already difficult situation. The purchase of twelve missile-armed Fast Attack Craft, upgrades to the Ghannatha fast troop carriers, and the conversion of four Bombardier Dash 8 aircraft into a maritime patrol configuration provide a capable force certainly able to mount an amphibious operation against the islands. The centrepieces of the new procurement programme, however, are the six multi-mission 72 metre corvettes, five of which will be built in the UAE by Abu Dhabi Ship Building (ADSB).

As part of its approach to maritime security, the naval forces of the UAE routinely conduct joint exercises with naval units visiting the area. This helps the UAE naval forces to build their own indigenous capacity and also gain from the cooperation with other navies. In a time of rising tensions and potential confrontation, this may well enable nations to quickly assemble a maritime coalition that is familiar with working together to try and defuse any tensions. Through both formalised permanent and ad-hoc arrangements, the UAE achieves strategic depth in its approach to maritime security. The combination of the elements of this naval force, and the allied close cooperation with indigenous coastguard units, provides an important capability to deter any unilateral action to close the Straits of Hormuz; a threat that has been issued by the Iranian government, apparently designed to deter any pre-emptive military action against its nuclear programme. Any multinational response to any closure, such as an attempt to mine the Straits of Hormuz, would be based upon a coalition of the willing, as any disruption of oil supplies in the area would be of global significance.

The UAE also has concerns about the impact of the piracy, pollution, illegal migration and levels of fishing in the area. These all have an impact upon local economies. Pirate attacks have been moving along the coastline from the Yemen to the shores of Oman. Mother ships are allowing the pirates to move further out from their traditional hunting grounds and also manoeuvre when weather conditions, such as the Monsoon winds, require a response. Piracy has an effect upon all of the economies in the region, with knock-on impacts on insurance premiums, security and transportation costs. The potential for the UAE to use some of its emerging naval prowess to branch out from the Gulf and provide assistance to the naval activities in the Northern Arabian Sea could well result in the UAE naval forces playing a wider regional role.

A21: UNITED KINGDOM

MULTI-AGENCY COOPERATION

The approach to maritime security being taken in respect of the coastal waters of the United Kingdom is fundamentally based upon a multi-agency approach, whereby different private and public sector organisations are encouraged to cooperate in sharing information. The May 2009 House of Commons Defence Committee report on The Defence Contribution to UK National Security and Resilience, provides some important insights into the issues this creates when faced by a complex threat environment. Where multi-agency responses are necessary in countries that have many organisations each holding their own specific responsibilities, it is sometimes difficult to see how the overall management of any threats or perceived weaknesses in maritime security are analysed. Coordinating multi-agency responses, whilst being very necessary, can be difficult and provide gaps that terrorists can exploit.

Through its direct support of the so-called 'Global War on Terror', the United Kingdom has placed itself at increased levels of risk from being targeted in terrorist attacks. The events of 7 July 2005 and the attempt to repeat those events on 21 July, two weeks later, highlighted how the social diversity of the United Kingdom can also create conditions in which people can become involved both directly and on the periphery of terrorism. Reports generated by the Security Services in 2009, estimate that over 2,000 people are either directly involved or very closely associated with planning attacks in the United Kingdom. It is not difficult to envisage some of these being directed at coastal locations.

The Parliamentary Intelligence Security Committee (ISC) Report issued in May 2009 highlighted the ever-present danger of terrorism and tried to draw out lessons from the attacks mounted in July 2005. It is hard not to conclude from any reading of the report that intelligence failures will still occur, as the sheer numbers of people involved in terrorism-related activities in the United Kingdom appears close to overwhelming the security system. Maritime security in the United Kingdom has to be seen through the lens of this problem, with people drawn to terrorism, and the vulnerabilities of certain important parts of the national critical infrastructure on the coastline, such as major oil and gas facilities, and nuclear power stations like those at Sizewell and Dungeness.

Terrorists increasingly use asymmetric forms of warfare to achieve their aims. The Tamil Tigers' use of the maritime domain to manoeuvre provides a good example of what those using terror tactics can resort to at sea. Whilst soft targets along the coastline, tourist hot spots and population centres help guarantee terrorists that they will be successful, hard targets also provide a clear indication of intent and commitment. The attack on Mumbai is an example of an asymmetric approach to terrorism, attacking a high profile target and achieving what has been called in the United States National Intelligence Estimate Report of 12 February 2009 as 'visually dramatic destruction'. The port of Leith in Scotland provides an excellent backdrop for an attack that would combine images of the Royal Yacht *Britannia* being seized alongside a move inland towards Edinburgh, some 3 km away. Google Earth imagery of the location provides detailed insights for attack-planning purposes. Grangemouth, on the east coast of Scotland, is also an attractive target.

Attacks on major United Kingdom infrastructure, launched from the sea, cannot be ruled out. Terrorists are capable of projecting power across the North Sea and English Channel, and targets such as Dungeness nuclear power station are attractive, as any threat to the local population arising from an attack launched from the sea would have a dramatic impact upon the local population and knock-on effects nationally. Terrorists with an apocalyptic view of the world would not have too many qualms about failing to achieve their goals if an attack was thwarted. The sheer audacity with which the attack were perpetrated would be sufficient to serve notice that any locations along our coastlines are at risk. Targets would range from urban population centres, through major port facilities and important nuclear, oil and gas installations, such as Milford Haven.

The United Kingdom's response to the threat has been to divide its coastal region into a number of areas or portals. These provide a basis for cooperation amongst agencies to ensure that indicators of people planning an attack, such as conducting reconnaissance, have an increased chance of being detected. Lessons drawn from Mumbai, however, suggest that terrorists increasingly use open sources of information, such as Google Earth, to study and develop their plans to attack targets that are seen to be high profile. Such attacks have both a short-term and medium-term aim. In the short-term, the objective is to immediately terrorise people as the attack unfolds. In the medium-term, the aim is to highlight how poorly defended a coastline actually is from a determined attacker.

A22: UNITED STATES

DEFENCE THROUGH MULTILAYERED INTERNATIONAL COOPERATION

Ever since the attacks of 11 September 2001, the United States has grown increasingly concerned about the potential for a maritime-based attack upon a major port or city. The 3,000-person death toll on that momentous day is seen by many in terrorist circles as being a bar that needs to be raised. The next major attack, which may take some time in the planning and execution, will need to be as spectacular as the last in appearing to come from nowhere and being totally unexpected. It must achieve massive media coverage and create lasting memories for everyone who either directly or indirectly witnesses it. One way to achieve this is to launch a Chemical, Biological, Radiological, Nuclear (CBRN) or large-scale conventionally-based attack, such as a Boiling Liquid Expanding Vapour Explosion (BLEVE) upon a major port.

Fearing the worst, the United States government has been taking a whole new look at its maritime security strategy. Its approach is to try and create a series of layers through which terrorists planning an attack must successfully penetrate if they are to succeed. One aspect of this multilayered system is the Proliferation Security Initiative (PSI). This is a multinational initiative to coordinate efforts across the world to identify and search vessels that are potentially involved in smuggling materials associated with Weapons of Mass Destruction (WMD). One focus of this is operations off the coast of North Korea.

The issue over North Korea is one dimension of the wider maritime security agenda being followed by the United States government. One concern that is well documented is the idea that Al-Qaeda operates a sea-basing approach to storage and supply of weapon systems to give it agility in the maritime arena and flexibility to withstand setbacks in the land environment. The idea of an Al-Qaeda fleet of 20 merchant vessels has been the subject of a great deal of speculation. The potential for one of those vessels, armed with a nuclear device, approaching the shores of America to attack a port facility is one that haunts maritime security planners in the United States, fuelled as it is by the efforts of Hollywood to make movies that appear to increase the credibility of such a scenario. The media also get involved in establishing the plausibility of such an attack. Brian Ross, an ABC News Reporter, pulled a stunt in the immediate aftermath of the 11 September attacks and arranged for depleted uranium to be smuggled into the port of Los Angeles. Given the sheer volumes of containers that arrive in major maritime hubs such as Los Angeles, this was not a difficult thing to achieve, but his scoop certainly created debate on the news wires.

In reacting to these concerns, the United States authorities have introduced a number of measures designed to make it harder for a terrorist group to achieve an aim of attacking a major port facility. Crew Identity Cards are one initiative that seeks to biometrically tag crew-members who are aboard merchant vessels visiting the United States. Vessels intending to dock in the United States must radio ahead their manifests twenty-four hours before arrival. These measures are all part of this multilayered approach, which also declares some ports of origin as being safer, as they are involved in the Ports Security. In 2002, the International Maritime Organisation (IMO) issued a statement requiring its 158 members, within eighteen months, to show they were compliant with the guidelines outlined in the International Ship and Port Facility Security Code. The adoption of this code worldwide does not entirely prevent another terrorist attack, criminal activity within a port or environmental problems, but it is a start and provides something upon which to build.

Of course, the United States does not simply face the problem of nuclear terrorism in its coastal waters. Major issues also exist with the smuggling of drugs and people into the United States. The Florida coastline is a destination sought by many looking for a new life and leaving behind the poverty of countries such as Haiti. Many Caribbean countries have poor economies and the attractions of a life in the United States are obvious and the risks appear to be worth it. This is a major issue for the United States Coastguard who have to police the extensive waters of the south and southeast of the United States to try and intercept people making these journeys.

Another element of the United States response is based upon a move upstream. The African Partnership Station (APS) initiative is a medium to long-term programme designed to transfer key maritime skills and equipment to African countries to help them better police their maritime security issues. The APS programme is multifaceted and involves donations of vessels, shore-based radar equipment and routine port visits, and training exercises aimed at building and maintaining local capacity. By helping African countries develop that capacity, the United States is building another layer of its defence system, making it harder for transnational terrorist groups to operate.

Drugs-smuggling by sea is a well known problem for the United States authorities. Major routes come overland, through Mexico via Guatemala, Honduras, Nicaragua, Panama and Belize. Sea routes use the waters of the Caribbean, launching fast boats containing drugs up through routes that cover Jamaica and the Dominican Republic. In 2008, the drugs cartels started to use mini submarines that are crewed by four to five people to move cocaine up the coastline of Mexico. The drugs smugglers are reacting to the increased intercepts being made by the United States Coastguard authorities. The re-establishment of the Fourth Fleet in the United States Navy is another development that seeks to improve maritime security through a defence-in-depth approach. Despite having limited resources at its re-inception, the US Fourth Fleet is a part of a longer-term plan to improve maritime security in the waters off the coast of South America, where other drugs routes across the Southern Atlantic Ocean ship cocaine through Africa to Western Europe. The United States approach to maritime security is rapidly evolving, driven on in part by the vivid memories of the events of 11 September 2001, and involves an international response to the potential threats from the sea in a multilayered architecture.

A23: VENEZUELA

IDEOLOGICAL DIFFERENCES AND TACTICAL COOPERATION

The approach to maritime security by the Venezuelan government appears to have a contradiction at its heart. Outwardly, the rhetoric of the regime of Hugo Chavez is hugely anti-American and quite specifically vitriolic, and yet Venezuela depends upon American consumption of oil for a significant part of its overseas income. In the maritime arena, it is not difficult to think that the relationship between the United States and Venezuela has echoes in the Cuban Missile Crisis. Paradoxically, Venezuela is a signatory to the 1947 Inter-American Treaty of Reciprocal Assistance (Rio Treaty), which is a United States sponsored mutual defence agreement designed to protect the western hemisphere from the perceived communist threat at the end of the Second World War. With the reformation of the United States Fourth Fleet in 2008 to patrol the coastal waters of the South Atlantic and the Eastern Caribbean Sea, it is not hard to think that Venezuela feels threatened by such posturing. Yet despite what are obviously ideological fault lines that are at the heart of the problem, the government of Venezuela actively cooperates with United States Counter-Narcotics efforts in the region; this is an implicit acceptance that the coastal waters of Venezuela have become hugely important to Columbian drugs cartels as they seek to use the 6,762 km (the United Nations' official figure for the coastline of Venezuela) coastline to manoeuvre, avoid coastguard patrols and react to the clampdown in Columbia upon their activities.

On 7 April 2009, in what is an increasing occurrence, the United States Coastguard—operating outside the immediate EEZ of Brazil—arrested a fishing vessel, the *Don Andres*, 513 miles northeast of Brazil. The United States Coastguard immediately requested permission from the Venezuelan authorities to board the vessel and conduct a search for drugs. The Venezuelan authorities granted this request and over 2,000 pounds of cocaine were seized. The vessel was possibly en route across the Atlantic Ocean to the west coast of Africa to drop off the drugs in a country such as Guinea-Bissau. Major ideological differences fuel the strategic differences, but at the tactical level cooperation is good and focused upon the many problems associated with drugs smuggling in the area.

Oil has been, and remains, the major driver behind the Venezuelan economy. Fishing is insignificant, by South American standards, with a reported catch of just under 350,000 metric tonnes a year of the 17.5 million metric tonnes caught in the region. Oil, however, is a different story. In 2008, Venezuela announced that it had increased its assessment of its proven reserves from 80 to 87 billion barrels. Some estimates place the total potential reserves at levels that would eclipse Saudi Arabia, making Venezuela the largest oil producer in the world. The oil is located in four sedimentary basins at Falcón, Apure, Oriental and Maracaibo. 80 per cent of the oil produced is exported. Venezuela has been increasing its oil supplies to countries such as China to reduce its dependency upon the United States as a major trading partner. This shift is not, however, straightforward. The oil Venezuela produces is a form of heavier crude oil, which requires specific refining capacity, and shipping costs to China are far higher than over the short distance to the United States across the Gulf of Mexico.

Recent efforts to modernise the Venezuelan Navy (The Venezuelan Bolivarian Navy) are a clear reaction to what may well be perceived as hostile American intent under the Bush administration to apply military power against what it sees as a rogue regime in Venezuela. The role of the Navy is perceived as that of protecting national sovereignty over its territorial waters, rivers and lakes, and conducting oceanographic research. The emphasis upon the purchase of submarines as part of the emerging naval capability is significant as part of what is emerging as a fleet that has a blue-water capability, is able to operate in the littoral and has a riverine capacity to mount amphibious landings. Covering all of these aspects would require an ongoing commitment to building up the Navy, and President Chavez does have major social and economic programmes to fund. Whilst the Navy is important, it has to take its place in the funding queue.

In reaction to this strategic posturing, the Venezuelan government has certainly strengthened ties with Russia. Whilst for some commentators, the idea of Russian missiles being based in Venezuela may sound far-fetched, with a new and apparently robust Russian leadership, anything may well be possible. Russia is a significant supplier of arms to Venezuela. In 2009, Russian warships conducted joint naval exercises with the Venezuelan Navy. The Venezuelan government is also actively courting its neighbours in the Eastern Caribbean Sea, with overtures being made to the Dutch and French governments. It has also been trying to leverage its position as a regional player, trying to create new local trading blocks with countries with similar ideological viewpoints to that of the government of President Chavez. Relations with Brazil, however, are strained. The recent significant oil finds off the coast of Brazil have raised it to a position of prominence and provide an alternative source of energy for countries that might wish to distance themselves from Venezuela.

Disputes arising over the ownership of Aves Island (Bird Island), which is 350 miles north of the Venezuelan coast but only 90 miles to the north-west of Dominica, have also created tensions in the region. Ironically, given the state of US-Venezuelan relations, the United States has explicitly recognised the claim made by Venezuela to Aves Island and the position that gives Venezuela over an expanded EEZ. Countries like Dominica, Saint Kitts and Nevis, and their island neighbours, reject Venezuelan ownership of Aves Island as the new boundaries of the EEZ that that would give Venezuela would impinge upon their own coastal zones. Given this situation, it is surprising that the Venezuelan government has not signed the UNCLOS Agreement and formalised its claims to the 385,674 km^2 of its EEZ. Perhaps the more pressing issue for Venezuela is its border dispute with Guyana and its claim to all of the territories to the west of the Essequibo River. This represents approximately 70 per cent of the total land area of Guyana or 160,000 km^2 of its territory. Many commentators believe that this is the most likely flash point for a traditional state-on-state conflict in the region. Should such a conflict occur, it would quite likely be based, in part, upon the application of the Venezuelan Navy at sea and along the rivers in the area.

B1: ECONOMIC MIGRANTS

Economic migration is a growing problem for maritime security. It particularly challenges the SAR capabilities of countries that have obligations to save lives in their coastal waters. In March 2009, reports emerged from various organisations, such as the International Organisation for Migration that more than 300 African migrants had drowned when their boat had sunk near the Buri oil platform off the coast of Libya. The timing of this was important as it represents the start of a weather window for smuggling in the Mediterranean Sea, which lasts from March/April to October. One of the boats involved was believed to be carrying 257 people, many of whom were women and children. Another boat, reported to be carrying 356 people, was rescued by the Libyan authorities. Having been alerted by radio, the Italian Coastguard informed the Libyan authorities and helped coordinate the rescue. Two boats, of an original three that were also reported to have been in difficulty, are believed to have sunk.

Following this incident, a further rescue had to be coordinated in May 2009 when an Italian tanker responded to a distress call and rescued economic migrants from three boats 56 km to the southeast of Lampedusa Island. Two Italian Coastguard vessels and a tax and customs boat immediately returned the people to Libya. These are examples of what is rapidly becoming a litany of events that highlight the scale of the problem. What is difficult to assess is the number of occasions when boats are lost without any reporting. The organisation Fortress Europe estimates that over 14,600 have died since 1988 in trying to make the journey.

Most of the people on board the vessels involved in these incidents were believed to have been economic migrants who had come from Sub-Saharan Africa and North Africa looking to gain a passage across the

Mediterranean Sea to a new life in Europe, possibly to join up with friends and family who had already successfully made the journey. The journeys the migrants make are often fraught with danger, as vessels are overloaded and have only very basic safety equipment. In difficult weather conditions, people are lost overboard and vessels can become swamped. The burden for their safety shifts to passing vessels that pick up survivors, to coastguard organisations and naval vessels, and allied aircraft operating within reach of an incident.

In an attempt to address this problem, the Libyan and Italian authorities are now collaborating through the framework of a broader maritime security initiative in the Mediterranean Sea called FRONTEX, an organisation based in Warsaw that started work in October 2005. The mission of FRONTEX is to help European Union states implement the agreed rules concerning the management of external borders. Whilst each state has its own responsibilities to manage its borders, the aim of FRONTEX is to ensure that this effort is coordinated and that best practice is shared across Europe. In April 2007, European Union Ministers approved the creation of a deployable force of border guards that could rapidly be mobilised to areas where economic migration was of immediate concern. A pool of 450 national experts was created to deploy to European Union countries whose borders were seen to be under 'urgent and operational strain' as a result of illegal migration. All twenty-seven member states of the European Union contribute to this effort, which can call upon twenty aircraft, thirty helicopters and over a hundred vessels.

Patterns of economic migration tend to follow areas of the world's oceans where maritime security infrastructures have gaps in their capabilities. States that have weak legal frameworks, such as those that have not signed the 1951 Refugee Convention and have no domestic asylum law, are particularly vulnerable. Organised criminal gangs use these gaps in the maritime security infrastructure to diversify their business interests, smuggling people alongside other commodities. The attractions of well paid work in Saudi Arabia make many journey across Africa, using Eritrea as a launch point to land on the shores of the Yemen, using that as a staging post to their final destination. Another known area for this is off the west coast of Africa and is used to move migrants through to the Canary Island as a means of gaining access to Spain. In 2006, it was reported that 31,000 illegal immigrants reached Spanish territory; a six-fold increase over the previous year. This route was one of the first that was focused upon by FRONTEX. Patrols mounted by European Union nations commenced in the area in May 2007. These cases are symptomatic of the international nature of the trade in human beings. The draw of a better life in the United States of America lures many people across the Caribbean Sea from countries such as Haiti, to escape poverty.

Historically, the Vietnamese boat people created huge problems trying to leave the situation in Vietnam and gain access to places like Australia. A number of high profile standoffs resulted, where ships had rescued people from drowning only to be told to stay away from the nearest country with naval vessels aggressively patrolling their own coastal waters to prevent people landing. In the case of Australia, holding camps were established where those who wished to claim political asylum could be processed. In Europe similar solutions are being developed with the holding camp on the Island of Lampedusa. The March 2009 incident off the coastline of Libya is one example of many that are believed to occur each year in the Mediterranean Sea. The island is a destination or gateway used by people smugglers who make large sums of money, exploiting people's desire to move into Europe for a better life. In 2008, it is estimated that over 37,000 people made it ashore on the island arriving from the coast of Libya and that 75 per cent of these were asylum seekers. With its poorly equipped Navy and its 1,770 km coastline, Libya is seen as an excellent location from which to launch boats across the Mediterranean Sea. Malta is another member of the European Union that experiences difficulties with current patterns of migration. Given the scale of migration, it is clear that no single state can address the problems alone. Through coordinated efforts, such as FRONTEX, states can cooperate in developing new approaches to illegal immigration and the challenges that poses to maritime security.

B2: ARCTIC AND ANTARCTIC OCEAN

Antarctica shall be used for peaceful purposes only. There shall be prohibited, inter alia, any measure of a military nature, such as the establishment of military bases and fortifications, the carrying out of military manoeuvres, as well as the testing of any type of weapon.

Article 1 of the Antarctic Treaty of 1959—Peaceful Purposes

Given the scale of the claims of sovereignty over the Antarctic Region, and the specific overlapping claims of Chile, Argentina and the United Kingdom over the area from the Bellingshausen Sea to the Weddell Sea including the South Shetland and South Orkney Islands, it is remarkable that the Antarctic Treaty uses the form of language in Article 1. Argentina, Chile and the United Kingdom are hardly countries with a long-standing tradition of friendship. Tensions underlie the bilateral relationships that exist between Chile and Argentina, and the Falkland Islands (Malvinas) remain a source of potential conflict between the United Kingdom and Argentina.

Notwithstanding the outcome of the Falkland Islands dispute, and the war that was fought over its sovereignty, the Antarctic Region, as a whole, has been a peaceful area. The aims and language of the Antarctic Treaty have been respected and multinational scientific research has been the focus of the various bases created in the region. It is one of the few areas in the world where international collaboration for the greater good of mankind—such as the pioneering work on the depletion of the ozone layer—has been carried out. As such, it is a model from which insights should be drawn. The potential for confrontation over the Arctic Region, however, is a very different story, with claims and counter-claims centring on a subterranean structure called the Lomonosov Ridge. Here the full might of a number of countries is being played out militarily and diplomatically to establish and delimit the extents of various countries' claims to the area.

It is believed that some 10 billion tonnes of oil and gas reserves exist under the Lomonosov Ridge—alongside diamond, zinc, copper and possibly uranium deposits—that are clearly extremely valuable. Defining the 200-mile economic zone, and how that determines claims made to the United Nations over ownership of areas of the sea, is of international interest. The vast reservoir of oil and natural gas reserves beneath the Arctic Ocean is thought to represent 20–25 per cent of the world's total remaining undiscovered resources with the United States Geological Survey placing an estimate upon the reserves of around 160 billion barrels, enough to supply the world's resources for five years. At the other end of the scale, however, the reserves could be as low as 40 billion barrels. The variance arises from problems of estimating the amount of oil in the region due to its inaccessibility.

A little known sub-surface feature extending over 1,800 km from the East Siberian Sea to the Ellesmere Islands off the coast of Greenland, called the Lomonosov Ridge, holds the key to what may be an ongoing international dispute over who owns these reserves and has the right to exploit them. The Lomonosov Ridge was first discovered in 1948 and was named after Russian scientists and writer Mikhail Lomonosov who, inter alia, explained in 1760 the formation of icebergs.

Recent efforts by the Russians, building upon a claim made to own this area submitted in 2000 which was rejected by an international panel of scientists, have brought the potential for competition over such reserves into sharp relief. Russia already has the world's largest economic development zone spanning its coastal waters. In April 2007, the Russians and Canadians, two of many parties with interests in the Lomonosov Ridge, mounted a joint exploration of the area. Recently a Russian expedition has returned from a follow-on survey claiming they have conclusive proof that under the definitions of established international law this area clearly belongs to Russia. In June 2008, the Russian ice-breaker, the *Akademik Fyodorov*, suffered a major engine failure as it was returning to plant a flag at the North Pole—in effect claiming it as part of Russia. After some engineering work, it resumed its journey and was due to start its exploration close to the North Pole at the beginning of August. This apparent stunt—planting a flag underwater—is all part of a new assertive stance being taken by Russia. Following the evidence collected in recent surveys, Russia is preparing a detailed legal claim to extend its coastline by an area of some 460,000 square miles—an area equivalent to the combined land masses of Germany, Italy and France.

With the Arctic Ice cap receding at a rate of 9 per cent per year, the long-standing vision of a maritime route avoiding the Panama Canal through the Northwest Passage linking the United States Eastern Seaboard with China, Japan and the other emerging economies in the Far East offers major prospects of shortening journey times and also associated economic benefits. With the vast reservoirs of the Arctic Ocean within reach and the reduction of sea ice, there is a huge potential for the navies of the United States, Denmark, Norway, the United Kingdom, Canada and Russia to come into conflict. Clearly NATO will have a role to play in providing a framework through which countries can support each other in projecting naval assets into the Arctic Ocean. The northern Norwegian air base at Bodo would again become strategically important in delivering long-range maritime patrol and air-to-surface combat projection capabilities. Norway's renewed interest in the High Arctic (explored in Case Study A16) is also explained by these developments. Canada's decision to invest in new bases and infrastructure in the area is also driven by similar considerations (see Case Study A4).

A resurgent Russian Navy, based upon its traditional Northern Fleet at Murmansk, would also be capable of rapidly projecting power into the Arctic Sea; it alone today has that potential. It is possible to see the Iceland-Greenland Gap re-emerging as a major strategic location and naval facilities in Iceland again being at a premium, with long range maritime patrol aircraft operating well above 75°N. Facilities on the Spitsbergen Islands would also become important for Norway in monitoring activities in the Arctic Ocean. The Barents Sea, with all of its previous focus in the Cold War as a major place that NATO forces would forward deploy to confront the Russian Northern Fleet, would again emerge as a major area of interest for naval operations and associated maritime security concerns. The contrast between the peaceful agreements over the South Pole and the potential for confrontation over the Lomonosov Ridge could not be clearer. With the Arctic ice cap appearing to be in retreat, the area is also becoming important as a new SLOC with the promise of faster voyage times and other allied benefits in terms of reduced operating costs for vessels making passage through both the North East (over the top of Siberia) and its more famous sister, the North West Passage.

B3: CLASHES OVER DEFINITIONS OF CONTINENTAL SHELF BOUNDARIES

The confrontation between the People's Republic of China, Taiwan, Vietnam, Philippines and Malaysia over the ownership of the Spratley Islands is symptomatic of a wider range of territorial disputes in the South China Seas with access to natural resources being a key motivator for economies that have, until the global recession of 2008/2009, been growing rapidly. The area of the South China Seas covers an area of the Pacific Ocean that stretches from Singapore and the Malacca Strait in the southwest to the Strait of Taiwan in the northeast. It covers an area of more than 200 small islands, rocks and reefs, with the majority located in the Paracel Islands and the Spratley Islands.

The Paracel Islands are simultaneously claimed in full by The People's Republic of China, Vietnam and Taiwan. In 1974, the People's Republic of China unilaterally seized the Paracel Islands. The People's Republic of China also claims the Pratas Islands, to the northeast of the South China Sea. These claims are underpinned by archaeological evidence that dates human occupation of the islands back to the Han (110 AD) and Ming (1403–1433 AD) dynasties. Whilst not making claims over the ownership of the Spratley Islands specifically, Brunei and Indonesia also look on from the sidelines with more than a passing interest. Arguably, this is the most extensive and complicated area where disagreements exist over maritime boundaries, other than perhaps the Lomonosov Ridge in the Arctic Ocean.

The Spratley Islands are a group of approximately 600 reefs, islands and cays that lie in the middle of the strategically important seas lanes from Japan to the Middle East. Vessels that make passage through the Malacca Strait will inevitably pass close to the Spratley Islands. The islands themselves comprise less than 5 km^2 of landmass but lie over an area of 400,000 km^2 of sea. They are part of three archipelagos of the South China Sea. In their own right, they have little to no economic value. They also have no indigenous population. Their value arises from their location, which is at the juxtaposition of a number of important claims over ownership rights concerning potential rich subterranean oil and gas reserves in the area.

Malaya's claim to areas of the South China Sea is based upon its definition of the continental shelf. Malaysia claims three of the Spratley Islands and has already populated one of the islands and built a hotel. The Philippines government claims eight of the Spratley Islands based upon similar arguments of the extent of its EEZ arising from the boundaries of its continental shelf. The discovery of the some of the islands by a Filipino fisherman in 1956 is also used to reinforce the claims.

On 16 March 2009, the People's Republic of China defended a decision it had taken to send a patrol boat into the area. Several days beforehand an American ocean surveillance ship, the United States Naval Ship *Impeccable* (T-AGOS 23), was harassed by five Chinese fishing vessels as it conducted oceanographic research 75 miles to the south of Hainan Island. This clash occurred after a period of relative calm in the area with the last reported confrontation occurring in 2002 when Vietnamese troops fired warning shots at a Filipino reconnaissance plane circling the Spratley Islands. Historically, the People's Republic of China can document a series of military clashes, of varying severity, back to the seizure of the Paracel Islands in 1974.

Since that date, several other exchanges have occurred, such as the naval battle between the Chinese and Vietnamese navies in 1988 at Johnson Reef, when several Vietnamese vessels were sunk and over seventy sailors were reported to have died. In 1992, in an attempt to widen the dispute, Vietnam accused the People's Republic of China of drilling for oil in Vietnamese waters off the Gulf of Tonkin. This accusation also included a charge of landing amphibious forces on Da Luc Reef. Further tensions in the area spilled over in 1994 when naval confrontations occurred over disputed oil exploration blocks. In 1995, the problems in the South China Sea widened when the People's Republic of China occupied the Mischief Reef then claimed by the Philippine government. A Philippine naval force was immediately dispatched to eject the Chinese people who had landed on the reef. This dispute continued into 1996 when in January, three Chinese naval vessels engaged in a ninety-minute gun battle near to Campones Island. During the first three months of 2001, the Filipino Navy boarded 14 flagged fishing vessels from the People's Republic of China and confiscated their catches, ejecting them from the disputed areas of the Spratley Islands. A gunboat was also dispatched to the Scarborough Shoal, to deter any attempt by the People's Republic of China to erect structures on the rock. This incident followed a previous clash in the same area in 1997, when the Philippine Navy ordered a Chinese speedboat and two fishing boats to leave the area. In retaliation, the People's Republic of China sent three warships to survey the Philippine-occupied islands of Panata and Kota.

Recent attempts at reconciliation by the People's Republic of China, Vietnam and the Philippines, through plans to conduct a Joint Marine Seismic Undertaking (JMSU) over the area to delimit the continental shelf, have had their legitimacy questioned with particular harsh criticism coming from with the Philippine Islands. Despite the obvious multilateral approach that is being adopted in this difficult matter, the JMSU seems to have opened up a debate over ownership of a large area of the EEZ already claimed by the Philippines. The Kalayaan Islands are of particular concern as they are currently claimed by the Philippine Islands government and have a small but established population, which is administered as a municipality in the province of Palawan. In an annex to the JMSU, the area to be explored includes approximately 80 per cent of the Kalayaan Islands, which had previously not been in dispute. Despite clear efforts at mediation and reconciliation, the disputed waters of the South China Sea pose a real problem for maritime security.

B4: BIOSECURITY

NEW ZEALAND'S AQUACULTURE INDUSTRY

The term biosecurity is often used in the context of biological weapons and their potential access and use by terrorists. Some uses of the term are very narrow, implying that it covers measures to reduce the theft of biological material, which may have a military application. Securing materials used for research into biological warfare is crucial and an important part of a wide range of measures to be undertaken to be able to react and cope with an attack using WMD. This case study, however, focuses on a much wider definition of the term in the particular context of the maritime domain.

Australia and New Zealand have been leading proponents of this dimension, being added into the wider definitions and holistic approach to maritime security adopted within this book. The Australian government defines compromises to biosecurity as being of threat to its maritime security; through deliberate or accidental introduction of foreign species fundamental imbalances can arise in local indigenous species and the biota. The statistics bear some examination: Australia inspected 1.6 million sea cargo containers in 2006–2007, which rose to 1.8 million in 2007–2008, a 10 per cent increase in a single year, while the United States, in comparison, inspected over 315,000 ships in the period 1991–1996, looking for pests that might harm local produce and disrupt the local environment.

Some species may initially appear to be unproblematic, but situations can change as environmental balances shift and a species can reach a tipping point at which it can multiply quickly, as in the case of harmful algae blooms. These threats to local aquatic environments are known an invasive species and they are new to a region and are capable of having a negative impact on it, with ecological and potentially economic implications as they displace and, in some cases, destroy local inhabitants. In some cases they are able—due to favourable environmental condition—to establish themselves, aggressively displacing native species. Maritime biosecurity is the term used to describe all of the measures taken to minimise the introduction of these harmful effects and includes measures such as quarantining potential suspect carriers, barring their entry into territorial waters and fining on those that do not follow the appropriate reporting procedures.

New Zealand has specific concerns about the introduction of such invasive species as they threaten the rapidly developing aquaculture industry, which is worth over $300 million a year and accounts for 40 per cent of domestic consumption. Flagship species include Greenshell™ Mussels, King Salmon and Pacific Oysters. The waters of New Zealand are particularly suited to the development of a major aquaculture industry and the authorities have embarked upon an ambitious plan to develop the industry, further targeting revenue of over $1 billion by 2025 from the sector. This development is firmly based upon a number of key guiding principles, such as that growth must take place within an environmentally sustainable framework.

In terms of New Zealand's economy, this growth in earnings from the aquaculture industry is significant, rivalling earnings from the wine industry. The development of aquaculture also helps replace wild fish stocks that have become severely depleted as a result of overfishing. Other countries, notably Chile and Norway, have suffered major setbacks when their fisheries have been devastated by a series of events. In August 2009, a major algal bloom was detected by satellite-based sensors systems on the NASA Aqua satellite. Norway has a history of such events over the last twenty-five years and observations suggest that they are increasing in frequency. Due to their scale and distribution, satellite-based sensor systems can help understand the area infected by the bloom and, when tied in with tidal and ocean current forecasts, enable some prediction of its likely growth to be made; this enables aquacultures that might become affected to be moved. Norway was the location of the world's first successful salmon farm, which was established in the early 1970s. Since then it has developed close ties with a number of countries around the world that also use this approach to supplement wild fish stocks that are in decline.

New Zealand does not want to see a repeat of such events. Red Tides or other harmful algae blooms can spread rapidly, and in Norway, losses of salmon have threatened local livelihoods. In the Aysen province of Chile, algae blooms have had a major impact at a number of important sites where Chilean Salmon is produced with quite devastating local consequences for economies and employment. The introduction of invasive species or naturally occurring algae blooms, sometimes fuelled by a combination of environmental conditions—where nutrients appear from run-off from the land or as a result of upwelling—could set back the development of a long-term industry.

The vectors, or pathways, by which non-indigenous species can be introduced into local areas, are many and varied, but the consequences can be quite catastrophic for local marine wildlife and fauna. With increased levels of shipping moving trade over increasing distances, the opportunities for accidental introduction of invasive species has increased. Maritime authorities have responded to this threat with the introduction of measures designed to reduce the risks associated with such events. One of these possible vectors concerns the discharge of ballast water. It is an area that the maritime authorities in New Zealand are specifically focused upon, with rules controlling such discharges being very clear. Ballast water loaded in other countries' waters cannot be discharged inside New Zealand's territorial waters. To enforce these rules New Zealand has deployed four of the 55 metre Inshore Patrol Vessels (IPV), with ranges in excess of 3,000 nm, to intercept vessels that may be flouting the restrictions. Working in cooperation with aircraft from the New Zealand Air Force, the IPV operate at the fringes of the New Zealand EEZ to board suspected vessels as far away from the territorial waters as possible. Yachts are a particular source of concern as they can travel long distances and pick up specific pests and diseases that are harmful to the local marine population.

In recognition of this work, New Zealand was elected to the IMO Council in November 2007. As a specialist agency of the United Nations, the IMO is charged with developing and promoting common international standards for maritime safety and security in the marine environment. New Zealand's election allows it to bring their specific focus, which they share with Australia, to the work of the IMO increasing international awareness of the issues involved in maritime biosecurity. In one example of the problem, New Zealand authorities were alerted in March

2007 to what appeared to be an abandoned container floating on the surface of the ocean near Cape Brett in the Bay of Islands, but an inspection of the vessel revealed it was the remains of a fishing vessel lost in the Indo-Pacific region five years earlier. When marine biologists inspected the vessel, they discovered a range of exotic fish, bivalves, crabs and other species had hitched a lift. The authorities immediately undertook a risk assessment on the wreck, which it is estimated had travelled 8,000 miles. The sheer scale of the potential vectors by which invasive species might become introduced into an area creates problems for the development of a comprehensive approach to maritime security.

B5: CLIMATE CHANGE AND MARITIME SECURITY

It would appear beyond doubt that changes are occurring to the climate. Increased frequencies of category five hurricanes, inundations and unexpected and severe weather conditions all point to a human signature modulating the well established climatic cycles, which are linked to variances in levels of solar illumination as the Earth orbits the sun. Whilst such changes have the potential to create highly localised and very difficult situations, the wider global interactions of the climate have started to become more widely understood.

The United Kingdom Meteorological office expects 2009 to be one of the top-five warmest years on record, despite the cooling that arises from global weather phenomena such as El Niño. Research is pointing to links between El Niño events and the upwelling of currents off the coast of South America, with other disturbances to weather patterns and droughts. The warmest year on record was 1998 and that coincided with an extreme El Niño event. Insights being developed by scientists into the impact of El Niño now point researchers to categorise the events. Weak and strong El Niño phenomena are not discernable and their impacts are being better understood in the short and medium-term. American scientists point to increasing levels of precipitation in the west-central tropical Pacific Ocean and drier-than-average conditions in Indonesia. Research is also pointing to links between El Niño and the Atlantic hurricane activity, with El Niño acting to increase the vertical wind shear in the Caribbean Sea and tropical Atlantic Ocean. Whilst the science is far from perfect, it does offer the potential to give guides as to what kind of hurricane seasons to expect; this aids the planning of possible humanitarian relief operations that may need to be conducted by naval forces located in the area.

With naval assets in increasingly short supply, anything that can provide some reliable indicators in this regard would be helpful.

The human race is, however, moving into uncharted waters with respect to its understanding of how the Earth's atmosphere and the seas will react to increasing levels of carbon dioxide. The degree of coupling that occurs at the air-sea boundary is not fully understood and deep-sea ocean currents that routinely move major supplies of water around the planet may become suddenly disrupted. Such changes are possible and not simply the subject of inventive screenwriters in Hollywood. Unexpectedly severe events are likely to become a feature if weather conditions were to become increasingly changeable. One thing does, however, appear to be accepted: the impact of climate change will have far-reaching consequences for all mankind, not least of which will be those people who have made their homes by the sea and who rely on fishing to feed their families and those for whom tourism is an important source of income.

Riverine systems are another major area of concern. They are closely coupled with their environments and changes in the nature of their flows can fundamentally alter delta areas. The extraction of gas, groundwater and activities such as damming and diverting rivers can fundamentally alter the ways in which specific river systems operate. Recent scientific reporting suggests that the majority of the world's major deltas are sinking (some by up to 15 cm), increasing the threat of the displacement of hundreds of millions of people that rely upon these fertile areas for their livelihood. 85 per cent of the world's major deltas have experienced flooding in recent years and of the thirty-three studied, twenty-four were found to be sinking at rates faster than can be explained by rises in global sea levels that are attributed to climate change, which are variously reported at between 1.8 to 3 mm per year. This contrasts markedly with the 15 cm being reported as a result of deltas sinking. Delta areas such as the Yangtze, Nile, the Pearl River near Hong Kong, and Colorado rivers are most affected alongside the Rhone in France. The Mekong delta is also thought to be vulnerable in the future. The implications for maritime security in these areas are clear.

Cyclone *Aila*, which hit Bangladesh and the eastern Indian state of West Bengal, is one of the more recent examples of the kinds of extreme weather conditions that scientists working in the area of climate change have predicted. Every year it is estimated that 10 million people are directly affected by storm surges, with the impact of Hurricane Katrina likely to last in people's memories as one of the worst events of its type for many years. At least 500,000 people were made homeless by the effects of Cyclone Aila. Flooding and landslides are direct consequences of such an event, with short and medium term problems also arising in the devastation that occurs to local fisheries and water supplies. Bangladesh is particularly vulnerable as a low-lying country and when its sea defences are overwhelmed it can take many months to reconstruct viable protection against future inundations. Of particular concern is the increasing threat of salt water to areas of rice production. Scientists in Bangladesh have measured sea levels increasing at a rate of 5 mm per year over the last thirty years. This rate of increase is placing an estimated 20 million people at risk. Other factors also contribute to changes in coastal areas that threaten homes and livelihoods, and fundamentally change the nature of the maritime environment and its ability to sustain local people.

International concerted action in the matter of climate change has been a long time coming. The immediacy of the problems, with the depletion of the Ozone Layer and its obvious potential for increasing cancers, seemed to quickly spur the international community to act. The problems with gaining a scientific consensus, especially in the presence of a vociferous and noisy oil lobby in the United States questioning the validity of the science, has hampered progress since Kyoto. The delays in cutting carbon emissions and the problems of countries that need to use coal to continue to fire their economies, such as China and India who have between them massive coal reserves, is probably exacerbating the dynamic. Prevarication and delay may be causing irreparable harm to the environment, which may not be reversible. Simply reducing carbon dioxide emissions may not guarantee a return to what have until recently been seen to normal climate patterns.

One of the solutions being adopted, albeit slowly, is to move to renewable energy sources. Wind and wave power, coupled with harnessing solar energy, may provide an important and growing part of the future energy generation capacity in the coming decades. But land areas are increasingly difficult to use and offshore facilities will feature more and more as locations from where energy supplies are generated. These facilities will be vulnerable to attack and quickly become part of what is defined as Critical National Infrastructure (CNI). New trading routes are also appearing as the Arctic Sea ice recedes, opening up both the Northwest Passage over the top of Canada but also the Northeast Passage around

Siberia. This will have a profound impact upon the nature of maritime trading routes and the potential for conflict to occur in areas such as the High Arctic. With competing claims to the underwater environments and all its riches, the Arctic is likely to emerge as a new focus for maritime security; a point that has not been lost on the Norwegian government with their plans for the development of the Norwegian Navy, and the Russian Naval plans to establish three carrier-based battle groups that can provide protection to the SLOC, which will all inevitably develop as a result of the exploitation of the huge gas reserves in Siberia.

B6: ENERGY SECURITY

For the foreseeable future, the world will depend upon oil as one it is primary sources of energy. In recent history, the movement of oil from key sources of supply, in places like the Middle East, which is believed to hold 60 per cent of the proven reserves, to the consumers in the West has been straightforward. Key choke points such as the Straits of Hormuz, the Bab al-Mandab and the Suez Canal have been focal points in a supply chain that has seen little change in terms of its maritime dimension. Some land-based pipelines have altered some of the flows of oil, but they have yet to have a significant impact on the amounts being carried by tankers to the consumer nations. The maritime environment is still the most important means by which oil is delivered from its point of extraction to its consumers.

That, however, is likely to change in the coming decade. In 2004, the list of major exporters of crude oil included countries such as Saudi Arabia (506 mt); Russia (458.7 mt); Iran (202 mt); Mexico (191 mt); Venezuela (153 mt); UAE (126 mt); Kuwait (120 mt); Iraq (100 mt); Nigeria (122 mt); and Norway (149.9 mt). Secondary players such as the United Kingdom (95.4 mt); Libya (70 mt); Angola (49 mt) and Indonesia (57.7 mt) also contributed to the world's supply. Analysing the seaborne trade in crude oil in 2004 provides some interesting insights on the supply chains, which tend to be based upon a number of quite specific routes.

In 2004, maritime trade in oil also plied the Caribbean, where by far the majority of Venezuelan oil production was bound for the United States. In the future it is likely that new routes will open as Venezuela increasingly diversifies its consumer market with China and Russia likely to become close trading partners. This will change the pattern of oil shipments moving in the Caribbean Sea and across the Atlantic Ocean. Brazil's emergence as a significant supplier of oil also has the potential to change the supply chain, with China an obvious potential market. Brazil's exports of oil grew from under 300,000 barrels of oil a day to nearly 500,000 barrels of oil a day in 2008, a growth of 73 per cent occurring between 2007 and 2008. With new supplies coming on stream, Brazil may well break into the top ten oil suppliers in the world in the next decade; although actual estimates on the total reserves that can be exploited vary, with some figures suggesting that Brazil has a proven reserve of 14 billion barrels. In September 2009, China agreed to loan Brazil's state-owned oil company, Petrobras, $10 billion in exchange for guarantees on oil supplies over the next decade. This was the largest loan Brazil had ever received from China and it came in the wake of China replacing the United States as Brazil's principal trading partner, after trade between the two countries had surged by more than 50 per cent in the period 2006–2008. A similar arrangement has been signed by China with Russia, except it is over a longer period of twenty years.

The United States relies on supplies from the Middle East (130 mt in 2004) and the Gulf of Guinea (92 mt) to supplement its own dwindling domestic production, which started to decline in the 1970s, with the United States becoming a net importer of oil in the mid 1990s. Japan relies almost exclusively on the Middle East for its source of oil, a somewhat perilous situation. These are trading routes that are based largely on bipolar relationships between sources and consumers. India is also a country whose energy demands and oil requirements are growing rapidly. India currently imports 60 per cent of its oil needs. This is projected to rise to 90 per cent by 2015, with India becoming the world's third largest energy consumer by 2030. This is bound to lead to tensions in the Indian Ocean as India and China seek to secure their energy supply chains, with India establishing close ties with the Sudan, Syria, Iran and Nigeria; their network of SLOC is increasing.

China has increasingly been reaching out to suppliers in Africa as part of its energy security strategy in an attempt to diversify its sources of supply from its current dependence on the Middle East, creating links with Angola and other West African countries that may have oil reserves. China accounted for 40 per cent of the total growth in demand for oil in the last four years, with countries such as Sudan, Chad, Nigeria, and Algeria being important sources alongside the West African states of Gabon, Equatorial Guinea and the Republic of Congo. China's growth rate has barely slowed, even during the recession of 2008, and China has a voracious appetite for oil. In 2005, China became the world's second largest oil-consumer in the world, using 6.6 million barrels per day whilst itself only producing 3.7 million barrels per day. Estimates suggest—based upon current growth projections—that China's net imports of oil will increase to 10.9 million barrels a year by 2025. This will inevitably place a renewed emphasis upon securing its SLOC from places like the Gulf of Guinea, around the Cape of Good Hope and through the Indian Ocean to the Malacca Strait or the other less well-known maritime choke points in Indonesia, the Lombok and Sunda Straits. India too is growing quickly and some analysts see its demand quadrupling in the period up to 2020. These demands emerge alongside new sources of oil coming on stream, further changing the nature of the supply routes.

The Falklands Islands, with estimated reserves of 60 billion barrels, new deposits in the Gulf of Guinea, the Lomonosov Ridge, areas off the coast of Greenland, and the Spratley and Paracel Islands, are all likely to be developing new supplies of oil in the period running up to 2020. Currently the South China region has proven reserves of 7.5 million barrels, with production levels at around 1.3 million barrels per day; this is hardly a major source of oil. However, optimistic estimates emerging from Chinese commentators suggest that the total reserves could range from 105 billion barrels of oil to 213 billion barrels, with industry commentators expecting 10 per cent of the proven reserves to be recoverable. With key developments in technology, it is entirely possible that this level of recovery may increase. Clearly, the long-term potential of the Spratley Islands has yet to be established, but the potential reserves make the area of obvious strategic interest; hence the competing claims to its ownership, which are explored in Annex B3 and in Annex B2, where a similar situation prevails in the High Arctic.

The situation on oil supplies and consumption is not going to change overnight. However, the increasing competition for oil from China and India makes the SLOC through the Indian Ocean of specific interest and, in part, explains the reasons for the arms build-up in the Indian Ocean. Extending the SLOC to Brazil and other increasingly important sources of supply will increase the importance of SLOC across the Southern Atlantic and the trading routes around the Cape of Good Hope and the Panama Canal, to use shorter routes from Venezuela and Brazil to China. The reduction in Arctic ice coverage will also open new trading routes in the High Arctic. While any immediate change in the major sea-trading routes used for conveying crude oil from their point of extraction to their consumers may be slow, the potential for significantly new SLOC to become involved in the trade of oil is clear. Russia's maritime security focus is likely to remain in the High Arctic and the Lomonosov Ridge. Whilst its links with Venezuela are clear, the Russian Navy's main focus will stay in the North, while keeping a watchful eye on its eastern seaboard and the rise of the PLAN. For the Indian and Chinese navies, a blue-water capability is an important element of developing a secure environment in which its vital energy supplies can be secured. For these countries, the nexus between maritime security and energy security could not be clearer.

B7: THE PROLIFERATION SECURITY INITIATIVE (PSI)

In June 2009, South Korean warships, working alongside United States naval vessels started to enforce a United Nations Security Council Resolution (UNSCR) 1874. The Resolution, which was passed unanimously on 12 June 2009, was a coordinated international response to North Korea's second nuclear test that was conducted on 25 May 2009 and its subsequent show-of-force demonstrations of multiple firings of ballistic missiles.

Within days of the passing of the Resolution, the United States Navy was reported to be tracking a North Korean vessel called the *Kang Nam*, which was suspected of being involved in the transportation of weapons, nuclear material or missile parts. Admiral Mullen, the Chairman of the United States Joint Chiefs of Staff, made it clear that the United States Navy was prepared to enforce the resolution. North Korea quickly issued a statement saying that any attempt to seize or board one of its vessels would be regarded as an act of war.

This would not be the first time that the international community had intercepted North Korean weapon shipments on the high seas. In 2002, a North Korean merchant ship the *So San*, was halted by two Spanish warships, an estimated 600 miles off the Yemeni coast. A search of the vessel revealed fifteen SCUD missiles and eighty-five drums of an undetermined chemical. The ship had apparently been tracked by United States intelligence sources since it left North Korea and appeared to be heading to the Yemen. Shipments of missiles have also been reported to Iran, Syria, Libya and Pakistan, and close ties continue between North Korea, Syria and Iran, two of whom were cited in President Bush's 2002 State of the Union speech as members of an 'axis of evil'.

Libya has recently sought a rapprochement with the international community after years of isolation and has declared that it wishes to give up its quest to obtain nuclear weapons. In the light of this shift, intelligence became available that showed the extent of North Korea's involvement in the shipment of uranium that could become the basis of a national nuclear weapons programme. When this was coupled with the international efforts of Professor Khan, the father of the Pakistani bomb, the scale of the proliferation problem—with its attendant risks of materials falling into the hands of terrorists—became apparent.

These specific examples are symptomatic of a much broader set of concerns that arose in the wake of the terrorist attacks on 11 September 2001 surrounding the use of the maritime domain to ship material and precursor chemicals associated with weapons of mass destruction. In response to this concern, President Bush launched the Proliferation Security Initiative (PSI) in May 2003. The aim of the PSI is to harness international cooperation to create a layer of security in the maritime domain whereby vessels can be searched at random if they are suspected of being involved in smuggling weapons or people associated with international terrorism. Whilst the aims of the PSI are laudable, many commentators have questioned their legality. The potential seizure of vessels on the high seas arguably stretches international law to its limits. The aim of PSI is clearly motivated by a desire to move upstream and intercept any threat before it reaches United States waters. It can be argued that under international law this is a pre-emptive action motivated by self-defence. This is one line of reasoning; UNSCR 1874 is another, and provides a limited mandate to search North Korean vessels. It does not, however, provide a broader framework, such as that envisaged by PSI. Initially South Korea was reluctant to sign up to the PSI, but in the light of North Korea's belligerence in the wake of its second nuclear test, the South Korean government joined it in May 2009.

To a large extent it can be argued that the PSI has not achieved what it set out to achieve. Its grand vision has not yet been seen in practical actions. Random boarding of vessels is not occurring all over the world. However, in some areas, maritime security of the high seas is being stepped up through coordinated action. NATO's contribution is provided under Operation Active Endeavor. Its mandate, the only operation conducted by NATO in recognition of the members of NATO to come to the aid of another NATO nation (Article 5 of the NATO Treaty), is part of a multifaceted response to the threat from transnational terrorism with contributions coming from more than fifty countries to help build Maritime Domain Awareness (MDA). The focus of the operation has been the eastern end of the Mediterranean Sea. This is an obvious area of concern, given the rate of incidents of smuggling recorded in Europe associated with the Caucasus and the associated concerns about Syria's long-term intentions. The initial deployment of vessels was based upon NATO's Standing Naval Forces, which came under the control of NATO's Maritime Component Commander in Naples. Whilst Operation Active Endeavor was initially a NATO-only activity, other nations, such as the Ukraine, have joined the effort. As of December 2008, over 100,000 merchant ships had been contacted and 148 had been boarded and searched at sea. Up until May 2004 488 vessels had also been escorted through the Straits of Gibraltar (STROG) as, at the time, it was known to have specific vulnerabilities from maritime-based terrorist threats emanating from North Africa.

It is likely that terrorists and criminals still make a great deal of use of the maritime domain to move people and goods. It is clear that a nexus is emerging between terrorist groups and criminality. This poses a threat as terrorist groups can leverage the established and wide-ranging social networks that underpin international criminal organisations. However, one benefit that has arisen is the closer cooperation and greater intelligence sharing that now occurs around the world concerning the maritime domain. Intelligence collection points have reportedly been established at various maritime choke-points to develop a comprehensive and long-term picture of the moment of maritime trade. MDA is being developed from which trends and anomalies can be derived, helping focus maritime-based assets into areas where the risks are thought to be highest, as part of a comprehensive approach to deterring the smuggling of WMD.

B8: HANS ISLAND

CANADA AND DENMARK IN DISPUTE

One of the underlying assumptions about maritime security is that it must be possible to define the extent of various nations' claims to what are or are not their own waters, as the case may be. UNCLOS outlines the ways in which sea boundaries are defined and agreed against and what are defined to be baselines from which measurements are to be taken. What if, however, even establishing the baseline is difficult, as the Earth's crust is in some form of constant, albeit tiny, motion? How do you define an approach to maritime security when the border is quite literally moving?

Hans Island is a rocky outcrop located in the Kennedy Channel off the Nares Strait that links Baffin Bay off the eastern coastline of Canada with the Lincoln Sea. Superficially it appears to be of little value. Its total area is only just over 1 km^2 and it has no permanent population. However, it has been the subject of an ongoing dispute between Canada and Denmark that dates back to the 1933 adjudication of the Permanent Court of International Justice declaring the legal status of Greenland in favour of Denmark. The subsequent dispute over the ownership of Hans Island has gone through many phases and on some occasions has appeared to be beyond reconciliation.

Since the early 1980s, a range of tit-for-tat landings have been staged on the island. In 1984, Tom Hoyem, the Danish Minister for Greenland, chartered a helicopter to the island. In 1988, the Danish Arctic Ocean patrol cutter, the HDMS *Agpa*, arrived off the coast of the island and raised the Danish flag. A catalogue of further visits occurred where the flags of Denmark and Canada were subsequently raised and removed. In

July 2005, the Canadian Defence Minister Bill Graham set foot on the island, provoking an outraged diplomatic protest from Denmark. In a subsequent chain of events, the Danish Ambassador was drawn into the dispute, writing in the *Ottawa Citizen* newspaper, defending his country's position.

So what really is behind this? As ever, oil and related natural resources appear to be at the heart of this dispute. Greenland has important deposits of gold, diamonds and natural gas alongside as-yet untapped potential for harnessing what are believed to be significant oil deposits. Reporting in the *Sunday Times* on 14 September 2009, Danny Fortson looked at the potential of Greenland in an article entitled 'Oil giants zero in on untapped Greenland' citing the 50 billion barrels of oil that the United States Geological Survey (USGS) believes can be extracted and contrasting that figure with the 38 billion barrels extracted from the North Sea after large-scale production began in the mid 1960s. Fortson noted that with the oil price above $40 a barrel the economics of exploration and extraction in the Arctic become interesting; hence the interest of many major oil companies in the area.

Political leaders, reluctant to admit that two NATO countries could come to blows over such a tiny outcrop of rock, dress up the issue in terms of its being a territorial dispute and the issue being one of the integrity of national boundaries. In practice, however, the dispute over Hans Island may be little more than a precursor to the much more significant debate that is emerging over the ownership of the Lomonosov Ridge and the definitions of where boundaries lie on the ocean floor. Both Canada and Denmark may be reluctant to back down over the Hans Island dispute in case it sets some sort of precedent that would hamper their positions over the much weightier matters of the potential riches of the Lomonosov Ridge. With the Arctic ice cap receding at a rate faster than predicted by most climate models, Denmark has started to lay out its claims in the area based upon what if defines as the extended continental shelf running north from the top of Greenland. Against this backdrop, Denmark has laid claim to the sovereignty of the North Pole. The Geological Survey of Denmark and Greenland (GEUS) has been receiving additional funding to derive the scientific data that supports the claims. A map has been developed showing the geological features of the Arctic Ocean.

This, however, may only be the start. Denmark clearly sees the potential of gaining access to the islands and the natural resources believed to lie on the sea floor around them. Denmark is pushing this agenda aggressively, and Greenland's Bureau of Minerals and Protection (BMP) invited companies to bid for exploration rights in the area of Hans Island and the Davis Strait in 2004. The potential for this to escalate into a wider dispute over ownership of territories that are part of the Arctic Archipelago—such as Canada's newest territory Nunavut—is clear, and despite agreeing in 2005 to seek arbitration the dispute runs on. Its resolution is complicated by the ever-changing geography of the local area.

Alfred Wegner, the father of plate tectonics, developed the idea that the Earth's current continents were originally part of a single giant landmass called *Pangaea* which started to break up just over 150 million ago, initially fracturing into two major sub-continents of *Laurasia* and *Gondwanaland*. 50 to 100 million years ago these two major landforms further divided as North America broke away from what became Eurasia. Standing back from the pictures of the earth, it is not difficult to see why Alfred Wegner devised his theory of plate tectonics. The pieces of the continents can be seen as a jigsaw puzzle that fit together; this assessment has been backed up by detailed analyses of rock cores and samples that clearly tie various landmasses together as an assembled puzzle. His claim that around 30 million years ago Greenland started to break away from North America is, however, unsubstantiated.

Between 1998 and 2001, scientists from the Geological Survey of Canada spent time mapping the high Arctic region collecting specific information on Hans Island. The project team, however, failed to find evidence of a fault line that was supposed to be indicative of an underlying plate in the Nares Strait. Over 30 million years, fault lines can move significantly and the team was looking for up to 300 km of displacement to verify the theory ventured by Alfred Wegner. They found 75 km of the 300 km they expected. They also found evidence of an ancient spreading ridge running along the route from Baffin Island and the Labrador Sea but rock samples taken onshore on Ellesmere Island and Greenland simply did not provide the conclusive proof.

This example serves to show that in the maritime security field a number of things have to be considered and some of those maybe be difficult to resolve geographically. In 2005, the Danish and Canadian governments agreed to take their dispute over Hans Island to arbitration. Time alone will tell if that finally resolves nearly eight decades of disagreement.

B9: THE MUMBAI ATTACK

A NEW PARADIGM FOR MARITIME TERRORISM?

We assess that Al-Qaeda will continue to pursue plans for Homeland attacks and is likely focusing on prominent political, economic and infrastructure targets designed to produce mass casualties, visually dramatic destruction, significant economic aftershocks and fear amongst the population.

United States National Intelligence Assessment (12th February 2009)

The terrorist attacks in the city of Mumbai between 26 and 28 November 2008 established a new paradigm which has sent reverberations around the world where law enforcement and military organisations responsible for coastal security have had to go back to the drawing board and reconsider their contingency plans. It has been described as India's 9/11, and it provides a new dimension to traditional thinking on maritime terrorism, which has tended to be governed by images of the USS *Cole* and the MV *Limberg*. The Mumbai attack was audacious and determined. It reflects the message of the United States National Intelligence Estimate published several months later, in that it could be said to be visually dramatic in capturing and holding hostages in the full glare of the international media, and it gained international prominence and saturation media coverage.

It was carried out by a group of men whose aim was to create havoc amongst the local population in what appeared to be a series of random attacks designed to terrorise the local population and specifically target Western businessmen and tourists. Mumbai was selected as a target because of its combination of being a financial centre and a location where multiethnic communities resided that could be targeted as part of the attack. The terrorists were told to make their attack last at least seventy-two hours. In lasting sixty-two hours and with the subsequent forensic analysis presented by the media, they largely achieved their objective, gaining repeated worldwide media coverage of their actions and subsequent coverage as the implications of the operation were considered and reported. Their message of terrorism was delivered to a local and international audience over an extended period of time. Subsequent reporting suggested that the terrorists had been taking a cocktail of drugs and steroids in order to extend the duration and apparent intensity of the attack.

Despite the intelligence warnings that were available, the Indian authorities were found wanting in the way they responded to the attacks and shortcomings in the approach to maritime security that were rapidly identified. In what is clearly a repeat of the failings that occurred in the run-up to the events of 11 September 2001, the Indian authorities clearly failed to join the pieces of the jigsaw puzzle together. This was an event waiting to happen. In 2001, a ministerial report in India warned that 'India's long coastline and coastal areas have been largely unprotected' and highlighted the apparent gaps in the responsibilities of agencies tasked with its protection. India's external intelligence service, the Research and Analysis Wing (RAW), claimed to have intercepted a satellite-telephone conversation on 18 November. The contents of this intercept were not made public, but it is believed it clearly indicated that a seaborne attack on Mumbai was imminent.

In spite of the strategic intelligence that was clearly available from the United States concerning the increased likelihood of an attack, the history of previous attacks on Mumbai—such as the sequence of bombs that affected the Mumbai railway system in 2006, and local concerns repeatedly raised by fishermen along the coastline about what they saw as unusual behaviour—the authorities' initial reactions were slow and somewhat confused. The scale and intensity of the attack left the police and military authorities overwhelmed and confused. Their lack of preparedness is surprising, given the warnings provided by local fishermen who for several months before the attacks had expressed concerns over the fate of a number of fishing vessels previously seized by the Pakistani coastguard. Over 380 such vessels had reportedly been seized and could have been used to deceive local coastguard authorities as to the true intentions of those aboard the vessels. The fishermen had written letters to the Indian Prime Minister, but their warnings had gone unheeded. This is a problem that is endemic in the maritime security environment of many countries. Creating a joined-up multi-agency approach, such as the Indians have now put in place in the wake of the attacks, is crucial and fast becoming a more general model for the approach to maritime security being adopted on the international stage.

The attack on Mumbai was conceived in Pakistan and mounted by a group of men with connections in the country. Embarking upon a small boat, the local Pakistani fishing vessel the MV *Al-Huseni*, on 22 November 2008 from a small creek near the southern port city of Karachi, the terrorists initially sailed south-easterly towards Mumbai. On 23 November, they intercepted the Indian fishing vessel the MV *Kuber* whose registered port was Porbander, off the Gujarati coast. The terrorists boarded the MV *Kuber* and reportedly killed four of the crew members. One day later they abandoned the MV *Kuber* and set off towards Mumbai on inflatable dinghies, landing at a fishing village at Badhwar Park in Cuffe Parade where they rapidly disembarked, split into their various teams, and made their way inland towards their initial targets. The ease with which the terrorists arrived on the coastline and used this as the platform for their attacks has deeply concerned many in the maritime security industry; as a new paradigm for attacks launched from the sea has developed. This could be repeated in the most unlikely places anywhere in the world.

The attack itself comprised several phases. The first, the attack on the main station and the Leopold Cafe, was random killing clearly aimed at getting the attention of the authorities. The attackers quickly moved on to secondary targets, maintaining that random element of killing as they moved to their final destinations where they would make their stand in front of the world's media. The iconic hotels in Mumbai created an important backdrop to the scenes before the final denouement of the operation.

In the immediate aftermath of the attack, the Indian Navy intercepted and boarded the suspect MV *Alpha*, a Vietnamese registered ship, which was initially suspected to have dropped the terrorists off the coast of Mumbai. The Indian Navy's Leander-class frigate *Vindhyagiri* and naval helicopters from the INS *Kunjali* were involved in pursuit of the merchant vessel alongside maritime patrol aircraft. An extensive search of the MV *Alpha* did not reveal any connection to the attacks on Mumbai and the vessel was allowed to go on its way to its destination of Panama. The attack on Mumbai was over, but the implications for maritime security across the world were just starting to be realised as governments asked the question, 'could that happen here?'

B10: BALLISTIC MISSILE DEFENCE

SOUTH KOREA AND JAPAN

In his 2002 State of the Union Speech, President George W. Bush defined North Korea as part of an 'axis of evil'. His concern, in the immediate aftermath of the terrorist attacks on New York and Washington, was focused upon the potential for a nuclear attack upon the United States. As he made that speech, his mind may well have briefly returned to an incident a matter of months before when the reality of a nuclear attack upon the United States suddenly became real and plausible. Writing in his book, *Nuclear Terrorism: The Ultimate Preventable Catastrophe*, Graham Allison recounts the tale of how credible intelligence became available to the Central Intelligence Agency (CIA) of a nuclear weapon having been placed in New York. The ultimate nightmare was playing out, not in some Hollywood blockbuster movie, but in real life. The pieces of the jigsaw puzzle seemed to show that they could be fitted together to make a chain of events that could mean the intelligence was plausible and could not be ignored. Tom Clancy had also explored the issue of a nuclear attack on the United States in his book *Sum of all Fears*, in which a nuclear bomb is shipped into the United States using a merchant vessel. The nuclear weapon, which is built from one located on a Israeli aircraft shot down in the Yom Kippur War, detonates at the Superbowl precipitating a potential showdown between the United States and Russia which is only narrowly averted. Clancy was so concerned by the potential for fiction to become fact that he added an afterthought into a new edition of the book to clear his conscience.

Looking around the world, it is not difficult to pick out the actions and manoeuvring that take place on the Korean Peninsula and the threats that poses to regional security as being one of the world's potential trouble spots. For some time now, North Korea has been embarked upon a nuclear weapon's programme and on 25 May 2009, it tested its second nuclear device. The implications of this for proliferation are addressed in the parallel case study on the Proliferation Security Initiative (PSI). This case study looks at another facet of the maritime security field, the potential for mobile, sea-based, Theatre Ballistic Missile Defence (TBMD).

This case study looks at maritime security from the viewpoint of delivering protection from the sea. Firstly, basing interceptor missiles in major silos is always likely to court controversy. Discussions in Western Europe about basing interceptors in Poland and the United Kingdom have stalled because of public resistance and associated political pressure. The arguments are always about the defence interceptors becoming targets; Russian concerns and media manipulation have helped create that uncertainty. Since the removal of the Thor Missiles from Turkey in the wake of the Cuban Missile Crises, the Intermediate Nuclear Forces (INF) Treaty signed by President Reagan and Soviet General Secretary Gorbachev on 8 December 1987 resulted in the destruction of 2,692 intermediate nuclear weapons systems, such as the Soviet Scud systems, by the ratification date of 1 June 1991. However, like most aspects of technology, by that time the cat was out of the bag and proliferation of the weapon systems technologies had already provided North Korea—through contacts in Egypt and Russia—with a base from which to develop its own indigenous capability, which it too could chose to proliferate.

North Korea's steady march to independence in the field of nuclear weapons and associated ballistic missile technologies is perhaps best illustrated by its frequent programme of testing. From its early beginnings in 1976, North Korea developed its Scud-B weapon system and by 1984 had its own Scud-C and Scud-D with ranges of 300 km and 500 km; both sufficient to cause concerns in South Korea and Japan. In July 2006, North Korea fired six of its missiles, out of an inventory believed to number in excess of 800 in total. One of these was the Taepodong-2 missile system, which is believed to have a range of 6,000 km; this particular launch, however, failed. This extended the range of the previous Taepondong-1 missile system, which could reach a distance of 2,200 km and posed a direct threat to the whole of Japan. US intelligence assessments believe that the Taepoding-2 missile system could have a range of up to 15,000 km if auxiliary boosters were attached to the initial stage of the vehicle. The reliability of the Taepondong-2 missile is yet to be fully proven.

At the same time that President Reagan was signing the INF Treaty, he was also encouraging the development of the 'Star Wars' system. Encouraged by the enthusiasm of Professor Edward Teller, the father of the H-bomb, the President announced the Strategic Defence Initiative (SDI) Programme in 1984, envisioning that it would consign the nuclear missile to history. A key component of the SDI Programme was to draw in international partners, and Japan and Israel became keenly involved in joint research activities. Japan's interest in the area of TBMD systems has continued as the threat from North Korea has crystallised. Its TBMD capabilities have also developed to the point where its government felt able to issue a warning to the North Koreans that it would shoot down any missile system whose trajectory is a threat to its country. The Japanese approach has been to build a combination of land and sea-based capability.

The threat to South Korea, however, is more immediate and comes from the many Scud missile systems that are part of the North Korean inventory. They fly at slower speeds, over much shallower trajectories and can be launched in ways that reduce the detection time of early warning satellites looking for the characteristic launch plume. In the First Gulf War, the Iraqis perfected launching under cloud cover when attacking Israel and Saudi Arabia. To defeat such a threat, a platform was developed, with an indigenous capability to both detect the launch, using a radar-based sensor system, and bring a defence missile system to bear to engage the threat. Closing speeds of the intercept exceed 1 km/s and therefore to achieve a hit-to-kill on the target, the tracking of the initial warhead must be accurate. Much of the technology developed on the Patriot systems that were used in the First Gulf War has moved to sea as the Aegis Missile Defence System, which is based upon the AN/SPY-1 radar system and the Standard Missile-3 (SM-3) missile system. As a result of successful testing and intercepts of unitary missile targets (a euphemism for a missile system that survives re-entry intact), the system has been given an operational status and the Japanese Defence Ship *Kongō* successfully intercepted a target missile system using this combination on 17 December 2007. Whilst some failures have occurred in the testing programme, the majority of the tests have been successful. A mobile, sea-based TBMD system is available that can be deployed at short notice to help protect the populations of South Korea and Japan from the threat of a nuclear armed Scud missile system. Given the unpredictable nature of the North Korean regime, this is an important capability and an additional element of a comprehensive approach to maritime security.

NOTES

PREFACE

1. National Customs Organisations had long believed that intervention upstream in the supply chain of those involved in smuggling was a valid tactic to disrupt those chains at source and at key vulnerable points en route.
2. On the 18 September there were thirty warships on patrol in the area at the expected start of the post-monsoon attack season in the autumn of 2009 from countries such as Australia, Turkey, Pakistan, India, Japan, South Korea and Saudi Arabia alongside vessels from Iran, Russia, China and Malaysia; all cooperating with the six vessels allocated to Combined Task Force 150 and the European Union activities being coordinated through Operation *Atalanta* and the NATO Operation *Ocean Shield*. Coordinating all of these contributions is a challenge, as each country is operating under its own political direction and specific national objectives.
3. A further illustration of the enduring nature of these concerns comes in a report issued on the 14 August 2009 by the Indian News Agency concerning the search Indian authorities had conducted on the North Korean MV *Mu San* at Port Blair to determine if the vessel had been involved in smuggling nuclear material. Their report found no traces of any form of Chemical, Biological, Radiological or Nuclear (CBRN) material, but the thoroughness of the search conducted and the time taken suggest an enduring concern about the potential for material from the North Korean nuclear programme to become available on the international market.

INTRODUCTION

1. Fukuyama, F. (1989), 'The End of History?', *The National Interest*.
2. These comments were made by President Obama on Saturday 11 July 2009, in a speech to Ghana's Parliament.
3. Sloggett, C. J., Sloggett, D. R. (2009), 'Reframing the narrative of the global war on terror', *Journal of Information Warfare*, vol. 8, issue 2.
4. International Institute for Strategic Studies (2009), 'Australia's new defence strategy', *IISS Strategic Comments*, vol. 15, issue 7, September.

5. Wilcocks, P. (2008), 'Future maritime security', *Naval Review*, vol. 96, no. 2.
6. Lagrone, S. (2010), 'US Navy's ideal fleet sails out of view' (3 Feb. 2010), *Jane's Defence Weekly*.
7. Tigner, B. (2009), 'EU reaches consensus on maritime security' (18 Nov. 2009), *Jane's Defence Weekly*.
8. Prins, G. (2006), 'What the Royal navy should do next to reclaim the seas', *Naval Review*, vol. 94, no. 4.
9. Till, G. (2009), 'Making waves—Naval power evolves for the 21st century' (12 Nov. 2009), *Jane's Intelligence Review*.
10. Frittelli, J. F. (2003), 'Maritime security: Overview of issues', *Congressional Research Service Report CRS 21079*.
11. See Case Study B6.
12. International Institute for Strategic Studies (2009), 'Obama's new missile-defence strategy', *IISS Strategic Comments*, vol. 15, issue 8.
13. McGreal, (2010), 'US raises stakes on Iran by sending in ships and missiles' (1 Feb. 2010), *The Guardian*.
14. Fish, T., 'South Korea to acquire "mini Aegis" destroyer' (13 Oct. 2009), *Jane's Navy International*.
15. Fish, T., 'France plans acquisition of four resupply ships' (15 Oct. 2009), *Jane's Navy International*.
16. 'Anti-missile test heralds advent of Chinese BMD capability' (15 Jan. 2010), *Jane's Defence Weekly*.
17. 'This week at war: China rules the waves' (29 Oct. 2009), *Foreign Policy*.
18. 'China's anti-piracy role off Somalia expands' (29 Jan. 2009), *BBC News*. The report notes how China is increasingly becoming involved in the day-to-day counter-piracy operations after lobbying for an increased role.
19. Joshi, S., 'Sixty-five thousand tonnes of ambition', *RUSI.org*. An analysis of the ambitions of the Indian Navy.
20. 'Power Struggle' (23 Dec. 2009), *Jane's Defence Weekly*. A briefing paper on the balance of power in the Indian Ocean.
21. 'Iran missile tests stoke tensions' (27 Sept. 2009), *BBC News*. The report notes that Iran has a range of short-range ballistic missiles that it routinely tests and that it has plans to test a longer-range variant of the Shahab-3 missile, which is thought to have a range of 2,500 km. This report was published directly after a second uranium enrichment plant was disclosed to the United Nations that had previously remained secret, creating disquiet as to Iran's intensions with respect to its nuclear activities.
22. 'Small boats', Robert Strauss Centre for International Security and Law, Austin: University of Texas.
23. Dryad Maritime Intelligence Service [www.dryadmaritime.com] carried a report on 17 September sourced from WC.net, which highlighted the specific nature of the problems of economic migrants trying to leave Somalia, where small fishing boats are being loaded with up to 125 people, each paying between $30–$50

out of the monsoon season and between $60–$100 during the monsoon, to get to the Yemen. In one account of a journey, 20 out of 65 passengers were thrown overboard. The report cited a specific incident on 13 September in which a boat carrying 142 Somali and non-Somali citizens experienced engine failure and capsized near the Yemeni coastal town of Radfan. It was reported that 98 passengers managed to swim ashore and 43 were missing, presumed drowned. The main season for smuggling people is in September when the monsoon winds decline, making the passage across the Gulf of Aden easier.

24. Detection of the threat by watch-keepers is all-important, especially given the skiffs used by the pirates are sometimes barely visible to radar sensors. Through a combination of speed (the skiffs can cruise at over 20 knots), camouflage and timing of the attacks, appearing at dusk against the backdrop of a slowly sinking sun, the timelines for detection can be reduced, making the option of increasing speed one that cannot be left until the threat is detected. After all, vessels take time to increase their speed. So called defensive measures now recognise the agility shown by the pirates in reducing the detection timelines and call for vessels to maintain as full a speed as possible through dangerous areas. This creates problems for attempts to brigade and convoy vessels, which would normally have to travel at the speed of the slowest vessel. The cost implication of the additional fuel burnt by running at speed through the area is also an economic consideration and part of a complex piece of analysis that must be conducted by masters as they face transitioning the Gulf of Aden and the northwest of the Indian Ocean.
25. 'Tracking Ships, Terrorists and Pirates' (11–17 Sept. 2009), *Maritime Sector: Open Source Week in Review*. The article referenced an original report in the Washington Post, describing a system that uses satellite-based sensor systems to track the 70,000 ships believed to be at sea each day on the world's oceans and identify unusual or unexpected behaviour or intelligence in the information collected by the system.
26. Burnett, J. (2009), 'Terror from the Deep', *Jane's Homeland Security Review*.
27. Reporting provided by Dryad Maritime Intelligence Service [www.dryadmaritime.com] on 4 February 2010 on the discovery of floating mines deployed by groups affiliated to HAMAS off the Gaza Strip that were clearly targeted at Israeli Naval Forces that are trying to impose a naval blockade to prevent weapons reaching HAMAS. The devices were apparently placed at sea to avenge the killing of Mahmoud al-Mabhouh, a veteran Hamas operative involved in smuggling rockets into Gaza. The devices appeared to be relatively unsophisticated but did include a mobile phone arming system. Reports suggest that several of the devices had been placed and that an oil rig in the area may have also been a target.
28. See Case Study B5.
29. The Royal Navy designation for this operation was the *Armilla Patrol*.
30. 'Canada in Arctic show of strength' (16 Aug. 2009), *BBC News*.
31. See Case Study B2.

32. Rosamond, J. 'China urges US to phase out EEZ surveillance' (2 Sept. 2009), *Jane's Naval International* [www.janes.com]. A report quoted efforts being made by China to encourage the United States to scale down and ultimately cease its maritime security and survey efforts within China's claimed EEZ. The aim is to reduce the tensions that have emerged from confrontations that have occurred, such as the intercept of the USNS *Impeccable* by five Chinese vessels 75 miles off Hainan Island, where China has built an underground base for its nuclear submarines.
33. 'Smugglers dump refugees in Corsica' (23 Jan. 2010), *Al Jazeera*.
34. The ReCAAP Information Sharing Centre [www.recaap.org] reported an attempted boarding of the vessels *Pacific Harmony* early on Monday 14 September, and the chemical tanker the *MMM Kingston* two hours later, near the southern Malaysian port of Tanjung Ayam which is just to the east of Singapore. This is regarded as a high-risk area by the IMB piracy reporting centre as several events have occurred in this region.
35. For the purposes of this book we shall refer to maritime piracy as 'an act of boarding or attempting to board any ship with the apparent intent to commit theft or any other crime and with the apparent intent or capability to use force in furtherance of that act'. This definition is taken from Peter Chalk's use in his presentation given in Cartagena in Columbia in November 2008.
36. Herbert-Burns, R. and Zucker, L. (2004), 'Drawing the line between piracy and terrorism', *Jane's Intelligence Review*.
37. It is unclear what currently the term Maritime Security Operations (MSO) actually means in practice, as it has not yet entered the lexicon of many documents covering the doctrine that defines the approaches states are taking to maritime security. It covers a multitude of activities that can be undertaken by navies in the maritime domain. Defining clear boundaries for MSO is difficult as in practice a security operation could be an amphibious landing to secure a piece of land adjacent to a maritime choke point that is a vital SLOC or it could be delivering humanitarian assistance in the wake of a major disaster. At present the term MSO appears to be a catchall phrase used to cover a wide range of different maritime operations.
38. See Case Study B10.
39. On 30 July 2009, the Aegis system underwent a test on board the USS *Hopper* when the ship's systems successfully detected, tracked, fired and guided a Standard Missile-3 (SM-3) Block-1A missile to intercept a ballistic missile target. The plan is that twenty-one vessels will have an operational ballistic missile defence capability by the middle of 2010 based upon this system.
40. The reaction to the deployment of a TMD capability is difficult to envisage as a country faced with having its primary means of attack diffused to some extent by the presence of the shield may well be tempted to pre-empt the deployment unless they are confident they have the sheer weight of numbers to defeat its effective operation.

41. Mann, M. E., Woodruff, J. D., Donnelly, J. P., Zhang, Z., 'Atlantic hurricanes and climate over the past 1,500 years', *Nature*, p. 460; 880–3.
42. 'Royal Navy helps clean up after Hurricane Gustav' (2 Sept. 2008), *United Kingdom Ministry of Defence*.
43. 'Hurricane Ike, Royal Navy heads for Turks and Caicos Islands with aid' (8 Sept. 2008), *The Times*.
44. Bhanu Krishna Kiran, R. (2009), 'Maritime security challenges: A changing role for the Indian Navy', *Naval Review*, vol. 97, no. 2.
45. Scott, R. (4 Sept.), *Jane's Navy International*. Scott's report stated that the Royal Navy was considering a new concept for its Sustained Surface Combat Capability (S2C2) platform that would provide a single solution to the requirement for future hydrographic, patrol activities and mine countermeasures. Similar concepts have been developed for the new Spanish patrol vessels such as the Buques de Acción Marítima (BAM) offshore patrol vessel.
46. See Case Study B6.
47. Androjna, A., 'Mediterranean maritime security threats and challenges' (28–29 May 2008), *International Conference on Transport Science*.
48. 'US Navy launches Operation Brimstone' (30 Jul. 2008), *Jane's Defence Weekly*.
49. The CENTRIXS facilities allow naval units equipped with some quite basic Internet-based systems to quickly establish connections into a number of data realms (areas of varying security access) that allows e-mail exchanges, web data access, file-sharing and collaboration services, such as areas where staff on warships can post information to share within the coalition. This simple, and yet effective means of data sharing, harnesses part of the much-acclaimed revolution in military affairs that was heralded at the end of the twentieth century, as a result of technological developments that were supposed to give Western military units battle-winning advantages in conventional combat situations and enable them to mass firepower as and when it was required. The ideas were based on the ubiquity of ISTAR and its ability to be all-seeing and detect enemy/adversarial formations providing commanders with an enviable position and lifting what was traditionally known as the 'fog of war'; the uncertain knowledge of what was often a chaotic battlefield. Unfortunately, as military writers since Sun Tzu have acknowledged, the enemy has a vote and can deceive ISTAR assets, denying vital information to commanders. The decision superiority that was supposed to arise from the implementation of Network Enabled Capabilities (NECs) has not quite lived up to their marketing hubris in recent campaigns, such as the Counter Insurgency campaign in Iraq where targets where often fleeting in nature placing a huge priority upon persistence in coverage. However, CENTRIXS is a pragmatic and practical way of sharing information with coalition partners that does help naval forces, for example, operating off the Horn of Africa, to coordinate their efforts. Its introduction has been hugely important and serves as a role model for future naval task force collaboration within the overall concept of the 1,000-Ship (virtual) Navy.

50. Dryad Maritime Intelligence Services [www.dryadmaritime.com] carried a report on 17 September 2009 noting the end of the monsoon season and the potential for attacks on commercial shipping to restart after a lull, as the weather conditions did not favour boarding operations. Other reporting, on 19 September, also suggests that pirates are increasingly looking to inflate the ransoms being paid for vessels with figures such as $2 million being regarded as small.
51. On 27 March, the Russian Navy announced it was stepping up its anti-piracy operations in the Gulf of Aden by sending a task force from the country's Pacific Fleet comprising the *Admiral Panteleyev* (a destroyer equipped with a Ka-27 helicopter), a salvage tug-boat and a tanker from Vladivostok.
52. Operation Ocean Shield is being mounted by NATO off the coast of Somalia and it is a continuance of the initial Operation Allied Protector which was NATO's first such coordinated effort in the area of counter-piracy activities. A key aim of the operation is not only to protect vulnerable shipping in the first instance but also to build indigenous capacity, where it can be created, to allow nation states such as Somalia to take responsibility for the situation and deploy their own coastguard services to arrest and prosecute those involved in piracy.
53. On 25 May 2009, it was announced in Tehran by the commander of the Iranian Navy, Rear-Admiral Habibollah Sayyari, that six Iranian warships and logistic vessels would be joining the international task force off the coast of Somalia and the Gulf of Aden. This deployment came in the wake of the attack by pirates on the cargo ship *Delight*, operated by the Islamic Republic of Iran Shipping Lines in November 2008 and an attack upon an Iranian fishing vessel allegedly fishing illegally off the coast of the semi-autonomous region of Puntland.
54. 'Pirates attack ship off Mogadishu' (25 Sept. 2009), *BBC News*.
55. There have been a number of reports that suggest that close ties exist between the pirates and Al-Qaeda. Much of this reporting is based upon speculation rather than fact. The Harmony Project from West Point in the United States produces a very careful appraisal of the difficulties encountered by Al-Qaeda in trying to establish bases in Somalia in their report 'Al-Qaeda's (Mis) Adventures in the Horn of Africa', which was published in 2006, by the Combating Terrorism Centre at West Point.
56. 'NATO warns India of Somali pirate attacks' (24 Sept. 2009), *Dryad Maritime Intelligence Service*.
57. '*Mexico acquires UAS for all-weather ISR capability*' (30 Jul. 2009), *Jane's Navy International*. The report documents a plan announced by the Mexican government to acquire Unmanned Aerial Surveillance (UAS) for a trials period to determine their effectiveness in countering criminal activities along the country's coastline.
58. 'Brazil plans procurement of ocean patrol ships' (24 Dec. 2009), *Jane's Navy International Report*.
59. The Yamal Peninsula in Siberia, where Russian estimates suggest that gas reserves may total 12 trillion cubic metres or be as high as 50 trillion cubic metres, is one

location where the changes in the local climate are providing an opportunity for major exploration and potential exploitation of reserves that might have been difficult to harness a decade ago. The prospect of LNG containers shipping gas from major facilities in Siberia to locations all over the world is a very real possibility by 2020.

60. One example of this is the impact upon house prices in Kenya as a direct result of the estimated $40 million income received by pirates in Somalia in 2008, which is used not only for buying expensive houses in Somalia, but is also flooding into the Kenyan property market, with potentially destabilising consequences.
61. On 3 May 2009, the Cruise Line Fred Olsen announced to its passengers who had booked a world cruise on board the *Balmoral* that they would no longer be stopping at ports in Dubai, Oman and Egypt, because of the risk from piracy in the area. This announcement came days after MSC had also announced it was not going to take its cruise liners north of Mauritius after the attack on the MSC *Melody* 200 nm north of the Seychelles.
62. An example of this was the attack mounted 237 nm to the east of the Seychelles Islands and 725 west-north-west of the Chagos Archipelago on the MV IVS *Cabernet* on 9 May 2009.
63. The approach taken in the book recognises the maritime environment in the widest possible sense and has parallels with the viewpoint being taken in Australia, which defines maritime security from the perspective of threats to Australia's national interests, covering topics such as: illegal exploitation of natural resources (unlawful fishing activities and the removal or destruction of wildlife); illegal activity in protected areas (designated marine reserves, such as the Great Barrier Reef, protected zones around offshore oil and gas installations and submerged cables and historic wrecks); unauthorised maritime arrivals (economic migrants); prohibited imports and exports; maritime terrorism; piracy; any compromise to bio-security (deliberately or accidentally) and pollution events.
64. McQuaid, J. V. (2009), 'Maritime security: Strengthening international and interagency cooperation', *CAN Analysis and Solutions*.
65. 'Israelis seize Iran arms ship' (4 Nov. 2009), *BBC News*.
66. See Case Study B3.
67. In July 2009, the US Secretary of State Hilary Clinton spoke in Thailand of developing an umbrella over the Middle East. Her rhetoric had echoes in President Reagan's 'Star Wars' concept of protecting the United States through developing a missile shield. The aim was to persuade Iran not to progress with its nuclear weapons programme. The real fear is that this will create pressures in neighbouring countries to develop their own nuclear programmes resulting in proliferation of nuclear programmes in an area known for its instability. The idea of a missile shield is one that can be deployed into a region, with a minimal local footprint, onboard warships that carry the radar, command and control and missile inventories that can intercept and destroy an incoming ballistic missile.
68. See Case Studies A2 and A21.

1. CONTEMPORARY PERSPECTIVES ON MARITIME SECURITY

1. This quotation is the result of a private communication with Commodore Niels Friis of the Royal Danish Navy in which he offered this definition of maritime security, dated 5 August 2009.
2. A fact made all the more relevant by the rate at which cyber-related issues are developing. Terms such as cyber-warfare, cyber-terrorism and cyber-crime may imply a move away from the physical environment, such as the maritime domain, but in fact simply highlight the opening up of yet another domain in which military specialists, terrorists and criminals believe they need to operate.
3. 'US Navy to stand up Fleet Cyber Command' (9 Oct. 2009), *Jane's Defence Weekly*. The report notes that an initial group of 182 personnel will form the nucleus of the formation. FLTCYBERCOM will be known as the tenth fleet, a functional command that was previously responsible for coordinating the military effort against German submarines in the Second World War. It was the first time the United States fielded a unified intelligence and operational command.
4. Snook, R. (2007), 'Violations of good order at sea and maritime security initiatives', *Naval Review*, vol. 95, no. 1.
5. Mullen, M, 'Keynote address: A global network of nations for a free and secure maritime commons' (21 Sept. 2005), Seventeenth International Seapower Symposium, Naval War College: Newport, Rhode Island.
6. Chalk, P. (2008) 'Maritime piracy, terrorism and drug trafficking: Overview and conceptualisation', *RAND Corporation*, Cartagena: Columbia.
7. Mugridge, D. (2009), 'Brothers in arms or a case of my enemy's enemy is my friend?', *Naval Review*, vol. 97, no. 3, pp. 215–22.
8. In this definition we shall include the notion of state on non-state (transnational actor) as an element to reflect the maritime security issues associated with evacuating non-combatants, such as occurred in July 2006 when European and Commonwealth citizens were evacuated from Beirut.
9. Kaplan, R. D. (2000), *The Coming Anarchy: Shattering the Dreams of the Post Cold War*, Vintage Books.
10. Hill, R. (2007), 'Deterring the undeterrable', *Naval Review*, vol. 95, no. 2.
11. Pelkofski, Captain J., 'Before the Storm: Al-Qaeda's Coming Maritime Campaign' (Dec. 2005), United States Naval Institute. Captain Pelkofski posits that 'rather than develop a false sense of security based on the belief that inherent difficulties will limit maritime terrorism [...] caution is warranted in the light of Al-Qaeda's adaptability, ingenuity, tenacity and audacity'.
12. Peter Chalk from the Rand Corporation offers suggestions for this, noting that operating at sea requires certain specialised skills and that these are often in short supply. He further notes that terrorist groups are, by their nature, conservative groups that like to reduce the risks of failure, relying on tried-and-tested techniques. Lastly, and perhaps most importantly, most of the high-value targets exist on the land where the potential for media coverage, such as was achieved over a

sixty-two hour period in Mumbai, can really help magnify the impact of the event.

13. O'Rourke, R., 'Homeland security: Coast Guard operations—background and issues for congress' (9 Dec. 2002), *Congressional Research Service Report RS 21125.*
14. Chalk goes on in his address in Cartagena, Columbia, to address trends which could result in terrorism developing in the maritime environment, such as the growing awareness of the anarchic nature of the maritime domain; the trends towards skeleton crews; the necessity to transit through a number of key choke points (there are nine recognised around the world) and the potential for terrorists to overcome their maritime skills deficit through access to the leisure market in the marine arena.
15. Grevatt, J., 'Mumbai attacks drive Indian Coast Guard modernisation plan' (29 Oct. 2009), *Jane's Navy International.*
16. See Case Study B9.
17. Parfomak, P. W., Frittelli, J. (2007), 'Maritime security: Potential terrorist attacks and protection priorities', *Congressional Research Service (CRS) Report RL 33787.*
18. See Case Study A22.
19. The report goes on to mention many other ways in which infrastructure, such as bridges, docks and storage facilities, could be attacked by hijacked fishing boats and other vessels, used as a Water Borne Improvised Explosive Device (WBIED) and the potential for multiple events to drain the resources of the responders.
20. Whilst a successful detonation would have a massive impact upon the country, even a weapon that only partially exploded would still create a major backlash. North Korea's first nuclear detonation has been reported as a 1 kt yield and yet the mere fact that it was exploded created a different atmosphere around the negotiations that have been occurring. North Korea got the international community's attention. Imagine the reaction if a terrorist group did the same?
21. Barnes, P. and Oloruntoba, R. (2005), 'Assurance of security in maritime supply chains: Conceptual issues of vulnerability and crisis management', *Journal of International Management*, no. 11, pp. 519–540.
22. Gooley, T. and Cooke, J. (2002), 'Shippers, carriers struggle with port-shutdowns aftermath', *Logistics Management.*
23. See Case Study B4.
24. This includes the potential for environmental terrorism.
25. Allows for man-made disasters as a result of acts of terrorism, the oil spill from the attack on the *Limburg* for example or an *Exxon Valdez* event created by terrorists in a key shipping lane.
26. This allows for natural disasters to make significant changes, for instance, to the bathymetry of an area.
27. 'Somalia: New navy task force takes aim at pirates' (23 Jan. 2009), *America.gov.*
28. See Case Study A9.
29. Gilpin, R. (2007), 'Enhancing maritime security in the Gulf of Guinea', *Strategic Insights*, vol. 6, issue 1, Centre for Contemporary Conflict.

30. Sloggett, D. R. (2008), 'Piracy and maritime terrorism: The achilles heel of the global economy?', *Naval Review*, vol. 96, no. 3.
31. 'Somalia: Pirates try to hijack North Korean ship' (10 Apr. 2009), *allAfrica.com*.
32. Fish, T., 'South Korea readies destroyer for Somalia patrol' (9 Feb. 2009), *Jane's Navy International*.
33. Morris, M., 'Warships foil hijack attempts in the Gulf of Aden' (19 Sept. 2009), ArabianBusiness.com. The report showed how Iranian Warships had opened fire on suspected pirate boats to prevent an attempted hijacking of three Iranian commercial vessels in the Gulf of Aden.
34. Mugridge, D. (2009) 'Globalisation and the new challenges for maritime security in North America', *SEUS CP*.
35. Huntingdon, S. P. (1996), 'The clash of civilisations and the remaking of world order', *Free Press*, Simon & Schuster.
36. See Case Study A1.
37. Sloggett, D. R. (2009), 'Maritime security challenges: A case study in the Gulf of Guinea', *Naval Review*, vol. 97, no. 2.
38. Carmel, S. (2008), *A Contrarian Perspective on Piracy*.
39. McGinley, J. E. and Berliner, J. P. (2009), *High Noon on the High Seas: A Proximity-Complexity Model of Maritime Piracy Threats*, Centre for Contemporary Conflict.
40. Gelfand, L., 'International shipping faces a longer-range Somali piracy threat' (12 Nov. 2009), *Jane's Defence Weekly*.
41. Mazumdar, M., 'Shaldag patrol craft delivered to Nigerian Navy' (27 Aug. 2009), *Jane's Naval International*. The report focussed on the acquisition by the Nigerian Navy of its first Shaldag fast patrol boat to work alongside two other vessels and several smaller craft to help counter piracy off the coast of Nigeria; thirty-seven pirate attacks have been reported here in the second quarter of 2009 by the International Maritime Bureau's Piracy Reporting Centre most of which were directed at vessels involved in the countries economically vital oil sector.
42. Revenues earned through charging tariffs to transit the Suez Canal have dropped by 25 per cent in February 2009 as a result of the combined effects of the downturn in the global economy and the piracy in the Gulf of Aden with arms manufacturers specifically re-routing vessels around the Cape of Good Hope. While some cruise operators have decided to follow suit, liners such as the *Legend of the Seas, Queen Mary, Queen Elizabeth*, the *Princess Dawn* and the *Pacific Princess* will all be using the Gulf of Aden as part of their cruise schedule. The owners believe that a combination of additional security measures will enable them to avoid being hijacked.
43. The New York State Office of Homeland Security runs an information campaign under the headline 'if you see something say something', which is aimed at engaging the widest possible range of maritime users highlighting the seven signs of terrorism (surveillance, suspicious questioning, tests of security, acquiring supplies, persons out of place, indications of trial runs/dress rehearsals and deploy-

ing assets prior to an attack) and documenting some specific suspicious activities that are good indications of malicious intent. The campaign emphasises the need to develop patterns of known activity from which suspicious behaviour can stand out and be readily detected.

44. The idea of the three-tiered model was introduced at The Shangri La Dialogue in 2008, by the Singaporean Minister of Defence, Mr Teo Chee Hean.
45. Shashikumar, V. K. (2009), 'Gaps in Maritime Security', *Indian Defence Review*, vol. 24, no. 1.
46. It is likely that as a ratio of vessels to the length of the coastline that, in practice, India had a higher density of coverage that many other countries around the world. Sheer numbers of craft are not the answer to the problem of maritime security; other factors, such as the cooperation between agencies and the effective deployment of airborne assets and coastal radar systems also need to be factored in to any overall solution.
47. Mazumdar, M., 'India commissions two more Car Nicobar-class craft' (11 Sept. 2009), *Jane's Navy International*. The report describes the commissioning of two Nicobar-class fast patrol boats into service and the development of eight inshore patrol vessels and the delivery of thirteen patrol boats to various coastal security and police agencies. The Indian Ministry of Home Affairs is also reported to have ordered seventy-eight FRP interceptors, of which forty-eight are 12-tonne and thirty 5-tonne variants for specific duties patrolling India's eastern coastline.
48. Mazumdar, M., 'Steady progress but no overnight success for India as it shores up coastal security' (23 Nov. 2009), *Jane's Navy International*.
49. Sloggett, D. R. (2009), 'The lessons of Mumbai for the maritime defence of the United Kingdom', *Naval Review*, vol. 97, no. 1.
50. Valencia, M. J. (2005), 'The proliferation security initiative: Making waves in Asia', *Adelphi Paper*, no. 376, International Institute for Strategic Studies.
51. Sugandha, S. (2008), *Evolution of Maritime Strategy and National Security of India*, Decent Books.
52. See Case Study A6.
53. Roy-Chaudhury, R. (2000), *India's Maritime Security*, Institute for Defence Analysis.
54. Singh, K. R., Singh, K. (2008), *Security for India: New Challenges and Responses*, New Century Publications.
55. Bhanu Krishna Kiran, R. (2009), 'Maritime security challenges: A changing role for the Indian Navy', *Naval Review*, vol. 97, no. 2.
56. Mugridge, D. (2008), 'A maritime malaise—The current UK approach to maritime security', *Naval Review*, vol. 96, no. 4.
57. It is clear that all of the measures introduced after 11 September in the area of airport security should have been in place beforehand but a lack of political will resulted in terrorists exploiting vulnerabilities that were, in hindsight, fairly clear to anyone who cared to look in some depth beforehand. Without doubt, 11 September changed a great deal in terms of mindsets and now the language is

focussed upon gaps in security. The security environment was transformed by the events of that dreadful day.

58. A comment attributed to Rear Admiral Tay at the Seventeenth International Seapower Symposium in Newport, Rhode Island on 21 September 2005.
59. Nye, J. S. (2002), *The Paradox of Power: Why the World's only Superpower Can't Go It Alone* Oxford: Oxford University Press.
60. Chen, Y., Edmonds, M. (2003), *Taiwan's Maritime Security*, London: Routledge.
61. 'Combating piracy off Somalia, swift naval response is only part of the solution' (2009), *Strategic Comments*, vol. 15, issue 1, International Institute for Strategic Studies.
62. On 7 April 2009, the United States Maritime Administration issues an advisory note to mariners operating in the Gulf of Aden recommending ships remain at least 600 nm (1100km) off the coast of Somalia.
63. Middleton, R., 'Piracy symptom of bigger problem' (15 Apr. 2009), *BBC News*.
64. 'The African Partnership Station: A new US approach to sub-Saharan engagement' (Aug. 2008), *International Institute for Strategic Studies Comments*, vol. 14, issue 6.
65. Hattendorf, J. B. (2007), *The Oxford Encyclopedia of Maritime History*, Oxford: Oxford University Press.
66. Vesky, J. P., (ed.) (2007), *Port and Maritime Security*, Nova Science Publishers.
67. Frittelli, J. F., Lee, M. R., Medalia, J., O'Rouke, R. and Perl, R. (2003) *Port and Maritime Security: Background and Issues*, Nova Biomedical.
68. By November 2002, eleven of the top twenty mega-ports in the world had agreed to take part in the CSI scheme, with the Canadian ports of Halifax, Montreal and Vancouver the first to join the programme when United States Customs Officials were deployed to those ports to screen the in-bound cargoes. In June 2002, Singapore joined the list, rapidly being followed by a number of European seaports; Rotterdam, Le Havre, Antwerp and Bremerhaven. Hong Kong is also amongst the list. This is important as the twenty mega ports generate 70 per cent of the container traffic that eventually ends up in the United States as part of the 16,000 containers a day that arrive by ship, truck and rail, of which only 2 per cent are inspected.
69. Corera, G. (2006), *Shopping for Bombs: Nuclear Proliferation, Global Insecurity and the Rise and Fall of the A.Q. Khan Network*, London: C. Hurst & Co.
70. Ibid., p. ix.
71. One incident concerned the motor vessel *Kang Nam 1*, supposedly bound for Myanmar, which was being closely monitored by the United States Navy. After some exchanges of increasingly bellicose rhetoric, Pyongyang seemed to back down and call the vessel home. There were some echoes in the incident of the Cuban Missile crisis.
72. See Case Study B7.
73. Jones, S. (2007), *Maritime Security: A Practical Guide*, The Nautical Institute.
74. McNicholas, M. (2007), *Maritime Security: An Introduction*, Butterworth-Heinemann Homeland Security Series.

75. Murphy, M. N. (2009), *Small Boats, Weak States, Dirty Money: Piracy and Maritime Terrorism in the Modern World*, London: C. Hurst & Co.
76. Young, A. (2007), *Contemporary Maritime Piracy in Southeast Asia: History, Causes and Remedies*, Institute of Southeast Asia Studies (ISEAS) Publishing
77. Herbert-Burns, R., Bateman, S. and Lehr, P. (2009), *Lloyd's MIU Handbook of Maritime Security*, London: CRC Press.
78. Detailed assessments of the threat from the Iranian Navy and the broader implications of attacks upon oil tankers in the Strait of Hormuz have been developed by the Robert Strauss Centre and can be found on their website http://www.hormuz.robertstrausscentre.org.
79. This is no way suggests that bombings in Iraq, and places such as Indonesia (July 2009), have been eliminated; however, the level of attacks is significantly down and disruptive efforts by security forces have clearly denied some organisations the space in which to operate.
80. Richardson, M. (2004), *A Time Bomb for Global Trade: Maritime-related Terrorism in an Age of Weapons of Mass Destruction*, Singapore: Institute of South East Asian Studies.
81. Al-Qaeda's navy is a dedicated part (Chapter two) of the work by Michael Richardson.
82. See case Study A19.
83. Stopford, M. (2009), *Maritime Economics*, 3rd Edition, London: Routledge.
84. Ibid. p. 55.
85. Nye, J. S. (2004), *Soft Power: The Means to Success in World Politics*, Public Affairs.
86. Ghosh, P. K. (2007), 'Maritime power projection for India: Is a rapid reaction force necessary?', *Naval Review*, vol. 95, no. 2.
87. In a spat over the North Korean nuclear programme, reported by the *Daily Mail* on 24 July 2009, the United States Secretary of State Hilary Clinton was described by the North Koreans as 'a funny lady' as she likes to use such rhetoric and that she was 'is by no means intelligent' and has made a number of 'vulgar remarks'. The Secretary of State replied accusing the North Korean Government of being like 'a child seeking attention' and 'having few friends left' and indicating that Washington had deliberately tried to play down the significance of a series of ballistic missile tests conducted by the North Koreans in order not to 'give them the satisfaction of being centre stage'. Previous verbal spats had seen President George W. Bush labelled as 'an incompetent and rude President who is senseless and ignorant'.
88. Nye, *The Paradox of American Power*.
89. Lexington Institute (2008), *Maritime Security*.

2. HISTORICAL PERSPECTIVES

1. Black, J. (2009), *Naval power: A History of Warfare and the Sea from 1500*, Palgrave Macmillan.

2. Gosse, P. (2007), *The History of Piracy*, New York: Dover Publications.
3. Aubet, M. E., Turton, M. (trans.) (2001), *The Phoenicians and the West: Politics, Colonies and Trade*, Cambridge: Cambridge University Press, Second Edition, p. 17.
4. Waterfield, R. (trans.), *Herodotus: The Histories*, Oxford: Oxford University Press.
5. The goods carried on these routes have been described in a Greek manual drawn from the period of the first century BCE called the *Periplus of the Erythraean Sea*.
6. Levathes, L. (1997), *When China Ruled the Seas: The Treasure Fleet of the Dragon Throne, 1405–1433*, Oxford: Oxford University Press.
7. Glete, J. (2000), *Warfare at Sea, 1500–1650: Maritime Conflicts and the Transformation of Europe*, London: Routledge.
8. Rodger, N. A. M. (2004), *The Safeguarding of the Sea: A Naval history of Britain, 660–1649*, London: Penguin Books.
9. Harding, R. (1999), *Seapower and Naval Warfare 1650–1830*, London and New York: Routledge.
10. Padfield, P. (2003), *Maritime Power and the Struggle for Freedom: Naval Campaigns that Shaped the Modern World 1788–1851*, London: John Murray.
11. Bauer, J. (1989), *A Maritime History of the United States: Role of America's Seas and Waterways*, Colombia: University of South Carolina Press.
12. Harding, *Seapower and Naval Warfare*, p. 37.
13. Adkins, R. and Adkins, L. (2006), *The War for all the Oceans: From Nelson at the Nile to Napoleon at Waterloo*, ABACUS.
14. Hore, P. (2005), *The Habit of Victory: the Story of the Royal Navy 1545 to 1945*, Pan Books and the National Maritime Museum.
15. In the early 1600s, the Dutch were well on their way to being the dominant commercial and economic power in Europe; they benefited from their geography, their enduring struggle with the sea, their location at the mouth of three rivers and their position with respect to access to the North Sea and the Atlantic Ocean and also the scarcity of natural resources. This almost unique set of conditions created a need for the Dutch people to become a blend of merchants, artisans, engineers and excellent sailors.
16. See Case Study B1.
17. 'Could 19th century plan stop piracy?' (9 Apr. 2009), *BBC News*.

3. THE MARITIME ENVIRONMENT

1. 'Cargo vessels navigate the legendary Northeast passage without using ice breakers' (13 Sept. 2009), *The Sunday Mail*. New sea lanes that may become available due to global warming may have a mitigating impact. *The Sunday Mail* reported the voyage of two merchant ships using the so-called North East Passage from Asia to Europe along the 2,000 mile stretch of coastline to the north of Siberia only encountering small scattered ice flows. The company behind the voyage

claimed it had saved £180,000 per vessels by cutting the journey by 3,500 miles in distance and by ten days in time.

2. New links between Columbian and Mexican drugs cartels and various groups in Nigeria and other countries in West Africa have been reported by CNN on 22 September 2009. The report claimed that at least nine top-tier Latin American drugs cartels had established bases in eleven West African nations hoping to exploit routes for narcotics through Europe's underbelly into the lucrative markets in the area. These West African countries are seen to have weak governance infrastructures and are vulnerable to being exploited by criminality.
3. The definition of the EEZ includes areas such as the waters surrounding overseas territories, which in the case of the United Kingdom includes locations such as Ascension Island and the Falklands Islands.
4. See Case Study A13.
5. The Director General of the Malaysian Maritime Enforcement Agency stated at an international conference in Melaka in Malaysia on 17 August 2009 that only one incident of piracy had been reported so far in 2009. He noted that three had been reported in 2008 and twelve in 2007. He attributed the drop to the increased levels of cooperation being undertaken under the auspices of the multinational Malacca Straits Sea Patrol.
6. Bradford, J. F. (2005), 'The growing prospects for maritime security cooperation in Southeast Asia', *Naval War College Review*, vol. 58, no. 3.
7. Issues such as the right for *hot pursuit* in the case of trying to make arrests of criminals can be fine when tension levels are low but should the potential for confrontation arise, an effort to arrest a criminal may well be seen as an infringement upon a state's territorial waters and a presage to conflict.
8. Sato, Y. (2007), *Southeast Asian Receptiveness to Japanese Maritime Security Cooperation*, Asia-Pacific Centre for Security Studies.
9. Reported from Metro TV, Jakarta on 2 February 2010 recounting the arrest of thirty-nine Afghan illegal immigrants in Southeast Sulawesi in the waters off Kabaena Timur Island in the Bombana District of Indonesia.
10. http://www.ips.org/roy-paper.pdf.
11. Fish, T., 'India launches second Kolkata-class destroyer' (18 Sept. 2009), *Jane's Navy International*. The report detailed the launch of the second Kolkata-class destroyer *Kochi* for the Indian Navy. This is the second of three ships scheduled to be in the class and follows the launch of the first-in-class *Kolkata* in March 2006. In 2009, India's Defence Acquisition Council approved the construction of a further four new destroyers under the umbrella of the Project 15 programme which is the follow-on to the Delhi-class destroyers which entered service between 1997 and 2001.
12. In his analysis Admiral Roy notes that between 200–250 major warships were planned for procurement by the end of the century and that more than thirty modern submarines have been ordered by Asian countries for delivery in the next decade, noting the impact of UNCLOS III on many smaller states which

have decided to modernise their naval capacity to protect their newly defined EEZ.

13. This is a term that implies financial linkages between those involved in the growth and smuggling of narcotics with groups and individuals involved in terrorism; a situation where funds raised from narcotics support those who carry out acts of terrorism. This is a nexus that had been explored by many authors and the links currently do not appear to be that strong when it comes to certain terrorist groups whose ideological motivation is simply not compatible with adopting any form of criminality to raise funds. That said, some terrorist groups find obscure religious justifications for temporarily turning a blind eye to this form of money-raising activity where it is proven to support their long-term ideological goals. Whilst many commentators rule out links because of this ideological divide, a pragmatic approach would note the agility of some groups to compromise on this position for short-term gains.
14. This need for transparency is an issue when one of the major developments of the PLAN is the new underground submarine base near Sanya, Hainan in China, which is estimated to have the capacity to hide up to twenty nuclear submarines and is strategically located to enable those submarines to be projected into the Indian and Pacific Oceans.
15. Bedi, R., 'India strengthens military cooperation with the Maldives' (21 Aug. 2009), *Jane's Defence Weekly*. The report described the deployment of two helicopters in the Maldives and additional patrolling by Dornier Do-228 sorties over the 600km north-south extent of the archipelago of the Maldives alongside supplying twenty-six radar systems on various atolls in the Maldives Island chain which will be linked to a command centre in Kochi in southern India. This is a response to the String of Pearls strategy developed by China, which is based on a number of regional defence and security arrangements in the Indian Ocean Region (IOR).
16. Chopra, R. (2004), 'The maritime dimension of energy security', *USI Journals*.
17. Venugopalan, U., 'Harbouring ambitions—China invests in Indian Ocean ports' (15 Oct. 2009), *Jane's Intelligence Review*.
18. See Case Study B6.
19. Pehrson, C. J. (2006), *String of Pearls: Meeting the Challenge of China's Rising Power Across the Asian Littoral*, see http://www.StrategicStudiesInstitute.army.mil/.
20. Chacko Joseph, C. 'China's "String of Pearls" strategy around India in tatters' (11 May 2009), FrontierIndia.net. The commentary suggests that far from being a successful approach the current situation is in tatters and not providing the encirclement of India that China seeks.
21. On 20 September 2009, China and Russia participated in joint naval manoeuvres as part of an exercise called 'Peace Blue Shield 2009' that explored cooperation in examining suspect ships with helicopters and surface vessels. China's flotilla of three surface ships tested communications links and coordinated re-supply efforts.

22. See 'Gunmen remain at large after Pakistan attack on Sri Lankan cricket team' (3 Mar. 2009), *The Guardian*.
23. Allen, T. (2007), 'New threats, new challenges: The Coastguard's new strategy', *US Naval Institute Proceedings*, p. 75.
24. Greenberg, M. D., Chalk, P., Willis, H. W., Khilko, I. and Ortiz, D. S. (2006), *Maritime Terrorism: Risk and Liability*, RAND Centre for Terrorism Risk Management Policy.
25. The Cunard Liner, *The Queen Mary 2*, has 1253 crew and can host up to 3056 passengers.
26. Monks, R., 'Falklands frontiers—Oil exploration at the ends of the earth' (6 Jul. 2009), *Jane's Intelligence Review*. The report states that oil companies are beginning a new round of exploratory drilling off the disputed Falkland (Malvinas) Islands in 2009 where initial exploratory drilling has suggested the existence of up to 60 billion barrels of reserves (greater than the combined assets of Nigeria and the Libya) and there is potential for gas reserves to be discovered in commercially viable quantities as well. In April 2009, the Argentinean Government presented a case to the UN Commission on the Limits of the Continental Shelf claiming sovereignty over the Falklands and a part of Antarctica, which is disputed by the United Kingdom and Chile.
27. See Case Study A20.
28. See Case Study A4.
29. See Case Study A7.
30. See Case Study A8.
31. See Case Study B7.
32. See Case Study A12.
33. Hammes, Colonel T. X. (2004), *The Sling and the Stone: On War in the 21st Century*, Minneapolis, MN: Zenith Press.
34. They are engaged in what is now referred to as an MSO operation which, whilst unclear in its doctrinal definition, seems to group together military activities that are conducted at a level below all-out industrial forms of warfare, such as the major forms of conflict in Korea, Vietnam, the Falkland Islands, and the First and Second Gulf Wars.
35. A definition offered by the United States Navy.
36. The most recent analysis of the world oil chokepoints published by the Energy Information Administration in the United States, dated January 2008, states that in 2007, world oil production amounted to 85 million barrels of oil per day, and 43 million barrels per day of that total were moved by tankers on fixed maritime trade routes.
37. Gosh, P. K. (2004), 'Maritime security challenges in South Asia and the Indian Ocean: Response strategies', Centre for Strategic Studies, American-Pacific Sealanes Security Institute Conference on Maritime Security in Asia, 18–20 January, Honolulu, Hawaii.
38. Energy Information Administration (EIA), January 2008, published its report on the world oil transit choke points.

39. 'Worldwide threat to shipping' (1 Apr. 2009), Office of Naval Intelligence, Civil Maritime Analysis Department.
40. Murphy, M. (2009), *Small Boats, Weak States, Dirty Money: Piracy and Maritime Terrorism in the Modern World*, London: C. Hurst & Co.
41. Young, A. J. (2007), *Contemporary Maritime Piracy in Southeast Asia: History, Causes and Remedies*, Singapore: ISEAS Publishing.
42. The Spanish Government announced on 9 September 2009 that it would be stepping up its protection of the tuna fleet that operates off the coast of Somalia after three attempts were made to hijack Spanish fishing vessels in the previous week. One event saw the *Intertuna dos* avoid capture when operating 420 miles from the Somali coast. The Spanish Government also issued advice to the trawlers about reducing the area in which they fish and also keeping in closer contact with one another whilst in the area.
43. Whilst patrolling in the waters of the southern area of the Bahamas, the United States Coast Guard Cutter (USCGC) *Bear* discovered a 40-foot sailboat with over 160 illegal migrants aboard. They were repatriated to Cap-Haitien in Haiti.
44. Analysis provided by the International Institute of Strategic Studies in the 2009 Chart of Conflict.

4. THREATS TO MARITIME SECURITY

1. Scott, R., 'Policing the maritime beat' (29 Apr. 2009), *Jane's Defence Weekly*. A briefing on the Combined Maritime Forces operating in the Middle East.
2. Russell, J. A. (2006), *Maritime security in the Gulf: Addressing the Terrorist Threat*, Gulf Research Council, issue 2.
3. Steinhäusler, F., Furthner, P., Heidegger, W., Rydell, S. and Zaitseva, L. (2008) 'Security risks to the oil and gas industry: Terrorist capabilities', *Strategic Insights*, vol. 7, issue 1, Centre for Contemporary Conflict.
4. 'North Korea's dangerous game: Nuclear test and missile launches go beyond usual brinkmanship' (Jun. 2009), vol. 15, issue 05, International Institute of Strategic Studies.
5. 'UAE seizes North Korea arms cargo' (28 Aug. 2008), *BBC News*. The report covers the story of the seizure of a North Korean ship bound for Iran containing a range of embargoed weapons that were covered by United Nations sanctions.
6. 'Gunmen storm Aqua Expeditions tourist cruise ship in Peru in dawn robbery' (6 Aug. 2009), *Daily Telegraph*.
7. See Case Study A11.
8. Greenwood, P. (2009), 'Maritime security: The underwater threat', *Naval Review*, vol. 97, no. 2.
9. See Case Study A17.
10. The more accepted term for these people is now 'irregular migrants'.
11. On 12 September 2009, the BBC carried a report by Will Ross in their pro-

gramme on one of these routes in a piece entitled 'Senegal's youths dream of Europe', in which an interview is conducted with a young man who explained his reasons for wanting to risk everything to enter Europe, where he hoped he would find a better life. He was not dissuaded from making the perilous crossing to the Canary Islands despite coverage of the global economic downturn, which he did not believe, contrasting the real situation on the ground in Senegal as a real economic crisis.

12. On 10 September 2009, the BBC reported that none of the 150 people aboard a boat that capsized off the coast of Sierra Leone had lifejackets, in direct contravention of local laws. The boat capsized just after it had left the port of Shenge to travel to Tombo, a journey of 65km and was carrying many children who were returning from their school holidays.
13. 'Australia PM seeks migrant help' (13 Oct. 2009), BBC News.
14. A report by the Chinese news agency Xinhua dated 11 September 2009, stated that the Indonesian Navy had detained fifty-six Afghan immigrants trying to enter eastern Indonesia. In March 2009, Indonesian Police arrested fifty-nine illegal migrants from Afghanistan and Pakistan who were reported to be travelling to Australia.
15. In March 2009, the United Nations Refugee Agency reported that the number of people crossing the Horn of Africa to Yemen was three times the number of arrivals for the same period in the previous year. Smuggling resumed earlier than is normal in the area due to calmer weather in the Gulf of Aden.
16. In April 2009, it was reported by the United Nations High Commissioner for Refugees partner agency the Society of Human Solidarity, that thirty-five bodies had been recovered from a boat that had capsized. The boat had been reportedly carrying 117 people. The agency further reported that 387 boats carrying 19,622 people had arrived in Yemen this year and that it believed 131 people have died and sixty-six others are known to be missing.
17. 'Mexico drug crew burn boat' (14 Oct. 2009), *BBC News*.
18. See Case Study A5.
19. See Case Study A3.
20. See Case Study A23.
21. Fish, T., 'Brazil orders second batch of patrol ships from EISA' (15 Sept. 2009), *Jane's Navy International*. The report noted the Brazilian Government's decision to order a second batch of the 54-metre Navio Patrulha (NAPA 500) patrol ships for delivery in 2012 at a cost of $27 million for each vessel. A third batch for a further six units has been announced at the same time as part of what is planned to be a force of twenty-seven vessels in total, within the framework of the 'Patrol Vessels Renewal Programme'.
22. 'Norway joins EU anti-piracy operation' (31 Jul. 2009), *Jane's Navy International.*
23. See Case Study A16.
24. Helmoed-Römer Heitman, H., 'Opinion: Africa and the maritime dimension' (25 Jun. 2005), *Jane's Defence Weekly*.

25. See Case Study B1.
26. 'Arctic has 90 billion barrels of oil' (24 July. 2008), *BBC News*.
27. 'Russia and NATO look to Arctic cooperation' (2 Apr. 2009), *Jane's Defence Weekly*.
28. Aryan, H., 'A new line of defence: Iran's Naval Capabilities Briefing' (28 Jan. 2009), *Jane's Defence Weekly*.
29. Detailed analysis on the Iranian Navy and its ability to conduct such attacks are provided by the Robert Strauss Centre on their website, where they provide an analysis of the ORBAT and command structures involved.
30. Haghshenass, F. (2008), *Iran's Asymmetric Naval Warfare*, Washington Institute for Near East Policy.
31. 'Tamil Tigers claim tanker attack' (31 Oct. 2001), *BBC News*. The report described the attack upon the MV *Silk Pride*, which was carrying more than 650 tonnes of diesel and kerosene to the port of Jaffna. The Tamil Tigers regarded any vessel operating within the coastal waters in support of the government of Sri Lanka as a legitimate target and attacked the vessel using a suicide vessel within a swarm of five boats.
32. 'Small boats', Robert Strauss Center for International Security and Law. The article cites the developing capabilities of the Iranian Navy to mount swarming attacks on vessels despite their lack of success in conducting such operations during the Iran-Iraq War due to the use of USAF. The United States Navy has maintained its interest in countering such attacks and an element of countering swarms of small boats is included in predeployment training through the development of Small Craft Action Teams (SCAT). This tests the ability of command teams on major combat units to discern the threat, which may suddenly arise from an area where many fishing vessels are operating.
33. Alexander, Y. and Richardson, T. B. (2009), *Terror on the High Seas: From Piracy to Strategic Challenge*, Westport, Connecticut: Praeger.
34. Rosamond, J., 'Italian Admiral points to vulnerability of commercial ports to terrorism' (22 Nov. 2007), *Jane's Navy International*.
35. Davis, A. M. (2008), *Terrorism and the Maritime Transportation System: Are we on a collision course?*, Livermore, CA: Wingspan Press.
36. Naylor, T. P. (ed.) (2009), *Maritime Tankers: Terrorist Threats, Consequences and Protective Measures*, New York: Nova Science Publications.
37. Sloggett, D. R. (2010), 'Asymmetric warfare: The maritime dimension', *Naval Review*, vol. 98, no. 1.
38. Heitman, H., 'Seychelles contributes to anti-piracy efforts' (7 May 2009), *Jane's Defence Weekly*.
39. 'Advisory Report issued concerning the MV *Pompei (Dredge)*', Dryad Maritime Intelligence Service.
40. 'Advisory Report 42/09—*Pirate Vessel Win Far 161 at sea*' (17 Aug.), Dryad Maritime Intelligence Service.
41. 'Somali pirates hijack Danish ship' (8 Apr. 2009), *BBC News*.
42. Freeman, C., 'Somali pirates becoming more sophisticated warns British naval commander' (18 Apr. 2009), *Daily Telegraph*.

43. Heitman, H., 'Harried Somalia pirates may plot course south' (11 Feb. 2009), *Jane's Defence Weekly*.
44. '"Ransom demand" for missing ship' (15 Aug. 2009), *BBC News*.
45. 'Death on the high seas as pirates put to the sword' (12 Apr. 2009), *The Times*.
46. Langewiesche, W. (2004), *The Outlaw Sea: Chaos and Crime on the World's Oceans*, London: Granta Books.
47. Stewart, D. (2006), *The Brutal Seas: Organised Crime at Work*, Bloomington, IN: AuthorHouse.
48. Reporting by Dryad Maritime Intelligence Service [www.draydmaritime.com] on 24 April 2009 highlighted the discovery of thirty-five dead people on the coastline of the Abyan Governorate of the Yemen on 22 April by a team from Medecins Sans Frontieres, with 120 survivors of Ethiopian and Somali origin.
49. The impact of the monsoons upon the activities of pirates off the coast of Somalia is a good example of this moderating effect upon criminal behaviour.
50. Barreira, V., 'Nigeria orders twenty high-speed catamarans' (28 Aug. 2009) *Jane's Navy International*. The report stated that Nigeria has ordered twenty high speed catamarans with a maximum speed of 45 knots and capable of carrying up to twelve fully equipped troops for operations to counter piracy and oil bunkering operations by MEND, as well as be capable of patrol and SAR operations.
51. Victor Barreira reporting in *Jane's Navy International* on 28 August 2009 reported that Nigeria has ordered twenty high speed catamarans with a maximum speed of 45 knots and capable of carrying up to twelve fully equipped troops for operations to counter piracy and oil bunkering operations by the Movement for the Emancipation of the Niger Delta (MEND) as well as be capable of patrol and SAR operations.
52. 'Italy ship thwarts pirate attack' (26 Apr. 2009), *BBC News*.
53. Tomberlin, R., L. (2008), 'Terrorism's effect on maritime shipping', *www.maritimeterrorism.com*, Maritime Terrorism Research Centre.
54. ICC Commercial Crime Services (15 Jul. 2009).
55. IMB reported that a total of 78 vessels were boarded across the world, 75 vessels were fired upon, and 31 vessels hijacked, with 561 crew taken hostage, 19 injured, 7 kidnapped, 6 killed and 8 missing.
56. Reuters reported comments made by a Farah Hussein, who was stated to be a pirate, highlighting the impact of the monsoon weather and its impact upon piracy operations (25 Apr. 2009).
57. *Somalia: Diaspora and State Reconstitution in the Horn of Africa*, Farah, Muchie and Gundel (eds.) (2007), London: Adonis & Abbey Publishers Ltd.
58. 'It's a pirate's life for me' (22 Apr. 2009), *BBC News*.
59. Roggio, W. (2007), 'The rise & fall of Somalia's Islamic Courts: An online history', *The Long War Journal*, www.longwarjournal.org.
60. Osman, A. A., Souaré, I. K. (2007), *Somalia at the Crossroads: Challenges and Perspectives on Reconstituting a Failed State*, London: Adonis and Abbey Publishers.
61. Iran's asymmetrical warfare

62. http://news.bbc.co.uk/1/hi/world/middle_east/7175325.stm
63. http://news.bbc.co.uk/1/hi/world/middle_east/7175325.stm
64. The legal requisite in Iraq for the presence of British forces in any capacity is due to expire on 1 August 2009 and has yet to be extended—although this expected to be provided in the fullness of time.
65. Kamal, A., 'Rose al-Yusuf divulges secrets of Al Azhar Engineers Organisation' (29 Jul. 2009), *Egyptian Weekly Rose al-Yusuf.*

5. MARITIME STRATEGY

1. The National Strategy for Maritime Security, September 2005.
2. The planned procurement of diesel submarines by navies across the world is one of the leading growth areas in the world's naval investment plans, alongside the procurement of OPV. Vietnam is buying 6 Kilo-class submarines from Russia for anti-submarine warfare and anti-surface-ship warfare. The Kilo-class submarines have been nicknamed *Black Holes* for their ability to avoid detection. China has also purchased eight more Kilo-class in 2002 for delivery in 2005 and 2007. The Russian state-run arms exporter Rosoboronexport has estimated that by 2015 Russia may have sold 40 Kilo-class submarines. The French arms industry also has a number of orders for the Scorpene Submarine from countries such as Chile, Malaysia and India.
3. Gates, R., M. (2009), 'A balanced strategy: Reprogramming the Pentagon for a new age', *Foreign Affairs.*
4. Friedman, N. (2001), *Seapower as Strategy: Navies and National interests*, Naval Institute Press.
5. Till, G. (2004), *Seapower: A Guide to the Twenty-First Century*, London and Portland: Routledge.
6. This has always been thought to be a factor that played on Lord Jellicoe's mind at the time of the Battle of Jutland when it was thought that only the Royal Navy 'could lose the First World War in an afternoon'.
7. The idea here is that you build maritime security from a simple premise that it starts at home and builds outwards from defence of the homeland's coastline. This can start at the boundary of the territorial waters and then develop in a series of apparent layers that allow maritime power, in varying forms, to be projected overseas in a number of types of operations that are collectively described as MSO, including the delivery of humanitarian relief to areas affected by disasters.
8. Despite the obvious attractions of the maritime environment, terrorists are often thought to be quite conservative in their adoption of new tactics, wishing to make certain that they achieve success. Only 2 per cent of the total recorded incidences of terrorism have, to date, involved a maritime element. However, this does not imply that this figure will not increase in the future, as the situation of the land may become increasingly challenging for transnational groups to operate.
9. The 2008 assessment by the World Bank published on 1 July 2009 ranks Eritrea

at 154th in the world with an estimated Gross Domestic Product (GDP) of $1,654 million; the IMF places it one position lower at 155th with a GDP of $1,476 million in its assessment published in April 2009. It is estimated that half of the Eritrean population lives on less than $1 a day and that one third live in extreme poverty (defined as subsisting on less than 2,000 calories per day).

10. This form of maritime competition is a practical example of the 'Balance of Power' theory developed in an essay by David Hume, remarking that it is as old as history and highlights how nation states that feel threatened seek a just equilibrium in order to be capable of resisting threats or intimidation from another state that seeks to impose its hegemony in a region. Professor Oppenheim highlighted that this is essential to underpinning the very existence of a notion of international law, as, if this idea breaks down, then a nation state can choose to impose its will upon others freely to suit its own needs. This idea of a balance of power is axiomatically at the heart of any maritime strategy and the development of a nation states' investment in any form of military capability.
11. Task Force 158 is a joint effort between the United States Navy, its Coastguard Service, the Royal Navy, the Royal Australian Navy and the nascent Iraqi Navy to protect Iraqi's oil terminals in the Persian Gulf from attack by terrorist groups seeking to disrupt the recovery of the Iraqi economy.
12. Harding, R. (1999), *Seapower and Naval Warfare, 1650–1830*, London: Routledge. Harding specifically notes the success of the idea of blockades in the French Revolutionary and Napoleonic Wars (1792–1801, 1802–1815) and how it became an 'essential part of maritime strategy based upon the existence of a powerful fleet of battleships'. The concept of the blockade has developed and while it remains a key part of any maritime strategy its role in the twentieth and twenty-first century is likely to be limited to the imposition of trade embargos sanctioned by the United Nations to reduce arms smuggling and try and contain local and regional conflicts.
13. It is possible to view the term 'concentration of force' through several quite distinct lenses. Historically, a concentration of force enabled one to defeat or deter an adversary. A contemporary analysis would suggest that a concentration of force might also apply to situations in which humanitarian relief operations have to be conducted or nationals evacuated from areas where their lives are at risk. Semantically, the issue is the use of the term 'force'. Operation Highbrow, conducted by the Royal Navy to remove nationals from Beirut was a concentration of six major naval units, including HMS *Illustrious* and HMS *Bulwark*, which had the potential to apply varying forms of force if they were challenged by either of the belligerents. Rules of Engagement were set for the operations that required naval vessels to enter Beirut and evacuate over 4,500 British and other nationals in what is termed doctrinally as a Non-Combatant Evacuation Operation (NEO). During the operation, negotiations with the belligerents established windows in which naval units could move alongside in Beirut and leave without being engaged by the protagonists. Given that one of these was a

transnational terrorist group the guarantees had to be taken with some caution, given the chaotic nature of the situation.

14. Handel, M. I. (2000), *Corbett, Clausewitz and Sun Tzu*, http://www.nwc.navy.mil/press/Review/2000.
15. It is difficult to sustain conflicts that are not about national survival. Where national survival is at stake, populations may well realise the implications of losing and fight on indeterminately. At the start of the twenty-first century that is a difficult argument to sustain, as governments in NATO are discovering as they try to secure public support for their operations in Afghanistan.
16. Historians may well view the outcome of the Battle of Jutland differently. In this context, a view is taken that while a major opportunity was lost to prolong the battle after the German fleet's withdrew, due to a failure in the assessment of the situation and some inaccurate intelligence, the Royal Navy had already taken some serious losses. However, the fact that the German High Seas Fleet withdrew to port and did not mount any further major operations, has been taken by some commentators to be a victory, allowing the Royal Navy to establish sea control over the North Sea in terms of its surface units. The continuing activity of the German Navy U-Boats for the remainder of the First World War illustrates Corbett's thinking that sea control is transitory.
17. 'Atmospherics' is an intelligence term used to describe the nature of relationships between groups of individuals that are protagonists in a conflict. Understanding the atmospherics and being able to exploit them to try and create the conditions where political progress can be achieved requires dedicated efforts to collect nuanced intelligence and then combining that with other insights gained from anthropological and social studies that reveal the nature of the social dynamics that exist in the societal landscapes that are the focus for the operations. Developing this capability is going to be a crucial aspect of future maritime strategy, as navies operate on a global scale and may have to participate in MSO, at short notice, in increasingly diverse areas of the world.
18. It is clear that the Taliban have developed their own form of influence activities, as they seek to deepen political and military tensions that surface within the NATO coalition in Afghanistan. The Taliban read press reports and understand public disquiet in the countries within NATO and seek to use their activities to exacerbate those tensions and fault lines.
19. This is not to suggest that the wider problems of maritime security concerning criminality and international terrorism will disappear; they will remain as before a problem in a number of regions.
20. Operation Palliser was mounted by the United Kingdom armed forces to evacuate United Kingdom nationals from Sierra Leone, which had a major naval contingent based upon HMS *Ocean*, HMS *Illustrious*, HMS *Chatham* and HMS *Argyll* operating with the support of the Royal Fleet Auxiliary *Fort Austin*.
21. Freedman, N. (2001), *Seapower as Strategy: Navies and National Interests*, Naval Institute Press.

22. Another term that has been used doctrinally is that of Military Operations Other Than War (MOOTW) to cover activities such as evacuating national subjects and providing humanitarian relief in areas of the world affected by disasters. If current predictions are anything to go by, the impact of climate change is likely to increase the need for being able to provide support to other nation states on a global basis.
23. In this context, the term peacemaking should be seen in a wider perspective covering military activities that include combat operations against a backdrop of an international crisis that are designed to create the conditions in which a conflict or confrontation can be resolved.
24. In this respect, the term 'military capability' is reflective of the combat capability of the vessels and its ability to project force into an area either to deter or defeat an adversary. Naval platforms have always enjoyed their inherent ability to provide support to places devastated by natural disasters, such as hurricanes, providing medical supplies, manpower and expertise to restore key services in the aftermath of an event. This latter aspects illustrate the application of soft power or influence by naval forces.
25. The obvious example of where this idea did not apply was in the so-called Atlantic Wall created by Field Marshall Rommel to protect France from an invasion by the Allies in 1944. His main idea was to defeat the enemy on the beaches and never let them gain a toehold in France. This strategy exposes the limits of German sea power at that time in the Second World War.
26. In effect, to target the naval resources effectively using intelligence and other patterns of behaviour, to place what are often limited resources to sea in specifically targeted parts of the maritime domain, so as to achieve an overall effect upon those a state seeks to dissuade from the use of its waters.
27. It has been reported in the press in several major newspapers, that in the run-up to the attack on Mumbai, local fishermen were troubled by what they saw as unusual patterns of activity in the local area. Their concerns were reported to the local security authorities, and whilst no direct linkage has been established with the attack on Mumbai, the information appeared not to have been acted upon at the time.
28. Vessels over 300 gross tonnes are mandated to carry an AIS capability to show their position, what they are carrying and their destination.

6. DELIVERING MARITIME SECURITY IN THE TWENTY-FIRST CENTURY

1. Fish, T., 'Merchant shipping cannot rely on naval protection warns CMF' (8 Apr. 2009), *Jane's Navy International*.
2. The international community is reacting differently to the problem of piracy off the Horn of Africa with the United States appearing to favour the deployment of Sea Marshalls on board vessels to frighten off pirates and the Spanish govern-

ment giving the go-ahead for private security firms to be hired by the Spanish tuna fishing boats operating in the Indian Ocean armed with high-powered rifles. Spain operates fourteen tuna fishing vessels in the Indian Ocean, most of which are based in the Basque country in Spain. In 2008 a reported ransom of $1.2 million was paid for the release of a tuna-fishing vessel after it had been held for six days. In a development reported on 18 September 2009, Valencia tuna fishermen have stated they are hiring thirty gunmen to protect their six vessels for three months, paying an estimated 15,000 Euros for three months work. The tuna-fishing season in the Indian Ocean closes at the end of December.

3. Boraz, S. C. (2009), 'Maritime domain awareness: Myths and realities', *Naval War College Review*, vol. 62, no. 3.
4. Jennings, G., 'BAMS-D completes first operational deployment' (21 Oct. 2009), *Jane's Navy International.* The United States Navy deployed its Broad Area Maritime Surveillance Demonstrator (BAMS-D) during 2009 as a result of a development programme initiated in 2006. The report states that during its initial deployment, it had been operating in support of the Commander Task Force 57 (CTF-57) with thousands of images supporting maritime intelligence and surveillance activities.
5. Hill, B. P. (2009), *Maritime Terrorism and the Small Boat Threat to the United States: A Proposed Response*, Naval Postgraduate School Thesis, Monterey, California.
6. 'Small boats threaten maritime security: United States Coastguard' (7 Aug. 2009), *AFP*.
7. New equipment is becoming available to help those trying to enforce a secure maritime environment. On 14 August 2009, the BBC carried a report headlined 'anti-Terror gun stops boats dead', highlighting the development of a new device that is capable of stopping a speedboat laden with explosives (WBIED) or perhaps pirates in a skiff. It deploys a net designed to become entangled with the propellers powering the target boat. Rosamond, J. 'DSEI: BAE Systems offers layered defence for commercial ships' (9 Sept. 2009), *Jane's Navy International.* Other developments include a laser dazzling device that aims to deter and disrupt piracy attacks over a range of 1 km, and a high-powered microwave device that tries to disable electronics being carried by the pirates, such as navigation equipment.
8. Bowcott, O., 'Britain lays claim to 200,000 sq km of the South Atlantic seabed' (24 May 2008), *The Guardian*.
9. The project to build these two ships was announced on 9 July 2009 by the Russian Federation Navy and the vessels are expected to be commissioned into service in 2011 and 2013. As an indication of the priority associated with this effort a partially completed frigate, the *Borodino*, was launched early in order to clear the slipway for the build of the first of the two vessels, which has already been named as the Seliger.
10. See Case Study A15.

11. 'Mexico acquires UAS for all-weather ISR capability' (30 Jul. 2009), *Jane's Navy International.*
12. Moss, T. 'Philippine troops battle Abu Sayyaf in Basilan assault' (14 Aug. 2009), *Jane's Defence Weekly*. An example of this is the attack launched by maritime forces from the Philippines against the Abu Sayyaf Group on 12 August on their base on the island of Basilan, reported by the government's News Service.
13. On 21 September, Dryad Maritime Intelligence Service [www.dryadmaritime.com] reported how an attack upon a bulk carrier was thwarted by a Yemini Coastguard unit and the cooperative actions of a Japanese P3 reconnaissance aircraft, the Australian warship HMAS *Toowoomba* that had recently joined CTF-15, assisted by a helicopter from the German warship the FGS *Bremen*, which brought the escaping pirates to a halt.
14. Scott, R., 'Policing the maritime beat' (29 Apr. 2009), *Jane's Defence Weekly*.
15. Blackmore, N., 'New tricks; Examining anti-piracy tactics' (Feb. 2010), *Jane's Intelligence Review*.
16. On 9 September, Dryad Maritime Intelligence Service [www.dryadmaritime.com] reported on developments announced at the international defence exhibition held in London: Defence Systems & Equipment International (DESI).
17. 'Philippines offers training for Somali coast guard' (1 Sept. 2009), Associated Press. The report stated that in the light of the high numbers of its nationals that are involved as seafarers, over 30 per cent of the world's 1.2 million merchant sailors, that President Arroyo had offered to provide training to the Somali Coastguard fearing another surge in attacks after the monsoon had passed. One of the vessels held the longest, the MV *Irene*, has a crew of twenty-two Filipino seamen aboard and they have been held captive since April 2009. In August 2009, a further twenty Filipino seafarers were also being held aboard another three vessels that at the time had yet to be released.
18. 'Maritime security enhanced with ship and satellite data integrated' (25 Oct. 2007), *Science Daily*. The report states that the Maritime Security Service (MARISS) was described as a capability that provides complementary sources of information to land-based sensors systems, such as AIS and VTMS.
19. The Chief of Staff of the European Union Naval Force operating in the area had earlier stated that the twenty-five warships patrolling the area on 23 May 2009 would have to be augmented to sixty in the Gulf of Aden alone and a further 150 off Somalia to effectively tackle the problem. A commitment of this level would require virtually the commitment of the entire 1,000-Ship Navy envisaged by Admiral Mullen, given the need to maintain ships on station and rotate others through training and allow for some time for leave for serving personnel.
20. Many of these parameters also read across into the second aspect of protecting the SLOC; but with the additional element of 'time-to-tasking' (the time taken to reach the patrol area) as an important consideration for units to operate remotely from the EEZ.
21. If the aim was to build a model of these various elements, duration would be a

sub-class of the platform type in an object-orientated hierarchy. As this text is not developing such a model the parameters are listed individually.

22. 'Sierra Leone Navy battles pirates' (28 Nov. 2008), *BBC News*.
23. 'Interview with Commodore Tim Lowe' (18 Feb. 2009), *Jane's Defence Weekly*.
24. The International Maritime Bureau's Piracy Reporting Centre reported on 30 August 2009 that ransoms totalling over $150 million had been paid to pirates operating from the coast of Somalia in the last year, and that notified attacks had grown from 114 in the first six months of 2008 to 240 in 2009. The Bureau further believes that only half of the unsuccessful attacks are actually reported by vessels' Masters. Individual ransom demands have grown from $5000 for a fishing vessel in the middle of the 1990s to $3 million for some of the more high profile vessels that have been taken in 2009. Pirates that put to sea on a skiff can earn up to $30,000 a year, which is a very large sum of money in Somali terms.
25. AFP has reported that Somali pirates have demanded a ransom of $20 million for the return of a Turkish bulk carrier, *Horizon 1*, which was seized on 8 July 2009 en route to Saudi Arabia with a cargo of 33,000 cubic metres of sulphide.
26. Hobsbawm, E. (2007), *Globalisation, Democracy and Terrorism*, New York: Little, Brown & Company.
27. Swain, J. and Gillard, M., 'Is Somalia the new Afghanistan?' (9 Aug. 2009) *The Sunday Times*, p. 14.
28. 'Reachback' is a term used in military circles to illustrate the value of being able to harness national technical means of intelligence collection, often conducted at a strategic level using advanced capabilities and platforms, to provide additional insights into the intelligence analysis process being conducted in theatre. This requires the intelligence picture to be assembled in theatre at the operational level of command.
20. The concept of a Virtual Assessment Team, is based on the idea that it is difficult for any one person to have all the expertise required to develop a detailed understanding of the anthropological history and associated creeds, customs and traditions of the kind of ethnic structures that form the societal landscapes against which twenty-first century military operations will be conducted. By identifying and then involving academics who have a deep knowledge in the various disciplines involved in delving into the societal landscape, the unintended consequences can be avoided, which can arise if this deep level of understanding is not available.
30. Warden, H. N. (2004), *Overcoming Challenges to the Proliferation Security Initiative*, Monterey, CA: Postgraduate Naval School.
31. Johnson, A. C. (2004), *The Future of the U.S. Navy in the Persian Gulf*, Monterey, CA: Naval Postgraduate School.
32. The various Task Forces operating in the Persian Gulf and the Gulf of Aden provide examples of what Johnson would have described as a continuous presence. This is reflective of the nature of the threat at present and is clearly a drain upon those countries that contribute to the operations as, to a first order, to

maintain a single ship on station requires one being worked up to replace that vessel when its deployment ends and another that is currently re-training and resting after it has completed a deployment.

33. Grove, E. (2006), 'The discovery of doctrine: British naval thinking at the close of the 20th century', in Till, G. (ed.), *The Development of British Naval Thinking: Essays in memory of Bryan Ranft*, London: Routledge.
34. Whilst some commentators may not like the apparent reference to the Suez Crisis and the invasion of the area around the Suez Canal by British and French forces in the wake of its nationalisation by President Nasser, with all of its repercussions, to deny that such a situation might not arise again would be to ignore the lessons of history.
35. *Jane's Navy International* reported on 12 August 2009, that the United States Navy is set to increase its funding for unmanned aircraft to $4 billion as part of the Future Years Defence Programme (FYDP), with a particular emphasis upon operations in harsh and difficult environments, such as in the Arctic.
36. On 2 September 2009, the United States Africa Command announced that it was going to deploy unmanned drones in the Seychelles Islands to provide ISTAR coverage of the Indian Ocean to detect the activities of pirates and locate potential mother craft from which attacks can be mounted. This is a clear reaction to the agility demonstrated by the pirates, as they have mounted attacks up to 1,000 km away from the shores of Somalia. The unmanned aircraft may also be based alongside P-3 Orion maritime patrol aircraft.
37. While these platforms carry an array of sensor systems that provide radar and electro-optical means of detecting vessels, the background against which the skiffs need to be detected can provide difficulties for the sensor systems, as the sea can provide a cluttered return that needs filtering and analysis to discover potential targets. It is likely that the main focus of the unmanned platforms will be the slightly larger mother vessels, typically previously hijacked trawlers, which carry the skiffs to a position close to where they can mount the attacks.
38. This is, of course, a subjective and fairly parochial assessment, as events in history can show that naval forces have conducted search operations for specific combat units over longer periods of time. It is probably best to regard this claim as being related to the longest pursuit of a vessel involved in alleged criminal undertakings in history. This more specific definition may stand a little more scrutiny.
39. 'Algeria looks hard at Brunei's unwanted OPVs' (5 Aug. 2009), *Jane's Naval International.*
40. 'BVT Surface Fleet to launch first corvette for Oman' (20 Jul. 2009), *Jane's Navy International.*
41. Some reporting has suggested that the actual requirement, over a fifteen year timetable, is for twenty-seven vessels in total, but this has not been confirmed publicly and may now have been scaled back given the economic situation.
42. Sloggett, D. R. (2009), 'Maritime security challenges: A case study in the Gulf of Guinea', *Naval Review*, vol. 97, no. 2.

43. A point echoed by the First Sea Lord, Sir Mark Stanhope, at a Defence Breakfast briefing in a law firm in the City of London on 19 January 2010.
44. 'Israel to confront Yakhont-capable Syrian challenge' (29 Jul. 2009), *Jane's Defence Weekly*.

INDEX